Health Care Policy

D0681095

Health Care Policy

David Calkins, MD, MPP
Chief, Division of Internal Medicine
New England Deaconess Hospital
Assistant Professor of Medicine
Harvard Medical School
Boston, Massachusetts

Rushika J. Fernandopulle, MD, MPP
Resident in General Surgery
Hospital of the University of Pennsylvania
Philadelphia, Pennsylvania

Bradley S. Marino, MD, MPP
Resident in Pediatrics
The Johns Hopkins Hospital
Baltimore, Maryland

b

**Blackwell
Science**

Blackwell Science

Editorial offices:
238 Main Street, Cambridge, Massachusetts 02142, USA
Osney Mead, Oxford OX2 0EL, England
25 John Street, London WC1N 2BL, England
23 Ainslie Place, Edinburgh EH3 6AJ, Scotland
54 University Street, Carlton, Victoria 3053, Australia
Arnette Blackwell SA, 1 rue de Lille, 75007 Paris, France
Blackwell Wissenschafts–Verlag GmbH
    Kurfürstendamm 57, 10707 Berlin, Germany
    Feldgasse 13, A-1238 Vienna, Austria

Distributors:

North America
Blackwell Science, Inc.
238 Main Street
Cambridge, Massachusetts 02142
(Telephone orders: 800-215-1000 or 617-876-7000)

Australia
Blackwell Science Pty Ltd
54 University Street
Carlton, Victoria 3053
(Telephone orders: 03-347-0300)
fax: 03 349-3016)

Outside North America and Australia
Blackwell Science, Ltd.
c/o Marston Book Services, Ltd.
P.O. Box 87
Oxford OX2 0DT
England
(Telephone orders: 44-865-791155)

Acquisitions: *Victoria Reeders*
Development: *Coleen Traynor*
Production: *Tracey A. Solon*

Manufacturing: *Kathleen Grimes*
Typeset by: *BookMasters, Ashland, OH*
Printed and bound by: *Braun-Brumfield, Inc,
Ann Arbor, MI*

© 1995 by Blackwell Science, Inc.
Printed in the United States of America
        97 98 5 4 3
All rights reserved. No part of this book may be reproduced
in any form or by any electronic or mechanical means,
including information storage and retrieval systems, without
permission in writing from the publisher, except by a
reviewer who may quote brief passages in a review.

Library of Congress Cataloging-in-Publication Data
Health care policy/edited by Rushika J. Fernandopulle, Bradley S. Marino;
    with David Calkins.
        p.   cm.
    Includes bibliographical references and index.
    ISBN 0-86542-447-0
    1. Medical policy—United States.   2. Medical care—United States.
I. Fernandopulle, Rushika J.   II. Marino, Bradley S.   III. Calkins,
David, 1948–   .
    [DNLM: 1. Health Policy—United States.   2. Delivery of Health
Care—United States.   WA 540 AA1 H43 1995]
RA395.A3H4124   1995
362.1'0973—dc20
DNLM/DLC
for Library of Congress
                                            94-45372
                                                CIP

Contents

Contributors

Colin Baker, MPP
Analyst
Health Economics Research, Inc.
Waltham, Massachusetts

Christopher Bencomo, MD, MPP
Resident in Obstetrics and Gynecology
University of California, Los Angeles,
   Medical Center
Los Angeles, California

David Blumenthal, MD, MPP
Chief, Health Policy Research and
   Development Unit
Massachusetts General Hospital
Boston, Massachusetts

Troyen Brennan, MD, MPH, JD
Professor of Health Policy and
   Management
Harvard School of Public Health
Boston, Massachusetts

David Calkins, MD, MPP
Assistant Professor of Medicine
Harvard Medical School
Boston, Massachusetts

Tamara L. Callahan, MD, MPP
Health Care Policy Fellow
Harvard Medical School
Boston, Massachusetts

Aaron Caughey, MD, MPP
Resident in Obstetrics and Gynecology
Brigham and Womens Hospital
Boston, Massachusetts

David Chin, MD, MBA
President and Chief Executive Officer
Novalis Corporation
Boston, Massachusetts

Deborah Cotton, MD
Assistant Professor of Health Policy
   and Management
Harvard School of Public Health
Boston, Massachusetts

Ronald David, MD
Lecturer in Public Policy
John F. Kennedy School of Government
Harvard University
Cambridge, Massachusetts

John Delfs, MD
Director, Deaconess Elder Care
New England Deaconess Hospital
Boston, Massachusetts

Jeanne M. De Sa, MPP
John F. Kennedy School of Government
Harvard University
Cambridge, Massachusetts

Robert Dorwart, MD
Associate Professor of Health Policy
 and Management
Harvard School of Public Health
Boston, Massachusetts

Penny Feldman, PhD
Lecturer in Health Policy and Management
Harvard School of Public Health
Boston, Massachusetts

**Rushika J. Fernandopulle,
 MD, MPP**
Resident in General Surgery
Hospital of the University of Pennsylvania
Philadelphia, Pennsylvania

Atul Gawande, MD
Resident in General Surgery
Brigham and Womens Hospital
Boston, Massachusetts

Linda G. Greenberg
PhD Candidate
Heller School, Brandeis University
Waltham, Massachusetts

Jill Horwitz, MPP
JD Candidate
Stanford Law School
Palo Alto, California

William Hsiao, PhD
Professor of Health Systems Economics
Harvard School of Public Health
Boston, Massachusetts

Lisa I. Iezzoni, MD, MSc
Associate Professor of Medicine
Harvard Medical School
Beth Israel Hospital
Boston, MA

Bradley S. Marino, MD, MPP
Resident in Pediatrics
The Johns Hopkins Hospital
Baltimore, Maryland

David Morales, MD
Resident in Plastic Surgery
University of Texas, Southwestern Medical
 Center
Dallas, Texas

Michael J. Murphy, MD, MPH
Resident in Psychiatry
McLean Hospital
Belmont, Massachusetts

Joseph Newhouse, PhD
John D. MacArthur Professor of Health
 Policy and Management
John F. Kennedy School of Government
Harvard University
Cambridge, Massachusetts

Elizabeth Onyemelukwe, MD, MPH
Resident in Medicine
Massachusetts General Hospital
Boston, Massachusetts

Adam Rosen, MPP
Health Care Policy Consultant
Boston, Massachusetts

Marjorie Ross
Policy Analyst
Principal Group
Bethesda, Maryland

James Sabin, MD
Associate Director, Teaching Programs
Harvard Community Health Plan
Boston, Massachusetts

Gretchen Schwarze, MD, MPP
Resident in General Surgery
Massachusetts General Hospital
Boston, Massachusetts

Douglas Staiger, PhD
Assistant Professor of Public Policy
John F. Kennedy School of Government
Harvard University
Cambridge, Massachusetts

Hugh H. Tilson, Jr., JD, MPH
Associate Attorney
Michaels, Wishner, and Bonner, P.C.
Washington, DC

Carlos Trejo, MD, MPP
Resident in Anesthesiology
Brigham and Womens Hospital
Boston, Massachusetts

Preface

The U.S. health care system is in a time of great change, and increasingly, broader health policy concerns are influencing how physicians practice medicine. Given this, what is health policy and why is it important for physicians to understand it?

The field of health policy is broad and a single definition of it is all too often elusive. We define it as those issues concerning the organization, delivery, and financing of health care from the level of the patient–doctor encounter to society as a whole, as well as those issues affecting public health, medical education, and biomedical research.

It is important for physicians to understand health care policy because policy decisions have a significant impact on how they practice medicine. Physicians and other health care personnel need to become educated consumers of health policy information in order to help shape their own future as well as their patients' through those who hold influence at higher levels of government.

After completion of our medical and health policy training, it became clear that many of our medical school classmates and the clinicians with whom we worked wished to know more about the system in which they practiced, its problems, and the potential solutions to those problems. Many of our colleagues, knowing of our interest in health policy, asked us to refer them to a text to address these questions that was short, complete, readable, and unbiased. After searching the bookshelves and consulting with health policy faculty, we realized that such an exposition did not exist.

To meet the need for a short, informative, readable primer, we organized a team of health policy students and faculty to write this book. Each chapter was written by a student with a faculty collaborator. Students were carefully selected based on their knowledge of health policy and their writing ability. Faculty were chosen from Harvard Medical School, the Harvard School of Public Health, and the John F. Kennedy School of Government, based on specific areas of expertise.

The purpose of this book is to teach the basic health policy concepts using our current system as an example. For example, Federal Proposals (Chap. 14) describes the five major health reform proposals before Congress in the spring of 1994. Our hope is that readers will come away understanding the different ways one can address cost, access, and quality, instead of the specifics of any one proposal. In addition, we hope the readers of this book will become familiar with the language of health care policy.

If one does not know what an MI is, one cannot talk to a cardiologist or be taken seriously by one. We have added a glossary of terms to help in this process.

American medicine is in a period of flux, and the issues are complex and controversial. The importance of knowing basic health policy concepts has never been greater and will continue to grow as the national debate on health care reform continues. We hope this book helps physicians and medical students understand better the system in which they practice, its problems, and potential solutions. The challenges ahead are great, and physicians need to be active participants to ensure the welfare of their present and future patients, as well as themselves. We hope this book teaches and empowers you. Remember, knowledge is power.

D.C.
R.J.F.
B.S.M.

Acknowledgments

We would like to thank, first and foremost, the contributing authors of this book, and their faculty advisors. Their phenomenal efforts ensured the breadth, depth, and quality of this book. We would also like to thank Victoria Reeders and Coleen Traynor at Blackwell Science for believing in the importance of this project and helping us bring the book to press so quickly, as well as David Morales, whose illustrations added so much to the project. We are indebted to our professors and colleagues at the John F. Kennedy School of Government, the Harvard School of Public Health, and Harvard Medical School for imparting to us the vital importance of health care policy, and to our friends for helping us survive our years as joint degree students. Finally, we would like to thank our families—without their support none of this would have been possible.

Glossary

Health care policy, like most other fields, has its own set of vocabulary that one must know to understand the issues involved. Below is a list of commonly used terms and acronyms. Because this book is basically for physicians, medical students, and other health care workers, we did not include terms generally familiar to these groups, such as primary care, teaching hospital, and MRI.

AAMC: Association of American Medical Colleges

AARP: American Association of Retired Persons—one of the strongest lobbying groups in Washington concerned with the issues of the elderly.

Actuarily fair price: The price of an insurance policy that would exactly equal the expected loss to the insurer—policies actually cost more because of administrative costs. See Chapter 4.

ADL: Activities of daily living—a method by which functional needs can be measured. IADL, instrumental activities of daily living. See Chapter 19.

Administrative costs: The overhead costs of running an insurance plan (i.e., money not paid out in benefits). Many argue that a major benefit of a single-payer system would be to drastically reduce administrative costs.

Adverse selection: The process by which people who know they are at a higher risk tend to buy more insurance than those at a lower risk. This is one of the inefficiencies of the health insurance market described in Chapter 4.

AFDC: Aid to Families with Dependent Children (also known as welfare)—a joint federal–state assistance program that provides cash grants to eligible families. Eligibility for AFDC also makes a family categorically eligible for Medicaid.

AHA: American Hospital Association

AHCPR: Agency for Health Care Policy and Research—a federally funded health services research group.

Allopathy: The system of western medicine most common in the United States, stressing mechanisms of disease and the scientific approach.

AMA: American Medical Association—the main trade group for physicians in the United States. Currently only about 40% of American physicians are dues-paying members.

Antitrust: Regulations to prevent businesses from engaging in anticompetitive behavior and controlling the prices of goods or services for an entire market. See Chapter 3.

Blue Cross: A series of state-wide, nonprofit insurance carriers covering hospital care and frequently taking on those who cannot buy insurance elsewhere; in return it gets favorable rates from hospitals. Now it is linked almost everywhere with Blue Shield plans. See Chapter 4.

Blue Shield: A series of state-wide, nonprofit insurance carriers covering physician services and frequently taking on those who cannot buy insurance elsewhere; in return it gets favorable rates from hospitals. Now it is linked almost everywhere with Blue Cross plans. See Chapter 4.

Capitation: A method of reimbursement where a provider is paid a certain amount per patient covered for a set of given services. Unlike fee-for-service, this contains incentives to minimize care.

Case management: A method of cost control that assigns case managers to examine the cases of only the most expensive patients and to devise ways to minimize the expense of their care.

Catastrophic coverage: Insurance that only pays for care over a certain, fairly high, threshold; for instance, it may only pay for expenses after the first $10,000. This coverage is much cheaper than traditional coverage, and some believe the state should guarantee it to all its citizens.

Categorical eligibility: One way to become eligible for Medicaid is to fit in a certain category of people, for instance, those eligible for federal welfare benefits (see AFDC). Some states allow people who spend down their assets to become eligible as well.

CDC: Centers for Disease Control—the major federal body dealing with issues of public health.

COGME: Council on Graduate Medical Education—one of the bodies that regulates residency programs.

Community health center: A local institution providing basic health care services to a particular community, usually located in underprivileged areas.

Community rating: A system of insurance pricing where everyone in a certain area is charged the same rate, regardless of previous health history or personal characteristics.

Comprehensive coverage: Insurance plans that cover a variety of services, usually including preventive services, hospital, and physician care.

CON: Certificates of need—a program started in many states to require preapproval for any large capital purchases by health providers such as hospitals. Many think, however, that these certificates have not been successful in containing costs. See Chapter 3.

Copayments: A frequent part of insurance contracts, which obligate the beneficiary to pay for a fixed percentage of his or her medical bills (frequently 20%).

Cost loading: The costs associated with forming and administering insurance pools. Similar to "administrative costs." See Chapter 4.

Cost shifting: The process of shifting the costs of taking care of some patients onto another group more able to pay. For instance, some argue that when Medicare reduced its reimbursements, hospitals simply charged more to patients with private insurance to make up their losses.

Cost sharing: Used to refer to a number of means of placing a part of the costs of medical care onto someone who is insured. The most common means of cost sharing include deductibles and copayments.

Cream skimming: The technique used by insurance companies to contract only with people who are healthy, and to exclude those who are more likely to get sick.

Deductibles: A part of many insurance contracts, which obligates the beneficiary to pay for the first part of any medical bill. For example, if someone had a $200 deductible per admission, he or she would have to pay the first $200 of a $2000 hospital bill, and the insurer would pay the rest (unless there was a copayment written in the contract as well).

Defensive medicine: The practice of ordering additional tests or performing additional procedures not for strictly medical indications but to prevent potential lawsuits. It is fairly controversial how much defensive medicine is practiced, and whether it is on the whole good or bad. See Chapter 15.

DRG: Diagnosis-related group—part of the Medicare Prospective Payment system used since 1993 to reimburse hospitals. Each patient is assigned to a DRG depending on his or her illness, and each DRG is assigned a different price, which the hospital is reimbursed.

DRG creep: The process by which patients are assigned a different diagnosis in a DRG that gives the hospital more revenue.

Employer mandate: A method of achieving universal access whereby employers are required to provide health insurance for their employees. Hawaii has had an employer mandate in effect for many years. See Chapters 13 and 14.

ERISA: The Employee Retirement Income Security Act of 1974, passed by the U.S. Congress.

Experience rating: A system of pricing health insurance whereby a person or group is charged a different rate depending on some demographic characteristics or health history.

FDA: Food and Drug Administration—the body responsible for, among other things, licensing pharmaceuticals and medical devices in the U.S.

Fee schedule: A method of paying providers whereby each service is compensated a fixed predetermined amount. The RBRVS is an example of a fee schedule.

FFS: Fee-for-service—the dominant system of physician reimbursement in the U.S. until recently, whereby providers are paid for each service they perform. Unlike capitation, many argue fee-for-service contains incentives to maximize the amount of care provided.

FMG: Foreign Medical Graduate

FQHMO: Federally Qualified HMO—an HMO that fulfills certain criteria outlined in the Federal HMO Act. See Chapter 5.

Gatekeeping: A cost-control technique used by many managed care organizations, whereby a patient cannot see a specialist or seek other such services without the approval of his or her primary care doctor.

GDP: Gross Domestic Product—defined as the value of all final goods and services produced in a particular country in a particular year. Thus for the U.S. it includes the value of goods and services produced in the U.S. by foreign companies, but does not include goods and services produced by U.S. companies abroad. It is used as a measure of the size of a country's economy, and in the U.S. it is very similar in magnitude to the GNP.

Global budgets: A method of cost control whereby a fixed budget is determined for the entire health sector, a region, or a particular institution like a hospital. The Canadian system and other systems make extensive use of global budgets. See Chapters 12 and 14.

GMENAC: Graduate Medical Education National Advisory Committee—asked to look at national medical manpower needs. See Chapter 2.

GNP: Gross National Product—defined as the value of all final goods and services produced by assets owned by a particular country in a particular year. Thus for the U.S. it includes the value of goods and services produced by U.S. companies abroad, but does not include goods made in the U.S. by foreign companies. It is used as a measure of the size of a country's economy, and in the U.S. it is very similar in magnitude to the GDP.

Group Model HMO:

An HMO that owns its own health care facilities but contracts with a medical group to provide the physician services needed. Kaiser Permanente in California is an example of such an HMO. See Chapter 5.

Hawthorne effect:

The observation that any group being studied may improve its outcome just because it is being studied. Some claim that U.S. health costs are being moderated in the 1990s not because of any lasting change, but because of all the attention being focused on the costs. See Chapter 11.

HCFA:

Health Care Financing Administration—responsible for the administration of Medicare.

Health Security Act of 1993:

The official name for President Clinton's health reform proposal of 1993.

Herfindahl Index:

A formula used to rate the amount of competition in a particular geographic area and used to determine if hospitals have violated antitrust laws.

HEW:

Department of Health, Education, and Welfare—a cabinet-level federal department which was later divided into the departments of Education and HHS (see below).

HHS:

Department of Health and Human Services—cabinet-level federal executive department responsible for, among other things, all federal health programs, including Medicare and Medicaid.

High-risk pools:

One method of improving access to health care, whereby people with a bad health status are provided subsidized insurance, usually by the state.

Hill-Burton Act:

A federal program started after World War II to encourage the expansion of hospitals in the U.S. See Chapter 3.

HMO:

Health Maintenance Organization—the prototype of managed care organizations. There are now several types, including group and staff models. See Chapter 5.

Horizontal integration: Relationships between organizations at the same level of production (also known as mergers). Thus it is horizontal integration when a hospital buys other hospitals in the same town. These mergers are closely regulated to prevent antitrust violations.

Hospice: A service provided to the terminally ill, mainly consisting of pain relief and social support, without heroic or curative measures.

Indemnity insurance: Traditional insurance whereby patients or providers were simply reimbursed for whatever medical care they needed or provided, respectively. In some ways, it can be thought of as "unmanaged care."

Individual mandate: A method of achieving universal access by requiring everyone who can afford health insurance to purchase it.

IPA: Independent Practice Association—a type of managed care whereby an HMO contracts with various independent groups or individual physicians who provide care in their own facilities and manage their own staffs.

JCAHO: Joint Commission on Accreditation of Health Care Organizations

Job lock: The predicament some Americans find themselves in whereby they fear changing jobs because their current illness will not be covered by a new insurer, as it will be as a preexisting condition. See Chapter 12.

Long-term care: Health and other social services delivered over a sustained period of time to people requiring such services to function. In the health care debate, this frequently refers to nursing home and home care for the elderly and disabled. See Chapter 19.

Managed care: Any of several types of organizations in which specific measures are taken to provide care for a certain group of patients within a specific budget. Examples include HMOs, PPOs, IPAs. See Chapter 5.

Managed competition: A system of health financing which uses competition between insurance plans within a strict regulatory framework to drive down health costs—

	advocated strongly by Alain Enthoven, and the basis of President Clinton's Health Security Act.
Medicaid:	A joint federal–state program to provide funding for medical care for certain groups of poor Americans. See Chapter 6.
Medicare:	A federal program providing health insurance to all Americans over the age of 65. See Chapter 6.
Medigap policies:	Supplemental insurance policies sold by private companies to Medicare recipients to cover things not covered by Medicare (also known as wraparound policies).
Moral hazard:	The altering of behavior because one is insured; for instance, one may be more likely to see a doctor for a simple cold if one is insured and pays nothing for the visit, as opposed to if one had to pay a fee for the visit. See Chapter 4.
Municipal bonds:	A way for not-for-profit enterprises like hospitals to borrow money. Investors do not have to pay taxes on the interest they earn from these bonds, allowing the hospital to pay lower interest rates, and thus get capital cheaper than for-profit enterprises.
National Health Service Corps:	A federal program providing scholarships for medical students in return for an obligation to serve in underserved areas after graduation. See Chapter 9.
NIH:	National Institutes of Health—the preeminent biomedical research institution in the U.S. It both conducts its own research in Bethesda, Maryland, and funds research elsewhere in the country. See Chapter 17.
No-fault liability:	A proposed reform to the medical malpractice system to replace the current tort system. It would award damages based on the fact that an injury occurred regardless of who was at fault. See Chapter 15.

Not-for-profit: An institution without shareholders, where any residual income after expenses (i.e., profits) do not accrue to any individuals, but are invested back into the institution itself. Not-for-profit institutions are exempt from federal income tax and have other advantages as well. See Chapter 3.

NRMP: National Residency Matching Program—a computer-matching process by which most U.S. medical students are assigned to residency positions.

NSF: National Science Foundation—a government-sponsored research organization.

Nurse practitioner: A registered nurse with a master's degree who performs limited patient care functions either alone or with the supervision of a physician.

Osteopathy: A system of medicine that emphasizes the unity of all the body parts and provides additional training in musculoskeletal and spinal manipulation. See Chapter 2.

Outcomes research: An area of research that looks at the outcomes of various medical interventions and evaluates which ones work, and at what cost.

Pepper Commission: A bipartisan congressional commission led by the late Florida Congressman Claude Pepper, whose task it was to recommend changes in the provision and financing of long-term care in the U.S. See Chapter 19 for a summary of their findings.

Physician assistant: Works under the supervision of a physician after a 2-year training period; responsibilities vary from state to state.

Play or pay: A form of an employer mandate to guarantee universal coverage, where employers are given a choice to either cover their employees or pay a tax so that the state can cover them. This was passed in Massachusetts, but was never implemented. See Chapters 13 and 14.

POS plan: Point of Service plans are yet another managed care product that offers patients more freedom of choice than traditional HMOs. Patients are free to see any provider; however, they receive maximum coverage only if they see approved providers and only if they

	see specialists with a referral from their primary clinician. See Chapter 5.
PPO:	Preferred Provider Organizations—a managed care product whereby subscribers have freedom of choice of provider, but must pay higher copayments if the provider they want to see is not on a list of approved providers. See Chapter 5.
PPS:	Prospective payment system—a way to reimburse hospitals used currently by Medicare, which pays hospitals a fixed amount per patient depending on diagnosis.
Preexisting conditions:	Any health conditions that a person may have at the time they sign up for a new insurance plan, which are usually not covered for a certain period of time after enrollment—one reason for lack of access to care. See Chapters 4 and 9.
PRO:	Peer Review Organization—method of quality assurance used by Medicare.
Rationing:	Any method of limiting the use of possible health services. This can be done through ability to pay, limited availability of equipment, or an explicit system, like the one being tried in Oregon. See Chapter 13.
RBRVS:	Resource-based relative value scale—a fee schedule used by Medicare to pay physicians based on the time, skill, and training required for each task.
Redlining:	A technique used by some insurers to not sell insurance to entire groups of people because they are considered high risk, for instance, excluding male hairdressers because of the perceived high risk of HIV.
Risk aversion:	The willingness to pay a small amount of money up front to avoid risking a larger loss in the future, even though the expected value of the loss would be less than the risk. It is because people are risk averse that they choose to buy health insurance. See Chapter 4.
Risk pooling:	The ability of insurers to group similar people with similar risks to change their individual uncertainties of facing a loss into a known cost that can be predicted. See Chapter 4.

Risk spreading: The spreading of losses among a large group; thus, all in a given insurance pool face the same small loss instead of a few people facing large losses. See Chapter 4.

Self-insurance: The process by which large companies assume the financial risk of health insurance themselves. Because of ERISA, this exempts them from most state insurance regulations such as mandated benefits.

Single-payer plan: Health reform proposals that would create a single— usually government—payer for health care, similar to the Canadian system. See Chapters 12 and 14.

Social insurance: A government program in which everyone mandatorily contributes premiums, and therefore everyone, not just poor people, is eligible for benefits (e.g., Social Security and Medicare). While some believe it is a waste to spend public money on those able to afford services themselves, social insurance programs are much more politically popular than welfare-type programs. See Chapter 6.

Socialized medicine: The term usually used derogatorily in the U.S. for any health system or proposal in which the government has a large role. Technically it refers to a system in which the state directly runs the health system, as in Britain. See Chapter 12.

Spend-down: The Medicaid option chosen by some states whereby people not categorically eligible for Medicaid can become eligible after spending most of their assets on medical care.

Staff Model HMO: A type of HMO that employs physicians as salaried employees and owns or leases its own health care facilities. An example is Harvard Community Health Plan in New England.

Tort system: The legal framework under which medical malpractice law is thought of in the U.S. Torts refer to breaking of obligations not necessarily delineated in a contract.

TQM: Total quality management (also known as continuous quality improvement [CQI])—the application of certain management techniques to monitor and improve quality, first used in industrial processes and now being applied to health care. See Chapter 10.

Uncompensated care pools: One method of improving access to health care by compensating hospitals for care they provide for which they are not paid. The funds for this can come from general taxes, other paying patients, or other sources.

Universal access: Providing health insurance coverage of essentially the whole population. This is a goal of many health reform plans.

Utilization review: A method of cost containment frequently used by insurance companies whereby they review the appropriateness of certain medical decisions, either prospectively or retrospectively (before or after the fact).

Vertical integration: Relationships between organizations at different stages of production. For instance, it is vertical integration when a hospital acquires a physician group, a nursing home, a pharmacy, or an outpatient clinic.

ONE

The U.S. Health Care System

The Health Care Industry

Rushika J. Fernandopulle and David Chin

> The key question is: Will medicine now become essentially a business or will it remain a profession? . . . Will we act as businessmen in a system that is becoming increasingly entrepreneurial or will we choose to remain a profession . . . ?
>
> Arnold Relman, 1982

Arnold Relman, former editor of the *New England Journal of Medicine,* reflected in this quote the uneasiness of many physicians when thinking about health care as a business.[1] Indeed, many feel that somehow health care must be different than other industries, such as the housing or the automotive industries, because it deals with something that seems to transcend monetary value: life itself. Yet in many ways the provision of health care is very similar to the provision of other necessities, such as food or clothing. To understand many aspects of health care policy in the United States, we first need to make clear in what ways health care is like other services in the economy, and in what ways it is different.

This chapter brings the health care industry into perspective by comparing its magnitude with that of other large industries. The allocation of spending within the industry is then briefly discussed. Several sectors of the industry, specifically hospitals, physicians, private insurance, managed care, and the role of government, are examined in more detail in following chapters. After this description of spending in the health industry, we look at how health care is different from other industries, and we explore briefly how this difference affects the way health care is paid for and delivered in the U.S. Finally, we examine the recent trend in the

U.S. of treating health care more like a business, and we discuss briefly the effects of this trend on hospitals, the medical profession, and patients.

THE HEALTH CARE INDUSTRY IN PERSPECTIVE ❖
The Health Care Industry Compared with Other Industries

One of the main reasons why health care has attracted so much attention recently is its large role in our economy. As Table 1.1 shows, household spending on health care in 1991 was double that spent on food, three times that spent on clothing, nearly four times that spent on automobiles and other means of personal transportation, and seven times that spent on education. Table 1.1 also shows that the amount spent on health care relative to other parts of the economy has increased dramatically in the last few decades. The causes and ramifications of this are addressed more fully in Chapter 8.

Spending in the Health Care Industry

The U.S. health care system is massive. Indeed, in 1993, health spending took up 14% of the Gross National Product (GNP) (i.e., approximately one of every 7 dollars spent in the U.S. went toward health care). Chapters 5 to 7 describe in more detail where this money comes from; in this chapter, we concentrate on how it is spent (i.e., how the health care industry delivers care). Table 1.2 delineates the largest targets of health spending for 1991.

By far the biggest spending on the health care system goes to hospitals. This figure represents a diverse group of institutions, from acute-care general hospitals to specialty hospitals, such as pediatric or psychiatric hospitals, to rehabilitation and chronic care hospitals. Even within general hospitals, there are rural hospitals, sub-

Table 1.1   The Health Care Industry in Perspective[a]

	1991	1979
Food	330.019	180.486
Clothing and footwear	226.242	107.766
Medical care and health expenses	656.021	180.797
Personal transport equipment	168.967	81.331
Education	92.760	29.787
Totals	3,781.120	1,543.040

[a]Household consumption in U.S. at current prices (billions of dollars).
(Source: OECD National Accounts, vol 2: detailed tables 1979–1991. Paris, OECD Press, 1993.)

Table 1.2 Distribution of U.S. Health Care Spending in 1991

Hospitals	38%
Physicians	19%
Nursing Homes	8%
Pharmaceuticals	8%
Dentistry	5%

Five largest areas of health care spending in the United States in 1991, as a percentage of the total health care spending.

urban community hospitals, tertiary referral teaching hospitals, inner city county hospitals, and government-run veterans hospitals, to name a few. Chapter 3 describes in detail the hospital industry, as well as some of the issues concerning its organization and financing.

Physicians account for 19% of medical spending, but their influence is actually far greater. Most experts agree that physician decisions are directly responsible for more than 70% of health spending. Thus, much of health care policy is targeted at understanding physician behavior and offering proper incentives to change this behavior to achieve policy goals. Chapter 2 discusses many issues relevant to physicians, their training, behavior, and payment.

Eight percent of spending goes to nursing homes, which are largely private entities, many for-profit, and they are in higher and higher demand as the population ages. The financing of nursing home and other long-term care is particularly problematic, and Chapter 19 takes on these issues in more detail.

Pharmaceuticals also take up 8% of national health spending. The pharmaceutical industry is extremely capital-intensive, with huge sums required to research, develop, and bring a drug to market. Some estimate it costs more than $200 million to develop just one drug. The Food and Drug Administration (FDA) is responsible for licensing of pharmaceuticals, and drugs must go through a long process of animal and then human trials, and they must be proved safe and efficacious before they can be brought to market. Pharmaceuticals are different than much of the rest of the health industry in that they frequently are not covered by insurance, and they are paid for out-of-pocket by consumers. Thus, although pharmaceuticals comprise only a small portion of total spending on health care, it is the portion consumers actually pull out of their wallet; thus, prices of pharmaceuticals engender much controversy among the public.

Finally, 5% of U.S. health dollars go to dentistry. Because much of dental care is also paid for out-of-pocket, the policy issues are different than for the rest of the health care industry. A more detailed look at dental policy issues is beyond the scope of this book, but the references include some good sources for those interested in this subject.

The rest of health spending goes to a myriad of other sources, including administration, home health care, hospice, medical devices, eyeglasses, and research.

HOW HEALTH CARE DIFFERS FROM OTHER INDUSTRIES ❖

Although in some ways the health care industry delivers goods and services much like other industries, there are several reasons why it is unique.

Insurance

The most obvious factor differentiating health care from other industries is health insurance. Most people in the U.S. have health insurance. Thus, when they are sick, they do not face the true price (if any) of the goods or services they receive. This fact greatly changes consumer behavior. Imagine if one had restaurant insurance and whatever meal one ordered would be free. With such insurance, one would tend to choose more expensive dishes; indeed, one would likely choose more expensive restaurants. One would also tend to consume more meals than they would if they had to pay for their meals. Note that the presence of such insurance not only would affect consumer behavior, but also would influence the very structure of the industry; in a world with ubiquitous restaurant insurance, there would likely be few cheap dives left.

Tax Treatment

Not only might one consume more health care because of the presence of insurance, but also one might consume more insurance because it is tax-deductible. One buys insurance with before-tax dollars, whereas most other things are bought with after-tax money. Suppose, for example, a person earned enough to be in a 28% marginal tax bracket; of each additional dollar earned, the government takes 28 cents. Suppose this person's employer offers a choice: either an additional $1,000 worth of health insurance or $1,000 in cash. Because the cash would be taxed, the real choice, then, would be between the $1,000 of insurance and only $720 cash ($1,000 minus 28%). Naturally, this employee would take the insurance. Thus, the tax system has incentives to over-purchase insurance, basically because the government subsidizes it.

Expertise

Medical care, more than most other industries, involves a huge information inequality between doctor and patient. Even with other complex purchases, such as an automobile, there is a lot more consumer information. In medicine, patients rarely know enough to choose their treatments or work-up; indeed, they usually do not want to. Thus, doctors have far more market influence than sellers of most other goods and services. Economists call this information asymmetry.

Needs Versus Desires

Medical care differs from other goods in that some medical care is a necessity. Certain necessities, such as food and clothing, are allocated by normal market mechanisms. Although these commodities are necessities, substitution is usually possible. Therefore, no particular food or article of clothing is a necessity at any particular time. Similarly, most nonemergent medical care has ready substitutes; thus, the health industry can function like any other market. However, emergency care, such as treatment of a bullet wound to the chest or an acute myocardial infarction, is truly different from other services.

Government Involvement

To a larger extent than in most other industries, the government is quite heavily involved in the health care industry. The health sector is more regulated than most others; there are strict licensing laws for providers, facilities, and drugs, as well as other legal responsibilities placed on all in the system. In addition, government is a large subsidizer of health care, through research grants (see Chapter 17), tax deductions, and direct funding through Medicare and Medicaid (see Chapter 6).

Capital and Labor

In most industries, there is a trade-off between capital and labor as inputs of production. Thus, in the auto industry, if one wants to make more cars, one can either hire more workers or spend more capital to buy a more automated assembly line. In health care, new technology usually requires both new capital (to acquire the equipment) and new labor (trained to use the new machines). In most industries, new technology is cost-saving, because it eventually replaces older technology. In medical care, new technology is usually additive: Computed tomography scanners did not replace radiography machines, they simply added to the number of radiological procedures.

Local Industry

Finally, most industries have large economies of scale, meaning that it is cheaper and easier to have large national organizations delivering products and services.

What makes this approach possible is that, for instance, selling a car in Iowa is fairly similar to selling one in Massachusetts. Medicine, however, is in many ways still a guild, and utilization varies considerably from area to area due partly to variations in training and practice styles (see Chapter 2). The malpractice system (see Chapter 15) encourages this variation by holding practitioners to the standard of care practiced in their community. Thus, for all these reasons, national scale enterprises have a harder time in the health sector.

Fragmentation

Partly because of this local variation, and because the complementarity of capital and labor makes economies of scale hard to achieve, health care is a much more fragmented industry than others. Thus, in almost all aspects of the delivery and financing of health care, the biggest players have less market dominance than in other areas of the economy. The top five pharmaceutical companies control only 30% of the pharmaceutical market, whereas the top five beer companies control 90% of the beer market and the top five auto companies control 80% of the auto market.[2]

The implications of these differences in the health care industry are many. These factors help explain why health care costs are so high and are rising faster than general inflation. Chapter 8 discusses these factors in greater detail. These factors also influence the structure of the industry, especially the organization of hospitals and physicians, which are the subject of the next two chapters.

TRENDS IN THE HEALTH CARE INDUSTRY ❖

As discussed, there are many reasons why health care is different than other industries; as a result, for a long time health care was not thought of as a business. In the past few decades, however, several changes have taken place that have transformed health care more into a business and made it more like other industries.

Because health care involves basic human needs, the expertise of physicians, and a large amount of local practice variation, until about the 1960s, the health industry was dominated by voluntary not-for-profit hospitals and a strong, independent medical profession. The hospitals were run by their local communities, and they depended on philanthropy for much of their income. Physicians were well respected, very busy, and left to their own judgments in almost all medical affairs. There was a strong legal doctrine against the corporate practice of medicine, as well as strong professional norms against advertising or other competitive behavior among physicians. Many patients were uninsured, especially the elderly, and the sums of money to be made in the health sector were small. For these reasons, health care looked very little like an industry, and people viewed its provision more as a public service than as a business.

Starting around 1960, however, a series of changes took place that transformed the health sector into the industry as we see it today. The most important of these changes was the entry of government as a large-scale health purchaser through Medicare and Medicaid. Partly as a tactic to gain the support of providers, reimbursements for Medicaid were given on a generous, retrospective cost-plus basis. Essentially, providers submitted bills, and the government paid them without asking many questions. At the same time, there was an increase in the number of people covered by employer-provided insurance. These two changes injected huge amounts of money into the health care industry, and people began seeing the provision of health care not solely as a way to serve humanity, but as a way to make money. This change has affected all parts of the health care industry, but we concentrate on the effects on its two biggest parts: hospitals and physicians.

Effects on Hospitals

The introduction of Medicare and Medicaid, in addition to the expansion of private insurance, meant that providing hospital care was no longer solely a charitable proposition, and many astute entrepreneurs started providing hospital care on a for-profit basis. The most visible of these groups were large hospital chains like Humana, Hospital Corporation of America (HCA), and National Medical Enterprises (NME), which prospered in light of generous reimbursements from the government and private insurance companies. By 1980, both Humana and HCA made more than $1 billion each in annual revenue, and they were listed among the most profitable service industries in the nation.[3] This increase in the number of for-profit hospitals has been paralleled in other areas of the health industry. For instance, by 1986, 37% of psychiatric hospitals, 81% of nursing homes, 66% of health maintenance organizations (HMOs), 90% of free-standing surgical centers, and 63% of blood banks were run as for-profit entities.[4] Because not-for-profit hospitals have to compete with these for-profit centers for capital funds for expansion, many believe these institutions have started to act more like businesses and less like charities.

Effects on the Medical Profession

It was inevitable that the same forces active in the hospital market would also affect physicians. Generous reimbursements combined with the features of the health industry discussed earlier gave rise to increasing health care costs. By 1970, these increasing bills began to concern employers, and many felt they had to take more control of the health care they were purchasing. *Fortune* magazine reflected this concern when, in May of 1970, it published a lead article stating, "the majority of physicians constitute an army of pushcart vendors in an age of supermarkets. . . . The management of medical care has become too important to leave to doctors, who are, after all, not managers to begin with . . . ."[5]

This change in attitude by payers coincided with another phenomenon: the start of a perceived doctor glut, as described in Chapter 2. This oversupply of doctors, combined with corporatization of the health sector and other forces, have led to what John Stoeckle and others have called the "proletarianization" of medicine. This term refers to a historical concept developed by Marx of the transformation of much of the workforce during the industrial revolution. Like the guilds of tradesmen in the middle ages, these writers argue doctors are being first brought into "factories" (i.e., hospitals) as independent workers, and then gradually made into salaried employees controlled by the factory owners (i.e., hospital administrators).[6]

It is undeniable that physicians no longer control the health industry as they used to; often they are now employees of some corporate enterprise and they must take marching orders from nonphysician managers. Many managed care plans require them to see a certain number of patients each session, or they tie their compensation to certain desired behaviors, such as increased productivity or hospital admissions. Even physicians still independently practicing frequently have to get approval for many tests and procedures from a patient's insurer, a process that usually involves a long-distance phone conversation with a nonphysician reviewer. This change of practice, more than anything, has probably led to the dissatisfaction of so many physicians.

Effects on Patients

The health care sector is becoming more like an industry, as a result of the rise of for-profit institutions, the pressures on non-profit centers to act like businesses, and the submission of some physician authority to the management of this new industry. These changes have obvious ramifications on those who work in health care, but the real public policy question is whether these changes are beneficial to the people for whom the system is designed to serve.

There are many arguments for why we should be glad that health care is becoming more like a business. First, some argue that this change will lead to increased efficiency because the market will weed out the inefficient players. Second, some say a market system is more customer-driven and responsive to needs than the old, professionally dominated system. Two-hour waits in dingy doctors' offices will not be tolerated in the new environment. Third, a more business-like health sector may be better at controlling costs, because physicians under the old system showed no desire or ability to do so. Finally, in a complex world, perhaps the health system is better managed by professional managers than by doctors who may be good at seeing patients but little else.

In contrast, many believe that the process described is severely detrimental to our society. Arnold Relman is one of the most passionate of these critics, and in several editorials in the *New England Journal of Medicine,* he has decried the rise of business in health care. The profit motive and good patient care are fundamentally incompatible, he says, and health care is fundamentally different than other services, as discussed, and it should not be left to the market to allocate.

What is the final verdict? The answer is far from clear. The health industry continues to be in a state of rapid transformation in the 1990s, and there is no end in sight. There are an increasing number of private and government initiatives that will all change the industry, although how is not clear. Increasingly, there is a need for physicians to understand these changes and to be able to be effective advocates for themselves and their patients. We hope the rest of this book will help you start this process.

❖ Suggested Reading ❖

Jones R. The supermeds. New York: Charles Scribner, 1988.

Wohl S. The medical-industrial complex. New York: Harmony, 1984.

   Two easy to read but slightly sensationalistic looks at the for-profit health industry.

Relman AS. The new medical industrial complex. N Engl J Med 1980;303:963–970.

Relman AS. The health care industry; where is it taking us? N Engl J Med 1991;325: 854–859.

   The classic article by Relman about the rise of business in health care, and a follow-up one decade later.

Iglehart JK. The American health care system. N Engl J Med 1992;326:962–967; 326: 1715–1720; 327:10; 327:742–747; 327:1467–1472. 1993;328:366–371; 328:896–900; 329:372–376; 329:1052–1056.

   An excellent multipart series on different aspects of the U.S. health industry.

2

Physicians

Christopher Bencomo, Carlos Trejo, and David Calkins

As discussed in the previous chapter, although physicians directly account for less than 20% of the money spent on health care, their decisions are responsible for more than 70% of all medical spending. Thus, it is important to look at who comprise the physicians in the United States, as well as at some of the issues concerning how they practice medicine. This chapter is divided into four distinct sections: basic demographics, educational background, professional characteristics, and trends in the physician workforce.

In the basic demographics section, we discuss such characteristics of the physician workforce as age, gender, and ethnicity. Special consideration is given to the participation of women and minorities in medicine. The section on educational background summarizes physician training, including allopathic and osteopathic medical education, foreign medical graduates, and educational costs. The section on professional characteristics presents data on postgraduate training, areas of specialization, income, geographic distribution, and practice style of physicians in the U.S. The last section addresses current trends in the workforce and focuses on models of projected supply and demand for physicians in the year 2000.

DEMOGRAPHICS ❖

The American Medical Association (AMA) developed a comprehensive data base of all physicians in the U.S. who meet the primary educational criteria needed to be recognized as physicians. The AMA Physician Masterfile, originally used for

Table 2.1 Physician Distribution by Age and Gender, 1992

	Total Physicians	Under 35	35–44	45–54	55–64	65 and Over
Male	534,543	93,287	153,921	110,790	80,288	96,257
Female	118,519	40,431	44,336	18,026	7,224	8,502
Total	653,062	133,718	198,257	128,816	87,512	104,759

Source: AMA Physician Masterfile.

membership accounting purposes, is considered the most comprehensive data base of physician information available.[7]

Age

According to the AMA, in 1992 there was a total of 653,062 Doctors of Medicine (MD) in the U.S.[8] Table 2.1 shows the distribution of physicians by age and gender. Overall, slightly more than one half of all physicians were under the age of 45. Physicians under 35 years made up 20.4% of the workforce, whereas those between 35 and 44 years represented 30.3% of the total. In the remaining age groups, 19.7% were between the ages of 45 and 54 years, 13.4% were between 55 and 64 years, and 16% were 65 years or older (Figure 2.1).

Gender

Historically, medicine in the U.S. has been a male-dominated profession. In 1992, men still accounted for the vast majority of the physician workforce. Table 2.1

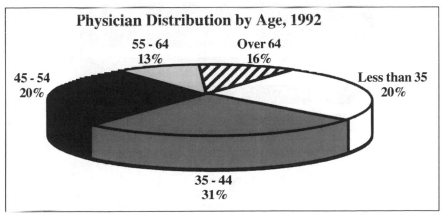

Figure 2.1 Distribution of physicians by age group, 1992. (Source: AMA Physician Profile.)

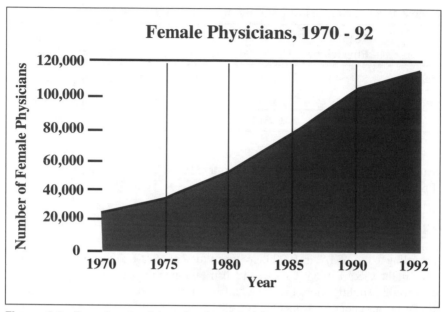

Figure 2.2 Female physicians in the U.S., 1970 to 1992. (Data source: AMA Physician Masterfile.)

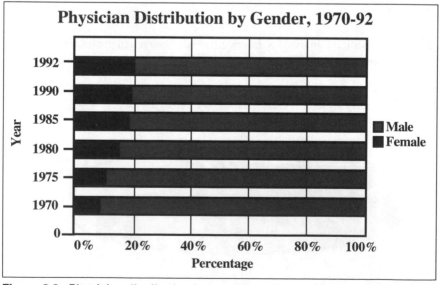

Figure 2.3 Physician distribution by gender, 1970 to 1992. (Source: AMA Physician Profile.)

Table 2.2 U.S. Medical School Graduates by Gender, 1987–1992

	1970	1975	1980	1985	1990	1992
Male	10,723	10,704	10,409	10,167	9,874	9,815
Female	5,107	5,215	5,221	5,231	5,553	5,550
Total	15,830	16,117	15,630	15,398	15,427	15,365

Adapted from AAMC.

shows that there was a total of 534,543 (81.9%) male physicians, compared with 118,519 (18.1%) female physicians. This represents a 450% increase in the number of female physicians since 1970, when the number of women in the profession was just more than 25,500, or 7.7% of all physicians. These trends are shown graphically in Figures 2.2 and 2.3.

These numbers, however, do not accurately reflect the growing increase in both the total number and the percentage of women applying to and graduating from U.S. medical schools. According to data collected by the Association of American Medical Colleges (AAMC), 2,734 women applied to U.S. medical schools in 1970, which represented 10.9% of the total applicants for that year. In contrast, for the academic year 1992 to 1993, there was a total of 37,410 applicants, of which 41.8% were female.[9] Data for the percentage of women graduating from U.S. medical schools, although not as striking, are nonetheless significant when compared with levels in 1970. Within the last 5 years, the percentage of female graduates has consistently increased at a rate of just less than 1% per year, from 32.2% in 1987 to 36.1% in 1992 (Table 2.2).

The gender distribution of medical school faculty approximates that of the physician workforce. Table 2.3 shows the gender distribution of U.S. medical school faculty. Women have a slightly higher percentage of representation in this area than in the field of medicine as a whole. Although men make up

Table 2.3 U.S. Medical School Faculty by Rank and Gender, 1992*

	Male	Female	Total
Professor	17,006 (92.0%)	1,471 (8.0%)	18,477 (100%)
Associate Professor	13,622 (82.0%)	2,993 (18.05%)	16,615 (100%)
Assistant Professor	18,483 (70.5%)	7,747 (29.5%)	26,230 (100%)
Instructor	3,480 (58.4%)	2,481 (41.6%)	5,961 (100%)
Total	52,591 (78.1%)	14,692 (21.9%)	67,283 (100%)

*Excludes faculty from Howard, Meharry, Morehouse and Puerto Rico Schools. (Adapted from AAMC: Faculty Roster Data System.)

81.9% of all physicians, they compose 78.1% of all faculty.[10] Women, in contrast, make up 18.1% of all physicians and 21.9% of all teaching positions. Although strides have been made in increasing the number of female physicians and faculty members, women are best represented at the Instructor and Assistant Professor level, as previously observed by Bickel in 1988.[11] She concluded that poorer representation of women at senior faculty positions translated to fewer likely female candidates considered for senior leadership positions and Deanships.

Ethnicity

The Council on Graduate Medical Education (COGME) recognizes the following as historically under-represented groups in medicine: African-Americans, Mexican-Americans/Chicanos, Native Americans, and mainland Puerto Ricans.[12] The AAMC compiles yearly statistics on the ethnic background of all applicants to and enrollees in U.S. medical schools. The number and percentage of total entrants to U.S. medical schools in each of the four minority groups are summarized in Table 2.4 for the years 1982 to 1992.

A total of 1,827 under-represented minorities entered U.S. medical schools for the academic year 1992 to 1993, or 11.2% of all new entrants. This figure has not changed significantly since 1982, when all minority entrants as a percentage of the total equaled 8.4%. Furthermore, until the academic year 1991 to 1992, minority enrollment as a percent of total enrollment had only increased 1.4% in the 10-year period since 1982 (data not shown).

In their second report to the U.S. Secretary of Health and Human Services in 1990, COGME commented on the discouraging trend in minority representation in the physician workforce. The Council concluded that most, if not all, minority groups remained severely under-represented within the U.S. physician workforce pool. They recommended the federal government encourage both private and public programs that promote a more equitable balance of racial and ethnic groups in medicine to ensure that minorities have equal access to health care services.

The data on minority representation within faculties at U.S. medical schools are even more discouraging. According to the AAMC Faculty Roster for 1992, African-Americans accounted for 1.9% of total medical school faculty, Native Americans made up 0.1%, and Mexican-Americans and Puerto Ricans were both 0.3% of the total. This trend is also reflected in the ethnic distribution of medical school department chairs. If historically black and Puerto Rican medical schools are excluded, in 1990 there were 27 African-American, 22 Puerto Rican, 6 Native American, and 4 Mexican-American department chairs in the United States.[12] Table 2.5 shows the breakdown of minority faculty in U.S. medical schools for 1992, excluding historically minority medical colleges.

Table 2.4 Minority Admissions to U.S. Medical Schools, 1982–1992

Year	African American Total	%	Native American Total	%	Mexican American Total	%	Puerto Rican Total	%	All URM Total	%	Total
1982	961	5.8	54	0.3	278	1.7	94	0.6	1,387	8.4	16,567
1984	971	5.9	67	0.4	290	1.8	112	0.7	1,440	8.8	15,927
1986	991	6.2	54	0.3	288	1.8	97	0.6	1,430	8.9	15,969
1988	997	6.2	68	0.4	260	1.6	106	0.7	1,431	9.0	15,867
1990	1,055	6.6	63	0.4	251	1.6	101	0.6	1,470	9.2	15,998
1992	1,203	7.4	102	0.6	409	2.5	113	0.7	18,827	11.2	16,289

URM = Under-Represented Minorities as defined by the Federal Government. (Source: AAMC Minority Students in Medical Education Facts and Figures VII, 1993.)

Table 2.5 Minority Faculty in U.S. Medical School, 1992*

	African American	Native American	Mexican American	Puerto Rican	
	Total (%)	Total (%)	Total (%)	Total (%)	Total
Professor	132 (0.7)	24 (0.1)	28 (0.2)	23 (0.1)	18,477
Associate Professor	227 (1.4)	13 (0.1)	41 (0.2)	30 (0.2)	16,615
Assistant Professor	655 (2.5)	22 (0.1)	114 (0.4)	112 (0.4)	26,230
Instructor	263 (4.4)	10 (0.2)	19 (0.3)	49 (0.8)	5,961
Total	1,277 (1.9)	69 (0.1)	202 (0.3)	214 (0.3)	67,283

*Excludes faculty from Howard University, Meharry, Morehouse and Puerto Rico Schools.
(Adapted from AAMC: Faculty Roster Data System.)

PHYSICIAN EDUCATION ❖

All practicing physicians in the U.S. must meet rigorous educational and licensing requirements. The training of most physicians in the U.S. is, on average, an 11- to 12-year process after the completion of high school, including four years of college, four years of formal training at an accredited allopathic or osteopathic medical school, and a one- to four-year postgraduate training program. Fellowship training can extend professional training an additional two to five years. Physicians trained in medical schools outside the U.S. are eligible for licensure only after satisfying eligibility criteria as determined by the individual licensing bodies.

Allopathic Physicians

There are 125 accredited, four-year *allopathic* medical schools in the U.S. with approximately 16,000 available positions. An undergraduate degree and a minimum basic science core curriculum are required for entrance to most U.S. medical schools. The selection process considers such factors as the Medical College Admission Test (MCAT), undergraduate GPA, letters of recommendation, research/ work experience, and personal interviews.

After five years of an increasing applicant pool, in 1993 the AAMC reported an all-time-record number of 42,808 applicants to medical schools[13] after a 15-year decline, which hit its lowest point in 1988 (26,721 applicants). This trend is shown in Figure 2.4. Unlike applications to medical schools, the number of new entrants has not varied substantially over the past decade, ranging from 15,867 to 16,567, which translates into an increasingly competitive field. In 1974, the acceptance rate was 35.3%, or 1 acceptance for each 2.8 applicants. By 1988, the acceptance

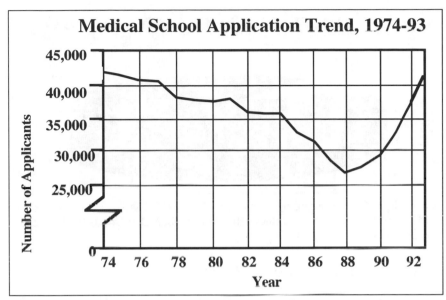

Figure 2.4 Minority students applying for medical school, 1974 to 1993. (Source: AAMC.)

rate increased to 64%, or 1 acceptance for each 1.6 applicants. By 1993, the acceptance rate had decreased to 40.6%, or 1 acceptance for each 2.5 applicants.

Osteopathic Physicians

Osteopathic medicine focuses on the unity of all the body parts, and it emphasizes preventive medicine and holistic patient care. The field was founded by Andrew Taylor Still, MD, in 1874. There are 15 Colleges of Osteopathic Medicine in the U.S., with a total first-year enrollment of approximately 1,800. The osteopathic curriculum is similar to that of allopathic medical schools, except that osteopathic schools provide additional training in musculoskeletal and spinal manipulation. Criteria for admission is similar to allopathic medical schools, including a four-year undergraduate degree, a set of basic science requirements, the MCAT, and personal interviews.

In 1993, there were 34,824 doctors of osteopathic medicine (DO) in the U.S.[14] Osteopathic physicians constituted approximately 5% of the total physicians (MD and DO) for that same year (Figure 2.5). As of 1993, women were estimated to make up approximately 17% of DOs. As with allopathic medical schools, the number of female first-year enrollees, total enrollees, and graduates has increased. In 1989, women comprised approximately 33% of first-year students, 28% of total enrollees, and 30% of graduates from osteopathic schools of medicine. Underrepresented minority enrollment has also increased; it totalled 8.8% of the first-year class in 1989.[15]

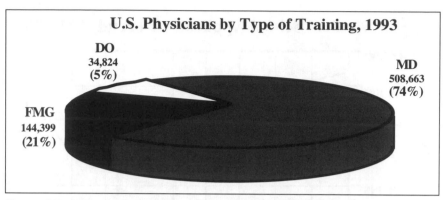

Figure 2.5 U.S. physicians by type of training, 1993. FMG = Foreign Medical Graduates; DO = Doctor of Osteopathic Medicine; MD = Doctor of Medicine. (Data source: AMA and AOA.)

Foreign Medical Graduate Physicians

Foreign medical graduates (FMGs) are defined as graduates from medical schools located outside the U.S., Canada, and Puerto Rico. They include U.S. and non-U.S. citizens. FMGs may apply to residency positions in the U.S. after satisfying state licensing and language requirements as outlined by the individual state boards. In 1992, FMGs accounted for 22.1% of all U.S. physicians.[8] In 1990, FMGs accounted for approximately 5,230, or 22%, of the applicants to the National Residency Matching Program (NRMP).[15]

Educational Costs

The average tuition cost in 1991 to 1992 to attend a public medical school was $6,943, whereas the average tuition cost per year at a private medical school was $19,618.[9] The primary source of financial aid for medical students is in the form of scholarships and loans. Parental contributions are generally minimal compared with the total cost. As recently as 1982, the mean educational debt for all graduates of allopathic schools was $21,028. According to the AAMC Graduation Questionnaire, the average debt was approximately $55,859 per graduating senior in 1992.[10] Figure 2.6 demonstrates the level of debt incurred by graduates of private and public medical schools in 1992.

Many experts believe that a high level of indebtedness may influence a medical student's choice of residency training.[16,17] Students with large debt burdens may favor procedure-oriented fields, which offer higher compensation. This may be an underlying factor in why students choose subspecialty training over training in a primary care field. The AAMC, in their graduating medical student questionnaire, is currently assessing how influential indebtedness may be when choosing a specialty. The results of this study and others like it may help policy-

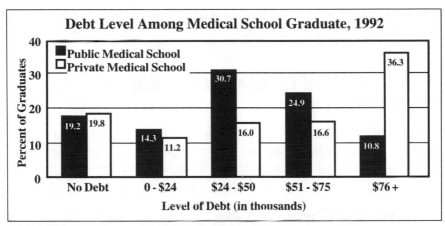

Figure 2.6 Debt level among medical school graduates, 1992. (Adapted from AAMC Medical School Graduation Questionnaire.)

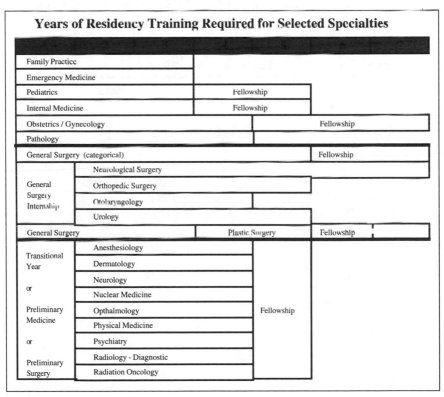

Figure 2.7 Schematic view of residency training program lengths for selected specialties. Note years of training noted above do not include years of biomedical research work required by many programs, and made optional in others. Fellowships, in most instances, are optional and vary between one and three years. (Adapted from The National Residency Program Directory 1993.)

makers structure incentives to increase the ranks of generalists in the field of medicine.

PROFESSIONAL CHARACTERISTICS ❖
Postgraduate Training

The majority of graduating students apply through the NRMP to one of the 22 specialties. Residency training programs vary in length (Figure 2.7).[18] Subspecialization is achieved through additional training in the form of fellowships.

Specialization Demographics

The AMA uses 38 specialty codes (SDPS) to describe physician practice (Table 2.6). The six specialties most often designated by physicians are internal medicine (18%), family/general practice (12%), pediatrics (8%), obstetrics/gynecology

Table 2.6 Number of Physicians in
Selected Specialties and Subspecialties, 1992

Specialty		Total
Anesthesia		28,148
Dermatology		7,912
Emergency Medicine		15,470
Family/General Practice		72,864
Family Practice	50,969	
General Practice	20,719	
General Preventive Medicine	1,176	
Internal Medicine		146,697
Aerospace Medicine	691	
Allergy/Immunology	3,441	
Cardiology	16,478	
Gastroenterology	7,946	
General Internal Medicine	109,017	
Occupational Medicine	2,787	
Pulmonary Diseases	6,337	
Neurology		9,742
Obstetrics and Gynecology		35,273
Ophthalmology		16,433
Otolaryngology		8,373
Pathology		9,742
Anatomic/Clinical	17,005	
Forensic Pathology	423	

Table 2.6 (continued)

Specialty		Total
Pediatrics		45,921
General Pediatrics	44,881	
Pediatric Cardiology	1,040	
Physical/Rehabilitative Medicine		4,469
Psychiatry		41,023
Child Psychiatry	4,618	
General Psychiatry	36,405	
Radiology		29,486
Diagnostic Radiology	17,253	
Nuclear Medicine	1,372	
Radiology	7,848	
Radiation Oncology		3,013
Surgery		81,481
Colon/Rectal	869	
General	39,211	
Neurological	4,501	
Orthopedic	20,640	
Plastic	4,688	
Thoracic	2,120	
Urological	9,452	
Other Specialty		7,295
Public Health		1,984
Inactive		55,656
Other (unspecified, not classified, address unknown)		27,407
Total		653,062

Adapted from AMA Physician Characteristics and Distribution in the U.S.

(6%), general surgery (12%), and psychiatry (6%) (Figure 2.8). COGME defines the primary care fields as family practice, internal medicine, and pediatrics. By this definition, 38% of all active MDs are in a primary care field. More than half of all DOs practice in a primary care field.

Geographic Distribution

The geographic distribution data available on physicians are divided into metropolitan versus nonmetropolitan areas. A Metropolitan Statistical Area (MSA) is defined in either of two ways: a city of at least 50,000 population, or an urbanized area of at least 50,000 population, with a total metropolitan population of at least

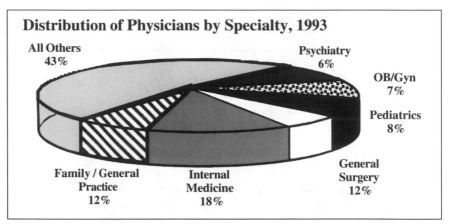

Figure 2.8 Breakdown of the six largest specialty groups among all active U.S. physicians. (Source: AMA Physician Characteristics and Distribution in the U.S., 1993.)

100,000.[8] The base units utilized throughout the U.S. for MSAs are counties, except for the six New England states, where town/cities are used due to the lack of county governments. In 1992, 88.4% of all physicians were located in metropolitan areas. This statistic has changed little since 1970, when 85.7% of total physicians were located in metropolitan areas (Table 2.7).[8] The majority of physicians located in nonmetropolitan areas are general/family practitioners. Figure 2.9 demonstrates further the stratification of physicians across MSAs of varying size.

The number and ratio of total physicians per 100,000 population in the U.S. has increased over the past 30 years. In 1960, there were 142 physicians per 100,000 population; in 1992, there were 248 physicians per 100,000 population. Figure 2.10 shows the physician-to-population ratio (MD/100,000) by state in 1992. Table 2.8 shows the states with the highest and lowest physician-to-population ratio. Finally, Tables 2.9 to 2.13 show the states with the highest and the lowest population per physician ratio for the following specialties, respectively: family medicine, internal medicine, pediatrics, general surgery, and obstetrics and gynecology. Tables 2.9 to 2.13 also note the percentage of total MDs that practice each specialty in each state.

There are several studies that suggest the U.S. has or will have a surplus of physicians before the turn of the century. In contrast, there is a large variation in the number of generalists and specialists across states (data on latter not shown). For example, in 1992, there were 2,148 people in the state of North Dakota for each general/family practitioner. In Massachusetts, an otherwise leader with high ratios of doctors in other specialties, there were 6,414 civilians per general/family doctor. A more striking example occurs between the two states with the highest and lowest civilian-to-obstetrician ratio. Delaware has the lowest ratio at 2,157 civilians per obstetrician, whereas Iowa has the highest ratio, with 14,552 civilians per obstetrician. Although nationwide there may be an overall surplus of doctors, within a given specialty there may be states with

Table 2.7 Urban and Rural Distribution of Physicians, 1970 and 1992

	General/Family Practice	Medical/Surgical Specialties	General/Family Practice	Medical/Surgical Specialties
	1970		**1992**	
Rural	16,457 (32.4%)	16,377 (11.9%)	16,451 (28.6%)	34,100 (11.3%)
Urban	34,359 (67.6%)	121,731 (88.1%)	41,120 (71.4%)	268,261 (88.7%)

Distribution above represents non-federal physicians only. The terms urban and metropolitan are defined as equivalent; similarly, rural and nonmetropolitan areas are equivalent. Metropolitan areas are defined as urban cities with a population of at least 50,000, or an urbanized area of at least 50,000 with a total metropolitan population of at least 100,000. (Source: AMA Physician Characteristics and Distribution in the U.S., 1992.)

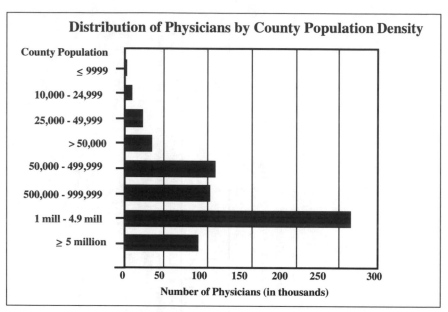

Figure 2.9 Physician distribution within counties in metropolitan and non-metropolitan statistical areas by population, 1992. (Source: AMA Physician Characteristics and Distribution in the U.S., 1993.)

physician shortages. Geographic variation is an important consideration when policy-makers consider limiting specialists to increase absolute numbers of primary care doctors.

Practice Variation

Similar to the geographic distribution of physicians, medical practice is not uniform throughout the U.S. Studies have noted large differences in the use of medical services in different geographical areas of the country. These services include surgical procedures, length of hospital stay, admissions to hospitals, and home health care visits, as well the number of office visits.[19]

Wennberg and Gittlesohn, in their study of six New England states, noted differences across regions, including the overall rate of surgery and the amount spent per capita on treatment in hospitals.[20] They found significant variation in care between cities as close as 20 miles apart. Furthermore, they found that this variation could not be explained by population characteristics, such as economic or general health status. In Maine, the probability of a woman having a hysterectomy by the age of 75 was 70% in one community, but it was only 25% in another.[21]

This extreme practice variation was not true for all diseases. Less practice variation was seen in diseases or procedures for which there was a consensus on the

Table 2.8 Ten Highest and Lowest
State Physician-to-Population Ratios, 1992

States with Highest Ratio		States with Lowest Ratio	
State	*Ratio*	*State*	*Ratio*
D.C.	705	Alaska	146
Massachusetts	380	Mississippi	149
Maryland	374	Idaho	150
New York	360	Wyoming	159
Connecticut	346	Nevada	166
Vermont	301	Oklahoma	168
Rhode Island	294	South Dakota	170
New Jersey	284	Iowa	175
Hawaii	283	Arkansas	179
Pennsylvania	275	Indiana	181

Ratios reflect the number of physicians per 100,000. (Data source: AMA, Physician Characteristics and Distribution in the U.S., 1993.)

preferred method of treatment. Examples cited included repair of inguinal hernia, management of an acute myocardial infarction, appendectomies, and treatment of hip fractures.[21]

Factors that explain practice variation may include variation in patient and physician characteristics, economic incentives, and the practice of "defensive"

Table 2.9 States with Highest and Lowest Population per Physician Ratio, Family Medicine/General Practice, 1992

States with Highest Ratio			States with Lowest Ratio		
State	*Ratio*	*% Specialists/ Total MDs*	*State*	*Ratio*	*% Specialists/ Total MDs*
Massachusetts	6,414	4	North Dakota	2,148	23
Rhode Island	5,859	6	Minnesota	2,204	18
Connecticut	5,621	5	Wyoming	2,363	27
New Jersey	5,492	6	South Dakota	2,392	25
New York	5,429	5	Washington	2,423	16
Missouri	5,087	9	Arkansas	2,460	22
Michigan	4,765	10	Nebraska	2,490	20
Nevada	4,599	13	Maine	2,767	17
Georgia	4,534	11	Kansas	2,781	18
Maryland	4,522	6	Indiana	2,886	19

Ratios reflect state population per physician. "% Specialists" reflects the percent of Family Medicine and General Practice physicians in each state with a specialty practice. (Data source: AMA, Physician Characteristics and Distribution in the U.S., 1993.)

Table 2.10 States with Highest and Lowest Population per Physician Ratio, Internal Medicine, 1992

States with Highest Ratio			States with Lowest Ratio		
State	Ratio	% Specialists/ Total MDs	State	Ratio	% Specialists/ Total MDs
Idaho	7,041	9	D.C.	712	20
Wyoming	6,706	9	Massachusetts	1,130	23
Alaska	6,360	11	New York	1,239	22
Mississippi	5,654	12	Maryland	1,348	20
Arkansas	5,251	10	Connecticut	1,348	21
South Dakota	5,118	11	Rhode Island	1,413	24
Iowa	4,902	12	New Jersey	1,704	21
Montana	4,647	11	Vermont	1,806	18
Indiana	4,523	12	Hawaii	1,978	18
South Carolina	4,517	12	Pennsylvania	2,059	18

Ratios reflect state population per physician, "% Specialists" reflects the percent of Internal Medicine physicians in each state with a specialty practice. (Data source AMA, Physician Characteristics and Distribution in the U.S., 1993.)

Table 2.11 States with Highest and Lowest Population per Physician Ratio, Pediatric Medicine, 1992

States with Highest Ratio			States with Lowest Ratio		
State	*Ratio*	*% Specialists/ Total MDs*	*State*	*Ratio*	*% Specialists/ Total MDs*
Idaho	16,694	4	D.C.	1,642	9
South Dakota	15,130	4	Maryland	3,109	9
Wyoming	14,710	4	New York	3,317	8
Nevada	12,704	5	Massachusetts	3,710	7
Montana	12,000	4	New Jersey	3,882	9
Iowa	11,043	5	Connecticut	3,996	7
Mississippi	10,742	6	Hawaii	4,269	8
North Dakota	10,246	5	Rhode Island	4,427	8
Indiana	10,025	6	Vermont	5,018	7
Oklahoma	9,686	6	California	5,314	7

Ratios reflect state population per physician. "% Specialists" reflects the percent of pediatric physicians in each state with a specialty practice. (Data source: AMA, Physician Characteristics and Distribution in the U.S., 1993.)

Table 2.12 States with Highest and Lowest Population per Physician Ratio, General Surgery, 1992

States with Highest Ratio			States with Lowest Ratio		
State	*Ratio*	*% Specialists/ Total MDs*	*State*	*Ratio*	*% Specialists/ Total MDs*
Alaska	16,088	4	D.C.	1,919	7
Idaho	11,500	6	New York	4,349	6
South Dakota	10,388	6	Massachusetts	4,406	6
Oklahoma	10,254	6	Maryland	4,880	5
Montana	10,177	5	Connecticut	5,073	6
Nevada	9,876	6	Rhode Island	5,082	7
Wyoming	9,500	7	Vermont	5,250	6
Mississippi	9,433	7	Hawaii	5,684	6
Indiana	9,294	6	Pennsylvania	5,769	6
Iowa	8,786	7	New Jersey	5,849	6

Ratios reflect state population per physician. "% Specialists" reflects the percent of General Surgeons in each state with a specialty practice. (Data source: AMA, Physician Characteristics and Distribution in the U.S., 1993.)

Table 2.13   States with Highest and Lowest Population per Physician Ratio, Obstetrics and Gynecology, 1992

States with Highest Ratio			States with Lowest Ratio		
State	*Ratio*	*% Specialists/ Total MDs*	*State*	*Ratio*	*% Specialists/ Total MDs*
Iowa	14,552	4	Delaware	2,147	6
South Dakota	13,647	4	D.C.	2,157	7
Alaska	13,024	5	Maryland	4,788	6
Idaho	12,938	5	Connecticut	5,144	6
Wyoming	12,324	5	Hawaii	5,268	7
North Dakota	12,019	4	New York	5,333	5
Montana	12,000	4	New Jersey	6,017	6
Indiana	11,531	5	Massachusetts	6,188	4
Arkansas	10,985	5	Louisiana	6,355	7
Oklahoma	10,818	6	Virginia	6,561	6
			Rhode Island	6,730	5

Ratios reflect state population per physician. "% Specialists" reflects the percent of OB/Gyn physicians in each state with a specialty practice. (Data source: AMA, Physician Characteristics and Distribution in the U.S., 1993.)

medicine. Professional uncertainty may also have a role. The sizable lack of data on effectiveness permits reasonable physicians to come to different conclusions regarding various health services. Advocates of change call for a renewed effort to realize the impact practice variation may have on health care costs and out-

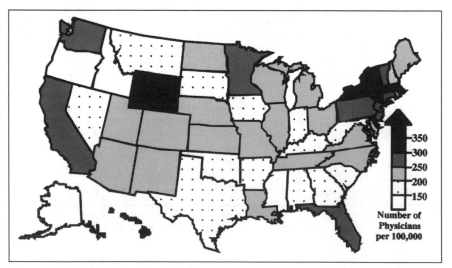

Figure 2.10   Physician to population ratios represent the number of physicians per 100,000 by state, 1992. (Data source: AMA Physician Characteristics and Distribution in the U.S., 1993.)

comes. Furthermore, they seek to increase the amount of research and evaluation of practice variation and outcomes.

Practice Activities

The AMA surveys physicians about their "major professional activities." Results of the 1992 survey are summarized in Table 2.14. In 1992, 59.6% of all active physicians designated office-based practice as their major professional activity. Twenty-four percent of surveyed physicians reported a hospital-based practice, and the remaining 6.6% were involved in nonclinical activities, such as administration, medical teaching, and medical research (Figure 2.11).

Income

Income for physicians varies by specialty. Figure 2.12 shows median income (after expenses and before taxes) for selected specialties in 1992. The highest median earnings were reported by radiologists ($240,000), followed by anesthesiologists ($220,000). The lowest median incomes were reported by general/family practitioners ($100,000) and pediatricians ($112,000). The median net income for all physicians was $148,000.

Table 2.14 Major Professional Activities of Physicians, 1992

Total Physicians	653,062	% of Total
Patient Care	535,220	82.0
Office Based Practice	389,364	59.6
Hospital Based Practice	154,856	23.7
Residents	86,468	13.2
Clinical Fellows	7,128	1.1
Full-Time Staff	56,260	8.6
Other Professional Activity	42,888	6.6
Medical Teaching	7,983	1.2
Administration	14,923	2.3
Research	16,367	2.5
Other Activity	3,615	0.6
Not Classified	16,589	2.5
Inactive	55,656	8.5
Address Unknown	2,709	0.4

Breakdown of all physicians by their major professional activity, 1992. (Adapted from AMA Physician Characteristics and Distribution in the U.S.)

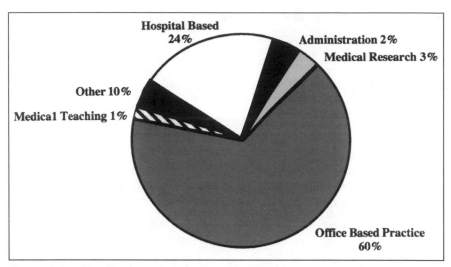

Figure 2.11 Distribution of all active physicians by major professional activity, 1992. "Other" = includes other activities, not classified, and address unknown. (Adapted from AMA Physician Characteristics and Distribution in the U.S., 1993.)

Figures 2.13 and 2.14 demonstrate that the median income for physicians also varied by region and practice size. In comparing solo and group practices, physicians working alone earned a median income of $140,000, whereas those in a practice of eight or more earned a median income of $220,000. Physicians working in the West South Central region of the U.S. (Arkansas, Louisiana, Oklahoma, and Texas) reported the highest average earnings ($193,300). Doctors living in the New England region (Maine, Vermont, New Hampshire, Massachusetts, Rhode Island, and Connecticut) reported the lowest average earnings ($124,000).

TRENDS IN THE PHYSICIAN WORKFORCE ❖

The period 1962 to 1971 was characterized by an explosion in the support for biomedical research and education, which provided the foundation for the current physician workforce. The "Kerr-Mills" Act of 1962 provided funds for the care of indigent elderly. The Health Professions Educational Assistance Act of 1963 provided support in the form of grants and funds to increase the number of enrolled medical students through expansion of class size and construction of new medical schools. In 1965, this Act was amended to provide for operating costs for medical schools, as well as scholarships for enrolled students. In 1965, Congress passed the legislation that would have the greatest impact on the medical establishment, the Social Security Act Titles XVIII and XIX, otherwise known as Medicare and Medicaid. The Health Manpower Act of 1968 and the Comprehensive Health Manpower Training Act of 1971 provided additional support to increase medical

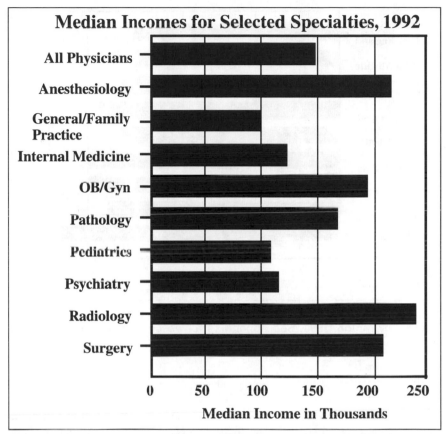

Figure 2.12 Median income in thousands after expenses, before taxes, for selected specialties, 1992. (Source: AMA Center for Health Policy Research.)

school enrollment, to develop departments of family medicine, and to increase the number of nonphysician health care providers.

The Graduate Medical Education National Advisory Committee (GMENAC) analyzed the total number and distribution of physicians within specialty groups. GMENAC designed forecasting models for both the future supply of physicians and the future demand for physician services in aggregate terms, as well as within selected specialties.[16] The conclusions of GMENAC were presented to the Secretary of Health and Human Services in September 1980, and they are briefly outlined in Table 2.15.

GMENAC concluded that there would be a surplus of 70,000 physicians by 1990 (536,000 supply; 466,000 required). This figure included 40,000 to 50,000 additional FMGs expected to be practicing in the U.S. by 1990. By the year 2000, the number of excess physicians was expected to double to 145,000 (643,000 supply; 498,000 required). Three years later, GMENAC published revised estimates,

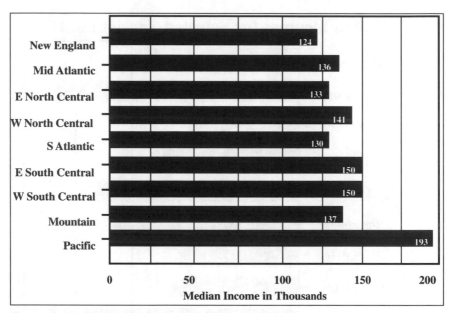

Figure 2.13 Median income in thousands of dollars, before taxes, after expenses, by region, 1991. See Appendix I for description of regions. (Source: AMA Socioeconomic Characteristics of Medical Practice.)

which included supply and demand models for six specialties that had been excluded in the original study.[22] The revised forecast projected an oversupply of 62,750 doctors by 1990 and 137,200 doctors by the year 2000.

GMENAC also made supply and demand projections for 1990 within selected specialties. Of the 34 individual specialties reviewed, only five were projected to have shortages by 1990, and an additional nine specialties were forecasted to be at equilibrium. All other specialties, mostly from surgical or medical subspecialties, were projected to have a surplus of physicians (Table 2.16).

GMENAC also attempted to document the uneven geographic distribution of physicians in the U.S. They found that the data information systems necessary for creditable geographic manpower planning did not exist. They observed a large variation in usage rates for many medical services in different specialty fields within different geographic areas. In the absence of studies of medical efficiency and agreed-on standards for designating a geographic area as adequately served, they concluded that local, regional, and national health workforce planning was seriously impaired, because workforce requirements for a given geographic area are dependent on utilization rates.

The AMA Center for Health Policy Research addressed this shortcoming of GMENAC and other needs-based studies in their 1988 publication, *Physician Sup-*

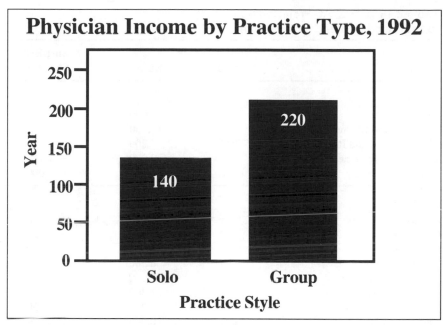

Figure 2.14 Physician median income by practice type, 1992. (Source: AMA Center for Health Policy Research.)

ply and Utilization by Specialty: Trends and Projections.[23] A major problem they saw in these types of studies was the lack of agreement, even among experts, as to what qualifies as appropriate "need" for physicians.

Instead of focusing on how much care "ought" to be provided, the AMA used ongoing utilization patterns as a basis for projecting future demand for physician services. Table 2.17 presents a summary of their analysis. It compares the projected percent change in supply expected in selected specialties with projected change of utilization within the same specialties for the period 1985 to 2000.

Table 2.15 Summary of Conclusions from the 1980 GMENAC Study

✦ There will be a surplus of physicians in 1990 and 2000.

✦ Shortages and surpluses will occur in some specialties by 1990.

✦ The U.S. may be training too many non-physician health care providers in light of the projected surplus of physicians.

✦ There will be an uneven distribution of physicians across the U.S.

✦ The factors influencing specialty choice are complex.

✦ The cost of graduate medical education is unknown.

✦ Economic motivation in specialty and geographic choice is uncertain.

Table 2.16   GMENAC Projected Supply
to Estimated Demand for Physicians, 1990

Specialty	Ratio	Required	Surplus + Shortage −
Shortage			
Child Psychiatry	45%	9,000	− 4,900
Emergency Medicine	70%	13,500	− 4,250
Physical Med. and Rehab.	75%	3,200	− 800
Preventive Medicine	75%	7,300	− 1,750
General Psychiatry	80%	38,500	− 8,000
Balance			
Hematology/Oncology	90%	9,000	− 700
Anesthesiology	95%	21,000	− 1,550
Dermatology	105%	6,950	+ 400
Gastroenterology	105%	6,500	+ 400
General Osteopathic	105%	22,000	+ 1,150
Family Practice	105%	61,300	+ 3,100
General Internal Med.	105%	70,250	+ 3,550
Otolaryngology	105%	8,000	+ 500
Pediatrics (& Subspecialties)	115%	36,400	+ 4,950
Surplus			
Urology	120%	7,700	+ 1,650
Pathology	125%	13,500	+ 3,350
Orthopedic Surgery	135%	15,100	+ 5,000
Ophthalmology	140%	11,600	+ 4,700
Thoracic Surgery	140%	2,050	+ 850
Infectious Diseases	145%	2,250	+ 1,000
Obstetrics/Gynecology	145%	2,400	+10,450
Plastic Surgery	145%	2,700	+ 1,200
Allergy/Immunology	150%	2,050	+ 1,000
General Surgery	150%	23,500	+11,800
Radiology	155%	18,000	+ 9,800
Neurology	160%	5,500	+ 3,150
Nephrology	175%	2,750	+ 2,100
Rheumatology	175%	1,700	+ 1,300
Cardiology	190%	7,750	+ 7,150
Endocrinology	190%	2,050	+ 1,800
Neurosurgery	190%	2,650	+ 2,450
Pulmonary	195%	3,600	+ 3,350
Nuclear Medicine	N/A	4,000	N/A

Required numbers for the specialties are estimates; full forecasting models were not performed. Projected surpluses and shortages represent national trends and do not take into account geographical clustering of physicians. (Adapted from the Graduate Medical Education National Advisory Committee, 1980.)

Table 2.17 Projected Changes in
Physician Supply and Utilization, 1985-2000

		Percent Change	
	Supply	**Population-Based Utilization**	**Difference**
All Physicians	23.8	14.5	9.3
General/Family	9.9	13.0	−3.1
All Internal Medicine	36.6	24.0	12.6
General Internal Medicine	27.0	24.6	2.4
Medical Subspecialists	51.8	23.4	28.4
All Surgery	13.1	17.0	−3.9
General Surgery	0.5	16.5	−16.0
Surgical Subspecialists	19.9	17.1	2.8
Pediatrics	38.8	7.0	31.8
Obstetrics and Gynecology	24.3	2.8	21.5
Radiology	18.2	—	—
Psychiatry	14.0	19.4	−5.4
Anesthesiology	41.7	—	—
Pathology	9.6	—	—
Emergency Medicine	69.4	6.2	63.2
Other Specialties	18.1	14.8	3.3

Source: AMA Center for Health Policy, 1988.

As with the GMENAC study, the AMA study indicates a mismatch between projected increases (or decreases) in supply within specialties and projected increases (or decreases) in utilization. For example, the fields of emergency medicine, obstetrics and gynecology, and pediatrics are projected to increase in supply at a higher rate than the anticipated increases in utilization. This finding is also true of all medical subspecialties taken in aggregate. The opposite is projected to occur in the fields of psychiatry, general surgery, and general/family medicine.

There are several precautions that need to be taken when interpreting the results of the AMA study. First, the results do not imply shortages or surpluses within any given field, but simply the projected percent increase or decrease in each category given the current trends in specialization and the current level of utilization. Second, the results are derived from projections based on past and current supply and demand trends. Unlike the GMENAC forecast, AMA projections do not consider any major changes in the health care delivery environment. AMA projections also do not assume major changes in technology or disease incidence and prevalence. For example, the impact of the growing number of patients with acquired immunodeficiency syndrome (AIDS) on the health system is not considered. Finally, these projections did not consider major realignments in health policy and their effect on supply and utilization. The latter would be an important consideration in the current political environment.

Although the AMA study stopped short of suggesting a surplus of physicians by the year 2000, one can extrapolate such a number from their data. By using the baseline number of active physicians in 1986 (544,308) and multiplying by the projected percent change in supply by the year 2000 (1.238), the AMA analysis would predict 673,853 physicians by the year 2000. Similarly, using the projected percent increase in utilization by the year 2000 (1.145) and multiplying by the baseline utilization figure (544,308), the AMA analysis would predict that 623,232 physicians would be needed to provide for the increased utilization. Therefore, the AMA data would predict a surplus of 50,621 physicians in the year 2000.

Using a similar model based on current physician utilization rates, the Bureau of Health Professions (BHPr), a division of the Department of Health and Human Services, published in March 1990 their physician supply and requirement forecast for the years 1990 and 2000.[17] Using data from a variety of sources, including the AMA and the National Center for Health Statistics' National Health Interview Survey and Hospital Discharge Survey, they forecasted an active physician supply of 721,600 by the year 2000. Physician requirements for this period were forecasted as 671,360, thus predicting a surplus of 50,240 physicians by the year 2000. Several other studies have been published on the topic of the physician workforce that support this conclusion. [24–26]

Although the models for predicting physician supply are fairly straightforward, the models for predicting physician demand or requirements are complex, and they are generally not agreed on by all experts. As such, it is difficult to determine which analysis is most credible. Despite this fact, the general consensus appears to be toward a surplus of physicians in a range of 50,000 to 150,000 by the year 2000, if not earlier.

CONCLUSION ❖

Whereas medicine was formerly an overwhelmingly white, male profession, it has gradually diversified to include more women and under-represented minorities. It includes physicians at all ranks in the medical hierarchy, although the data suggest that women have made greater inroads within the faculty ranks than members of under-represented minority groups.

Approximately one quarter of all doctors in the U.S. are graduates of foreign medical schools or schools of osteopathic medicine. The majority of physicians, however, are trained in U.S. allopathic medical schools. Furthermore, the number of applicants to U.S. medical schools continues to increase. With more than 42,000 applications, 1993 marked a record year. This is a considerable turnaround from the late 1980s, when applications reached a 15-year low. This renewed interest in the medical profession has occurred despite the increasing cost of medical education, which has translated into higher levels of indebtedness for graduating seniors.

The AAMC is currently studying how levels of indebtedness influence specialty choice.

The six specialties with the largest percentage of physicians are, in decreasing order: internal medicine, family/general practice, general surgery, pediatrics, obstetrics and gynecology, and psychiatry. Collectively, the primary care fields of internal medicine, family/general practice, and pediatrics contain 38% of all active allopathic physicians in the U.S.

The majority of physicians are located in metropolitan areas (approximately 88.4% of all physicians in 1992). This pattern has remained relatively stable since 1970. States differ not only in the total number of physicians, but also in their physician/population ratios. Medical practice is not uniform throughout the U.S. Geographic areas with similar demographic characteristics may have wide variations in the use of medical services, including surgical procedures, length of hospital stay, and hospital admissions.

Physicians with the highest incomes tend to be in procedure-oriented specialties, such as surgery, anesthesia, and interventional radiology. Other factors influencing income include practice size and regional location.

There is no widely accepted approach to determine future physician requirements. Despite this fact, there is general agreement that the U.S. is training an excess of doctors. The surplus of doctors by the year 2000 is estimated to be between 50,000 and 150,000.

❖ Suggested Reading ❖

Physician characteristics and distribution, 1993 ed. Department of Physician Data Services, Division of Survey and Data Resources, American Medical Association, 1992.
For more detail on general demographics of physicians.

Bergeisen L, ed. Minority students in medical education: facts and figures VII. Association of American Medical Colleges, Division of Minority Health, Education, and Prevention, August 1993.
Contains up-to-date trends and statistics of the most relevant topics concerning minority issues.

Council on Graduate Medical Education. Second report of the council: the underrepresentation of minorities in medicine. Rockville, MD: Department of Health and Human Services, Bureau of Health Professions, August 1990.
Contains complete historical summaries of the issues of under-represented minorities in medicine.

Report of the Graduate Medical Education National Advisory Committee to the Secretary, Department of Health and Human Services, vol 1, September 30, 1980.
For more information on the topic of physician workforce, the reader is directed to the 1980 and the 1983 studies.

3

Hospitals

Jeanne M. De Sa and Douglas Staiger

If one thinks of the structure of the health care industry in the United States as a wheel, its hub would be the vast network of for-profit and not-for-profit hospitals. Hospitals are tightly woven into the social fabric of communities, and they function as centers for what economists often call the production of medical care. However, they are also financial institutions with the same responsibilities as large corporations, and they have an enormous role in the country's economy. Indeed, national expenditures on hospital care total $282 billion in 1992, 34% of total national health care costs, which is an increase of 10.5% from 1991, when hospital expenses totaled $259 billion. Hospital costs are increasing at approximately two times the inflation rate.

We provide an introduction to the anatomy of the hospital system in the U.S. The first section describes the evolution of the modern American hospital, and the second section describes the overall characteristics of the current system, focusing on institutional features and recent utilization trends. In the following sections, the hospital's internal environment is examined, in terms of organizational structure, costs, reimbursement mechanisms, and financing options. Subsequently, the hospital industry's characteristics and behavior are examined under competitive and regulatory environments. Finally, the hospital's future role in national health care reform are discussed.

EVOLUTION OF THE HOSPITAL SYSTEM ❖

The modern U.S. hospital barely resembles the original hospitals of the nineteenth century. Prior to the late 1800s, hospitals were predominantly religious or charitable institutions run for the indigent and those without family or community. Medical treatment was delivered in the home by physicians. In *The Social Transformation of American Medicine,* Paul Starr extensively documents the changes that turned hospitals from social welfare institutions into professional, bureaucratic, and financially oriented centers for medical science.

Transformation: 1870 to 1910

Between 1870 and 1910, the hospital developed into a new kind of institution. Scientific advancements were the main impetus to change. The advent of antiseptic surgery in 1870 and the invention of diagnostic equipment, such as the x-ray machine in 1895, revolutionized medicine. Their use and proliferation allowed for the elimination of infection-ridden wards and the creation of centers that diagnosed and treated disease. Other factors contributed to this change: the industrial revolution, growth of the free-market economy, a subsequent increase in demand for hospital medical services, and the increasing power of physicians.

During this same period, industrialization caused an increase in the numbers of persons living in urban centers, which contributed to an increasing demand for medical care in centralized institutions. As with many other turn-of-the-century industries, hospitals grew quickly to respond to increasing popular demand for their services. In turn, physicians began to use hospitals for education, training, and patient care. The medical profession became incorporated into the hospital entity, shifting the practice of medical care from the home to the hospital.

Expansion: 1910 to 1965

By the early part of the twentieth century, hospitals were characterized as a mix of public and private institutions. These hospitals were financed by paying patients and run by administrators and physicians. The growing free-market economy, and not central national planning, was the main factor in the system's development throughout the century, as hospitals continued to grow in significance. The freestanding hospital maintained its independence under this organizational structure, thus avoiding the pressures other industries faced to merge into larger corporate entities. Financial crisis during the Depression spurred the development of private hospital insurance, a factor that contributed to increased utilization and the reputation of hospitals as the central place for the treatment of illness.

After World War II, the industry expanded significantly through implementation of the Hill-Burton program, a federal program that, under the 1946 Hospital

Survey and Construction Act, funded the construction of community hospitals. Under this program, the federal government required states to develop agencies to coordinate development. Over the next 30 years, approximately $12 billion was dispersed, benefiting middle-income communities and causing an enormous expansion in the supply of hospital beds.

Cost Escalation and Reform: 1970 to the Present

In the late 1960s, after Medicare and Medicaid were implemented, the industry grew again as insurance coverage for hospital care expanded. However, by the early 1970s, increasing costs of medical care caused government intervention and implementation of cost-containment policies in the hospital industry. In 1971, the Nixon administration enacted the Economic Stabilization Program, which imposed price controls on health care, as well as on the rest of the economy. Controls on health care remained until 1974. Under the Carter administration, the threat of more controls on hospital spending caused the industry to put forward a voluntary effort to hold back spending. However, because voluntary efforts failed to contain costs, the federal government implemented the Medicare Prospective Payment System in 1983 as a means of cost containment.

OVERALL HOSPITAL CHARACTERISTICS AND TRENDS ❖
Organization and Ownership

Currently, there are approximately 6,500 hospitals in the U.S., which comprise a complex system of financial and community organizations. Of these, approximately 5,300 are classified as community hospitals. Community hospitals are defined by the American Hospital Association (AHA)[27] as nonfederal, short-term (i.e., average patient stays under 30 days), general, and specialty hospitals. The balance include long-term psychiatric or chronic rehabilitation hospitals, federal hospitals, and chemical dependency institutions. This chapter focuses primarily on community hospitals because they comprise the vast majority of U.S. hospitals.

An important characteristic of hospitals is their ownership. There are three types of hospital ownership: *not-for-profit* or voluntary, *for-profit* or investor-owned; and *government*. Table 3.1 shows the number of community hospitals, the number of beds, and their inpatient admissions for 1992.

Not-for-Profit
Not-for-profit, nongovernmental hospitals, often referred to as voluntary hospitals, dominate the hospital market. Because not-for-profit hospitals comprise a large proportion of hospital employees, beds, and patients, they are the most im-

Table 3.1 Community Hospitals by Ownership Type, 1992

Type	Number of Hospitals	Inpatient Admissions	Beds
Not-for-Profit	3,173	23 million	656,000
For-Profit	723	3 million	99,000
State and Local	1,396	5 million	166,000
All Community Hospitals	5,292	31 million	921,000

Data source: AHA Hospital Statistics 1993.

portant institution to understand when discussing hospital behavior and performance. Not-for-profit, or volunteer, hospitals are often run by religious organizations, and they provide routine care to people living in their immediate area. Increasingly, they are forming multihospital systems.

A not-for-profit designation means that the hospital does not have corporate shareholders (i.e., individuals who own stock in the organization and divide up its profits). Profits are the difference between revenues of the organization and expenses, which include salaries, taxes, supplies, among others. Not-for-profit hospitals can legally earn profits, yet they cannot distribute these profits to shareholders.[28] In theory, because the community is viewed to be the hospital owner, those profits are distributed to the public in terms of expanded services and lower costs. However, legal rules do not clearly define how the profits earned by not-for-profit hospitals should be allocated. This allocational decision often rests with a state hospital regulatory agency.

A distinct feature of not-for-profit hospitals is that they have tax-exempt status (i.e., they do not have to pay federal income tax). Section 501(c)(3) of Internal Revenue Code is the source of not-for-profit tax-exemption. Other advantages of not-for-profit status come at the state and local level.[29]

◆ Exemption from property taxes
◆ Exemption from corporate income tax
◆ Better access to tax-exempt debt financing (i.e., raising money through bonds)
◆ Favored treatment under antitrust laws
◆ Eligibility to receive private donations

In the current cost-conscious environment, tax-exempt status for hospitals is being questioned. One argument is that not-for-profit status provides a public subsidy to the hospital industry and provides not-for-profit hospitals a competitive advantage over for-profit institutions. In addition, questions are raised as to whether not-for-profit hospitals are really benefiting their communities in terms of providing charitable care.

For-Profit

For-profit, or investor-owned, hospitals act as other private businesses. These hospitals distribute their profits to shareholders who own stock in the corporation. Unlike not-for-profit hospitals, for-profit hospitals are not tax-exempt. They have a large market share in a few states, and they are often part of national multihospital organizations with a centralized management structure. These organizations are located primarily in the sunbelt states, such as Florida and Texas, which have significant elderly populations.[28] With regard to bed size, for-profit hospitals tend to be smaller; they have between 100 and 200 beds, and they do not generally have teaching programs.

In the 1970s, for-profit hospitals and chains grew rapidly as certain institutions bought up small proprietary hospitals owned and run by physicians. By the end of the 1980s, however, many for-profit hospitals began to sell off unprofitable hospitals. Currently, for-profit hospitals are expanding into other health care services, such as long-term care providers.

There is an on-going debate over whether for-profit hospitals provide lower costs for the delivery of health care and lower prices for consumers than not-for-profit institutions. The variance of regulation across different regions of the country makes such an analysis difficult. Some studies find that costs do not differ significantly.[28] Others find that on a per-bed basis, for-profit hospitals have slightly higher costs, charge considerably more, and earn higher revenues.

Government

The other type of organization is government-run hospitals. State, county, and city hospitals account for a significant proportion of community hospitals across the country. These hospitals are a particularly important source of hospital care for local, indigent populations. The federal government runs 325 hospitals, most of which serve the Veterans Administration (VA). VA hospitals provide services to low-income veterans, often with drug dependency or mental illness. Within the system there are 122 general and 50 mental hospitals, as well as several clinics and rehabilitation centers.[30] The Departments of Defense, Army, Navy, and Air Force also operate hospital and clinic facilities on military bases.

Teaching Hospitals

An important characteristic of the U.S. hospital system is the presence of academic medical centers and teaching hospitals, institutions that serve as training centers for new physicians. There are currently 102 academic health centers, facilities that contain a medical school and one or more teaching hospitals. In addition, approximately 1,300 institutions participate in at least one residency

program.[31] According to evaluations done by the Prospective Payment Assessment Commission (PROPAC), which monitors the Medicare prospective payment
system, costs in teaching hospital are 28 to 41% higher than costs in community
hospitals. Although teaching hospitals tend to have more beds than nonteaching
institutions, they vary in terms of size and type of specialty. They are viewed as
having higher unit costs due to higher salary levels and compensation and more
intensive services.

Recent Trends in Hospital Utilization

Decline in the use of hospitals has been sharp since the early 1980s, because
patients spend fewer days in the hospital and turn to alternatives to inpatient
care. As shown in Table 3.2, inpatient days and occupancy in community hospital decreased between 1982 and 1992. Particularly because of incentives built
into the Medicare prospective reimbursement system, average length of stay
(ALOS) decreased (i.e., on average, patients spent fewer days in the hospital)
(Table 3.2).

During the same time that inpatient hospital utilization has been declining, outpatient services have been expanding. Technological advances in surgery have
allowed for more complicated surgical procedures to be done on an outpatient
basis. In addition, in response to cost-containment pressures, private insurance
plans have extended coverage to outpatient in an effort to decrease inpatient utilization services. Table 3.3 shows that the number of annual outpatient visits increased by 41% and the number of outpatient surgeries increased 16.7% from
1982 to 1992.

Table 3.2 Inpatient Utilization Measures
in Community Hospitals 1982 and 1992

	1982	**1992**	**% Change**
Community Hospitals	5,801	5,292	−8.8%
Admissions (millions)	36.4	31.0	−14.2%
Inpatient Days (millions)	278	221	−20.5%
ALOS (days)	7.6	7.1	−6.8%
Occupancy Rate	75%	66%	−12.8%

(ALOS) refers to patient "Average Length of Stay" in the hospital. As noted by the percent change
column, there has been a general decline in the use of hospitals from the early 1980s to 1992. (Data
source: AHA Hospital Statistics 1993.)

Table 3.3 Outpatient Utilization Measures
in Community Hospitals 1982 and 1992

	1982	**1992**	**% Change**
Outpatient Visits	248 million	349 million	+41.0%
Number of Outpatient Surgical Procedures	19.6 million	22.9 million	+16.7%

In general, outpatient hospital utilization has increased from the early 1980s to 1992. (Data source: AHA Hospital Statistics 1993.)

THE INDIVIDUAL HOSPITAL ❖
How a Hospital Functions

Hospitals have an organizational structure that is distinct from that of other firms, largely because of the hospital's unique medical mission.[32] Economists often refer to hospitals as multiproduct firms, which in essence are "workshops" that produce many "products" that contribute to care of patients and to the hospital's other functions.

Organizational Structure

The hospital is physically designed around the routine inpatient patient care areas, which are arranged into wards according to functional use (e.g., pediatrics, oncology, obstetrics, surgery). Depending on hospital size, each ward contains approximately 25 to 40 beds, with a nurses station in the center.[28] Additional areas related to patient care include the emergency department, the operating and recovery rooms, and the intensive care unit (ICU). In some instances, hospitals have a cardiac care unit (CCU) for the treatment of patients with severe heart disease.

Ancillary services are provided by individual departments within the hospital, and they are designed to respond to diagnostic and therapeutic daily needs of physicians and patients. These ancillary departments are generally operated by a physician or a professional within that field. Physical, occupational, and speech therapy facilities all provide various types of therapies prescribed by a physician, and they are operated under the direction of qualified therapists. Some ancillary departments provide materials, such as blood or pharmaceuticals. The blood bank is responsible for drawing, processing, procuring, and distributing blood, whereas the pharmacy provides drugs. When hospitals do not have the resources to maintain certain ancillary services in the hospital, they may contract out to nearby hospitals or health care providers that do have access to such facilities.

Hospitals may also have programs that provide special social and medical programs to the community.

◆ Hospice provides services to the terminally ill, mainly medical pain relief
   and social support for families.
◆ Home health services provide nursing, therapy, and social services through
   the hospital in the home.
◆ Chaplain/pastoral care provides spiritual support to patients and their
   families both in and out of the hospital.

In response to increasing outpatient admissions, hospitals have expanded the
amount and variety of outpatient services they offer to patients. These outpatient
services are for patients who do not remain in the hospital overnight. In 1992, more
than 94% of hospitals offered some kind of ambulatory surgery service.[28] Additional services offered on an outpatient basis include psychiatric care, rehabilitation, and chemical dependency treatment. Furthermore, hospitals have also
focused on developing long-term care services for the growing elderly population.
Skilled nursing facilities (SNFs) provide medical treatment and nursing care to recovering patients in long-term care facilities, intermediate residential housing, or
in beds specifically designated SNF.
   A significant part of hospital functions, however, do not take place around actual patient care. Even a small hospital has administrative needs, which demand the
presence of planning, finance, marketing, and medical records departments. As
with any hotel catering to overnight guests, hospitals require laundry and housekeeping departments, food service and cafeteria areas, purchasing, and security services. Plant maintenance is essential to the daily operating functions of the hospital.

Hospital Actors and Responsibilities
When patients enter a hospital, their primary contacts are their doctor and the
nurses. However, there are many other actors involved in patient care, each with
unique responsibilities demanded by their position.

The Medical Staff
The medical staff represents one of two major authorities controlling the hospital
organization. Unless they are part of the hospital's management, physicians on
the medical staff have no contract with the hospital and receive no income from
the hospital. This is a distinct feature for hospitals in comparison with other businesses. Although the medical staff is one of two premier players in hospital
decision-making, as well as the primary generator of service demand, its members are not actual hospital employees.[33] An important factor to consider when
analyzing hospitals is that within the hospital, the physician's role is that of
specialized decision-maker about patient care needs and the hospital resources
necessary for those needs.

The medical staff of a hospital, organized by specialty and subspecialty, has its own by-laws and decision-making hierarchy.[28] The medical staff reviews all applications and determines the granting of admission privileges. Problems with medical staff are determined through an internal peer review process, which has the authority to revoke admitting privileges.[28]

The Board of Trustees and the Administration

Not-for-profit hospitals are run by a Board of trustees, which the hospital's legal charter invests with the power to oversee and direct hospital management policy. In contrast to corporations, members of this Board do not own stock in the hospital. They are often prominent members of the community, and they provide donations to the hospital. The Board chooses an administrator to manage the hospital, usually designated as president, executive director, or Chief Executive Officer (CEO). Generally, this individual has a postgraduate degree in business administration, a public health degree, or a medical degree.[28] They run the administration, which is the other major player in the hospital organization. Within the administration, there are several vice presidents, who manage the various functional areas described in the previous section and their staffs. The Chief Financial Officer (CFO) is often one of the most important vice presidents, because they are responsible for the hospital's vast financial demands. The vice president of nursing is also a prominent figure in hospital administration and decision-making.

The Nursing Staff

The nursing staff has its own complex organizational structure that is often not apparent to the casual observer.[34] There are several kinds of nurses of varying education and skill levels and a hierarchy of assigned duties.

A clinical nurse specialist (CNS) is a registered nurse (RN) with a master's degree in a particular specialty area. CNSs teach other staff members about issues relating to their given specialty area. The CNS has the highest level of nursing training and medical education.

Nurse practitioners are RNs with a masters degree who perform limited patient care alone or with physician supervision. Similar to the CNS, nurse practitioners have the highest level of nursing training and medical education.

An RN typically has a Bachelor of Science in Nursing (BSN), which is a four-year degree from a university; an Associates Degree in Nursing, which is a two-year degree obtained from a community college; or a Nursing Diploma, which is a two- to three-year degree awarded by a hospital-based nursing program. An RN has also successfully passed the RN nursing Board examination. Depending on the region of the country they work in, RNs on average earn $20 per hour. Their patient care responsibilities are the most complex of all nursing types, and they generally oversee and manage the other nurses on their ward.

Licensed practical nurses (LPNs) typically have 9 to 12 months of education, and they are certified through a licensure examination. LPNs' role varies depending on the hospital and its staffing needs. They are paid less than RNs, they typically perform noninterpretive patient care tasks, and they must work under the supervision of an RN. In areas with shortages of RNs, LPNs have been found to be an economical replacement.

Technician nurse extender (NE) represent a new development in nursing, and they have been popular since 1985. They serve as technical assistants to nurses, but they mainly handle noninterpretive tasks, such as collecting vital signs and patient transport. Some hospitals with RN shortages have begun to delegate more tasks to them. They earn 20% to 45% less than nurses, and two thirds of NEs are men.

Physician assistants (PAs) are required to have a four-year undergraduate degree, two years of PA classes, and a PA diploma. They always work under the guidance of a physician. Use of PAs varies dramatically from region to region and hospital to hospital.

Unit assistants (UAs), clerks, and nurses aides are responsible for the extensive clerical work necessary for the functioning of the unit. Table 3.4 shows the distribution of attained education levels among nursing staff.

In the 1960s, nurses began to manage patient care responsibilities in their unit through an organizational style called team nursing. Under team nursing, RNs would manage a team of lesser-skilled LPNs. Under this process, nurses were able to run the hospital unit in a more cost-efficient and controlled manner than had been done previously under a system of one nurse for each patient. Primary nursing, developed by nurse educators, emerged in the 1970s, and it focused on RN autonomy over duties. This style called for decentralization of the nursing unit, and it increased the responsibility of the nurse to the patient. The RN would write and manage a 24-hour care plan for the patient. Although primary nursing improved continuity of care, higher costs resulted due to a ratio of fewer patients per nurse. Since 1985, NEs are commonly used for economic reasons, as well as in response to RN shortages in some regions in the 1980s. Nursing organizational styles vary with regard to hospitals, regions of the country and education, and age of the nursing staff. One important issue for nursing staffs concerns the division of labor over patient care tasks; some nurses want to perform more comprehensive patient-care tasks and others want to concentrate on medical and more technically oriented tasks.

Table 3.4 Education Level of Nursing Staff, 1991

Level of Education	% of all Nurses
Masters in Nursing	3.6%
Baccalaureate in Nursing (BSN)	30.8%
Nursing Diploma	27.9%
Associates Degree (2 year)	37.3%

Data source: Statistical Abstract of the United States 1993.

Table 3.5 Types of Nursing
Staff Utilized by Hospitals 1991

Staffing Type	% of Total
Per-Diem	31.2%
Float Pool	21.2%
On-Call	8.7%
Temporary Service	25.3%
Other	13.6%

Data source: Statistical Abstract of the United States
1993.

The head nurses coordinate the schedules and the task distributions for nurses in all the units. Due to the varying demands of patient acuity and volume, scheduling nurses is a challenging task, and it has heavy economic implications. In many hospitals, computer programs are employed to assist the nursing staff in this endeavor. Full-time nurses work 35 or more hours per week, whereas part-time nurses work fewer than 35 hours per week. Depending on scheduling demands, they split their time between the three shifts of day, evening, and night; staffing levels at night are approximately one half of those during the day. On any given shift, there will be a need for a particular mix of RNs, NEs, LPNs, and UAs. Because of this variance in nursing needs, the head of the nursing staff has to make short-term decisions regarding staffing, and they must utilize a mix of nurses to provide the most efficient and effective staffing level.

A nurse must sometimes be drawn from one unit to another if demand shifts suddenly. These nurses are in the float pool. Some nurses are on call, and they can be summoned from their homes by the staffing nurse with short notice. In many instances, nursing units utilize the services of a temporary nursing agency, which can provide additional nurses in high volume situations. As shown in Table 3.5, hospital nursing staffs utilize alternate staffing methods on a regular basis.

Other Hospital Workers

In addition to physicians and nurses, hospitals employ a variety of other health care workers. Dieticians and nutritionists plan nutrition programs and supervise the selection of meals in the hospital. They usually have a bachelors degree, as well as several months of supervised practice experience. Occupational therapists help individuals develop, maintain, or regain skills needed for work or daily living. Physical therapists concentrate on specific exercises to regain physical function after injury or illness. Related health workers include art, dance, and music therapists, each of whom uses these particular means to aid patients. These therapists have bachelors degrees, with a major in their respective fields, and many states now require them to have further training and licensing to practice.

Pharmacists prepare and dispense medications, as well as advise physicians on dosage, use, and side effects of pharmaceuticals. They must have graduated from an accredited pharmacy school, and they also need to complete a supervised internship and pass a state examination to earn their license. Other workers include lab technicians, radiology technicians, and medical records librarians. In addition, the hospital needs to employ numerous services workers, such as janitors, food service workers, and security guards.[35]

Internal Coordination

Although hospitals and their staffs have certain levels of tasks they must perform every day, as well as certain minimum staffing requirements for patient care wards, it is difficult to plan for the amounts and types of services that will be necessary on any given day. Particularly due to the unpredictability of clinical decision-making and the uncertainty of illness, it is essential that hospitals have the capacity to react to short-term problems. When a patient needs blood, the blood bank is called and mobilized to deliver the blood to the patient. A physician demands a radiograph for a patient, and radiology reacts to supply that radiograph. A local accident occurs and the emergency room is overcrowded, whereas the next day occupancy rates are below 50%.

The result is a complex dialogue that goes on between the hospital staff, the nurses coordinating the unit, the physicians ordering tests, and the ancillary departments. The uncertainty of short-term clinical needs makes overall decision-making difficult for hospital planners. Longer-term planning needs may cause tension with short-term needs as cost-reduction pressures continue to mount. Problems in this process may occur when the medical staff's demands for tests, supplies, or equipment exceed the short-run capacity of the hospital.[33]

Hospital Costs
Defining Hospital Costs

In the current debate on health care reform, there is much discussion about controlling hospital costs. Costs are often confused with charges (i.e., the price patients or insurance companies are charged for their hospital visit). Costs, however, mean something different. Hospital costs are the amount of money the hospital has to spend to operate and produce its patient care "product." Charges are the amount that insurers or patients are billed for a hospital service.

Hospital management needs to pay their employees a salary and benefits, purchase nonmedical as well as medical supplies, and pay for electricity and water. These daily costs are operating costs, and they are included in Table 3.6 as wages and salaries, employee benefits, and general administration. General administration covers food, utilities, housekeeping, purchasing, supplies, and administration. Professional fees refer to fees paid for services the hospital contracts to other organizations. Costs are often referred to as expenses. The hospital also has to make investments in the actual hospital structure (i.e., the plant and the equipment).

Table 3.6   Distribution of
Community Hospital Expenses 1992

Type of Expense	% of Total
Wages and Salaries	44.6%
General Administration	33.6%
Employee Benefits	9.5%
Capital Expenses	8.1%
Professional Fees	4.2%

"General Administration" expenses include food, utilities, housekeeping, purchasing medical and non-medical supplies, and administrative costs. "Professional Fees" refers to hospital service contracts to outside organizations. (Data source: AHA Statistics 1993–4.)

These costs are called capital costs. Capital costs include interest and depreciation on the plant and the equipment. Table 3.6 shows the distribution of costs within an average hospital, and it demonstrates that salaries and employee benefits are a high proportion of hospital costs.

Businesses and organizations break down their costs into different components to determine where to set prices so they can make a profit. The following economic terms are commonly used in describing costs, and they can be applied to hospital costs as well. A microeconomics textbook may provide further information on costs and prices.

◆   *Fixed Costs.* Fixed costs are those that do not depend on how much output a firm produces. In the case of a hospital, fixed costs are those that do not vary with how many patients the hospital admits. A hospital's fixed costs generally include investments in the plant and the equipment. In the short run, many other hospital costs are fixed because the hospital has a certain required staffing level for the number of beds, for example. In this instance, hospitals do not have much flexibility in changing labor and nonlabor expenses.

◆   *Variable Costs.* Variable costs are costs that change with the level of output. In a hospital's case, variable costs are those incurred to care for more patients, to hire more nurses, and to purchase more supplies and medicine. In the long run, most hospital costs are variable because hospitals can expand or cut back investment in a new wing or in new equipment.

◆   *Total Costs.* Total costs are the sum of fixed and variable costs, and they comprise the total amount spent at a certain level of output. Hospitals tend to measure total costs for inpatient and outpatient care.

◆   *Average Costs.* Average costs are total costs per unit of output. Sometimes a hospital will measure its output in terms of inpatient days.

◆   *Marginal Costs.* Marginal cost is the change in total cost that occurs for each one-unit change in output. In the case of a hospital, the addition of one patient will result in a change in the hospital's total costs. That change is the marginal cost of adding that patient, and it will vary depending on how many patients the hospital serves. Most businesses set their prices so that marginal revenue is equal to marginal cost to maximize profit.

Hospitals do not have control over some of the factors that impact their costs, such as physician admitting, quality and treatment patterns (most physicians are not on salary), regional wage levels, depreciation on past investments, and demographic characteristics of the service area population. The hospital does have control over administrative decisions, such as future capital investment, how to employ certain types of nurses, or whether they will open or close certain patient care areas.

Costs and Hospital Performance

Businesses look to costs to measure productivity and efficiency. Unit costs are the average amount hospitals spend on each patient for a particular department or service. Hospitals divide up their total costs in each department in a document called a *cost report*. Cost reports will show the amount of money a hospital spent during a given period in each inpatient and outpatient department. Each department that generates a cost report is considered a responsibility center. A responsibility center is an organizational unit headed by a responsible manager that uses resources called inputs, works with these resources, and produces outputs called goods (tangible) or services (intangible). A responsibility center is defined as an expense center, a revenue center, a profit center, or an investment center.

+ *Expense Center.* A responsibility center in which inputs are measured in monetary terms, and the manager is held responsible for those costs incurred, but not revenues.
+ *Revenue Center.* A responsibility center in which outputs are measured in monetary terms, and the manager is held responsible for those revenues, but not costs incurred.
+ *Profit Center.* A responsibility center in which both inputs and outputs are measured in monetary terms, and the manager is held responsible for both costs and revenues.
+ *Investment Center.* A responsibility center in which inputs are measured in terms of expenses, outputs are measured in terms of revenues, and assets employed are measured. The manager is held responsible for the return on assets invested.

Unit costs are used as comparison measures to other hospitals or to monitor a hospital's performance over time. In hospital inpatient departments, unit costs are costs per patient day or costs per patient admission. For outpatient departments, costs are measured in terms of surgical minutes or visits, depending on the nature of the service. Differences in hospital size, services provided, and use of outpatient facilities and level must be controlled for in cost-measurement comparisons among hospitals. To control for level of illness, hospitals adjust their discharges for case-mix.

Depending on the number of patients served, hospitals may perform differently. There is disagreement over whether larger hospitals are more cost-efficient due to economies of scale (i.e., the more patients a hospital treats, the lower its average costs are). At some point, however, hospitals become too large, and they are forced to address more complex administrative needs. Average cost per patient then begins to increase, and economies of scale no longer exist.

Cost Escalation and Cost Control

Because of the enormous economic role hospitals have in the health care system, hospital cost escalation is of particular importance to policy-makers, hospital administrators, and patients. After institution of the Medicare program in 1966, hospital cost increases accelerated and generated national concern. In response, the government implemented various price control mechanisms in the 1970s and the early 1980s. In the late 1980s, hospital prices and expenditures accelerated, increasing to 5% higher than inflation (almost 9% annually).

The factors that contribute to cost escalation in hospitals are currently under debate by health care economists and professionals. Empirical evidence is still being gathered on several fronts looking at technology, volume and severity, capital expenditures, labor productivity, and management. Hospitals have been active in trying to reduce their costs through relationships with other providers, labor reductions, and improvements in their operations. Although no one distinct cause of increasing costs has emerged, the cost-escalation dialogue has focused on increased intensity of care as the source of increased costs. Other components of cost escalation in the hospital industry include the following.

✧   *Capital Expansion.*[36] Hospitals often upgrade plant and equipment to have a competitive advantage over others. This approach can result in duplication of services within the local community.[37] Increases in particular types of equipment from 1982 to 1992 are shown in Table 3.7.

✧   *Reimbursement Incentives.* Traditional cost-based reimbursement systems reward hospitals for increased admissions and performance of additional services, including extra tests and invasive surgical procedures.

✧   *Volume and Severity.* Although some hospital inpatient volume is being directed to outpatient settings, patients who remain in inpatient care tend to be the more serious cases (i.e., cardiac patients), and they demand a greater intensity of care.

✧   *Patient Insensitivity to Costs of Care.* Because of the third-party payer insurance system, patients are not aware of the costs of their care; they therefore do not question the need for services or intensity of care.

Table 3.7 Percent of Community Hospitals with
Selected Equipment or Technology 1982 and 1992

	1982	1992
Computerized Tomography (CT) Scanners	55.5%	75.2%
Cardiac Catheterization	18.4%	31.3%
Magnetic Resonance Imaging (MRI)	4.7%	24.6%
Organ Transplantation	4.9%	11.8%

Data source: AHA Hospital Statistics 1993–4.

Reimbursement and Hospital Behavior
Revenue and Charges

Revenue sources for hospitals are varied. In the past, hospitals gained most of their revenue from patient charges. As a result of increases in private health insurance and institution of the Medicare and Medicaid programs, this method of revenue generation has changed considerably. In contrast to most businesses, hospitals do not receive revenue for their services directly. They receive payment for their goods and services through third-party payers. A small portion of revenue comes from private donations, government grants, and in-kind subsidies in the form of services.

Hospital financial statements refer to revenue in several ways. According to the AHA:

✦ *Gross patient revenue* is the amount of money a hospital would receive if all patients paid full price.
✦ *Net patient revenue* is gross patient revenue less adjustments negotiated with different payers, bad debt, and uncompensated care.
✦ *Net total revenue* is net patient revenue added to all contributions, government grants, and other nonpatient payments.

Charges are the amount that hospitals determine patients (or their insurance company) should pay for the provision of hospital care. In most businesses, prices for goods and services are set to cover the costs of providing those services. Hospitals, however, have a more challenging time determining charge levels due to the varying reimbursement methods of third-party payers.

Reimbursement

Although some payments are made by patients directly to the hospital, most payments are reimbursed to the hospital by a third-party, such as private or government insurance. More than 90% of a hospital's operating budget comes from third-party reimbursement. The amount of money reimbursed for each patient depends on the insurer, the particular insurance plan, and the reimbursement formulas for different groups. Even Blue Cross plans reimbursement levels vary across different states.

The overall result of this system is that a hospital cannot charge the same amount for all patient services, and it gains more revenue from some than from others. Charge levels are often negotiated with third-party payers. Two important terms to know are *allowable charges* and *allowable costs.* Allowable charges are the maximum fee a third-party payer allows a hospital to charge for a particular service. Allowable costs are the costs that a third-party payer will reimburse. For example, some payers will not pay for a single room or other amenities.

Medicare payments accounted for a large percentage of all hospital revenue in 1992. Prior to 1983, hospitals were reimbursed for the cost of each service delivered to the patient. This system, however, resulted in cost escalation because hospitals kept patients for long stays and treated them with expensive tests and services. The Medicare Prospective Payment System (PPS), instituted in 1983, paid hospitals on a per-case basis, essentially assigning a fixed budget for each patient. It categorized patients' illnesses into **diagnosis-related groups** (DRGs), thereby fixing the price per admission for specific services.

As shown in Table 3.8, Medicaid payments account for 13.9% of hospital revenue. Government payers comprise an increasing portion of hospital revenue. In 1988, the percentage of hospital days accounted for by Medicare and Medicaid was 57.9%. By 1992, it was 65.2%.[38] Nongovernment and self-pay sources of revenue accounted for 34.1 and 6.7% of hospital revenues, respectively.

Hospitals also have uncompensated care (i.e., care that does not get reimbursed), which accounts for approximately 5% of all hospital costs.[28] Uncompensated costs fall disproportionately on public hospitals, including uninsured individuals who go to a hospital clinic or an emergency room for medical care. Bad-debt care is the value of care delivered to patients judged by the hospital as able to pay but who did not. Charity care is rendered to patients whom the hospital judged unable to pay. Hospitals have two methods of handling this type of issue: they can either pay for the care as charity or write off the expenses as bad debt.

Table 3.8 Gross Patient Revenue to
Community Hospitals by Payer Source, 1992

Payer	% of Gross Patient Revenue
Medicare	40.4%
Private Insurance	34.1%
Medicaid	13.9%
Self-Pay	6.7%
Other Payers	4.9%

Data source: AHA Statistics 1993–4.

In some states, uncompensated care pools, comprised of excess revenue from hospitals in the state, are divided among hospitals that have disproportionate shares of uncompensated care.

Reimbursement and Hospital Behavior

Implementation of the Medicare PPS brought about significant changes in hospital behavior, and it is the subject of extensive studies. Because fees are fixed for each service, the average length of stay for each patient, and hence hospital occupancy rates, has begun to decrease. The efficacy of this reimbursement system is currently under debate in the health care field. Critics argue that patients are released "quicker and sicker." In addition, inflation of the severity of some cases may occur. This situation, called *DRG creep,* suggests that hospitals categorize patients as sicker to receive more reimbursement. Furthermore, hospitals may also transfer the unreimbursed costs of caring for Medicare patients to those with private insurance. This phenomenon is called cross-subsidization or *cost-shifting.* This shift also occurs when other third-party payers negotiate discounts from charges. Hospitals have also begun implementing better electronic billing systems to reduce reimbursement delays and mistakes.

Financing: Hospitals and Public Sector Capital Markets[39]
How Does a Hospital Raise Money?

When a hospital wishes to expand a service line, build a new wing, or purchase new equipment, it needs to borrow money because funds from its own income may be insufficient. Prior to the 1960s, hospitals funded new construction or facility upgrade through local philanthropic donations, federal *Hill-Burton grants,* or their own income.[40] Sometimes they would take out a bank mortgage if other funds proved inadequate. Since then, however, the capital needs of hospitals have changed dramatically. Largely due to changes in technology, hospitals have to upgrade their facilities more often and purchase the newest equipment necessary for patient care needs. These factors, combined with declining philanthropy and the end of the Hill-Burton program, resulted in increased financial pressures on hospitals to find other sources of money to borrow for their capital projects.

In addition to donations and use of internal reserves, profit-making businesses have two main ways to finance new projects. They can raise money through equity financing or debt financing.

♦ *Equity Financing.* In the private sector, businesses raise money through issuing shares (equity) in the company. The investors in these shares earn dividends and capital gains on their investments. Not-for-profit hospitals, however, cannot issue equity because they do not have shareholders. For-profit hospitals may use this method.

✧   *Debt Financing.* Debt financing means that the organization borrows the amount of money it needs and pays the borrowers back in increments over a pre-set period. To gain access to money for a project, organizations issue debt or bonds in return for funding. These bonds are promises to pay back the money with interest. There are two kinds of bonds: revenue bonds, which are paid back mainly by revenues from a project and are backed by insurance; and general obligation bonds, which are borrowed by a public entity and are guaranteed by the faith that the seller can always raise taxes to cover the debt. Servicing the debt means paying off the principal and interest every year.

✧   *Tax-Exempt Debt Financing.* Some bonds are tax-exempt (i.e., the investor does not have to pay taxes on the earnings), making them more profitable for investors than some other investments with higher yields. Non-profit organizations and state and municipal governments can gain access to tax-exempt bonds. Subject to a few restrictions, these kind of bonds are generally called *municipal bonds.* Hospitals and universities, due to their not-for-profit status, can borrow up to $100 million tax-exempt. Currently, there is pressure on Congress to lift this borrowing ceiling.

Tax-Exempt Bonds for Hospitals

Tax-exempt hospitals do most borrowing through the issuance of tax-exempt revenue bonds. They offer health facilities longer payback periods, and they may have no or a minimal down payment or equity requirements and lower interest rates than taxable bonds. For-profit hospitals have limited access to tax-exempt bonds. Government hospitals use general obligation tax-exempt bonds as their primary source of capital. Federal hospitals, such as those run by the Veterans Administration, finance through federal taxes.

In the 1970s, there was an explosion of tax-exempt debt financing by hospitals that wanted to expand their facilities and upgrade their equipment. Medicare and Medicaid policies in the early 1970s reduced the risk involved with debt financing because they reimbursed 100% of interest. President Nixon further encouraged the development of tax-exempt financing authorities to help hospitals issue tax-exempt bonds.

Throughout the 1980s, tax-exempt revenue bonds have grown into the primary means of financing new hospital projects. Currently, hospitals tend to rely on borrowing more money than other sectors of the economy. Whereas most public sector organizations, such as power plants, are approximately 60% debt-financed, hospitals carry debt loads in excess of 80%, largely because of the unique, technology-intensive nature of the industry. Typical investors in tax-exempt hospital bonds are municipal bond funds, casualty companies, and individuals. The hospital market, however, has fewer buyers than for city-issued bonds for sewers or water improvements.

How Does the Financing Process Work?

The first step for a hospital to raise money for capital expansion or improvements is to survey organizational requirements. There may be changes in patient demand for a service line or modernization and expansion needs. After the hospital administration determines what projects need to be done, the feasibility of the project needs to be determined. The life of the project, its benefits, and the costs of alternative investments need to be considered. Most importantly, however, whether the project will be able to pay off its debt is crucial. "Does the return on investment exceed the cost of the capital?" is the main question asked.

After the project's feasibility is determined, the hospital administration assembles a financing team of lawyers, financial advisors, bankers, investors, creditors, and community members to determine how much money they need to borrow. The banker generally oversees the process. During this time, rating agencies make an assessment of how credit-worthy the hospital is. This process is called a debt rating, and it is important to hospitals seeking to borrow money because a low rating raises the hospital's payments on their debt. Tax-exempt bonds for hospitals are issued by states, municipal hospitals, counties, or cities; sometimes they are issued by a health-financing authority under a state agency. In some states, the hospital must go to a state-wide authority, whereas in others, a local hospital authority will serve as the issuer.

The Problem of Hospitals and Debt

As stated, hospitals carry heavy debt loads, which means they are over-leveraged. Indeed, throughout the 1980s, bond ratings for hospitals have worsened. Questions have arisen as to whether the hospital sector has reached the limits of debt capacity. Because of these questions regarding capital and cost-escalation, Medicare started prospective payment mechanisms for capital expenses in 1992. In the face of these pressures regarding debt financing, hospital administrators have begun to find alternative means of financing equipment purchases, such as leasing. Leasing is essentially a contract that grants possession of an asset to a hospital for a period, in return for some form of compensation for its use. In addition, many hospitals are refinancing their debt at lower interest rates.

Financial Management

Hospitals must maintain financial stability if they want to be able to raise money for projects or large purchases. In managing a hospital's finances, the hospital administrator has to focus on several issues. Primarily, the hospital must have enough revenues to match the cost of its daily operations and to maintain its facilities and equipment. To accomplish these goals, the hospital must prepare an annual budget, which accounts for estimates of revenues and expenses. Hospitals may also develop capital budgets, which may extend for longer periods than one year. The hospital must also decide, in the case of a revenue shortfall, how much money to borrow. Also, the financial manager must bear in mind that some hospital costs are not reimbursable, such as capital investments, paying for the uninsured, and research costs.

There are many ways a hospital manager can look at a hospital's financial health. Often this task entails looking at ratios from the hospital's financial statements. Financial statements are a collection of documents that show hospital financial information. They include an income statement, which shows revenues and expenses during a given period, and a balance sheet, which shows the hospital's assets and obligations (liabilities) at a given point in time. A basic accounting textbook that focuses on not-for-profit organizations may serve as further reference for understanding hospital accounting mechanisms. The following definitions are a collection of the most important terms used in assessing a hospital's financial well-being.

✧   *Profitability.* Profitability, the excess of revenues over expenses, is an important measure of a hospital's health. In the 1980s, profitability declined as costs increased, utilization declined, and revenue decreased due to limitations in DRG reimbursement. The *operating margin,* a measure of profitability, is the ratio of profits from operations over the revenue from operations, and it defines the proportion of operating revenue retained as income. Other important profitability ratios include the *deductible ratio,* which measures the proportion of gross patient revenues that is not expected to be realized in cash because of contractual allowances, bad debts, or charity care; and the *markup ratio,* which shows how much hospitals have elevated their prices above their cost to provide services. Two other helpful ratios include *return on equity,* which is the ratio of profits after taxes to owner's equity, and it indicates how profitably the hospital is utilizing shareholders' funds; and *return on assets,* which is the ratio of pretax profits to total assets, and it indicates how efficiently the hospital is utilizing its assets to generate profits.

Overall, U.S. hospitals have showed improved profitability during the 1990s. The reasons for improved profitability include hospital efforts to reduce costs and to develop more efficient operations, higher income from investments, and installation of operation improvement strategies.

✧   *Liquidity.* Liquidity, which is a measure of a hospital's ability to meet current obligations, is determined by the *current ratio,* which is the ratio of current assets to current liabilities. Of particular concern for hospital financial managers is that they do not receive most patient payments at the time of service due to the third-party payer system. The result is that hospitals do not receive cash for services. This category is called *accounts receivable* on the balance sheet. Three other useful liquidity ratios include the days in patient accounts receivable, the average payment period, and days cash on hand ratios. A measure of the average collection period for accounts receivable is *days in patient accounts receivable,* which is a ratio expressed in days between the net patient accounts receivable and the net patient service revenue, divided by 365 days. A measure of how quickly hospitals are meeting their current liabilities is the *average payment period,* which is a ratio expressed in days between current liabilities and operating expenses, divided by 365 days. *Days cash on hand* is a ratio expressed in days between cash and operating expenses, divided by 365 days, and it measures the number of days a hospital could operate if all income ceased on that particular day.

Average hospital liquidity has improved over the past several years. Reasons for this improvement include improved profitability, the build-up of cash reserves, cost-control measures, and improved electronic billing systems.

◇ *Capital Structure.* Capital structure ratios, such as long-term debt ratio and debt service coverage, give information about a hospital's debt load and its ability to pay it. The *long-term debt ratio* defines the proportion of long-term debt to equity. Higher values for this ratio imply a greater reliance on debt financing, and they may imply a reduced ability to carry additional debt. The *debt service coverage ratio* measures total debt service coverage (interest + principal) from the hospital's cash flow. Higher values for debt service coverage indicate better debt repayment ability.

Capital spending is slowing, which is likely to continue until health reform transpires. The result is that hospitals have not been taking on additional debt.

◇ *Measures of Physical Plant and Equipment.* In this age of rapidly changing technology, the age of the hospital facility and its equipment is important to the quality of the service it is providing, and it is a measure of financial health. The *accounting age of assets* is a measure of the average age of the assets of the hospital, including the plant and the equipment.

The average accounting age of fixed assets for the hospital industry increased in 1992. Reasons for this increase include slowing of new construction, caution in investing in expensive new technology, and off-balance sheet financing.

◇ *Full-time Equivalents (FTEs).* For a financial manager, evaluating staffing levels per bed is also essential to evaluate the health of the organization. FTEs per bed is one way of looking at this indicator.

In addition, salary and benefit expense as a percent of operating expenses declined in 1992. This factor is a reflection of hospital trends to save by modifying labor forces.

COMPETITION ❖
Industry Structure

An industry is a group of organizations that produces the same or similar products. Although the hospital industry does meet this definition in that hospitals all produce and deliver a similar kind of medical care, it is far more expansive and complex. As stated at the outset of this chapter, hospitals have different kinds of ownership, provide different kinds of services, and vary significantly in size. They also differ by their distribution across regions. Approximately half of all

Table 3.9 Admissions to Urban and
Rural Community Hospitals, 1982 and 1992

	1982	1992	% Change in Admissions/Hospital
Urban Community Hospitals	3,041	3,007	
Admissions	28 million	26 million	−6.1%
Rural Community Hospitals	2,760	2,285	
Admissions	8 million	5 million	−24.5%

Data source: AHA Hospital Statistics 1993–4.

community hospitals are located in Metropolitan Statistical Areas (MSAs), geographic areas that contain at least 50,000 people. Hospitals in MSAs are classified as urban hospitals. However, 80% of total hospital beds are located in urban hospitals. An urban hospital has specific problems its administration has to handle, including poverty, crime, emergency room traffic, and needs for security.

There are currently 2,285 rural hospitals in the U.S., a 17% decrease in this category since 1982. Rural community hospitals are often the only hospital within a scattered resident population, and they serve regional needs. Sometimes these hospitals have specialty services and are part of multihospital systems. In many towns across the U.S., there is only one hospital in the market with no substitutes for services. In most urban areas, however, there are high concentrations of hospitals that provide numerous services. These dense hospital areas often attract patients from outlying rural areas with specialty services and teaching facilities. Table 3.9 is a comparison of urban and rural hospitals from 1982 to 1992.

Prior to the 1980s, most hospitals were independent, not-for-profit, and local. A distinct industry trend is that now many hospitals are part of multihospital systems. These organizations generally have centralized corporate management structures. Between 1987 and 1990, the number of hospitals in health care systems increased significantly as free-standing hospitals combined into systems (Table 3.10). By 1990, 53% of the acute-care hospitals in the U.S. were part of systems.

The majority of systems are metropolitan area–based or local hospital systems (i.e., they operate within a small geographic area [60 mile radius] and control two or more of that area's hospitals).[41] Los Angeles, Dallas, Houston, Detroit,

Table 3.10 Multi-Hospital Systems, 1987 and 1990

	1987	1990	% Change
Number of Systems	303	311	+ 2.6%
Total Staffed Beds	435,422	558,664	+22.1%
Number of Acute Hospitals in Systems	2,567	2,906	+11.7%

Adapted from Modern Healthcare, March 9, 1992 (AHA Data).

Tampa, and Atlanta have more than eight systems within their metropolitan areas. Although these systems range in size, 80% have only two or three hospitals. Some, however, can have more than 5 hospitals in one small geographic area. In terms of ownership, 41% were reported to be not-for-profit; half were run by the Roman Catholic Church. For-profit systems accounted for 37% of these local hospital systems.

Hospital Market Areas

Individual hospitals refer to the area from which they draw their patients as a service or a market area. Sometimes they will have sole control over a service area, and other times their service area will overlap with that of other hospitals. Determining the precise market area is an important question for hospitals because it enables the hospital to know its market share, as well as its competitive power in certain areas and in certain services. Where are their patients from? Who are the patients whom a hospital serves? Which hospitals are competitors for patients?

Geopolitical boundaries, such as a county or a town, are one means of determining a hospital's market area. Another approach is a fixed-distance approach, which essentially draws a 15-mile radius from the hospital and uses that geographic circle as its service area. A more detailed method of service area determination is the patient-origin approach. By looking at the home ZIP codes of its patients, a hospital can get a broader picture of where its patients are coming from and what its market share is in any specific geographic area. This latter approach is particularly useful to determine a hospital's market share of specific service lines and to assess the utilization of health services within a specific market.

How Do Hospitals Compete?

Although there is a perception that community hospitals act independently in their medical care mission, hospitals are part of a large competitive industry in which decisions are based on the behavior and the activities of other nearby hospitals. Hospitals in essence compete with each other for patients and the revenue they bring. The market for hospital services is often a local one, restricted to a specific geographic area. However, for some specialty services (i.e., cardiac care and oncology), the market is regional or even national.

Whereas businesses strive to maximize their profits (i.e., their revenues minus their expenses) and to minimize their costs to compete with other businesses, hospitals act in a somewhat different manner. Businesses engage in price competition to gain customers (i.e., they offer lower prices than their competitors). However, price has not been the major competitive issue for hospitals when attracting patients. One reason for this factor is that the third-party payer reimbursement mechanism insulates patients from the cost of their care. In addition, patients often choose a hospital because their physician referred them or because it is the sole provider in their geographic area. This nonprice factor is amplified by the incomplete information that patients have about the quality of their medical care.

One theory is that hospitals act to gain revenue by maximizing the quality of their service and consequently gain more patients. Quality, rather than price, is the main form of competition between hospitals. This phenomenon of nonprice competition may be seen in hospital reputation, local proximity, and perceived quality of service, often gauged by the medical staff characteristics and the hospital's equipment and plant. Nonprice competition leads to increases in costs. Because physicians have the power to admit patients, hospitals must attract physicians by investing in the quality of facilities, new medical technology, expanded service lines, and provision of office space so that physicians will choose their hospital. The overall result will be higher investments in technology and physical plant and increasing costs for patient care.

Increasingly, as cost-containment pressures grow stronger, hospitals are beginning to engage in price competition by offering lower prices to insurers. In response to competitive pressures, hospitals are also seeking alliances with other hospitals and forming local monopolies to improve their bargaining power. These new kinds of relationships between hospitals are discussed in more detail in the next section.

Relationships Between Hospitals

In reaction to cost-control pressures, hospitals have joined into multiorganization arrangements to become more efficient and to gain market power. As stated previously, hospital systems are already a significant part of the hospital industry. In recent years, there has been further growth in horizontal integration in the hospital industry. *Horizontal integration* is when firms at the same level of production join together in some formal, legal relationship.

The most common form of this kind of relationship is the merger. When two hospitals merge, they become one legal entity and one organizational structure, combining their boards of trustees. Often, a merged hospital will maintain two sites, although sometimes hospitals are completely merged into one institution. Mergers allow hospitals to increase their patients, revenue, and reputation, and to develop efficiencies that come from a larger institution. Sometimes a hospital, or a parent company that owns a hospital, will acquire another hospital, resulting in a relationship similar to a merger. Other legal arrangements between hospitals are affiliations, whereby two hospitals will make a contract, but there is no change in ownership or hospital control. These cooperative agreements may include joint purchasing agreements or shared services, a legal arrangement whereby providers agree to share provision of services, such as laundry and food service.

Vertical integrations are relationships between organizations at different stages of production. In the hospital industry, vertical integration occurs when a hospital acquires a physician group, an HMO, a clinic, or a long-term care facility. These types of relationships have become more popular in recent years as inpatient utilization has declined and moved to alternative settings.

Impact of Competition

Heated debate continues over the outcome of a competitive environment on hospitals. Potential negative effects of competition on the hospital industry impact costs, access, and quality of care. Competition may lead to increased spending on duplicative services and equipment as hospitals compete for patients. Also, patients may be concentrated in larger and more costly facilities. In addition, a competitive environment may force hospitals to close, particularly those in poorer financial health. Concern exists as to whether those hospitals closed will be located in poor communities or whether hospitals closed will reduce needed outpatient services. Finally, as hospitals strive to gain more profits, there is concern that quality may suffer. Individuals concerned about hospital mergers suggest that they reduce competition and thus raise the cost of medical care. Yet, mergers may also reduce the economic impact on a community by becoming more efficient and reducing service duplication.

REGULATION ❖

In the mid 1970s, regulation of medical industry proliferated. Regulation of an industry is primarily intended to lower the price of goods and services and to improve the efficiency of the delivery of those goods and services. Regulation in the hospital field aims to inform and empower consumers, reduce duplication of expensive services, hold down governmental expenses, and improve access to care.[38]

Antitrust

Two federal agencies, the Department of Justice (DoJ) and the Federal Trade Commission (FTC), monitor hospital integration to see whether horizontal or vertical relationships violate *antitrust laws.*[42] Antitrust laws are generally designed to prevent businesses from engaging in anticompetitive behavior, thus controlling and setting the prices of goods and services for an entire market. The FTC has the authority to enforce antitrust law, whereas the DoJ prosecutes criminal violations.

To evaluate whether a hospital merger is anticompetitive, these government organizations first define the geographic boundaries of a hospital patient service area (sometimes focusing on selected services such as cardiac care) and look at the percentage of patients hospitals have from that service area. To measure the extent of competition between hospitals in that service area, they use an indicator called the

Herfindahl Index, which attempts to rate the degree of a geographic area's competitiveness. Because hospitals are a unique type of business (i.e., not-for-profit, civic purpose, and nonprice competition factors), the government also looks at the financial health of a hospital and the benefits a merger might have on a particular community. Increasingly, government merger analysis also looks at the legality of joint ventures of hospitals with physician groups.

Licensing and Accreditation

Since the middle of this century, states have regulated hospitals through licensure statutes and regulations. State agencies design requirements hospitals must follow to get operating permits. Typically, these state regulations have not focused on quality of care. Instead they have focused on hospital adherence to safety regulations and building and fire codes.

Throughout most of the U.S., private accreditation of hospitals overlaps or replaces the authority of state licensure. The most important accreditation organization is The Joint Commission on Accreditation of Health Care Organizations (JCAHO), which is a private group that imposes detailed organizational and procedural standards for each hospital. The JCAHO has significant power among the hospital industry, and it is sponsored by the AHA and the American Medical Association (AMA). It evaluates all aspects of hospital functions, including the staffing ratio, the adequacy of the plant, and the efficiency of the organizational structure. Although currently it does not evaluate quality of care outcomes, it is beginning to include outcome criteria. Many states delegate accreditation to the JCAHO. In addition, the Medicare program uses its standards and requires that hospitals have JCAHO certification.

Certificates of Need

Certificates of Need (CON) are regulatory tools designed to reduce state or regional hospital cost inefficiencies that result from duplication of services, investment in expensive medical equipment, and construction of new facilities. They include rules that limit service-line expansion, construction of new hospital facilities, or purchases of new technology exceeding specified amounts (these amounts vary among different states). In addition, they specify the number, category, and location of beds allowed for each hospital.

Under CON regulations, health care facilities must submit an application to an official state planning agency before undertaking an expansion project. Criteria the agency uses to determine whether to allow a hospital to proceed with its plans include community need, financial feasibility, quality of care, alternatives, and accessibility to the indigent. Public hearings are generally held to allow community members to review the hospital plans. After this hearing, the state agency renders a decision. In summary, CON rules attempt to find the actual needs of a community the hospital serves before allowing the hospital to make capital expenditures or to proceed with expansion plans.[28]

States passed CON laws in the early 1970s to control hospital expenditure increases. In 1975, the National Health Planning and Resources Development Act made CON laws a provision of funding for state and local agencies. Under President Reagan, federal support for CON regulation fell on hard times, and the law was repealed in 1987. As of 1992, however, 38 states and the District of Columbia still had CON laws.

Effectiveness of these regulations varies from state to state, and it is a controversial subject. In *Health Care Economics,* Paul Feldstein remarks that CON laws have not been that helpful in reducing the costs of health care. He suggests that they have resulted in a reduction in hospital competition and that they protect existing hospitals rather than encourage lower cost, new hospitals to compete. Although states appear to be keeping CON laws, they may be abandoned in a more competitive hospital system.

Rate Regulation and Expenditure Limits

In addition to federal government controls through Medicare, many states established agencies for regulation of hospital prices in the 1970s. The main reasons for state regulation were to combat rising Medicaid costs, to minimize overall costs of patient treatment, and to achieve system efficiency. Until recently, eight states were regulated, mainly in the Northeast, including Connecticut, Maryland, Massachusetts, New Jersey, New York, Rhode Island, Washington, and Wisconsin.[28] Massachusetts and New Jersey deregulated within the last three years. New York is known for having one of the most rigorous regulatory systems, which uses a mechanism called the New York Prospective Hospital Reimbursement Methodology.

Rate-setting programs vary in characteristics: some are voluntary, others are mandatory. Some are required for all payers, whereas others are for Medicaid only. There are several different methods for regulating hospital rates and setting overall expenditure limits. Under a budget review process, the rate-setting agency reviews an individual hospital's budget and determines whether it is reasonable. The second method sets reimbursement levels for a hospital according to the hospital performance in comparison with other state hospitals. Under a third method, the hospital determines a maximum increase in expenditures allowable for the hospital each year.[30]

The impact of price controls in hospital settings has been sharply debated as to their efficacy or their impact on the quality of care. In *Health Care Economics,* Paul Feldstein offers a detailed description and analysis of the impact of hospital rate regulation. Feldstein finds that state health planning agencies lack technical competence, rely heavily on providers for data, and use a reactive approach to planning. He finds that although mandatory rate regulation held down hospital cost increases in the pre-DRG period, evidence has been less clear since that time. The effects of regulation depend on how much power is vested in particular state agencies. In addition, price regulation by rate regulatory commissions does not address the physician role in demanding services.

FUTURE TRENDS IN THE HOSPITAL INDUSTRY ❖

The U.S. hospital system is changing in response to financial constraints, a more cost-conscious health care environment, and the prospect of national health care reform. Several major trends characterize these changes.

❖ *Continued growth of national multihospital systems, mergers, and affiliations.* Hospitals are increasingly seeking these relationships with other hospitals to achieve efficiency, greater access to patients, and shared technology. Minneapolis is a good example of a city in which there have been numerous hospital mergers. However, one potential problem with numerous mergers is that local monopolies may be created where one hospital or hospital system is the only provider in a geographic area. In addition, increased merger activity may force many hospitals to close, thus reducing access for many communities. In 1992, the AHA reported that 39 hospitals closed.[37]

❖ *Expansion of integrated health care networks.* Another strong trend in the hospital system is that hospitals are seeking to form legal and informal relationships with physician group practices, insurers, and HMOs to have control over all levels of care and not just the acute phase. These integrated delivery systems allow hospitals to gain more patients and revenue, to achieve greater efficiency, and to diversify into for-profit ventures. In the latter situation, a hospital can become a parent company for subsidiaries while protecting its tax-exempt status.

❖ *Continued expansion of outpatient facilities and satellite clinics.* Hospitals are expanding outpatient services as the demand for inpatient hospital care declines.

❖ *Managed care plans.* The continued proliferation of managed care plans will direct patient volume toward hospitals with lower costs and higher quality of care.

❖ *Workforce reduction.* Layoffs and attrition will continue to provide a means of cutting hospital costs.

❖ *Computer information systems, networks, and telemedicine.* These technologies will also impact hospital organization and production dramatically in the near future. Improved data collection, purchasing management, and information sharing with other hospitals through better computer systems will help hospitals manage their operations better, reduce labor, and integrate with other facilities. The advent of telemedicine (i.e., two-way audiovisual communications networks) will allow hospitals to exchange radiographs and other diagnostic procedure results. This exchange will particularly benefit rural hospitals, which have limited access to technology. It will also allow for cost savings in that it will reduce needs for specialized labor and equipment duplication.[43]

❖ *Clinical utilization improvements.* Hospitals will decrease costs by reducing length of stay, unnecessary testing, and improving clinical protocols.

❖ Suggested Reading ❖

Eastaugh SR. Health care finance: economic incentives and productivity enhancement. New York: Auburn House, 1992.

Eastaugh SR. Medical economics and health finance. New York: Auburn House, 1981.
   Excellent source on the economics of the hospital industry and hospital finance.

Feldstein P. Health care economics, 4th ed. New York: Delmar Publishers, 1993.
   Comprehensive chapters on hospital competition and regulation.

Starr P. The social transformation of American medicine. New York: Basic Books, 1982.
   Best source for the evolution of the U.S. hospital system.

American Hospital Association (AHA). Hospital statistics, 1993.
   Provides extensive aggregate information on the performance of the hospital industry.

4

Private Health Insurance

Adam Rosen and Douglas Staiger

To a greater extent than in any other country, the financing of health care in the United States is left up to the private health insurance market. Most Americans receive their health coverage through this private market, and it is largely because of problems in this market that we currently face a "crisis" in health care.

In this chapter, we look at the private health care industry in the U.S., both from the point of view of a historian and that of an economist. First, we look at the historical development of the private health industry, from the start of the Blue Cross/Blue Shield plans, to the rise of the commercial insurers, to the proliferation of managed care in recent years. Then we take an economist's view of health insurance by describing the market for insurance, looking at some factors that affect the cost of premiums, and ending with a discussion of some of the major imperfections in the market. These discussions are designed for readers with no prior background in economics. An appendix at the end of the chapter goes into more depth for those with more background or interest in the subject.

HISTORY OF PRIVATE INSURANCE ❖

Like most parts of the social system in the U.S., the private health insurance system was not designed as a comprehensive, logical system, but rather it evolved through the years in response to a series of historical forces.

Blue Cross

The beginnings of the modern American system of private insurance are traced to the creation of **Blue Cross** in Dallas in 1929. At that time, hospital services were not a large component of health care costs; most people did not receive their health care from hospitals, and hospital costs were quite low compared with their current levels. As a result, the average expenditure per person on hospital services was also quite low ($5.36 per year in 1929).[44] However, for those who did require hospital services, the cost burden could still represent a considerable portion of their wealth. Because of the burden imposed by these costs, defaults on hospital debts were common. Hospitals sought a way to stabilize their revenues and insulate themselves from the vagaries of these bad debts. Dr. Justin Ford Kimball of the Baylor University Hospital, the man credited with creation of the original Blue Cross plan, devised a solution.

In exchange for a prepayment of $.50 a month, 1,250 Dallas schoolteachers were offered hospital insurance. A $6 annual premium bought the teachers 21 days' worth of hospital care in a one-year period. These teachers would be largely relieved of the risk of hospital costs, and the Baylor hospital could rely on the stream of monthly payments.

Thus, the impetus for the original Blue Cross plan was not to protect patients from the hardships of high health care costs, but to stabilize the revenue streams of hospitals. The result of the Baylor plan was greater security for both hospital and patient. From that original plan, many of the dominant characteristics of the American private insurance system are traceable. First and foremost was the fact that this was an employer-based system. The Baylor hospital sought the pre-formed pool of the Dallas schoolteachers rather than attracting their own pool, patient by patient. Second, what the Baylor Hospital offered the teachers was not an indemnity plan, in which patients are reimbursed for health care costs incurred, but rather the teachers were guaranteed hospital services, directly, in exchange for their prepayment.

The Baylor plan was not the first private health insurance initiative in the country, but it proved far more successful than its predecessors. Partly, its success was due to the appeal of the plan. Patients enjoyed the benefits of the insurance. Unlike other plans at that time, this plan also catered to the medical community by providing them with a way to stabilize their revenues without subjecting themselves to external cost controls. Furthermore, because this system of offering hospital service in exchange for prepayment was not strictly considered insurance, the Blue Cross plan was able to avoid state insurance regulations that hampered early indemnity health insurance plans. The plan's success was also due to the economic environment into which it was born. In an economy of increasing incomes, there was less demand for cost savings schemes like the Blue Cross plan. But the Great Depression that commenced following the crash of the stock market in 1929 wreaked havoc on the American economy. In that economy of spiraling unemployment and plummeting income, hospitals were pushed to the financial brink, and any and all cost-savings schemes were highly sought after. By 1942, 6 million people were enrolled in Blue Cross plans, and the number was growing rapidly.[44]

Commercial Insurers

The success of Blue Cross spurred the interest of commercial firms already providing life, fire, and home insurance, and it demonstrated the potential for expansion by these commercial firms into the health insurance market. The Blue Cross plans were built around their connections to the hospitals. Whatever services were needed by the patients under their plan would be provided by their affiliated hospitals. The commercial entrants into the health insurance market were more typical of conventional insurance plans. These plans were cost-based indemnity plans. Individuals under these plans received reimbursements from the insurers according to the expenses incurred for the services they received. The difference between being service-based and cost-based had critical ramifications for the development between the two types of insurance.

Because the Blue Cross plans were service-based and because their original purpose was to stabilize the revenues of hospitals, these plans were less concerned with cost minimization. Accordingly, their premium schedules were based on community rating systems. This manner of rate setting transfers costs from high-risk to low-risk customers; low-risk customers pay more than their actuarially fair premium. The commercial insurers under cost-based plans typically relied on experience rating in an effort to tailor the costs of the insurance plan to the expected health care costs of the individual to whom the plan would be offered. This difference in pricing schemes between Blue Cross and the commercial firms had and continues to have an important role in the development of the two systems.

Another difference between the commercial firms and Blue Cross plans lay in the range of services offered. Unlike Blue Cross, the commercial insurers provided coverage for a wide range of health care needs beyond hospital services. In part to better meet the competition posed by the commercial firms, Blue Cross plans fostered the development of physician-based plans rather than hospital-based plans. These new entities, **Blue Shield** plans, started in California in 1939, and they expanded rapidly to become full siblings of the Blue Cross plans.

The Growth of Private Insurance

In the 1930s and through the 1940s, the private insurance market grew at a huge rate. In 1934, there were 15,000 people enrolled in commercial plans. In 1938, the commercial firms had 100,000 people enrolled. By 1941, the commercial firms had enrolled 3.7 million, and Blue Cross plans covered 6 million. In 1951, 40 million people were covered by the commercial firms, and 37 million were covered by Blue Cross.[44]

In part, the rapid growth in private insurance was spurred by federal policy during World War II. During the war, consumer goods were scarce because industrial output was geared toward the war effort and its demands. The government feared an upward spiral of price inflation, as consumers competed for what scarce goods were available. In an effort to prevent this price inflation, the government took the extreme step of controlling the wages of private industry workers.

With wages controlled, management was constrained in the increased benefits it could offer to attract labor. Expanded health insurance coverage became a desirable way of increasing compensation without violating the wage controls imposed by the government. This use of increased health benefits had another appeal to both management and labor. Health benefits were (and remain) tax-deductible. Employers were able to consider health benefits for their employees a cost of doing business; they were therefore not taxable. At the same time, employees did not have to pay income tax on benefits received as health care. Thus, a dollar paid in health benefits was more valuable to employees than a dollar of taxable wages.

This tax effect also had a crucial role in the expansion of health insurance after the war. It also contributed greatly to the employer-based system that has developed. Because of the tax policy, it was cost-effective for employers to provide their workers with health benefits, in contrast to employers paying a greater portion of wages and employees purchasing insurance with their own after-tax dollars. Thus, throughout the 1940s and the 1950s, collective bargaining agreements between management and labor relied on expansion of health benefits as a means of increasing compensation. Health benefits became a mainstay and an expected perquisite of employment.

The Current Insurance Market

Private health insurance of all types pays for approximately one third of all health expenditures in the U.S. The traditional commercial insurers continue to represent the largest segment of this market (86.7 million enrollees in 1990). The managed care sectors represented by the health maintenance organizations (HMOs), preferred provider organizations (PPOs), and point of service (POS) plans represent a large and growing segment. Combined enrollees in HMO-type arrangements and those in self-insured plans total 86.2 million. The Blue Cross/Blue Shield plans remain a dominant force in the market; 70.9 million people are enrolled in these plans. The increasing cost of health care has prompted the rise of another segment; the self-insuring large firm. Many large employers feel they employ large enough numbers of people to create their own well-diversified risk pools. These firms have chosen to become their own insurer and to administer their own plans directly. In so doing, these firms hope to save a large portion of the cost load of insurance by reducing administration costs and eliminating the profit margins they would pay commercial insurers. Figure 4.1 shows the market shares of the components of the private health insurance market in 1993.

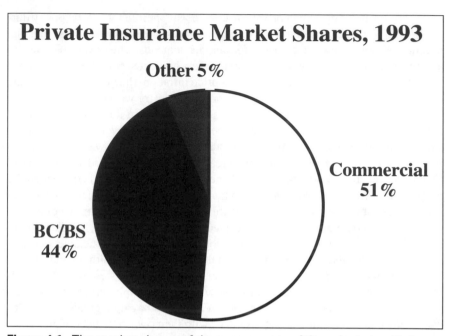

Figure 4.1 The market shares of the components of the private health insurance market in 1993. BC = Blue Cross; BS = Blue Shield. (Data Source: Bureau of Labor and Statistics, The Health Care Book of Lists, 1993.)

Of the $430 billion expended on health care in 1990 by the private sector, $110 billion was expended by business (not including business' $30 billion contribution to Medicare). Another $43 billion was extended by individuals to cover their employee contribution to their employer-sponsored private health insurance plans. In 1990, 29% of total health care expenditures and 43% of private health care expenditures were paid by business.[45] The legacy of the original health insurance plans in the 1930s and 1940s remains with us; ours remains largely an employer-based system of health insurance. Within that context, the changing face of medical care and the battle against increasing costs have caused dramatic change in the forms of private insurance available in the marketplace. The continuing development of medical science and the concomitant continuing increase of health care costs will likely force still greater changes in the future.

ECONOMIC ANALYSIS OF HEALTH INSURANCE   ❖

Many of the problems facing the U.S. health system can be traced to failures in the market for health insurance. To understand these problems, then, we need to look more closely at the market for health insurance. The most important tool for doing so is microeconomics, which attempts to describe how markets work and whether they are working efficiently. In the rest of this chapter, we take an economist's view of the insurance market by first describing why the market exists, then discussing some issues in pricing policies, and finally pointing out some of the reasons why the market may not work efficiently. These discussions, as mentioned earlier, are meant to expose noneconomists to important economic concepts useful in understanding the health system and its problems. The Appendix at the end of the chapter, as well as some of the key references, contain a more rigorous treatment of some of these issues for readers who already have a working knowledge of microeconomics.

The Market for Health Insurance

Economists define a market as having buyers and sellers who are exchanging certain goods. The good in question is health care insurance, but what exactly do we mean by this? In general, health care constitutes a range of services that enable us to avoid or attempt to alleviate illness or life-threatening conditions. Some of us may never find ourselves in these situations, but all of us face that risk, and these risks are associated with large, potentially exorbitant health care costs. Health insurance can be seen as paying money up front to avoid some of the risks associated with the financial costs of health care.

Is Health Care Like Other Goods?

Before we begin applying an economic framework to health care and health insurance, we need to ask whether we can treat these goods as simple commodities, such as cars, houses, or widgets. Is health care different? The answer we give to this question is typical of economists: yes and no. In some sense, our health is like few other "commodities." It affects our ability to appreciate anything else. How we view the world and the economic decisions we make are fundamentally determined by our level of health. In this sense, trade-offs between health and other simple commodities are difficult to make. How many dollars would a dying man pay for health? In some cases, health is simply priceless.

But even in this extreme case, some will choose to die rather than impoverish their dependents. In other less extreme cases, making trade-offs between health and other more worldly commodities is far easier. How much would you pay to avoid a bad cold? In this case, your health is clearly not priceless. No one would impoverish themselves to avoid a cold, but they would likely pay something. If a cold costs you one day's wage while you are sick in bed, perhaps you would be willing to pay some amount just less than one day's wage. Between these extremes of imminent death and a trivial inconvenience lie a spectrum of health risks. Economic frameworks provide useful tools for considering how we are likely to respond to these risks.

Health insurance can also be thought of as a good for which people are willing to pay a certain price. The amount of insurance I would buy for an expensive and uncommonly required procedure (e.g., kidney dialysis) will reflect the likelihood that I will need this procedure. Because I think I will not require this type of care, I will not insure heavily for it, despite its high cost. The amount of insurance I will purchase will properly reflect the economic valuation of these risks. This amount will obviously differ tremendously from the amount of "kidney dialysis insurance" I would buy after I learned I required the procedure. Economic frameworks, then, can provide useful tools for describing the "efficient" level of insurance.

Why Do People Buy Insurance?

As discussed earlier, a market requires both buyers and sellers. We must first ask the question: why are people willing to buy health insurance? The key concept here is called **risk aversion.** Those who are risk-averse are more willing to pay a small, certain amount of money now, than to stand a risk of losing a larger amount of money in the future. Imagine this game: I will put the numbers 1 through 1,000 in a hat and draw one out. If I pick the number 1,000, you will have to pay me $1,000. How much would you be willing to pay me in advance not to play the game? If you were risk-neutral, you would pay me the expected value of the loss. Expected value in this case is simply defined as the amount of the loss ($1,000) times the probability of that loss (0.001), or $1. If you were willing to pay me less than $1 not to play the game, you would be risk-loving, and if you were willing to pay more than $1 not to play, you would be called risk-averse.

There are much data to show that most people are risk-averse because of what is called the diminishing marginal utility of wealth. Simply put, we value the first few dollars we own more than the last few. Thus, we are more than 1,000 times as reluctant to lose $1,000 than we are $1. The Appendix at the end of this chapter contains a more rigorous look at this important concept.

Why Do People Sell Insurance?

The discussion provides a rationale for the demand for insurance. But what is the incentive to sell insurance? We define the **actuarially fair price** for insurance to be that price that equals the expected loss—$1 for the game described. At this price, consumers will demand insurance against their losses. If insurers can charge the actuarially fair price plus some additional fee to cover their administrative costs and a desirable return on their investment (known as the insurer's cost load), there then exists the basis for an insurance market where both consumers and providers of insurance gain. Insurers, then, will choose to provide insurance to risk-averse consumers if they can profitably offer that insurance at premiums at or greater than the actuarially fair price. Because of risk pooling and risk spreading, they are able to do so.

Risk Pooling

We described the actuarially fair price as the premium that reflects the expected losses of a risk. Insurers are able to group together large populations with similar characteristics. Individually, the members of these populations face a particular expected cost. As a population, these expected costs approach a certain, predictable cost because of the law of large numbers.[46] If 1,000 people face a 25% chance of a $200 loss, and if the risks faced by these 1,000 people are independent of each other, then the average loss faced by these 1,000 people will be $0.25 \times 200 = \$50$. An insurer who incorporates these 1,000 people into a single **risk pool** can confidently expect an exposure of $50 × 1,000 people = $50,000. Insurers, of course, cannot tell which of the 1,000 people will suffer losses, but they are confident that among them are 250 (0.25 × 1,000) people who will. Thus, by grouping similar people with similar risks together into large pools, insurers are able to change these individual uncertainties into known costs that can be predicted with great confidence.

Risk Spreading

Having grouped consumers of insurance into these risk pools, insurers can then charge these individuals the same premiums. Some of these consumers will actually suffer a loss, and the insurers will compensate them. Others will not suffer the loss, and they will not require compensation. All these customers—those who suffer the loss and those who do not—are left facing the same small, known costs. In effect, the losses that some of the risk pool suffer are spread across all the members of the pool in the form of premiums; hence the term, **risk spreading.**

What Affects Insurance Premiums?

We have just seen why health insurance can be thought of as a good, and why there are buyers and sellers of it in the market. We now turn to discussing some of the issues that influence insurance premiums. The level of premiums are important, because it affects both the cost of health care and access to it, two of the major issues facing the U.S. health system.

The Competitive Market

In a competitive marketplace, price is driven down to the lowest price the suppliers can sustain and still remain profitable. In the insurers' market, this price must be the actuarially fair premium plus the insurer's cost load. If some insurers charge more than this premium, competitors who charge lower premiums to customers will win them over. If they charge less, they will not receive enough revenues in premiums to cover both administrative and transaction costs plus the losses of their customers for which they must compensate. To the extent then that insurance markets are competitive (i.e., several suppliers competing for the business of consumers), suppliers will provide insurance at the actuarially fair premiums plus the insurer's load. Also, it can be seen that at the actuarially fair price, risk-averse individuals will choose to fully insure themselves.

Deductibles and Copayments

Most private insurance plans require deductibles or copayments for health care expenditures. Both these mechanisms more closely align the full costs of health care with those costs paid by the individual. As a result, these mechanisms reduce the level of costs of health care expenditures, thus allowing the insurer to charge lower premiums to consumers.

Deductible

Most insurers charge deductibles to their consumers. A deductible is a fixed level of health care expenditures below which insurers will not compensate their insurance consumers; only after consumers have expended an amount on health care equal to or greater than the deductible will insurers begin to reimburse the customers for expenditures. If my insurance policy has a $1,000 deductible, that first thousand dollars of care are paid for out of my pocket. Anything I spend after that $1,000 will be reimbursed by my insurer.

For small health care costs, transaction costs incurred in risk pooling and administration may outweigh the benefits received from risk spreading; the actuarially fair price plus cost load may exceed the customer's willingness to pay to avoid the risk of small costs. Deductibles provide a means for individuals to effectively self-insure for risks of small costs (below the deductible) and to maintain insurance for greater risks (costs that exceed the deductible.) In addition, insurers save money because they reduce the amount of expenditures for which they must compensate their customers. This savings may be passed on to consumers in the form of lower premiums.

Copayments

Deductibles are frequently combined with another form of cost reduction called copayments. In exchange for charging lower premiums, providers of insurance charge their customers a portion of the marginal cost of all the customer's medical care expenditures. The copayment by the consumers increases the individual marginal cost they face. In effect, the larger the copayment, the smaller the subsidy by the insurer to the consumer. Because consumers with copayments pay a percentage of the marginal costs of their care, they have the incentive to seek out cheaper care and to refuse care they deem unnecessary. The extent to which health care is price-elastic (i.e., individuals alter their consumption patterns of health care according to changes in the price for health care) will determine how much savings this cost sharing yields.[47] Insurers also save costs by shifting a portion of the costs from their own ledgers to those of the consumer. In both these ways (i.e., cost-shifting and reduction in expenditures by the insurer), copayments reduce insurers' costs and enable them to charge customers lower premiums.

Cost Loading

Another important determinant of insurance premiums is **cost loading** (i.e., costs associated with forming and administering the insurance pools). For commercial for-profit firms, these loads will also include an extra "mark-up" from which the insurers derive their profit. We noted that competition in the market for insurance drives prices to the actuarially fair premium. At this premium, individuals will choose to fully insure against losses. Because, in practice, insurers in a competitive market charge a premium above the actuarially fair premium by the amount of their loads, individuals who are free to choose their own level of coverage will not choose to insure completely. The level of cost loading, then, may have a significant impact on how much insurance people choose to purchase. As we have seen, the level of insurance people have affects the amount of health care people consume. Thus, cost loading is a critical issue in considering health insurance because it affects the price of insurance all consumers face and the amount of health care consumed.

What determines the level of cost loading? Insurance firms will be able to reduce costs by increasing the efficiency with which they administer their organizations. In addition, for-profit firms will be able to reduce their loads to the extent that they reduce their own profit margins. In both cases, competition among suppliers of insurance will reduce the cost loads these firms offer. Competition forces firms to be as efficient as possible because firms that fail to offer consumers the lowest possible price will be driven from the market. Therefore, insurers in a perfectly competitive market will attempt to minimize cost; profits, administrative costs, and transaction costs will be as low as possible to allow firms to offer the lowest possible premiums. The extent to which insurance markets truly are competitive will have a large role in determining the cost loads of insurers.

Although competition reduces inefficiency in an insurance firm, it may increase inefficiency within an insurance market, or it may prevent the firms from reaching greater efficiency by changing the scale of their operations. Some industries operate more efficiently the larger the amount of production is from an individual firm. Such industries are said to have increasing returns to scale and are said to be natural monopolies. It is worth considering whether health insurance is such an industry. Larger insurance firms, for example, may gain greater returns out of the administrative costs they incur if the risk pools they operate serve far more customers. The administrative costs can be spread out over more customers, and they can reduce the per premium cost load.

Monopolies may result not only from these efficiencies, but also from barriers to entry into the insurance market. These barriers may arise from regulatory control over who gets to offer insurance or because of special relationships between large insurers and hospitals. In this case, monopoly obstructs the efficiency of competition, and it may lead to higher-than-necessary premiums.

Thus, the market structure and the degree to which insurers operate efficiently will determine the cost loading of an insurance company. Because of these important implications of the structure of health insurance markets, much attention and research have been devoted to determining the extent to which insurance markets are competitive.

Cream Skimming

Another manner by which an insurer may reduce the premiums it charges individuals is to offer insurance only to lower risk customers. Because these lower risk customers will face lower actual losses as a group, insurers are able to charge lower actuarially fair premiums to risk pools consisting of these types of customers. The process in which these low-cost consumers are offered insurance and higher risk customers are refused is called **cream skimming.**

Insurers gain the requisite information with which to distinguish the risk individual customers face in a variety of ways. They may screen potential customers for pre-existing conditions. Pre-existing conditions are ailments or health characteristics that customers have before they enter an insurance program. Because of this condition and the costs it will likely impose, insurers may be reluctant to offer insurance to this consumer. For example, older patients with a history of heart disease will have a harder time finding new health insurance programs. Insurers may also rely on tailoring the insurance packages they offer to attract healthier customers. For example, a firm with a low premium but a high copayment will attract customers who judge themselves to be healthy and who will not need a great deal of health care. In this way, customers signal to the insurer that they are confident about their own levels of health. Other means of screening are more surreptitious. For example, insurers catering to older clientele may recruit customers at senior citizen dances with the intention of seeking out the healthier elderly.

Cream skimming raises serious equity concerns. In particular, it raises the question of what is an appropriate criterion for weeding out high-risk customers. For example, it may be appropriate for an insurer to act on the belief that smokers face a greater risk of health care problems than nonsmokers do. The insurer may screen applicants to determine whether they smoke and reject them on that basis. The argument has been made that this approach is proper; why should people who choose to harm their health in this way impose this cost on those who do not by increasing their health insurance premiums?

In contrast, it is far less clear whether this selection process is appropriate for conditions about which the applicant has no control. For example, only people of African descent face a risk for development of the disease sickle-cell anemia; only people of eastern European Jewish descent face the risk of acquiring Tay-Sachs disease. If an insurer were to charge higher premiums or to reject applicants on the basis of risk for developing these diseases, the insurer would be discriminating on the basis of race and religion. Although cream skimming may allow low-risk individuals to receive insurance that more accurately reflects the risks they face, cream skimming may achieve this by discrimination.

Determining legitimate criteria for risk pooling is critical. At the same time, because of the numerous and subtle ways firms may select low-risk individuals, preventing cream skimming presents a vexing policy challenge.

Community Rating Versus Experience Rating

Policy considerations with regard to community versus experience rating are closely linked to discussions about cream skimming. **Community rating** refers to the practice of not judging people by the risk they actually represent but by the average risk of the community as a whole. **Experience rating** refers to the process by which people are grouped into risk pools according to individual determinations of risk.

Community rating has its history in the evolution of health insurance under Blue Cross and Blue Shield. Community rating is often defended as a more equitable system of risk pooling because higher risk individuals are often those who are less able to pay for health care; they therefore benefit from the lower premiums they receive by being grouped with healthier individuals. Furthermore, supporters of community rating argue that charging people for incurring risks beyond their control (e.g., genetic pre-existing conditions, such as heart conditions) is also inequitable. President Clinton's health care proposal, for example, maintained the necessity of a community ratings–based system for these reasons.[48]

Critics of community rating and advocates of experience rating point to the basic inefficiencies in a community-based rating system and its encouragement of adverse selection and cream skimming. If insurance firms are prevented from experience rating, low-risk customers will be charged premiums higher than their actuarially fair price. If this price exceeds their willingness to pay for insurance, they may choose not to insure, instigating the adverse selection problem. If low-risk persons are grouped with high-risk persons in community-rated pools, then they will be subsidizing the higher risk consumers of health care. Critics contend that this transfer is not necessarily equitable.

Many of these advocates argue for more efficient risk assessment and a more efficient means of subsidizing the health care premiums of those least able to pay.

Inefficiencies in the Market for Insurance

In practice, insurance markets do not operate as smoothly as our discussion implies. There are many "inefficiencies" in insurance markets that have contributed to the cost and access problems faced by the American health care system.

We have seen how insurance can be viewed as a natural outgrowth of the marketplace. However, the presence of health insurance markets fundamentally changes the behavior of market participants. Some of these changes account for many of the concerns plaguing the health care market. This section explores the ways in which health insurance changes the marketplace for health care. Two of the inefficiencies in the health care marketplace that result from information asymmetry in the health insurance market are discussed: **moral hazard** and **adverse selection.**

Adverse Selection

Competitive markets lead to efficient outcomes when, among other things, consumers and suppliers act with full information. In the market for insurance, this full information implies that the insurer can accurately assess the risk of individual insurance purchasers. Recall that insurers are able to charge an actuarially fair premium that equals the expected losses of the insured because the insurers are able to reduce their uncertainty through risk pools of large numbers of people with similar risks. The law of large numbers transforms their individual risks into relatively certain aggregated costs.

For people to be placed in the proper risk pool and to be charged the actuarially fair premium that reflects their expected losses, the insurers must have good information about the consumer's expected losses. There is a limit, however, to how precisely insurers can assess the risk of individual insurance purchasers. In forming their risk pools, insurers can feel confident about their total exposure, because on average their assessments are likely to be accurate. Within risk pools, however, there will be a variation of the actual risk individuals face; some members of the risk pool will be riskier than average, and others will be less risky. Because all the members of the same risk pool pay the same premium (i.e., the actuarially fair premium for the average member of the pool), riskier members of the pool will pay premiums below their expected costs, and less risky individuals will pay more than their expected costs. In this way, less risky members of the risk pool subsidize the premiums of risky members by paying more for their own premiums.

The accuracy and precision with which insurers can assess the risk of the insurance purchasers, then, will determine the extent to which these less risky customers will pay premiums higher than their expected costs. If information is poor and insurers cannot assess the risk of their customers, the additional premiums the less risky pay may be substantial. In fact, this additional amount may be so substantial that less risky consumers decide that insurance is no longer worth it to them. The actuarially fair premium for the risk pool to which they are assigned may so greatly exceed their own expected loss that the premium exceeds their willingness to pay. In this case, these individuals will choose not to insure or to purchase less insurance. This decision by less risky individuals to drop out of the insurance market because of imprecision in the assessment of risk in the risk pools results in high-risk individuals making up a disproportionately high percentage of those insured by the market. This process by which individuals who know they are most at risk of having an insurance claim disproportionately purchase insurance is called adverse selection.

Moral Hazard

In our discussion of the demand for health care, we described why we believe the consumption of health care is price-elastic (i.e., the amount of health care people consume depends on its cost to them). Imagine that you are fully insured and have paid your health insurance premium for the period. Imagine an illness develops for which you may require medical care. You will weigh in your mind the costs and benefits of seeking care for this illness. In this case, because your full insurance is already paid, the additional (i.e., marginal) financial cost of seeking this care is zero (ignoring for the moment other factors, such as time out of work). In effect, you have already paid for the care when you paid your premium. Thus, any positive benefit you expect to receive for this care will outweigh the costs.

Alternatively, if you were not insured and you faced the same illness, your cost-benefit comparison would be different. You would weigh the benefits of avoiding or alleviating the illness against whatever medical fees you expected to incur. If the ill effects of the illness were small, you may decide that the medical costs exceed the benefits you would receive. In this case, you would choose to not receive the care. Thus, when individuals are insured, they purchase more health care than if they were not insured. This altering of the behavior of consumers by the presence of insurance is called moral hazard.[49]

Although insurance lowers the costs borne by the consumers of health care, the full costs of producing the health care have not been reduced. Rather, the burden of the costs has been shifted from the consumer of the care to the insurer. Because insurers pass costs on to all purchasers of insurance in the form of higher premiums, moral hazard causes everyone to pay more for insurance. Individual consumers, however, base their consumption decisions not on the full costs of care, but only on the portion of the costs they bear. Thus, with insurance, individuals "over-consume" health care, in the sense that they consume more than they would in the absence of insurance. This overconsumption results in what economists call a deadweight loss to society. Another example illustrates the effect of moral hazard on health care demand.

Imagine you are presented with the option of a new operation. The operation would reduce the odds that farsightedness develops. The operation involves no real risk or ill effects; it is not dangerous or painful, but it is exorbitantly expensive. In this case, in the absence of insurance, you may decide that the risk of wearing reading glasses is not worth impoverishing yourself. However, if you were fully insured for this procedure and the physician determined you were eligible for it, the marginal cost to you of this procedure would be negligible. The benefits, although not enormous, are significant. Under these circumstances, you may choose to have the operation performed; in fact, it would be the rational thing to do. This extreme example demonstrates one of the critical ways in which insurance and third-party payer schemes increase the amount of health care consumed.

Under what circumstances could moral hazard be prevented? If the insurer had complete information about the likely behavior of each health care consumer, the insurer could control moral hazard. Each insurance policy could be contingent on certain guidelines governing the behavior of each consumer. For example, an insurer could establish guidelines that said consumers will not be covered for care that they would not have sought in the absence of insurance. Such guidelines are, of course, foolish because they are unenforceable. The insurer has no way of knowing how the insurance is altering the behavior of consumers. However, this discussion makes the point that moral hazard could be controlled if the insurers had precise information about the risks each individual consumer truly faced.

CONCLUSION   ❖

It is critical for us to understand private health insurance, because it forms the basis of most of the health financing in the U.S. In this chapter, we looked at the historical development of insurance, as well as at some economic analysis of the market, how it operates, and some of its inefficiencies. The results of many of the characteristics we discussed in this chapter will become evident in the next section, in which we discuss the challenges that face the U.S. health system: cost, access, and quality.

APPENDIX: RISK AVERSION   ❖

The following is a more technical discussion of risk aversion, one of the most important concepts in understanding the insurance market, because it is the primary motivation for people to insure.

Economists usually assume that we all behave in ways that maximize our own individual utility, where "utility" means happiness or well-being. Economists also generally assume that having more goods to consume or having better health raises our utility. Our *utility function* (i.e., the collection of factors that determine our level of utility) may also include such things as the utility of others, but we focus on the wealth aspect of our utility. Clearly, the more wealth we obtain, the more our level of utility is increased, or, at worst, our utility remains unchanged (all else equal.) However, the higher the level of wealth we have, the fewer changes in our wealth increase or decrease our level of utility. One hundred dollars increase everyone's utility, but these dollars increase the utility of a starving pauper by a greater amount than if he were a millionaire. In this sense, people are said to possess a *diminishing marginal utility to wealth.*

Because people have diminishing marginal utility to wealth, they are said to be *risk-averse.* To define risk aversity, we need to define the concept of expected value. *Expected value* is a probability term that means the average of all possible outcomes. If when you role a die there is a 67% chance that you win $100 and a 33% chance that you win nothing, the expected value to you of rolling the die is $(0.67) \times \$100 + (0.33) \times 0 = \$67$. How much would you risk for the opportunity to take this chance? If you would be willing to pay exactly the expected value ($67) for this chance of winning $100, you are risk-neutral; if you are willing to pay more than $67, you are risk-loving; and if you are only willing to pay less than $67 or no amount at all, you are risk-averse.

Being *risk-averse* can be defined as having a preference for a certain outcome of known value relative to an uncertain outcome with an expected value of the same amount. In other words, even if both the known outcome and the risky outcome have the same expected value in dollar terms, risk-averse people prefer (i.e., derive a higher level of utility from) avoiding the uncertainty. This is equivalent to saying people are willing to pay some positive amount (and thereby incur a known, certain loss) to avoid the risk of a greater loss. This willingness of consumers to pay to convert uncertain but potentially high costs into known, certain smaller costs is the basis for the demand for insurance.[50] How much, exactly, would people be willing to pay for insurance?

Figure 4.2 describes an outline of the demand for insurance by risk-averse individuals. Imagine that you are risk-averse and you possess an initial level of

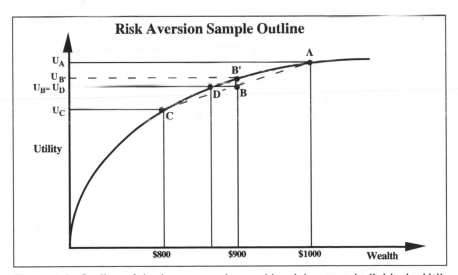

Figure 4.2 Outline of the insurance demand by risk-averse individuals. Utility, on y-axis, is defined economically as individual well-being or happiness, or having greater goods to consume or better health, etc. Utility is said to increase as monetary wealth increases.

wealth equal to $1,000, with a corresponding level of utility of U_A, point A in the diagram. Imagine that you face a 50% risk of a $200 dollar loss, reducing your wealth to $800 and your utility to U_C, point C. Your expected loss is $0.50(0) + 0.50(200) = \$100$. Thus, your expected outcome is $900 ($1,000 − $100.) Note that this expected outcome can be found by point B, in this case the midpoint of the secant between point C and point A. Point B is halfway between C and A, because both C and A are equally likely outcomes (50% probability of both.)

The level of utility associated with this expected outcome of $900 is U_B. Note that this point lies below the utility function, $U(W)$. If you were to possess $900 of wealth, with certainty your level of utility would be U_B', where $U_B' > U_B$. Similarly, there is some smaller amount of wealth received with certainty, indicated by point D on $U(W)$, that would give you the same level of utility than the uncertain but potentially greater amount of wealth at point B. The difference between point A and point D is your *willingness to pay* for insurance. Imagine you were to pay the amount of this difference to an insurer in exchange for the promise that the insurer would compensate you fully in the event that you actually suffered the $200 loss. In this case, you would be indifferent between being fully insured and paying this premium (i.e., A–D) versus having no insurance; your utility is the same in either case. If the insurer charged you a premium of any amount less than the difference between point A and point D, you would prefer buying the insurance to risking the $200 loss.

As we described, the expected loss you face is $100. The actuarially fair price for insurance is defined as the price equal to this expected loss ($100), the difference between point A and point B. Any price above $100 would exceed the expected loss you face; any price below $100 would fall short of that expected loss. Note that if you were to pay this actuarially fair price as a premium, your level of utility would be U_B', which, as noted, is greater than the level of utility of your expected wealth if you were uninsured (U_B). *Thus, there exists a range of prices, from your willingness to pay threshold to the actuarially fair price, which you would pay with certainty to avoid the risk of the larger loss of $200.*

From Figure 4.2, we can also determine what factors are involved in our willingness to pay for insurance. The further the secant joining the possible outcomes lies below the utility function, the greater amount we would be willing to give up with certainty to avoid the risk of a greater loss. In other words, the greater this distance, the greater is our willingness to pay for insurance. What factors determine this outcome? First, the size of our initial wealth, point A, and the size of the potential loss (i.e., the distance between points A and C) are factors. Where point B lies along the line joining A and C is determined by the probability of the bad outcome; therefore, this probability also determines the willingness to pay. Second, the shape of the curve of the utility function above point B will affect the size of the willingness to pay; therefore, our degree of risk aversion (i.e., the extent of the concavity of the utility function) will also matter. All these factors combine to determine the extent to which we can be made better off with insurance against a particular risk.

❖ **Acknowledgment** ❖

The author is indebted to Professor Douglas Staiger of the John F. Kennedy School of Government, and to Jeffrey Leibman, Department of Economics, Harvard University, for their useful comments.

❖ **Suggested Reading** ❖

Feldstein PJ. Health care economics. New York: Delmar, 1993. Chapter 6: The demand for health insurance.

Phelps CE. Health economics. New York: HarperCollins, 1992.
   Chapter 2: An overview of how markets interrelate in medical care and health insurance.
   Chapter 4: The demand for medical care—a conceptual framework.

Newhouse JP. The economics of medical care. Reading, MA: Addison Wesley, 1978.
   All three references have excellent discussions on the economics of insurance.

Fein R. Medical care, medical costs, the search for a health insurance policy. Cambridge, MA: Harvard University Press, 1989.
   Best source for history of the American private insurance market.

Starr P. The social transformation of American medicine. New York: Basic Books, 1982.
   Readers are directed to Paul Starr's book for a further analysis of the development of the insurance market and an excellent general history of American medicine.

5

Managed Care

Aaron Caughey and James Sabin

From 1960 to 1990, the number of managed care plans and the number of persons enrolled in them increased at an astounding rate. Currently, almost 80 million Americans receive their health care from a health maintenance organization (HMO) or some other prepaid health plan. Many believe HMOs to be the answer to spiraling health costs, whereas others believe them to be a band-aid on a bleeding and broken health care financing system.

This chapter first defines ***managed care*** and gives a history of managed care in the United States (U.S.). Against this background, the discussion then focuses on the different types of managed care plans available: ***HMOs***, *preferred provider organizations* (*PPOs*)*,* and *point of service* (*POS*) plans. The analysis turns to the cost-control measures used by managed care plans, and finally to the issues facing physicians practicing in managed care plans.

MANAGED CARE DEFINED ❖

Managed care describes many different medical care constructs. A managed care organization is one in which specific measures are taken by the provider system or health insurance program to provide health services to a given population within a specific budget. This loose definition can encompass any of the many types of prepaid group practices and health plans that have evolved over the years and the methods they employ to keep medical expenditures under control.

The methods used to keep costs controlled include different financial disincentives aimed at decreasing unnecessary care. These disincentives include copayments for office visits and pharmaceuticals, increased cost sharing when seeking care outside a defined group of caregivers, use of primary care providers as gatekeepers, and replacing hospital care with outpatient therapy. In addition, costs are also theoretically controlled by decreasing administrative costs.

Another way to define managed care is to consider two other forms of health care delivery: *fee-for-service* (**FFS**) and indemnity health insurance. Under FFS, patients may see any physician they choose, provided that they can pay the fees charged by that physician. This is a reasonable approach for yearly physicals and routine tests, but it quickly becomes cost-prohibitive if a serious medical condition develops that requires multiple follow-up visits, expensive therapies, or hospitalizations, which can cost up to $1,000 per day.

Health insurance is an indemnity product (i.e., financial protection against future medical costs). If a patient with health insurance requires medical care, the health insurance company either reimburses the patient for expenses incurred or pays the health care provider directly.

Health insurance has three aspects of payment: premiums, copayments, and deductibles. Premiums are often established on an annual basis, and they involve experience rating, which is price differentiation based on differences in each individual's demographic make-up. Copayments are utilization fees that are paid when the patient receives medical care, whereas deductibles are maximum limits on costs that a patient will incur for any particular procedure or in any particular year.

Managed care incorporates aspects of health insurance, such as annual premiums and copayments; however, these premiums are often community-rated (i.e., medical costs for a large group of enrollees is actuarially predicted and then spread equally among all members of the group). In addition, copayments are required by law not to make medical care inaccessible, and they are often just $5 to $10.

THE HISTORY OF MANAGED CARE ❖
The Rise of HMOs

The concept of prepaid medical services has existed in the U.S. since 1798, when the federal Marine Hospital Service was established to contain communicable disease spread by the transient seafaring labor force. It was mandatory and funded by the merchant seamen who had 20 cents taken from their monthly paychecks.[51] Voluntary prepayment plans emerged in San Francisco during the Gold Rush in 1849, and the Southern Pacific Railroad Company's health plan, established in 1868, survived into the twentieth century.[51]

During the first half of the twentieth century, the number of prepaid medical plans increased rapidly. In 1929, 1,500 Dallas schoolteachers paid 50 cents per month to join a prepaid hospitalization plan at Baylor University Hospital.[52] In the same year, two physicians, Donald Ross and H. Clifford Loos, established the Ross-Loos Clinic, a prepaid plan designed to serve 2,000 members of the Los Angeles County Employees Association of the Department of Water and Power. It was also around this time that organized medical associations, long-time proponents of solo fee-for-service practice, began their extensive attack on prepaid group plans, which lasted over the next few decades. Specifically, the Los Angeles County Medical Association (LACMA) and the California Medical Association (CMA) brought charges of unethical advertising against Drs. Ross and Loos.[51]

In this setting of prepaid practice infancy, Dr. Sidney Garfield, a young surgeon, contracted with Industrial Indemnity to care for the 5,000 "medically neglected" men working along the Colorado River Aqueduct that ran 190 miles from the Parker Dam to the outskirts of Los Angeles.[53] He built a small 12-bed hospital with such modern conveniences as air conditioning and radios. Initially, Dr. Garfield found himself unable to collect much more than the fees provided by the workman's compensation insurance, and that even this was difficult with insurance companies' objection to claims.

Harold Hatch and Alonzo B. Ordway, officers of Industrial Indemnity Exchange, saw that despite Garfield's dedication, he was losing money, so they proposed to prepay him $1.50 per worker per month. Furthermore, the three men developed the idea that workers could also prepay for illness and injury unrelated to work at the rate of 5 cents per day. Nearly 100% of the workmen joined, and Garfield was able to employ 10 additional physicians and built two additional hospitals.[51]

Riding on the success of the prepaid medical plan on the aqueduct, Garfield accepted the offer of Edgar Kaiser in 1938 to develop a similar plan at Mason City in eastern Washington, where 5,000 employees of the Henry J. Kaiser Company were building the Grand Coulee Dam. He brought six other physicians with him and oversaw $100,000 of renovations to the current 85-bed hospital. Financially, the arrangements were similar to his previous plan: The company prepaid for industrial accidents, and workers were charged 50 cents per week for a non-work-related voluntary prepaid health care plan. However, the workers' families had no health plan or the means to pay the hospital bills incurred when a family member became ill. In response, Garfield created a family prepaid health plan, charging 50 cents for wives and 25 cents for each child.[51]

The prepaid health plan at Mason City was popular with both workers and physicians, and it was a financial success. It was here that Kaiser and Garfield met and discussed the possibility of expanding prepaid health plans across the country.[51] Thus began a working relationship that spanned almost 30 years until Kaiser's death in 1967, and that was responsible for developing the largest HMO in the country—The Kaiser Foundation Health Plan.

In January 1941, Kaiser requested Garfield to develop a prepaid medical plan for the 20,000 workers at the Kaiser shipyards in Richmond, California. In ad-

Table 5.1 Kaiser Health Plan Membership Trend 1945–1958

Date	Northern CA	Southern CA	Portland–Vancouver	Total
1945	11,500	0	15,000	26,500
1950	120,000	20,000	14,000	154,000
1955	291,000	188,000	22,000	501,000
1958	337,000	245,000	30,000	618,000

Membership trend in three selected Kaiser Permanente Health plans over a thirteen year period. Includes 6,000 members from Hawaii in 1958. (Data source: Hendricks R, A Model for National Health Care: The History of Kaiser Permanente, Rutgers University Press, 1993.)

dition, he had plans to develop the Portland–Vancouver and San Francisco areas. In 1942, The Permanente Foundation was created, and it built or renovated hospitals in Oakland and Richmond.[51] This same year, the Northern Permanente Foundation was formed to finance construction of a new hospital for the care of the workers in the Portland–Vancouver area. The Southern Permanente Foundation soon followed to provide health care for 3,500 workers and their families at the Kaiser Fontana mill. Table 5.1 shows the growth in the Kaiser plan on the West Coast from 1945 to 1958.

Although Kaiser's Permanente Health Plans enjoyed success, they endured continuous attack from local and national medical associations. Physicians who worked at the Kaiser facilities were denied membership in medical societies, and they were in some cases barred from becoming specialty Board licensed. Members of the American Medical Association (AMA) objected to the recruitment of patients and the socialized medicine aspects of prepaid group plans. Furthermore, they claimed that the prepaid plans denied access to free choice of physicians and provided poor quality service to make a profit.[51]

Despite the objections of the AMA, growth in the Kaiser Permanente continued, and membership increased to 808,000 in 1960. By 1967, there were more than 1.5 million members. In 1992, Kaiser Foundation Health Plans had a membership of more than 6.6 million.[51] Although acceptance was slow, the AMA grew to coexist with managed care plans, and it eventually recognized managed care plans and the physicians who worked in them as legitimate.

The AMA Recognizes Group Practice Physicians

The AMA suffered a series of legal defeats, beginning in 1943 with the landmark U.S. Supreme Court decision against the AMA for "restraint of trade" against GHA of Washington, D.C.[54] These decisions, combined with favorable economic conditions and the realizations that prepayment plans posed only a small threat, led the AMA to relax its opposition, and it " . . . became reconciled to vigilant coexistence with prepaid group practice."[55]

In 1955, the Commission on Medical Care Plans was created by the AMA. In its 1959 report, it found that although the plans were seen to be dehumanizing and intruded in the doctor-patient relationship, "free choice of medical plan was an acceptable substitute for free choice of physician."[55] Most importantly, the physicians in prepaid group practice were totally absolved by the AMA's report.[51] Finally, in an effort to curb skyrocketing health care costs, the federal government enacted the HMO Act of 1973, which legitimized managed care.

The HMO Act of 1973

The Health Maintenance Organization Act of 1973 mandated that employers of 25 or more persons offer a prepaid group practice plan to their employees, in addition to a traditional indemnity plan. This became known as the "dual choice" mandate. To assist in the creation of such plans, the federal government authorized loans and grants to HMOs that met certain federal requirements. The HMO Act received bipartisan support. The conservatives could point to its efficiency and its potential to reduce government spending, and liberals advocated the humanitarian aspects of increasing access to health care.[54]

Federal Requirements

Specifically, the federal requirements to qualify as an HMO under the HMO Act of 1973 included the following.[56]

✧   Payments for the health plan were to be periodic, without regard to use of services; fixed under a community-rating system; and possibly supplemented by a nominal copayment.

✧   Basic services were to be provided to each member of the plan by health professionals who are members of the staff of the HMO, group practices contracted to provide care to HMO members, or individual practice associations contracted to provide care through the HMO.

✧   Enroll members who are broadly representative of the geographic area it represents.

✧   Ensure fiscal solvency.

✧   Members cannot be expelled or refused renewal of the plan.

✧   Members shall make up at least one third of the policy-making body of the HMO.

✧   Furthermore, the HMO Act defined the "basic services" that a plan must provide. These services included general medical services, such as specialist care, laboratory and diagnostic tests, inpatient and outpatient hospital services, and emergency care. In addition, they included short-term (< 20 visits) mental health care, alcohol and drug abuse treatment, home health services, and preventive health services.

Although the federal requirements placed an increased financial burden on HMOs, there were still two strong incentives for HMOs to enter the marketplace. One was the loans and grants given by the federal government to *federally qualified HMOs* (*FQHMOs*); the second was that the employers required to offer HMOs to their employees were required to offer FQHMOs, which led to a huge market advantage over non-FQHMOs.

HMO Growth

The incentives provided by the HMO Act of 1973 led to an increase in the growth of both the number and the size of HMOs. When the Act was passed in 1973, there were only 72 plans, which enrolled 2% of the population (≈3.5 million individuals). By 1980, there were 235 plans providing care to 5% of the population.[57] In 1992, the enrollment was 17.3% of the U.S. population in more than 500 HMOs.[58] Growth in the number of HMOs and the number of enrollees from 1985 to 1992 is depicted in Table 5.2, and HMO penetration by state in 1992 is shown in Figure 5.1.

Current Status of the HMO Act

Because of this large growth in HMOs, the federal government stopped financial support, and the "dual choice" requirement of employers will become voluntary after 1995. These amendments to the HMO Act are primarily a result of the stability of HMOs and predictions of their ability to maintain market share regardless of the loss of employer mandates. In addition, it is believed if there is more freedom given to individuals and organizations developing plans, then more cost savings can be created by tailoring plans to consumer preferences.

Table 5.2   HMO Growth Trends, 1985–1992

Date	Number of HMO's	% Change from Previous Year	Enrollment (Millions)	% Change from Previous Year
1985	490	—	22.7	—
1986	632	+22.5	26.6	+14.7
1987	707	+10.6	31.0	+14.2
1988	659	− 7.3	33.7	+ 8.0
1989	623	− 5.8	35.0	+ 3.7
1990	610	− 2.1	37.5	+ 6.7
1991	581	− 5.0	40.4	+ 7.2
1992	562	− 3.4	43.7	+ 7.6

Growth trend in HMOs over a seven year period. (Data source: Marion Merrell Dow Managed Care Digests, 1993.)

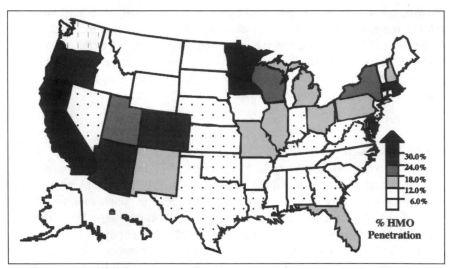

Figure 5.1 HMO penetration by state, 1992. (Data Source: Marion Merrell Dow Managed Care Digests, 1993.)

EVOLUTION AND SPECIATION OF MANAGED CARE ❖

In evolutionary terms, managed care is undergoing speciation, as health care plans evolve to fill every consumer niche. When the Office of HMOs (OHMO) was re-named the Office of Prepaid Health Care (OPHC) in 1982, it reflected the growth within the managed care field. The OPHC was given the responsibility of directing not only HMOs, but also all of the other forms of prepaid, competitive, and capitated health plans.

HMOs

As evidenced by Kaiser, HMOs have been around for decades before the Federal HMO Act of 1973, but they grew even faster in number and enrollment after its passage. In the late 1980s and early 1990s, although enrollment in HMOs has continued to increase, the actual number of HMOs has been decreasing annually. In 1992, there were 562 HMOs, with a total enrollment of 43.7 million.[58] This seemingly counterintuitive decrease in the number of HMOs is a result of mergers and consolidations. For example, Harvard Community Health Plan (HCHP) in Massachusetts merged with both MultiGroup in Massachusetts and Rhode Island Group Health Association (RIGHA) to become a larger health plan, both in terms of enrollment and geographic distribution.

HMOs are seen as existing in four different designs: staff, group, individual practice association (IPA), and network models. Staff and group models represent two forms of prepaid group practice. Both are considered closed-panel HMOs because the physicians see HMO patients only. Physicians within IPAs and networks often see patients on a FFS basis as well, which is designated an open-panel design.

Staff Model

A staff model HMO directly hires individual physicians to provide care at facilities that are owned or leased by the HMO. The HMO maintains the facilities, hires support staff, and pays for malpractice insurance. Physicians are paid salaries, sometimes augmented with bonuses based on the HMO's ability to contain costs or other measures of its performance. In this model, the physician is truly an employee of the HMO. In 1992, there were 56 staff models (10% of the total HMOs), which accounts for 10.8% of total enrollment.[58]

Group Model

In the group model, the HMO again provides the facilities for care delivery. Instead of hiring individual physicians, the HMO contracts with a group practice to provide health care. The group practice is either paid on a capitated basis or garners a fixed percentage of the HMO's premium. The distribution of the remuneration is then left up to the group of contracting physicians. This arrangement is exemplified by the contract between the Kaiser Foundation Health Plan and the Permanente Medical Group. In this model, physicians are members of a partnership or a corporation, not employees of the HMO. The 71 group model HMOs accounted for 12.6% of all HMOs and for 25.9% of total HMO enrollment in 1992.[58]

Individual Practice Associations

In the confusing milieu of acronyms, IPAs are also known as independent practice associations. In this model, each of the group or individual practices that constitute an IPA is independent of the other. IPA model HMOs consist of an HMO contracting with either a group practice association or individual physicians (known as direct contracting). However, in this scenario, the physicians provide care out of their own facilities, and they manage their own staff.

The HMO may reimburse IPA physicians either on a capitated or a fee-for-service basis. Sometimes primary care physicians are reimbursed on a capitated basis, whereas specialists receive some form of fee-for-service payments. Alternatively, providers may receive a portion (perhaps 80%) of their fee; the remainder of the fee is placed into a bonus account. On a regular basis, if the HMO's budget is maintained, the providers receive the bonus. Initially, it was thought that IPAs would not have the incentives to keep costs down, but it has been shown that IPAs in which the providers bear some of the financial risk have rates of hospital days that are similar to rates of traditional prepaid group practices.[59]

The IPA model is popular with providers, consumers, and insurers because it has aspects of both traditional HMOs and private practices. Providers keep their own offices and staff, and they retain control over many of the day-to-day issues in their practice. However, as members of an HMO, they have a guaranteed patient population. Patients receive the more personal attention of a small practice that might be lost in a large staff or group model HMO, and they are 10% more likely to rate a small practice "excellent" than an HMO.[60] Sponsors have no need to build and staff large facilities. There were 363 IPA model HMOs in 1992 (64.6% of all HMOs), and they accounted for 47.6% of all HMO enrollment in the U.S.[58]

Networks

Networks are HMOs that use any combination of the other models. For example, a network model HMO may have its own facilities and contract with a group practice to provide primary care services, but it may also contract with independent specialists or IPAs to provide additional care. In 1992, 12.8% of all HMOs were networks. These 72 network model HMOs accounted for 15.7% of all enrollment.[58] Table 5.3 provides a summary of the different HMO types.

Preferred Provider Organizations

Although HMOs restrict choice by only offering care through specified providers, PPO benefit plans provide incentives, such as additional benefits, to use providers on a preferred list, and disincentives, such as higher copayments when other providers are used. In PPO arrangements, health care providers are generally reimbursed on a discounted FFS payment schedule. However, providers have two important incentives to join PPOs. First, they are assured of prompt payment without extensive billing procedures. More importantly, they gain access to a larger market share of patients as a result of practicing within a PPO. In 1992, there were 681 PPOs available to more than 120 million individuals.[61]

Table 5.3 Summary of HMOs by Model Type

Model	Number	% of All HMOs	% of Total HMO Enrollment
Staff	56	10.0	10.8
Group	71	12.6	25.9
IPA	363	64.6	47.6
Network	72	12.8	15.7

Summary of the four different designs of HMOs. IPA = Individual Practice Association. Figure based on data from 1992. (Source: Marion Merrell Dow Managed Care Digests, 1993.)

Point of Service Plans

POS plans, similar to PPOs, expand the choices available to consumers, at a cost. Patients are able to choose to stay within a select group of providers at a lower cost or to go outside that group at a higher cost. The difference between PPOs and POS plans is that POS plans are fundamentally an HMO product. Patients receive maximum coverage for specialists' services only if they obtain a referral from their primary care physician. PPOs, in contrast, provide the opportunity for self-referral to specialists; patients receive full coverage as long as the specialist is on the preferred list.

POS plans are a good compromise for HMOs because they provide access to a greater market share than the traditional HMO. They offer expansion possibilities to rural areas with reduced population concentrations. Consumers are less wary of joining a POS plan because they are still left with the choice of provider. Membership in POS plans increased 44% in 1992 to 5 million; there was a concomitant 69% increase in HMOs offering POS plans. Of these plans, HMOs reported that 75% of the total dollar value of claims stayed within their own physician and hospital network.[58]

COST-CONTROLLING MEASURES ❖

One of the reasons that prepaid group health plans have been able to garner an increasingly larger share of the health care and health insurance markets is because they have been able to reduce costs. HMOs employ a number of cost-controlling measures.

Gatekeeping

HMOs utilize the concept of *gatekeeping* to prevent self-referral. Patients either choose or are assigned a primary care physician (PCP). This physician can then coordinate care of the patient with increased efficiency by reducing the number of redundant and excessive tests, procedures, and referrals to specialists. In an established, long-term patient-doctor relationship, physicians, knowing the reliability of the patient as a historian, can rely on follow-up as opposed to diagnostic tests. In systems that utilize gatekeepers, patients cannot see specialists or get second opinions without getting a referral from their PCP gatekeeper.

Decreasing Hospital Use

It has been noted that hospital admissions and average length of stay (ALOS) are both lower in HMOs than in traditional medical practices.[62] Because the cost of inpatient care is much higher than outpatient care, this approach reduces medical expenditures. Inpatient admissions are being converted to such entities as day surgery in ambulatory care centers. ALOS is also being decreased by greater utilization of home health services.[63]

Utilization Review

Utilization review is used for both cost-containment and quality assurance, including activities such as preadmission certification, concurrent review, precertification of referrals, and physician review.

- ✦ In *preadmission certification,* an HMO reviews cases prior to admission and determines whether hospitalization is appropriate.
- ✦ *Concurrent review* investigates the necessity of a hospital admission and the length of stay during the hospitalization.
- ✦ *Precertification of referrals* to specialists can decrease redundant care if specific guidelines regarding the referral process can be delineated.
- ✦ *Physician profiling* tracks practice patterns of physicians, including therapeutic regimens, referrals, hospitalizations, and ALOS.

These methods lead to continuing cost control by decreasing hospitalizations, procedures, and referrals. It is clear that these methods must have some recognized ability to achieve cost control because health insurers in the FFS sector have adopted many of these methods, which may be the best support of managed care's ability to control costs. However, if this trend continues, the cost control achieved by these methods may actually decrease as they are increasingly incorporated into other sectors of the health care system (e.g., hospitals, health insurers).[64]

Decreasing Administrative Costs

By eliminating the health insurance middle man, administrative costs are decreased. HMOs only need to bill for premiums that are predictable entities, rather than billing for every use of services, as in a traditional FFS plan. The HMO need only collect the small copayments on provision of services.

Although HMOs theoretically may decrease administrative costs at the level of the individual plan, the increasing diversity and the numbers of plans overall actually may be increasing administrative costs within the system. These costs, which are a significant portion of health care expenditures, could possibly be decreased by increased consolidation and universal paperwork standards.

Critiques of Cost Control

In addition to the possible cost-controlling methods presented, there is also literature supporting claims of HMO cost shifting (i.e., rather than actually cutting costs
from the health care system, they are finding ways to pass these costs along to consumers via other routes). One way often cited is that HMOs have found a variety
of ways to recruit the healthier members of the communities they serve.[66] This
"cream skimming" or "cherry picking" of healthier patients then shifts the costs
of more expensive patients onto the FFS providers and insurance companies.
Other techniques include negotiated discounts with pharmaceutical companies
and hospitals, mandates on delivery of care, and restriction of services.

It has also been demonstrated that although HMOs do reduce costs, demonstrated by decreasing hospital admissions and LOS, these reductions are one-time
adjustments. It has been shown that HMO costs continue to increase at the same
rate as FFS plans.[66] Therefore, although initially beneficial, HMOs do not provide
a solution to the problems of long-term increases in health care costs.

Other critics of HMOs, prepaid medical practices, and managed care claim that
although some costs are reduced by decreases in hospitalization usage, this approach leads to lower client satisfaction and poorer health status.[67] In reply, other
studies have shown that patients are pleased with their care at HMOs.[68] However,
evidence on both sides of the argument has its strengths and weaknesses. In the
end, it seems that the truth may fall somewhere between the extreme views.

PHYSICIANS IN MANAGED CARE ❖

As HMOs, PPOs, and POS plans increase in size and market share, there will be
a concomitant increase in the number of physicians who practice medicine within
the managed care context. Among these physicians, the experience of practicing
managed care will vary. Practice within an IPA will be quite different from that in
a traditional staff model HMO. Because managed care plans depend quite heavily
on quality physicians committed to managed care, they need to expend effort both
in recruitment and in encouraging the particular managed care techniques they utilize to contain costs.

Managed care plans focus their efforts in recruitment toward young physicians
in primary care fields. Younger physicians are less likely to have established practice patterns, and they can be more easily influenced to utilize the cost-containing
practice guidelines. Primary care physicians perform the gatekeeping role in managed care systems.

HMOs utilize methods such as profiling, financial incentives, and practice
guidelines to encourage physicians to control costs. The financial incentives can
entail withholding a percentage of physician fees until the physician stays within
a specific budget, or bonuses paid from a pool that increases as a result of efficient
cost control. In profiling, individual physicians are informed of their performance

compared with the rest of the HMO. Comparisons to the HMO average include the following.[64]

- ✦ Total panel size
- ✦ Number of office visits per member
- ✦ Average amount of money received per visit
- ✦ Number of specialty referrals as a percent of total visits
- ✦ Number of specific tests ordered per member
- ✦ Number and type of prescriptions per member
- ✦ Number of admissions to the hospital, ALOS, and days of care per member.

Although HMOs give physicians less autonomy and often a lower income than could be earned in the FFS sector, there are a number of benefits to physicians working in HMOs. In FFS, a young physician must build up a clientele via referrals from colleagues, learn the extensive billing procedures of different insurance companies, and essentially participate in the management of a small business. In an HMO, the patient population has already been recruited, the paperwork is uniform if not less, and management is left to those who choose to participate. Call schedules are easier and more flexible. In general the hours spent working are often less.

These benefits need to be considered in light of the context of each. An HMO patient-physician relationship is often less permanent than that in traditional practice, although it need not be. Less involvement in management means less control over decisions affecting the workplace conditions. Fewer call and working hours again means that physicians are less likely to see their own patients on admission to the hospital for acute illnesses.

The biggest contrast to consider is that of the fiduciary responsibilities to place the patient's well-being above all else, compared with the "employee" responsibilities of cost control to the HMO. This dilemma is one that is difficult to resolve, and it is one of the most challenging aspects of a physician's role in an HMO.

THE FUTURE OF MANAGED CARE ❖

It is clear that managed care will continue to evolve over time. Increasing patient enrollment with declining numbers of managed care plans indicates a trend of increasing numbers of enrollees per HMO. This trend is likely to continue, particularly if managed care companies continue to arborize and consolidate to gain increased access to less traditional markets.

The recent increase in HMOs that offer POS plans (a 69% increase from 64 to 108)[58] will most likely continue. These plans, combining aspects of IPAs and PPOs, give HMOs increased flexibility and ability to market their product.

Because there is more overlap in the markets supplied by different plans, there should be more competition between health plans with regard to both price and services. Even without mandates specifying managed competition, current purchasers of health care services, big business, government, and insurance companies will increasingly act as purchasing cooperatives and encourage competition on price, as well as better evaluation of quality of care.

As managed care continues to increase its market share, its gatekeeper emphasis on PCPs will increase demand for general internists. In contrast, the demand for specialists is likely to decrease.

National health care reform promises to have a large effect on managed care. If managed competition is mandated, then health plans will need to compete on the basis of cost, quality, and customer satisfaction, and they will continue to pursue cost-controlling measures to enable this competition. If universal coverage is guaranteed, an additional 37 million individuals will need a specified health plan, and these new consumers will likely cause the managed care industry to continue to speciate to attract them.

❖ Suggested Reading ❖

Berkowitz ED, Wolff W. Group Health Association: a portrait of a health maintenance organization. Philadelphia: Temple University Press, 1988.
An excellent history of Group Health Association.

Fein R. Medical care, medical costs; the search for a health insurance policy. Cambridge, MA: Harvard University Press, 1989.
A briefer history, primarily of twentieth-century developments in health care financing.

Hendricks R. A model for national health care: the history of Kaiser Permanente. NJ: Rutgers University Press, 1993.
An excellent history of Kaiser Permanente.

Moore P. Evaluating health maintenance organizations. New York: Quorum Books, 1991.
Similar in content to the lawyers' book, but it spends more time on analysis of HMOs in particular, looking at utilization, quality, and cost control.

The National Health Lawyers Association. The insider's guide to managed care. An NHLA Education in Print Publication, 1990.
A concisely written book with very clear definitions and concepts about managed care.

Starr P. The social transformation of American medicine. New York: Basic Books, 1982.
The definitive history of health care in this country.

6

Medicare and Medicaid

Hugh H. Tilson, Jr., Marjorie Ross, and David Calkins

The last time the health care system in the United States was reformed on a national scale was in 1965, when the Medicare and Medicaid entitlement programs were created. Over the last 30 years, the costs associated with these programs have increased at an astounding rate, taking up an alarmingly larger percentage of federal and state budgets each year.

This chapter covers the history, eligibility criteria, benefits, and financing of Medicare and Medicaid. More importantly, it focuses on the current and future challenges to these two entitlement programs.

HISTORY OF MEDICARE AND MEDICAID ❖

Although both Medicare and Medicaid provide insurance coverage for people unable to obtain insurance, they use very different approaches. Similar to Social Security, *Medicare is social insurance.* By making mandatory contributions to the Medicare Trust Fund through a payroll tax, U.S. citizens are automatically eligible for Medicare benefits, regardless of their income, when they reach the age of 65 or become permanently disabled. Because Medicare is a federal program, all Medicare beneficiaries are entitled to identical coverage regardless of the state in which they live. *Medicaid, however, is welfare.* Qualifying for state welfare cash assistance is dependent on meeting certain eligibility criteria that center on low income and assets. Because Medicaid is a joint federal-state program, the criteria used to determine eligibility and the benefits covered vary among states beyond certain federally mandated minimum criteria.

Why did these two entitlement programs, which were enacted simultaneously, use such different philosophical approaches? When designing and enacting the Medicare and Medicaid programs, Congress had to address three issues.

+ Should a national health insurance program provide guaranteed coverage to all U.S. citizens, or should the program target a limited population?
+ Should eligibility be means-tested, or should it be universal?
+ Should the program be administered at the federal, state, or both levels?

Furthermore, they needed to consider why past attempts at health reform had failed, the political climate at that time, and any related legislation already in effect when addressing these issues.

After attempts in the late 1940s under Truman to enact universal health insurance through national health reform failed, Congress in the late 1950s and 1960s debated over how best to provide coverage to the uninsured poor and elderly. Proponents of national health insurance for the elderly generally took one of two approaches: expand the social insurance provided through Social Security coverage to include health insurance, or provide a welfare-type program for those elderly too poor to purchase coverage.

The advantages of the social insurance approach were that coverage would be universal and guaranteed, and it built on the existing Social Security structure. Furthermore, because everyone would age and become eligible, a plan offering coverage for all elderly people was politically feasible. The advantages of the welfare approach were primarily financial. Selectively targeting assistance for health insurance coverage to those who needed the most assistance would be a more efficient use of tax dollars.

Another part of the debate was to determine whether the federal or state governments would be best to administer the programs. A uniquely federal program such as Social Security would allow consistency across the country with regard to benefits and eligibility. It was argued, however, that a national program would not allow the flexibility needed for those Americans still opposed to compulsory insurance. As a political compromise, the Chairman of the House Ways and Means Committee, Wilbur Mills, suggested expanding the federal *Old Age Assistance Program.* The Old Age Assistance Program amended the Social Security Act in 1950 to help states pay for medical care to the elderly who were also on welfare.

In 1960, Congress enacted the **Kerr-Mills Act,** a joint federal-state, means-tested program that was the precursor to the Medicaid program. It provided federal assistance to states to purchase medical care for indigent persons over the age of 65, whether or not they were welfare recipients. Because participation was optional, and because any state could elect not to participate due to the financial impact on their budget, coverage of the elderly poor varied by state residence.

In 1964, after campaigning to establish broader medical coverage for the elderly through Medicare, President Johnson was re-elected by a sufficient majority to provide the mandate he needed to pursue his Great Society agenda. Johnson's Great Society in the 1960s, building on Roosevelt's New Deal in the 1930s, refocused the national agenda on the health care system.[69] In 1965, Congress passed Titles XVIII and XIX of the Social Security Act, establishing Medicare and Medicaid, two federal entitlement programs that would fund health insurance for the elderly and the indigent, respectively.

The origin of each of these programs dictated the populations they would serve, and ultimately, the social stigmas they would earn. Medicare expanded the social insurance provided to retirees and the disabled to include health insurance through Social Security. Medicaid replaced two earlier programs of federal grants to states, the Social Security Amendments of 1950 and the Kerr-Mills Act, to assist states in providing health insurance for the poor. Medicare became an "earned right" like Social Security, and Medicaid became synonymous with welfare.

In 1965, the climate was one of political unrest and social change. Because of the intensity with which the interests of senior citizens were represented in Congress, the program that demanded the most attention was Medicare. As a result, the focus on Capitol Hill ended up being primarily on Medicare and the benefits associated with its enactment. Medicaid became an appendage to the Medicare legislation, and it is regarded as somewhat of an afterthought in the eyes of many historians.

Medicare coverage was ultimately established in two parts: Part A, mandatory hospital insurance financed through social insurance; and Part B, supplemental medical care with federally subsidized premiums. Although the initial Medicare proposal included predominantly hospital-intensive services, various groups expressed concerns that hospital insurance alone was insufficient for the needs of the elderly. To assuage these concerns, Mills expanded the program to include Part B coverage of physician services, which provided Americans over 65 years with access to a much richer benefit.[70]

Because of Medicaid's evolution from two programs providing federal grants to states, programs were state-designed and state-implemented. The federal government established minimum standards for the classes of individuals to be covered and the services to be offered. State compliance with federal guidelines was achieved by making federal reimbursement of state expenditures under Medicaid contingent on compliance with those federal guidelines. Despite these minimum standards, a wide variety of eligibility standards and coverage currently exist among the states. As a result, access to health insurance coverage for the poor still depends substantially on the state in which they reside.

The populations enrolled in these programs have increased from 19.5 million (Medicare) and 10 million (Medicaid) in 1967 to an estimated 36.3 million (Medicare) and 32.6 million (Medicaid) in 1993.[71] Expenditures for these programs have increased from $3.2 billion (Medicare) and $1.9 billion (Medicaid) in 1967 to an estimated $145 billion (Medicare) and $135 billion (Medicaid) in 1993.

National health expenditures have increased from 6.3% of the gross domestic product (GDP) in 1967 to an estimated 14.4% of the GDP in 1993. Of the estimated $903.3 billion spent on health in 1993, 32.1% ($290 billion) were federal expenditures and 14.5% ($131 billion) were state and local expenditures. Medicare and the federal component of Medicaid are administered by the Health Care Financing Administration of the U.S. Department of Health and Human Services. For more details concerning the role of government in health care, refer to Chapter 7. Table 6.1 contrasts philosophies, target populations, eligibility criteria, benefits, and financing of the Medicare and Medicaid programs.

MEDICARE ❖
Eligibility

In general, anyone over the age of 65 years or who is permanently disabled is entitled to be enrolled for coverage under the Medicare program.[72] Medicare is a federal program that entitles beneficiaries to a set of benefits defined in legislation to be reimbursed, on a fee-for-service basis, by any qualified provider of their choosing.[73] Medicare consists of Part A (mandatory hospital insurance) and Part B (supplemental medical insurance).

Part A Eligibility

An estimated 35.1 million individuals are enrolled for coverage under Part A.[74] Individuals are entitled to Part A benefits if they receive benefits under the Social Security or the railroad retirement systems, could receive benefits under those systems but have not filed for them, or had Medicare-covered government employment. Most individuals establish entitlement to Part A on the basis of at least 10 years' work under either the Social Security or the railroad retirement system. Enrollment in Part A for those who are eligible is automatic. Those over 65 years who are not automatically covered can voluntarily purchase Part A benefits at their actuarial value. As of January 1, 1993, the monthly premium for those purchasing Part A coverage was $221.

Those under 65 years who are disabled establish entitlement in a similar fashion. An individual is entitled to premium-free Part A benefits if they have been a disabled beneficiary under Social Security or the railroad retirement Board for more than 24 months. Individuals receiving continuing dialysis for permanent kidney failure or who have received a kidney transplantation are generally eligible for premium-free Part A benefits.

Part B Eligibility

All resident citizens age 65 years or older, regardless of eligibility for Part A, can enroll in Part B, and, after paying the monthly premium, they can receive Part B

Table 6.1

	Philosophy	Target Population	Eligibility	Benefits	Financing
Medicare	—Social Insurance an "earned right" —Uniform National Program for the Elderly	The elderly and the permanently disabled	Uniform eligibility— all over the age of 65 and the permanently eligible Permanent eligibility	Not total coverage of all health care expenses Prescription drugs, long-term care not covered Co-payments and deductibles required	Federally financed through payroll tax, general revenues and beneficiary premiums (Part B)
Medicaid	—Welfare or Charity —Federally guided, state controlled program for the poor, disabled, aged, blind, etc.	Categorical eligibility Federal mandate for coverage of certain categories of individuals States have option to cover additional categories (and receive federal matching funds)	Broad variation among states regarding income and asset eligibility determinations Beneficiary's eligibility may change over time	Federally specified core benefits which must be covered Broad variation among states regarding the optional services to be covered Nominal co-payments and deductibles may be required from some beneficiaries for certain services	Joint federal-state financing Federal financing ranges from 50% to 85%

Data Source: Penny Feldman, Harvard School of Public Health.

benefits. An estimated 34.1 million beneficiaries received coverage under Part B in 1993.[74]

End-Stage Renal Disease Program

The Medicare *End-Stage Renal Disease Program* (**ESRD**) program is the only federal program that entitles people of all ages to coverage under Medicare on the basis of their diagnosis.[75] Although the need for the program arose in the 1960s after the development of hemodialysis and renal transplantation, it was not until 1971 that coverage for end-stage renal disease treatment through the Medicare ESRD program was enacted. The legislation that created the Medicare ESRD program was never formally considered in the relevant House and Senate committees. Rather, it was attached, after 30 minutes of discussion in the Senate, as a floor amendment to a broader measure that President Nixon signed into law.[75]

The ESRD program provides full coverage under Parts A and B of Medicare for eligible beneficiaries. Individuals are eligible for Medicare ESRD coverage if they are medically determined to be suffering from end-stage renal disease, they apply for benefits, and they fit into one of the following categories: (1) an individual who is fully insured for old age and survivor insurance benefits, (2) an individual who is entitled to monthly Social Security benefits, or (3) an individual who is a spouse or a dependent of a person in the first two categories.[76] Approximately 93% of patients with end-stage renal disease are eligible.

When the ESRD program was established in 1972, approximately 10,000 beneficiaries were eligible for coverage, and it was assumed that the number of eligible beneficiaries would level off at approximately 90,000.[75] Medicare ESRD expenditures, however, were estimated to be $6.6 billion in 1993, for 184,257 beneficiaries.[76]

Benefits

Medicare Part A reimburses participating institutional providers for acute-care inpatient hospital, skilled nursing facility, home health, and hospice services rendered to beneficiaries who are enrolled. Medicare hospital insurance services for 1993 are shown in Table 6.2.

Part A—Hospital Insurance

Medicare will reimburse for up to 90 days of inpatient hospital care for each spell of illness or *benefit period.* Each benefit period begins when a beneficiary first enters the hospital, and it ends when there has been a break of at least 60 consecutive days since inpatient hospital or skilled nursing care was provided. There is no limit on the number of benefit periods available to any beneficiary, as long as there

Table 6.2 Medicare Part A: Hospital Insurance Services for 1993

Services	Benefit	Medicare Pays	Beneficiary Pays
Hospitalization			
Semiprivate room and board, general nursing and miscellaneous hospital services and supplies.	First 60 days	All but $676	$676
	61st to 90th day	All but $169/day	$169/day
	60 reserve days	All but $388/day	$388/day
	Beyond 150 days	Nothing	All costs
Skilled Nursing Facility			
Beneficiary must have been in a hospital for at least 3 days and enter a Medicare-approved facility within 30 days after hospital discharge.	First 20 days	100% of approved amount	Nothing
	Additional 80 days	All but $84.50/day	$84.50
	Beyond 100 days	Nothing	All costs
Home Health Care			
Medically necessary skilled care	Part-time or intermittent care for as long as conditions met	100% of approved amount; 80% of approved amount for durable medical equipment	Nothing for services; 20% of approved amount for durable medical equipment
Hospice Care			
Support services for the terminally ill	As long as doctor certifies need if hospice option elected by beneficiary	All but limited for outpatient drugs and inpatient respite care	Limited cost sharing for outpatient drugs and inpatient respite care
Blood			
	Unlimited if medically necessary	All but first 3 pints per calendar year	For first 3 pints

Source: HCFA, Medicare, 1993 Highlights.

are the requisite 60 days between benefit periods. Should a beneficiary exceed the 90-day benefit period, they may draw on a nonrenewable 60 day *lifetime reserve.* Medicare *inpatient hospital benefits* include the following.

+ Semiprivate room
+ Regular nursing services
+ Operating and recovery room costs
+ Intensive care
+ Drugs
+ Laboratory tests
+ Radiographs
+ All other medically necessary services and supplies

Medicare will reimburse up to 100 days of care per benefit period for skilled nursing facility care for continued treatment or rehabilitation if it is certified by the physician as medically necessary and if it follows within 30 days of a hospitalization of three days or more. The services covered are similar to those covered under the inpatient hospital benefit, but they also include rehabilitation services and appliances.

Home health care, including a homemaker aide, may be furnished by a home health agency in a home-bound beneficiary's residence if intermittent or part-time skilled nursing, physical therapy, or rehabilitation care is necessary. Although there is no time limitation for these services, there must be a plan of treatment and periodic review by a physician.

Hospice care provided to terminally ill patients, if diagnosed by their physician as having less than 6 months of life expectancy, is also reimbursed by Medicare. The patient must elect to forego traditional medical treatment for the terminal illness and elect to receive only the more limited hospice care. Hospice care specializes in making a terminally ill patient more comfortable in their final months, and it is usually provided in their own home. It includes the following:

+ Pain relief
+ Supportive medical and social services
+ Physical therapy
+ Symptom management for a terminal illness

Medicare will cover medically necessary services not related to the terminal illness while the beneficiary is receiving hospice services.

Part B—Supplemental Medical Insurance
Part B medical insurance helps pay for physician services, outpatient hospital services (including emergency room visits when the patient is treated and released), diagnostic tests, durable medical equipment, ambulance services, and many other

health services and supplies that are not covered by Part A. Medicare Part B medical insurance services for 1993 are listed in Table 6.3.

What's Not Covered

Although coverage provided to Medicare beneficiaries under Parts A and B is quite comprehensive, there are a number of limitations and exclusions. There are limits, for example, to the duration of the services to be covered, and exclusions generally exist both because Medicare is designed to cover acute-care services and to contain the costs of this entitlement program.

Certain prescription drugs delivered in certain settings are covered by either Part A or B. Prescription drugs delivered to a Medicare beneficiary while in the hospital are covered under Part A. Self-administered prescription drugs obtained by a Medicare beneficiary as an outpatient and certain vaccines are covered under Part B. The remainder of the prescription drugs taken by Medicare beneficiaries must be purchased directly by the beneficiary (i.e., there is no coverage for these drugs). Similarly excluded are eyeglasses, hearing aids, dentures, and dental care.

Custodial care is also excluded from coverage under Medicare. Care is considered to be custodial when it is primarily for the purpose of helping with daily living and if it could be provided safely and reasonably by people without professional skills or training. The long-term care provided in nursing homes is often considered to be custodial care; it is therefore excluded from Medicare reimbursement.

Also excluded from coverage under either Parts A or B are routine physical examinations, preventive care, any services not related to the treatment of an illness or injury, and all services provided for care not "reasonable and necessary" under Medicare program standards.

Although Medicare entitles beneficiaries to a defined set of benefits and pays for premiums for those eligible under Part A, it does not pay for the copayments and the deductibles that are required. An increasingly larger percentage of beneficiaries elect to enroll in managed care plans, which cover more services with lower copayments and deductibles.

Supplemental Insurance

Because Medicare provides only basic protection against the cost of health care but does not pay all medical expenses or long-term care expenses, many beneficiaries obtain supplemental coverage for their health care. Many employers, although diminishing in number, offer their retirees supplemental coverage as a retirement benefit.

The remainder of those purchasing supplemental coverage elect to purchase their supplemental coverage under the so called *Medigap policies.* Medigap policies are private insurance policies designed to pay, within limits, most of the health care service charges not covered by Part A or B. Most states have adopted regulations limiting the sale of Medigap insurance to only 10 standard policies, one of

Table 6.3 Medicare Part B: Medical Insurance Services for 1993

Services	Benefit	Medicare Pays	Beneficiary Pays
Medical Expenses			
Doctor's medical and surgical services, medical supplies, tests and more	Medicare pays for medical services in or out of the hospital	80% of approved amount (after $100 deductible)	$100 deductible, plus 20% of approved amount (and limited charges above approved amount)
Clinical Laboratory Services			
	Unlimited if medically necessary	100% of approved amount	Nothing for services
Home Health Care			
Medically necessary skilled care	Part-time or intermittent care for as long as conditions met	100% of approved amount; 80% of approved amount for durable medical equipment	Nothing for services; 20% of approved amount for durable medical equipment
Outpatient Hospital Treatment			
	Unlimited if medically necessary	80% of approved amount (after $100 deductible)	$100 deductible, plus 20% of billed charges
Blood			
	Unlimited if medically necessary	80% of approved amount (after $100 deductible and starting with 4th pint)	For first 3 pints plus 20% of approved amount for additional pints (after $100 deductible)

Source: HCFA, Medicare, 1993 Highlights.

which may be the basic policy offering the "core package" of benefits. Like Medicare, beneficiaries complying with the enrollment criteria may not be refused coverage under a Medigap policy for a pre-existing condition.

Despite premium-free Part A benefits, many Medicaid beneficiaries cannot afford Part B coverage. The Medicaid programs of each state provide additional coverage for those Medicare beneficiaries poor enough to meet the state's income and assets standards. *Dual eligible* individuals, or those Medicare beneficiaries eligible for coverage under both Medicare and Medicaid programs, receive assistance with payments for the Part B premiums and the cost-sharing requirements under both parts. Coverage for supplemental services, such as long-term care, eyeglasses, and prescription drugs, may also be provided if those services are available under the state's Medicaid program. Medicare beneficiaries who do not qualify for Medicaid because their income or assets are not within a state's standards, but who are still below the federal poverty line, may receive assistance through the *qualified Medicare beneficiary (QMB)* program. As a QMB, a Medicare beneficiary receives assistance from Medicaid for premium and cost-sharing requirements, but they are ineligible to receive coverage for Medicaid program services.

Financing
How Is Medicare Financed?

Medicare beneficiaries are responsible for the cost-sharing requirements under Parts A and B, the premium payments under Part B, and all health care charges not covered under the Medicare program. Similar to Social Security, Part A is financed through mandatory payroll deductions, the so called *Medicare tax.* Employers, employees, and the self-employed are required to pay 1.45% of payroll, or 2.9% total. The cap on income subject to the Medicare tax was removed in 1993; therefore, all income is now subject to this tax. Revenues generated from this payroll tax are placed into the *Hospital Insurance Trust Fund,* and they may be used solely for payment of health care expenses for Medicare beneficiaries.[77] In 1992, the Hospital Insurance Trust Fund had a balance of approximately $120 billion.[74]

Part B is financed through premium payments that are usually deducted from the monthly Social Security checks of those Medicare beneficiaries electing Part B coverage. Twenty-five percent of Part B funds, or $14.2 billion, is derived from premium payments; 72% of Part B, or $41.5 billion, is financed from general federal tax revenues. The remaining 3%, or $2.0 billion, of Part B financing comes from interest on trust fund assets.

It was estimated in 1993 that approximately 31.3 million aged and 3.7 million disabled individuals received protection under Part A and that 6.9 million aged and 800,000 disabled will actually receive reimbursed services.[76] The cost of delivering these services is estimated to be more than $90 billion.[76] It is also estimated that 30.8 million aged and 3.4 million disabled individuals will be enrolled in Part B and that 26.0 million aged and 2.7 million disabled will actually receive reimbursed services in 1993.[76] These services are estimated to cost more than $54.6 billion. Total Medicare expenditures are estimated to be approximately 9.4% of the federal budget for fiscal year 1993.

How Are Providers Paid?

Providers are reimbursed for the health care services they deliver to eligible beneficiaries through the public or private agencies or organizations that contract with the Health Care Financing Administration (HCFA) to serve as the fiscal agent between government and providers. Medicare *intermediaries* process Part A claims and Medicare *carriers* process Part B claims. In addition to processing the claims and reimbursing providers, these agencies and organizations also have the responsibility to

+ Determine costs or charges and reimbursement amounts
+ Maintain records
+ Safeguard against fraud, abuse, and excessive use and assist in investigations of fraud or abuse
+ Make payments to providers for services
+ Assist both providers and beneficiaries as needed

Peer Review Organizations (PROs) are used to promote effective, efficient, and economic delivery of health care services to the Medicare population. PROs are groups of practicing health care professionals who are paid by the federal government to review the care provided to Medicare beneficiaries in each state. Their responsibilities include deciding if the care provided is reasonable and necessary, deciding if the care is provided in the most appropriate setting, deciding if quality standards are being met, and reviewing the appropriateness of care for which additional payment is sought.

How Much Is Paid?

In an effort to win the support of physician and hospital groups, the original Medicare legislation reimbursed providers on a "reasonable cost" basis. Hospitals were reimbursed for the reasonable cost, including capital, overhead, and administrative costs, of delivering services to beneficiaries. Physicians were reimbursed under a fee-for-service method based on the "customary, prevailing, and reasonable" charge for a service. As the cost of delivering health care to Medicare beneficiaries skyrocketed, Congress changed the way providers are reimbursed in an effort to control the costs of the Medicare program.

In 1983, Congress changed the way hospitals are reimbursed from the reasonable cost basis to the prospective payment basis. Under this system, a hospital is paid a predetermined amount, whose formula is fixed by Congress based on its clustering within a ***diagnosis-related group (DRG),*** for providing whatever medical care is required during a person's inpatient hospital stay. Like all capitated payments, in some cases the payment is less than the hospital's costs, and in others it is more—the hospital either absorbs the loss, makes a profit depending on the efficiency with which it can deliver the care, or charges other patients more for the services reimbursed under private insurance. This transfer of costs onto privately funded patients coined the term *cost shifting.* Although one might expect the quality of care to decline under this system, no study has uncovered either a systematic pattern of diminished quality or reduced access to medical treatment since its enactment in 1983.[78]

A new payment system for Part B physician services was recently adopted in 1989, and it will be phased in from 1992 to 1996. The new fee schedule is based on the ***resource-based relative value scale (RBRVS),*** which assigns relative values to health care services. The relative values reflect three things—physician work (i.e., time, skill, and intensity), practice expenses, and malpractice costs—and they are adjusted for geographic variations in the costs of practicing medicine. Once these relative values are calculated, they are converted into a dollar payment amount by a conversion factor. The conversion factor is intended to ensure that cognitive services and procedures are reimbursed more appropriately than they have been in the past.

Medicare payment is made either on an "assigned" or an "unassigned" basis. By accepting assignment, physicians agree to accept the Medicare-approved amount as payment in full. If assignment is accepted, beneficiaries are not liable for any out-of-pocket costs other than standard deductible and coinsurance payments. In contrast, if assignment is not accepted, beneficiaries may be liable for charges in excess of the Medicare-approved charge. This process is known as balanced billing.

MEDICAID ❖
Eligibility

Unlike the federal Medicare program, both the services covered by Medicaid and the categories of individuals eligible for Medicaid coverage vary considerably from state to state, as well as within each state over time. Medicaid is a federal-state matching entitlement program that provides medical assistance for certain individuals and families with low income and resources. Within broad guidelines the federal government provides, each of the states establishes its own eligibility standards; determines the type, amount, duration, and scope of services covered; sets the rate of payment for services; and administers its own program.

Medicaid does not provide medical assistance for all poor persons. Even under the broadest provisions of the federal statute, the Medicaid program does not provide health care services, even for very poor persons, unless they are in one of the categories designated. Accordingly, Medicaid eligibility is called ***categorical eli-***

gibility. Low income is only one test for Medicaid eligibility; assets and resources are also tested against established thresholds determined in each state.

States generally have broad discretion in determining which groups their Medicaid programs will cover and the financial criteria for Medicaid eligibility. However, to be eligible for federal funds, states are *required* to provide Medicaid coverage for most individuals who receive federally assisted income-maintenance payments, as well as for related groups not receiving cash payments. The following are *federally mandatory Medicaid eligibility groups.*

+ Recipients of Aid to Families with Dependent Children (AFDC)
+ Supplemental Security Income (SSI) recipients (or aged, blind, and disabled individuals in states that apply more restrictive eligibility requirements)
+ Children under age 6 who meet the state's AFDC financial requirements or whose family income is at or below 133% of the federal poverty level
+ Recipients of adoption assistance and foster care under Title IV-E of the Social Security Act
+ All children born after September 20, 1983, to families with incomes at or below the federal poverty level
+ Certain Medicare beneficiaries
+ Pregnant women whose family income is below 133% of the federal poverty line (services are limited to pregnancy, complications of pregnancy, delivery, and three months of postpartum care)

States also have the *option* to provide Medicaid coverage for other "categorically needy" groups. These optional groups share characteristics of the mandatory groups, but the eligibility criteria are somewhat more liberally defined. The broadest *optional groups that a state may cover* (and for which they will receive federal matching funds) under the Medicaid program include the following.

+ Infants up to age one year and pregnant women not covered under the mandatory rules whose family income is below 185% of the federal poverty level
+ Certain aged, blind, or disabled adults who have incomes above those requiring mandatory coverage, but below the federal poverty level
+ Children under 21 years who meet income and resources requirements for AFDC but who are otherwise not eligible for AFDC
+ Institutionalized individuals with income and resources below specified limits
+ "Medically needy" persons

The option to have a *medically needy program* allows states to extend Medicaid eligibility to additional qualified persons who have income in excess of the mandatory or optional categorically needy levels. The income and assets level of the medically needy category is higher than the usual categorical level. This option allows beneficiaries to retain more of their income and assets so they are not required to *spend down* into Medicaid categorical eligibility. Some states allow families to establish eligibility for medically needy coverage by paying monthly premiums to the state in an amount equal to the difference between family income and the threshold allowance for income eligibility.

In addition to providing health insurance to the low income individuals, Medicaid also finances two other programs. Ten percent of Medicaid funds pay for institutional and community-based services for mentally retarded and developmentally disabled persons. In addition, Medicaid finances long-term care for the elderly, including home health care, nursing home services, personal care, and home and community-based waiver services. Seventy-five percent of all Medicaid expenditures for the elderly ($21.5 billion) funded nursing home services ($14.5 billion) and home care ($1.7 billion) in fiscal year 1990. Because most private policies are very limited in their scope of coverage, Medicaid serves not only low income elderly, but also those elderly who either spend down for these benefits or who exhaust their own savings and meet eligibility requirements.

An estimated 32.6 million Americans will receive benefits under the Medicaid program in 1993.[79] Because more than 70% of those eligible for Medicaid are families and children and less than 10% are age 65 years or older, Medicaid is often thought of as a program for poor families. However, Medicaid expenditures for these two groups were approximately equal in 1991.

Benefits

Title XIX of the Social Security Act requires that to receive federal matching funds, *certain basic services must be covered* for the categorically needy populations in any state program. These services include the following.

✦ Inpatient and outpatient hospital services
✦ Prenatal care
✦ Physician services
✦ Nursing facility services for individuals aged 21 years or older
✦ Home health care for persons eligible for skilled nursing services
✦ Family planning services and supplies
✦ Rural health clinic services
✦ Laboratory and radiographic services
✦ Pediatric and family nurse practitioner services
✦ Certain federally qualified ambulatory and health center services
✦ Early and periodic screening, diagnosis, and treatment (EPSDT) services for children under the age of 21 years

States may also receive federal assistance for funding if they *elect to provide other optional services* (currently 31 options). Some of the most commonly covered optional services under state Medicaid program programs include the following.

✦   Nursing facility services for aged and disabled individuals
✦   Intermediate care facilities for mentally retarded individuals
✦   Optometry services and eyeglasses
✦   Prescription drugs
✦   Prosthetic devices
✦   Dental services
✦   Clinic services

The Omnibus Reconciliation Act of 1981 (OBRA 81) created two waiver programs that would give states more flexibility to deliver care to Medicaid patients more cost-effectively. States may now provide, through section 1615 (c) waivers, home and community-based care to individuals who have limitations in specified activities of daily living (e.g., toileting, transferring, and eating), who are at least 65 years old, and who are either medically needy or eligible for Medicaid due to receipt of SSI benefits. Another option allows up to eight states (as a demonstration project) to establish and provide community-supported living arrangement services for individuals with mental retardation or a related condition.

Financing
How is Medicaid Financed?

The Medicaid program is part of our social welfare net. Unlike Medicare, for which contributions are made over one's lifetime and eligibility is automatic on reaching the age of 65 years, Medicaid is available only if income and assets are sufficiently low to meet the states' requirements for assistance. Although Medicaid is generally perceived as medical assistance for poor families, approximately 70% of Medicaid program expenditures go to Medicare beneficiaries who have "spent down" into Medicaid eligibility. In 1993, the Medicaid program provided medical services to more than 32 million eligible poor persons who were aged, blind, disabled, or pregnant, or children in certain families, at a total cost of more than $135 billion.

The Medicaid program is financed by both the federal government and the states. The federal portion of the Medicaid program is financed through general tax revenues. Because it is an entitlement program, the amount of total federal outlays for Medicaid has no set limit. The federal government must match, at a predetermined percentage, state expenditures for mandatory services and any optional services provided for eligible recipients. The portion of the Medicaid program paid by the federal government for services, known as the *Federal Medical Assistance Percentage (FMAP),* is determined annually for each state by a formula that compares the state's average per capita income level with the national average. By law, the FMAP cannot be lower than 50% or greater than 83%. Administrative costs for the Medicaid program are shared equally by the states and the federal government. In 1993, total Medicaid expenditures were $135 billion, of which $77 billion were federal funds and $58 billion were state and local funds.

States may impose nominal deductibles, coinsurance, or copayments on some Medicaid recipients for certain services. Certain Medicaid recipients must be excluded from this cost sharing: pregnant women, children under the age of 18 years, hospital or nursing home patients who are expected to contribute most of their income to institutional care, and categorically needy health maintenance organization enrollees.

How Are Providers Paid?

The method by which Medicaid providers are paid is left up to each state, within some broad federal guidelines. In general, the federal government requires that payment levels are sufficient to induce providers to see Medicaid patients. Despite this requirement, however, aggregate Medicaid payments were only 80.3% of the estimated costs for beneficiaries in 1990.[80]

Inpatient hospital services are currently almost universally reimbursed under a prospective payment similar to the DRG system used by Medicare. Some states have established a prospective system in which hospitals are reimbursed a flat rate per day regardless of the patient's diagnosis. Other inpatient services, such as psychiatric and other specialized hospitals, are often still reimbursed under a cost-plus system. Hospitals that treat a disproportionate number of Medicaid patients, known as disproportionate share hospitals (DSH), receive additional Medicaid payments.

Physicians or other independent practitioners are usually reimbursed at the lesser of the provider's actual charge or a maximum allowable charge set by the state. The adequacy and timeliness of these payments vary from state to state. Finally, Medicaid does reimburse for prescription drugs, using a formula that encourages use of generic drugs when available.

How Much Is Paid?

The method to determine payment to providers is decided by each state. Medicaid usually pays hospitals and physicians on a fee-for-service basis, capped at the maximum allowable charge, which is set by each state. States can either set a *fee schedule,* pay on a prospective basis like Medicare, or use other methods of cost containment, such as capitation or managed care. By law, Medicaid is a "payer of last resort," meaning all other means of reimbursement for health care services must be exhausted before Medicaid will reimburse for the services. The Physician Payment Review Commission (PPRC) estimated that in 1989, Medicaid reimbursed 73.7% of services Medicare would have paid had it covered those services.

States were required to use the same method for hospital services as Medicare, and they were paid based on actual cost until 1980. Many states now use the Medicare Prospective Payment System using DRGs, or they have negotiated rates directly with hospitals. States are still required to make payments to hospitals that serve a disproportionate number of low income or Medicaid patients. These DSH hospitals incur higher costs, presumably from the notion that poverty is positively correlated with illness, and that these populations tend to have no primary care provider.

Soon after the enactment of Medicaid, states began to devise methods other than a fee schedule to reimburse for services to contain costs. Many states have entered into contractual arrangements with managed care organizations, primarily *Health Maintenance Organizations (HMOs)*, thus enabling Medicaid patients to enroll for treatment of nonemergency care. Many states have gone even further and have implemented Medicaid-managed care programs, in which all Medicaid beneficiaries are required to enroll in HMO plans for health care coverage. Other methods of cost containment include reducing reimbursement rates, covered services, or eligibility, all of which have become controversial. In many cases, states are required to seek a waiver from the federal mandates to implement their reforms. The most publicized was the waiver sought by the state of Oregon, which attempted to ration care (see Chapter 13).[81]

The gross underestimate of the revenue source needed to finance medical assistance for the poor was realized almost immediately after Medicaid's enactment. Because any outlay would be matched by federal funds, states were provided with incentives to spend more under the program. Medicaid was phased in on a state-by-state basis beginning in 1966, and federal and state program spending increased 43% between 1966 and 1967. As an example of the power of these incentives, in 1966 New York set income protections for which 45% of its residents would have qualified.[82] Spending has continued to increase at dramatic rates, and fraud and abuse concerns prompted Congress to enact Medicare-Medicaid Anti-Fraud and Abuse Amendments in 1977.

Despite federal and state efforts to contain costs, the Medicaid program cost inflation has been in the double digits, with only a short reprieve in the early 1980s. Although the number of beneficiaries has increased, only part of the increased costs have been due to increased utilization. In an attempt to subsidize their costs, states have devised ways to increase DSH payments to hospitals, to impose provider taxes, and to increase federal matching payments. In 1991, Congress passed an Act that would limit DSH payment adjustments to 12% of Medicaid spending beginning in fiscal year 1992. However, actual spending in 1992 totaled approximately 16%.

Effects of Medicaid Reimbursement

Many physicians have chosen not to accept Medicaid patients in their practices because Medicaid reimburses for services at a lower rate than private insurance and because Medicaid serves the nation's poor, whose illnesses are often more severe. Although the program entitles beneficiaries to a range of health care services, the law does not mandate that all providers accept Medicaid patients. Although the Medicaid legislation provided these vulnerable populations with health insurance coverage, they still were not able to access the care they needed. As the number of patients qualifying for Medicaid has increased, and the number of providers accepting them has decreased, the low income population has been forced to seek care in the one place where they knew they would not be turned away: the emergency room. This approach has been especially true for public hospitals and for academic medical centers because of their location in inner cities.

In the absence of a primary care provider, the uninsured and the Medicaid population have been using the emergency room as a source of primary care. Many hospitals are forced to provide these services without reimbursement, or with reduced reimbursement for Medicaid recipients, thus increasing the level of *uncompensated care* they provide. This inappropriate use of the emergency room by these populations contributes to the escalating costs of health care. As the level of uncompensated care increases, hospitals shift the costs of providing this care to privately insured patients through higher rates.

Congress has realized that health insurance through Medicaid was not enough to ensure that the low income populations receive the care they need. The Omnibus Reconciliation Act of 1989 increased monitoring reimbursement of providers in OB/GYN and pediatric specialties to prevent the number of physicians avoiding care for Medicaid patients. In addition, the Act required Medicaid to reimburse nonphysician providers (i.e., nurse practitioners, midwives) for their services, as well as services provided by *Federally Qualified Health Centers (FQHC),* such as community and migrant health centers. Other barriers to care, such as geographic isolation and the need for transportation and translation services, have prevented these populations from getting the care they need. In addition, other deterrents for beneficiaries include longer waiting times and shorter visits than their private paying counterparts.

CONCLUSIONS ◆

Although both Medicare and Medicaid are under a lot of scrutiny due to soaring costs, they still provide a valuable role in providing health insurance to many Americans. Some, such as Rep. Pete Stark, have proposed simply expanding Medicare to all the population as a means of providing universal access. It is unclear what will happen to Medicare and Medicaid if there is health reform, but the lessons learned from these programs will surely inform the next round of changes in the U.S. health care financing system.

❖ Suggested Reading ❖

Committee on Ways and Means. 1993 green book: overview of entitlement programs. Washington, DC: U.S. Government Printing Office, 1993.

Prepared by the House Committee on Ways and Means, this book contains brief descriptions of the entitlement programs over which the Committee has jurisdiction. The descriptions are both substantive (e.g., describing the program's eligibility, coverage) and quantitative (e.g., describing appropriations, expenditures, trends).

Congressional Research Service. Medicaid source book: background data and analyses (a 1993 update). Washington, DC: U.S. Government Printing Office, 1993.

Prepared by the Congressional Research Service for the Subcommittee on Health and the Environment of the House Committee on Energy and Commerce, this 1,127-page book contains everything you ever wanted to know about the Medicaid program but were afraid to ask.

Health Care Financing Administration. The Medicare handbook.

Prepared by the Health Care Financing Administration to explain the Medicare program to Medicare beneficiaries, this pamphlet is easy to read, and it provides basic program information.

7

The Role of Government

Bradley S. Marino and David Calkins

The role federal, state, and local governments have in financing and delivering health care has changed dramatically over the course of this century. Whereas in the early 1900s federal and state governments paid little for the health of their citizens, health financing currently takes up an ever-increasing percentage of deficit-ridden federal and state budgets.

This chapter outlines the evolution of the governmental role in health care and describes the role federal, state, and local governments currently have.

The discussion of the role of the federal government begins with an analysis of federal expenditures on health, its rate of growth, and how this impacts debt reduction and the ability to produce balanced budgets in the future. The specific agencies within the Department of Health and Human Services and their budgetary allocation for 1994 are then defined. Finally, the discussion of the federal role focuses on how federal health policy is made. In this section, the Kingdon Paradigm is delineated, and the roles the executive branch, Congress, and interest groups have in making federal health policy are defined. This topic is of particular importance because of recent discussions of possible health care reform. Given what we have learned about this policy-making process, we then look at the failure of the Clinton Health Security Act.

After the federal role is delineated, we offer a description of the evolution and current roles of state and local governments in health care.

THE EVOLUTION OF THE ROLE
OF FEDERAL GOVERNMENT ❖

Over the course of the past 200 years, the role of government in organization, financing, and delivery of health care services in the United States (U.S.) has evolved from that of a highly constricted provider of services and protector of public health to that of a major financial underwriter of an essentially private enterprise, the policies and procedures of which have increasingly encroached on the autonomy and prerogatives of the providers of care.

Although extensive, such growth has not come about capriciously or because legislators or bureaucrats have had any great desire to interfere in health services, but rather because providers, consumers, insurance carriers, and politicians realized the need for government assistance. The reason given to justify this intervention was usually market failure. That is, people believed the free market would not provide health services either efficiently or fairly.

In the early days of the republic, there were few organized government health programs at either the state or the national level. There were no state health departments, foreign quarantine was the responsibility of each port, and programs for communicable disease control and environmental sanitation were the responsibility of local government. Government intervention in health was confined to protecting society from epidemic disease and to meeting the essential needs of the destitute. Local governmental aid for the poor was coupled with support provided by religious groups, charitable agencies, fraternal societies, lodges, and clubs organized by immigrant groups.[83]

The federal government's first health care legislation was the Marine Hospital Service Act of 1789, which established the Public Health Service (PHS) and authorized it to care for U.S. merchant seamen and members of the armed forces. During the first half of the nineteenth century, the mission of the PHS was extended to include Native Americans, who were held in protective custody on reservations as wards of the state. This role was eventually formalized through creation of the Indian Health Service. Throughout the 1800s, with the exception of the activities of the PHS, the federal government's role in matters of health could be characterized as minimal. A citizen's health and how he or she procured their health care was a private matter.

This pattern continued until the 1920s, when, with the passage of the Sheppard-Towner Act on Maternity and Infancy of 1921, the federal role in health and medical affairs began to grow and to evolve dramatically. This act established the first continuing program of federal grants-in-aid to state health agencies for direct provision of services to individuals, the forerunner of the current maternal and child health program. Federal intervention into health care continued with the Agriculture Appropriations Act of 1931, which established the Food and Drug

Administration (FDA). The deteriorating quality of the food supply during the Great Depression provided the impetus for this bill. Enactment of the Social Security Act in 1935, which marked the beginning of the U.S. system of social welfare, provided the next major development in the growth of the federal involvement in matters of health. The law provided for federal grants to the states for public health, maternal and child health, as well as for public assistance for aged, blind, and families with dependent children. From this legislation, two concepts of social welfare emerged: (1) social insurance for the working population in the form of unemployment insurance, workers compensation, and guaranteed retirement benefits; and (2) public assistance in the form of direct financial aid provided by the states for those unable to work.[83]

The Hill-Burton Construction Act of 1946 provided federal assistance to update and to modernize hospitals whose physical plants had grown obsolete in the post-World War II era. The act resulted in a dramatic increase in the number of teaching and community hospitals. This bill would serve as the prototype for federal involvement in health care because it established the principles of local initiative, state review, federal matching funding, and, for the first time, mandated state planning. Federal support was later extended to medical education and research in the 1950s and 1960s.

In 1950, the Social Security Act was extended to include the permanently disabled, and in 1960, the Kerr-Mills Act was enacted, which provided, for the first time, for a federal-state program of medical assistance for the elderly.

Under the Johnson Administration, the federal government became inextricably tied to health financing with passage of the Medicare and Medicaid programs in 1965. Both entitlement programs would grow rapidly over the next 30 years, and they consume an ever-increasing percentage of the federal budget. Taking into consideration the Johnson "Great Society" legislation, the Medicaid bill was considered an afterthought. It was passed as an extension and an improvement of the earlier Kerr-Mills program that relied on the existing welfare system. Its architects never delineated clear goals for the program or came to grips with the problems inherent in the welfare system, particularly determination of

Table 7.1   National Health Expenditure Trends 1970–91 (in thousands)

Year	Total National Health Expenditure	Private Expenditure	% of Total	Public Expenditure	% of Total	% of Public Expenditure that is Federal $
1970	74,377,000	46,703,000	62.7	27,674,000	38.3	64.1
1980	250,125,000	144,966,000	57.9	105,159,000	42.1	68.4
1990	675,037,000	389,973,000	57.7	285,063,000	42.3	68.2
1991	751,771,000	421,811,000	56.1	329,980,000	43.9	67.5

Adapted from Statistical Abstracts of the U.S. 1993, 113th ed., The Reference Press, Inc., Austin, Texas 1994, p. 108.

eligibility, which was left to the states. Like the Kerr-Mills Act before it, Medicaid tended to epitomize the problems inherent in relying on a states rights approach to resolving broad social problems. In attempting to retain state autonomy and decision-making under the program, the rich states tended to get richer and the poor states either took no action or had minimal participation in the program. As a result, there was a considerable lack of uniformity, both between and within states, which became even further exacerbated during recessions in the late 1970s and late 1980s. Growing concern on the part of federal and state governments over administration of the program led to enactment of several provisions to improve its management, including guidelines requiring states to review on a continuing basis cost, administration, and quality of the health care services rendered under their programs in the late 1960s, as well as withholding of federal funds from states that failed to implement the utilization review and Early Periodic Screening, Diagnosis, and Treatment programs mandated by Congress in the 1970s.

Legislation in the 1980s and 1990s has focused on cost-containment. To stem the rising tide of Medicare reimbursement to hospitals, the diagnosis-related group (DRG)-based Prospective Payment System was put into place in 1983. To constrain and to redistribute reimbursements to physicians, the Resource-based Relative Value Scale was implemented in 1993.

After attempts by Presidents Nixon and Carter to increase access and to contain costs failed in the 1970s, President Clinton made health care reform one of the cornerstones of his candidacy in 1992. Although hopes initially were high for system-wide reform, the attempt failed for reasons discussed at the end of this chapter.

ROLE OF THE FEDERAL GOVERNMENT ❖
Federal Expenditures on Health Care

Table 7.1 summarizes federal government expenditures for health care in the U.S. in 1970, 1980, 1990, and 1991. Total expenditures are broken into private and pub-

Total Federal $ spent on Public Expenditure	% of Federal $ spent on Public Expenditure	Medicare Expenditure	Medicaid Expenditure	Total Medicare/ Medicaid	% of Total Federal $ spent on Medicare/ Medicaid
17,711,360	23.8	7,633,000	3,155,000	10,788,000	60.9
71,928,756	28.8	37,533,000	14,003,500	51,536,500	71.6
194,412,966	28.8	110,736,000	39,842,500	150,578,500	77.4
222,723,000	29.6	122,803,000	52,470,500	175,273,500	78.7

lic components. Notable is the significant increase in total national health expenditures and the shift of spending from the private to the public sector. The percentage of total expenditure that the private expenditure represents has decreased from 1970 to 1991 from 62.7 to 56.1%, whereas the percentage of total expenditure that the public expenditure accounts for has increased from 38.3 to 43.9%. Although the public portion of the health care bill has increased over the last two decades, the percentage of the public expenditure that is federal dollars has also increased from 64.1 to 67.5%. As a result, federal expenditures from 1970 to 1991 as a percentage of the total national health care expenditure have increased from 23.8 to 29.6%. Of the federal dollars spent on health care, the two largest ticket items are the Medicare and Medicaid entitlement programs. The percentage of the federal expenditure devoted to Medicare and Medicaid, if Social Security Administration expenditures are not taken into consideration, has increased during the period 1970 to 1991 from 60.9 to 78.7%.[84]

Department of Health and Human Services

The vast majority of the health care dollars spent by the federal government is managed by the Department of Health and Human Services (HHS). The organizational chart for HHS is shown in Figure 7.1.[85] HHS major subdivisions include the Public Health Service, the Health Care Financing Administration (HCFA), the Social Security Administration (SSA), the Administration for Children and Families, and the Administration on Aging. Estimated total outlays for HHS in fiscal year (FY) 1994 are $709 billion dollars, which represents 47% of the $1.5 trillion federal budget in FY 1994.[86] Figure 7.2 itemizes how the $709 billion HHS budget is divided among its major subdivisions, as well as what percentage of the total these expenditures represent.

An entitlement program is a federal program that guarantees a certain level of benefits to persons or other entities who meet requirements set by law (e.g., Social Security, Medicare, or Medicaid programs). Entitlement programs therefore leave no discretion with Congress with regard to how much money to appropriate, which makes these programs extremely difficult politically to amend, reduce, or cut. A discretionary program is a federal program that Congress may fund or cut at its pleasure. *Note that $672 billion of the entire $709 billion HHS budget (94%) is allocated to entitlement programs.*[87]

As shown in Figure 7.2, 92% of the HHS budget consists of SSA, Medicare, and Medicaid expenditures. Estimated outlays for the Department of Defense (DoD), a discretionary program, in FY 1994 are $300 billion, which represents 20% of the federal budget in 1994.[84] Interest that must be paid on the national debt for FY 1994 is estimated to be $202 billion, which represents 13% of the federal budget.[88] Therefore, between SSA, Medicare, Medicaid, the DoD, and interest on the national debt, 81% of federal expenditures for FY 1994 are accounted for. If one considers DoD

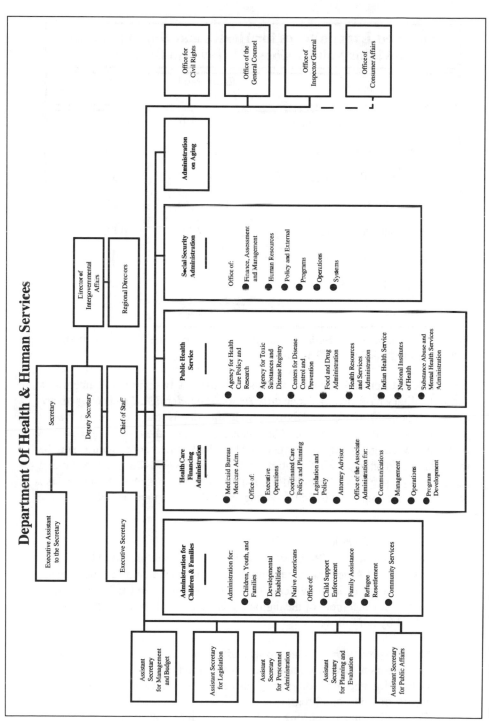

Figure 7.1 Organizational map of Department of Health and Human Services. (Data Source: U.S. Government Manual, 1993–94.)

Estimated Expenditures for Health and Human Services by Major Subdivisions, FY 1994 (in thousands)

Division	Estimated $ Expenditure	% of Total
Social Security Administration	354,546,535	49.97
Health Care Financing Adm.	303,727,187	42.80
Adm. for Children and Families	30,953,795	4.36
Public Health Service	19,050,264	2.69
Administration on Aging	823,110	0.12
Departmental Management	186,525	0.03
Offices of the Asst. Secretaries	134,790	0.02
Total..	709,422,206	

Figure 7.2 Adapted from Budget of the U.S. Government, U.S. Government Printing Office, Washington, D.C., 1993, p. App. 601–637.

as a "quasi-entitlement" program, because it is extremely politically damaging to support military base closings, then *only 19% of the federal budget is truly discretionary.* This 19% represents all the other functions of government, and it is the first to be capped or cut when the federal budget is tight. Given the fact that almost 50% of the federal budget is currently consumed by HHS entitlement programs and that this number will only grow in the future (further eating away at discretionary spending), it would appear that health reform that will contain these burgeoning costs is critical to avoid continued deficit spending and a worsening national debt.

Public Health Service

The Public Health Service (PHS) was established in 1798 to provide Marine Hospitals for the care of American merchant seamen. Subsequent legislation has vastly broadened the scope of its activities. The broad mission of the PHS is to promote protection and advancement of the nation's physical and mental health, which are accomplished by the following.

   ◆   Coordinating with the states to set and to implement national health policy and to pursue effective intergovernmental relations.
   ◆   Generating and upholding cooperative international health–related agreements, policies, and programs.
   ◆   Conducting and supporting medical and biomedical research.
   ◆   Sponsoring and administering programs for the development of health resources, prevention and control of diseases, and alcohol and drug abuse.

◆ Providing resources and expertise to the states and other public and private institutions in planning, direction, and delivery of physical and mental care services.

◆ Enforcing laws to assure safety and efficiency of drugs and protection against impure and unsafe foods, cosmetics, medical devices, and radiation-producing projects.

Estimated total outlays for the PHS in FY 1994 are $19 billion, which represents 2.7% of the budget for HHS.[89]

The major subdivisions of the PHS include the Agency for Health Care Policy and Research, the Centers for Disease Control and Prevention, the Agency for Toxic Substances and Disease Registry, the FDA, the Health Resources and Services Administration, the Indian Health Service, the National Institutes of Health, and the Substance Abuse and Mental Health Services Administration.[90] The Surgeon General is the titular head of the Public Health Service. While the position carries little statutory authority, it is a bully pulpit from which to educate the public and bring attention to different health issues. Previous Surgeon Generals have focused on cigarette smoking, AIDS, and teenage pregnancy. Figure 7.3

Estimated Expenditures for the Public Health Service by Agency or Adm., FY 1994 (in thousands)

Agency or Administration	Estimated $ Expenditure	% of Total
National Institutes of Health	9,906,574	52.0
Health Resources and Services Adm.	2,669,764	14.0
Substance Abuse and Mental Health Services Adm.	2,293,336	12.0
Centers for Disease Control and Prevention	1,763,813	9.3
Indian Health Service	1,568,743	8.2
Food and Drug Adm.	670,937	3.5
Agency for Health Care Policy and Research	117,097	0.6
Agency for Toxic Substances and Disease Registry	60,000	0.3
Total..	19,050,264	

Figure 7.3 Adapted from Budget of the U.S. Government, U.S. Government Printing Office, Washington, D.C., 1993, p. App. 601–615.

itemizes how the $19 billion HHS budget is divided among its agencies and administrations, and what percentage of the total these expenditures represent.

Agency for Health Care Policy and Research

The Agency for Health Care Policy and Research (AHCPR) was established by the Omnibus Budget Reconciliation Act of 1989 as the successor to the National Center for Health Services Research and Health Care Technology Assessment. The agency is the federal government's focal point for health services research. The AHCPR is the only federal agency charged with producing and disseminating scientific and policy-relevant information about quality, medical effectiveness, and cost of health care. Its programs focus on maximizing the value of our national health care investment by analyzing costs and improving the outcomes of health care. Estimated total outlays for the AHCPR in FY 1994 are $117 million, which represents 0.6% of the budget for the PHS.[91] Its priorities include the following.

✧   Reducing health care costs through studies on the interaction of cost, quality, and access; microsimulation modeling to understand the effect of proposed health care reform; and analyzing health care costs affected by acute ambulatory, long-term care and the acquired immunodeficiency syndrome (AIDS).

✧   Expanding clinical practice guideline activities by increasing production of important guidelines and evaluating their effect on cost and quality of health care.

✧   Enhancing the scientific evidence base for cost-effective clinical practices by expanding research to improve clinical decision-making and by strengthening clinical information systems for effectiveness research.[90]

Agency for Toxic Substances and Disease Registry

The Agency for Toxic Substances and Disease Registry (ATSDR) was established as an operating agency within the PHS by the Secretary of HHS in 1983. The agency's mission is to carry out the health-related responsibilities of the Comprehensive Environmental Response, Compensation, and Liability Act of 1980. The agency provides leadership and direction to programs and activities designed to protect both the public and the workers from exposure or the adverse health effects of hazardous substances in storage sites or released in fires, explosions, or transportation accidents. Estimated total outlays for the ATSDR in FY 1994 are $60 million, which represents 0.3% of the budget for the PHS.[92] To carry out this mission, the Agency, in cooperation with states and other federal and local agencies, performs the following.

✧   Collects, maintains, analyzes, and disseminates information related to serious diseases, mortality, and human exposure to toxic or hazardous substances.

✧   Established appropriate registries necessary for long-term follow-up or specific scientific studies.

✧   Established and maintains a complete listing of areas closed to the public or otherwise restricted in use because of toxic substance contamination.

 ✧ Assists the Environmental Protection Agency in identifying hazardous waste substances to be regulated.

 ✧ Assists, consults, and coordinates with private or public health care providers in the provision of medical care and testing of exposed individuals.[93]

Centers for Disease Control and Prevention

The Centers for Disease Control and Prevention (CDC), established as an operating health agency within the PHS by the Secretary of Health, Education, and Welfare in 1973, is charged with protecting the public health of the nation by providing leadership and direction in prevention and control of diseases and other preventable conditions and by responding to public health emergencies. It is composed of 10 major operating components: the Epidemiology Program Office, the International Health Program Office, the Public Health Practice Program Office, the National Center for Prevention Services, the National Center for Environmental Health, the National Center for Injury Prevention and Control, the National Institute for Occupational Safety and Health, the National Center for Chronic Disease Prevention and Health Promotion, the National Center for Infectious Diseases, and the National Center for Health Statistics. The agency administers national programs for prevention and control of communicable and vector-borne diseases and other preventable conditions. It develops and implements programs in chronic disease prevention and control, as well as programs to deal with environmental health problems, including responding to environmental, chemical, and radiation emergencies.[94] Estimated total outlays for the CDC in FY 1994 are $1.8 billion, which represents 9.3% of the budget for the PHS.[86]

Food and Drug Administration

The FDA, which was created through the Agriculture Appropriations Act of 1931, is charged with protecting the health of the nation against impure and unsafe foods, drugs, and cosmetics, as well as other potential hazards. Estimated total outlays for the FDA in FY 1994 are $671 million, which represents 3.5% of the budget for the PHS.[95] Its subdivisions include the following.

 ✧ The Center for Drug Evaluation and Research develops policy with regard to safety, effectiveness, and labeling of all drug products for human use, and it reviews and evaluates new drug applications. It develops and implements standards for the safety and effectiveness of all over-the-counter drugs, and it monitors the quality of marketed drug products through product testing, surveillance, and compliance programs.

 ✧ The Center for Biologics Evaluation and Research inspects manufacturers' facilities for compliance with standards, tests products submitted for release, establishes written and physical standards, and approves licensing of manufacturers to produce biological products. It also coordinates the AIDS program, which is working toward development of an AIDS vaccine and AIDS diagnostic tests.

✦   The Center for Food Safety and Applied Nutrition conducts research and develops standards on composition, quality, nutrition, and safety of food and food additives, colors, and cosmetics.

✦   The Center for Veterinary Medicine develops and conducts programs with respect to safety and efficacy of veterinary preparations and devices.

✦   The Center for Devices and Radiological Health inspects manufacturers' facilities for compliance with standards; tests products submitted for release; and establishes and develops programming to control unnecessary exposure of humans to, as well as ensure the safe and efficacious use of, potentially hazardous ionizing and nonionizing radiation.

✦   The National Center for Toxicological Research conducts research programs to study the biological effects of potentially toxic chemical substances found in the environment, emphasizing determination of the health effects resulting from long-term, low-level exposure to chemical toxicants and the basic biological processes for chemical toxicants in animal organisms.[96]

Health Resources and Services Administration
The Health Resources and Services Administration (HRSA) has leadership responsibility in the PHS for general health services and resource issues relating to access, equity, quality, and cost of care. Estimated total outlays for the HRSA in FY 1994 are $2.7 billion, which represents 14% of the budget for the PHS.[97] The administration is subdivided into the following Bureaus.

✦   The Bureau of Primary Health Care serves as a national focus for efforts to ensure availability and delivery of health care services in health professional shortage areas, to medically underserved populations, and to those with special needs.

✦   The Bureau of Health Professions provides national leadership in coordinating, evaluating, and supporting development and utilization of the nation's health personnel.

✦   The Bureau of Health Resources Development develops, coordinates, administers, directs, monitors, and supports federal policy and programs pertaining to health care facilities; a national network of activities associated with organ donations, procurements, and transplantations; and activities related to AIDS. These responsibilities include financial, capital, organizational, and physical matters.

✦   The Maternal and Child Health Bureau develops, administers, directs, coordinates, monitors, and supports federal policy and programs pertaining to health and related care for the nation's mothers and children. Programs administered by the bureau address the full spectrum of primary, secondary, and tertiary care services and related activities conducted in the public and private sector that impact on maternal and child health.[98]

Indian Health Service
The Indian Health Service (IHS) provides comprehensive health service delivery for American Indians and Alaskan Natives with opportunity for maximum tribal

involvement in developing and managing programs to meet their health needs. The service's goal is to raise the health status of American Indians and Alaskan Natives to the highest possible level.[99] Estimated total outlays for the IHS in FY 1994 are $1.6 billion, which represents 8.2% of the budget for the PHS.[100]

National Institutes of Health

The National Institutes of Health (NIH) is the principal biomedical research agency of the federal government. Its mission is to pursue knowledge to improve human health. To accomplish this goal, the institute seeks to expand fundamental knowledge about the nature and behavior of living systems, to apply that knowledge to extend the health of human lives, and to reduce the burdens resulting from disease and disability. The NIH is composed of the following Institutes: the National Cancer Institute; the National Heart, Lung, and Blood Institute; the National Library of Medicine; the National Institute of Diabetes and Digestive and Kidney Diseases; the National Institute of Allergy and Infectious Diseases; the National Institute of Child Health and Human Development; the National Institute on Deafness and Other Communication Disorders; the National Institute of Dental Research; the National Institute of Environmental Health Sciences; the National Institute of General Medical Sciences; the National Institute of Neurological Disorders and Stroke; the National Eye Institute; the National Institute on Aging; the National Institute of Alcohol Abuse and Alcoholism; the National Institute of Arthritis and Musculoskeletal and Skin Diseases; the National Institute on Drug Abuse; the National Institute of Mental Health, Clinical Center; the National Center for Human Genome Research; the National Center for Nursing Research; and the Fogarty International Center.[99] Estimated total outlays for the NIH in FY 1994 are $9.9 billion, which represents 52% of the budget for the PHS.[101] See Chapter 17 for a more detailed description of Biomedical Research Policy.

Substance and Mental Health Services Administration

The Substance Abuse and Mental Health Services Administration (SAMHSA) provides national leadership to ensure that knowledge, based on science and state-of-the-art practice, is effectively used for prevention and treatment of addictive and mental disorders. SAMHSA strives to improve access and to reduce barriers to high quality, effective programs and services for individuals who suffer from or are at risk for these disorders, as well as their families and communities. Estimated total outlays for the SAMHSA in FY 1994 are $2.3 billion, which represents 12% of the budget for the PHS.[102] Major components include the following.

✧   The Center for Substance Abuse Prevention provides a national focus for the federal effort to prevent alcohol and other drug abuse.

✧   The Center for Substance Abuse Treatment provides leadership for the federal effort to enhance approaches and to expand programs focusing on the treatment of substance abusers, as well as associated problems of physical illness and comorbidity.

✧ The Center for Mental Health Services provides national leadership to ensure the application of scientifically established findings and practice-based knowledge in prevention and treatment of mental disorders; to improve access, reduce barriers, and promote high quality, effective programs and services for people with or at risk for such disorders, as well as their families and communities; and to promote the rehabilitation of people with mental disorders.[103]

Health Care Financing Administration

The HCFA was created by the Secretary of HHS in 1977 to combine under one administration oversight of the Medicare program, the federal portion of the Medicaid program, and related quality assurance activities. HCFA currently serves 67 million persons, or one in four elderly, disabled, or poor Americans through Medicare and Medicaid.[104] Estimated total outlays for HCFA in FY 1994 are $304 billion, which represents 43% of the budget for HHS.[105] Figure 7.4 delineates how HCFA spends its resources.

Medicare

The Medicare program provides health insurance coverage for people age 65 years and older, younger people who are receiving Social Security disability benefits, and persons who need dialysis or kidney transplantations for treatment of end-stage renal disease. For a detailed analysis of the Medicare program, see Chapter 6.

Estimated Expenditures for the Health Care Financing Administration, FY 1994 (in thousands of $)

Payments <u>out of</u> Federal Hospital Insurance Trust Fund (Medicare Part A)	101,206,576
Grants to States for Medicaid	91,960,800
Payments <u>out of</u> Federal Supplementary Medical Insurance Trust Fund (Medicare Part B)	63,565,274
Payments <u>into</u> the Hospital Insurance (Medicare Part A) and Supplementary Medical Insurance Trust Funds (Medicare Part B)	46,625,440
HCFA Program Management	369,097
Total	303,727,187

Figure 7.4 Adapted from Budget of the U.S. Government, U.S. Government Printing Office, Washington, D.C., 1993, p. App. 617–622.

Medicaid

The Medicaid program is a medical assistance program jointly financed by state and federal governments for eligible low-income individuals. Medicaid covers health care expenses for all recipients of Aid to Families with Dependent Children, and most states also cover needy elderly, blind, and disabled individuals who receive cash assistance under the Supplemental Security Income program. Coverage is also extended to certain infants and low income pregnant women, as well as, at the option of the state, other low income individuals with medical bills that qualify them as categorically or medically needy. For a detailed analysis of the Medicaid program, see Chapter 6.

Quality Assurance

HCFA also carries out the quality assurance provisions of the Medicare and Medicaid programs, develops and implements health and safety standards for providers in federal health programs, and implements the End-stage Renal Disease Program.

Social Security Administration

The SSA was established in 1946, and its predecessor, the Social Security Board, was abolished at the same time. In 1953, the SSA was transferred from the Federal Security Agency to the Department of Health, Education, and Welfare, which later became the HHS. As of March 1995, the SSA will be removed from HHS and will become an independent agency. The SSA administers a national program of contributory social insurance, whereby employees, employers, and the self-employed pay contributions that are pooled in special trust funds. When earnings stop or are reduced because the worker retires, dies, or becomes disabled, monthly cash benefits are paid to partially replace earnings the family has lost.

Principal programs administered by the SSA include the Old Age, Survivors, and Disability Insurance programs (OASDI) and the Supplemental Security Income program (SSI). The umbrella OASDI program administers specifically the Old Age Retirement program, through which retirees who have paid into the system receive Social Security checks; the Survivor program, in which the spouse or child of a deceased person who has paid into the system receives their benefits; and the Disability program, through which a person who is disabled, has paid into the system for at least 10 years, and has paid for at least five of the last 10 years, receives benefits. The SSI program is a disability program for aged, blind, or disabled persons who are not eligible for the OASDI program. SSI is financed with general revenues, rather than a special trust fund.[106] Estimated total outlays for the SSA in FY 1994 are $355 billion, which represents 50% of the budget for HHS.[107] Figure 7.5 delineates estimated SSA spending for FY 1994.

Estimated Expenditures for the Social Security Administration, FY 1994 (in thousands of $)

Payments <u>out of</u> the Old-Age and Survivors Program Trust Funds...	283,283,232
Payments <u>out of</u> the Disability Insurance Trust Fund...	37,384,850
Payments from the Supplemental Security Income Program...	27,331,775
Payments <u>into</u> the Old-Age and Survivors, and Disability Insurance Trust Funds (OASDI)................	6,546,678
Total...	354,546,535

Figure 7.5 Adapted from Budget of the U.S. Government, U.S. Government Printing Office, Washington, D.C., 1993, p. App. 622–623 and 635–637.

Administration for Children and Families

The Administration for Children and Families (ACF) was created in 1991, and is divided into the Administration on Children, Youth, and Families; the Administration on Developmental Disabilities; the Administration for Native Americans; the Office of Community Services; the Office of Child Support Enforcement; the Office of Refugee Resettlement; and the Office of Family Assistance. Estimated total outlays for the ACF in FY 1994 are $31 billion, which represents 4.4% of the budget for HHS.[108]

✦   The Administration on Children, Youth, and Families (ACYF) administers state grant programs; discretionary grant programs providing Head Start services and facilities for runaway youth; the Child Abuse Prevention and Treatment Act; the Child Care and Development Block Grant; Child Welfare Services training, research, and demonstration programs; and the Runaway and Homeless Youth Act.

✦   The Administration on Developmental Disabilities (ADD) serves as the focal point in HHS for supporting and encouraging provision of quality services to persons with developmental disabilities, as well as in assisting states through design and implementation of state programs in the furthering of independence, productivity, and community inclusion of persons with developmental disabilities.

✦   The Administration for Native Americans (ANA) represents the concerns of Native Americans, and it serves as the focal point within HHS on the full range of developmental, social, and economic strategies that support Native American self-determination and self-sufficiency. Native Americans include

American Indians, Alaskan Natives, Native American Pacific Islander, and Native Hawaiians.

✧ The Office of Community Services (OCS) provides leadership on matters relating to community programs that promote economic self-sufficiency and personal responsibility in low income and needy individuals. It administers the Community Services Block Grant, the Social Services Block Grant, and the Low Income Energy Assistance Program, as well as a variety of discretionary grant programs that foster family stability, economic security, responsibility, and self-support.

✧ The Office of Child Support Enforcement (OCSE) provides direction, guidance, and oversight to state child support enforcement. The OCSE assists states to develop programs for establishing and enforcing support obligations, establishing paternity when necessary, and obtaining child support.

✧ The Office of Refugee Resettlement (ORR) plans, develops, and directs implementation of a comprehensive program for domestic refugee and entrant resettlement assistance. The office provides direction and technical guidance to programs, including the Refugee and Entrant Resettlement Program, State Legislation Impact Assistance Grants, and the U.S. Repatriate Program.

✧ The Office of Family Assistance (OFA) advises the Secretary, through the Assistant Secretary for Children and Families, on economic self-sufficiency programs. The Office provides leadership, direction, and technical guidance in administering the AFDC program.[109] Estimated total outlays for the OFA in FY 1994 are $17 billion, which represents 54% of the budget for the ACF.[110]

Administration on Aging

The Administration on Aging is the principal agency designated to carry out the provisions of the Older Americans Act of 1965. It is the leading agency within HHS on all issues concerning aging. Estimated total outlays for the administration in FY 1994 are $823 million, which represents 0.1% of the budget for HHS.[111] Its mission is to

✧ Advise the Secretary, Department components, and other federal departments and agencies on characteristics, circumstances, and needs of older people.

✧ Develop policies, plans, and programs designed to promote the welfare of the elderly, and to advocate their needs in HHS program planning and policy development.

✧ Administer a program of grants to states to establish state and community programs for older persons.

✧ Administer a program of grants to American Indians, Alaskan Natives, and Native Hawaiians to establish programs for older Native Americans.

✧ Administers ombudsman, legal services oversight, and protective services for older people.[112]

Making Federal Health Policy

The making of public policy is a complicated, dynamic process that is affected by multiple variables. What determines which of the many competing policy proposals gets enacted or even considered by the government? John Kindon, in *Agendas, Alternatives, and Public Policies,* created a useful framework with which to answer this question. Our analysis first looks at the Kingdon Paradigm to delineate how public policy is made, and it then focuses specifically on the making of federal health policy. Federal health policy is made by three key players, each of which wields power that ebbs and flows, depending on a host of other factors and interactions.

The Kingdon Paradigm
According to Kingdon, public policy-making includes setting the agenda, specification of alternatives from which a choice is to be made, making an authoritative choice among those specified alternatives, and implementation of the decision.[113] The governmental agenda is the list of subjects or problems to which governmental officials, and people outside government closely associated with those officials, are paying serious attention at any given time, whereas the decision agenda is a list of subjects that are moving into position for an authoritative decision, such as legislative enactment or presidential choice. In general, two categories of factors affect agenda-setting: the participants who are active, and the processes by which agenda items and alternatives come into prominence.

Participants
Participants in the process can be divided into visible and hidden clusters. The visible cluster includes such actors as the President and his high-level appointees, prominent members of Congress, the media, and such election-related actors as political parties and campaigners. The hidden cluster includes career bureaucrats, academic specialists, and congressional staffers. They affect the specification of alternatives from which authoritative choices are made.

Processes
The three processes by which agendas are set and alternatives are specified include problem recognition, policy generation, and the political process. Each can be seen as an independent stream of ideas and possibilities.

Problem Stream   In the problem stream, conditions are brought to the attention of people in and around government by systemic indicators, by focusing events such as crises and disasters, or by feedback from the operation of current programs. Conditions come to be defined as problems, and they have a better chance of rising on the agenda, when they violate important values of the nation or when they compare unfavorably with conditions in other countries or other relevant units.

Policy Stream   The generation of policy proposals resembles a process of biological natural selection. Many ideas are possible in principle, and they float around in a "policy primeval soup" in which specialists try out their ideas in a variety of ways: bill introductions, speeches, testimony, papers, publications, and conversation. Proposals are floated, come into contact with one another, are revised to form combinations and recombinations, and are floated again. Proposals that survive to the status of serious consideration meet several criteria, including their technical feasibility, their fit with dominant values and the current national mood, their budgetary workability, and the political support or opposition they might receive. Thus, the selection system narrows the set of conceivable proposals and selects from that large set a short list of proposals that is actually available for serious consideration.

Political Stream   The political stream is composed of swings in national mood, administration or legislative turnover, and interest group pressure campaigns. Potential agenda items that are congruent with the current national mood, that enjoy interest group support or lack organized opposition, and that fit the orientations of the prevailing legislative coalitions or the current administration are more likely to rise to agenda prominence than items that do not meet such conditions. Turnover of key participants, such as a change in administration or the ideological makeup of the Congress, also may have a powerful effect on the policy agenda. Interest groups may affect the alternatives considered. They may block consideration of proposals they do not prefer, or they may modify a policy initiative already high on the governmental agenda by adding elements a bit more to their liking. They less often initiate policy or set agendas on their own. When organized interests come into conflict with the combination of national mood and elected politicians, the latter combination is likely to prevail, at least as far as setting the agenda is concerned.

Kingdon's thesis is that these separate streams of problems, policies, and politics come together at certain critical times. Solutions become joined to problems, and both are joined to favorable political forces. This coupling, which is accomplished by policy entrepreneurs, is most likely when policy windows are open. Policy windows can be defined as brief opportunities to push pet proposals or to bring attention to particular problems. Windows are opened either by the appearance of compelling problems or by happenings in the political stream. Thus, agendas are set in the problem and the political streams, and by visible participants, and alternatives are generated in the policy stream and by hidden participants.

Often there are partial couplings: solutions to problems, but without a receptive political climate; politics to proposals, but without a sense that a compelling problem is being solved; and politics and problems both calling for action, but without an available alternative to advocate. Only the complete joining of all three streams dramatically enhances the odds that a subject will become firmly fixed on a decision agenda. Partial coupling is less likely to result in an issue rising to the decision agenda.

Policy windows can open predictably, for example, when legislation comes up for renewal on a schedule creating opportunities to change, expand, or abolish certain programs; or without warning, for example, when a national disaster happens or when an unexpected election result produces turnover in key decision-makers. Predictable or unpredictable open windows are scarce, and they usually last for a short duration.

Policy entrepreneurs are people willing to invest time and resources to advance future policies they support. Entrepreneurs are seen at three junctures: they highlight the indicators that so importantly dramatize a problem they want dealt with, they are central to the softening-up process their policy proposals need to be successful, and they make the couplings between problem recognition, policy development, and politics when policy windows open. Entrepreneurs can be elected officials, career civil servants, lobbyists, academics, or journalists. No one type of participant dominates the pool of entrepreneurs. Entrepreneurs bring several key resources into the action when policy windows open: their claims to a hearing, their personal connections and negotiating skills, and their sheer persistence. An item's chances of moving up onto the decision agenda are enhanced considerably by the presence of a skillful entrepreneur, and they are dampened considerably if no entrepreneur takes on the cause, pushes it, and makes the critical couplings when policy windows open.

Given this paradigm, we look at the three key players who make or influence federal health policy: the executive branch, the Congress, and interest groups.

The Role of the Executive Branch

Despite Congress' predominant role in the legislative process, the executive branch has many ways in which it can impact health care legislation and policy. In addition to proposing, lobbying, and vetoing legislation, it can effectively thwart legislative intent in its implementation of governmental programs.

The President

The President of the United States occupies what many term the *bully pulpit*. By the nature of the position, many influential persons, both politically and economically, as well as domestically and internationally, will listen to what the President has to say. The President, through the use of the bully pulpit, can move items up to the decision agenda and function as a policy entrepreneur coupling the streams by spearheading new domestic and foreign policy initiatives that meet certain needs of the American people. The President is a visible participant and a mover in the political stream who can do much to set the decision agenda. Domestic examples of this power include Roosevelt's "New Deal" in the 1930s in response to the Great Depression, Johnson's "Great Society" initiatives of the 1960s in response to the undercurrent of social reform that swept the country, and the Clinton Health Security Act, which responded to the growing belief that the health care system of the U.S. was in crisis and needed significant reform.

The President may also veto legislation or select appointees who would render particular legislation ineffectual.

The Department of Health and Human Services

HHS is critical to policy generation and to problem recognition. Within each component of HHS are staffers whose sole purpose is to follow and to analyze the impact of their programs. They produce the indicators and analyze the feedback that define conditions which may be deemed problems. Once problems have been identified, these same HHS staff begin and continue the policy generation that needs to take place to address these problems. Clearly, congressional staffers, academics, interest groups, and think tanks also have a vital role in problem identification and policy generation, but the importance of HHS cannot be underestimated because its leaders are political appointees who have the ability to influence the President, who in turn has a decisive impact on agenda-setting. Similar to the President, high-ranking officials at HHS, such as the Secretary, the heads of the PHS, the CDC, the FDA, and the NIH, also have the ability to set agendas and to function as policy entrepreneurs.

The Role of Congress

Although the word *health* does not appear in the official title of any congressional committee, at least 14 committees and subcommittees in the House and 24 in the Senate have been identified as having some direct or oversight responsibility for health.[114] Of these, six committees (three in the House and three in the Senate) control much of the legislative activity in Congress.

House Committees

❖ *The Ways and Means Committee* is an authorizing committee that has the power to tax, and it was the launching pad for much of the health financing legislation passed in the 1960s and the early 1970s. It oversees the Medicare program.

❖ *The Committee on Energy and Commerce and its Subcommittee on Health and the Environment* is an authorizing committee that has jurisdiction over the PHS programs and the Medicaid program. It shares jurisdiction with the Ways and Means Committee for Medicare.

❖ *The Committee on Appropriation and its Subcommittees on Labor, Health and Human Services, and Education* appropriates funds for individual health programs.

Senate Committees

❖ *The Committee on Labor and Human Resources* is an authorizing committee that has jurisdiction over the PHS programs.

❖ *The Committee on Finance and Subcommittee on Health* is an authorizing committee that has jurisdiction over Medicare and Medicaid.

❖ *The Committee on Appropriation and Subcommittees on Labor, Health, and Human Services, and Education,* like its counterpart in the House, appropriates funds for individual health programs.

It has been estimated that although the tax committees (House Ways and Means and Senate Finance) have jurisdiction over only 15% of all health program legislation, they control approximately 70% of all federal health dollars expended. In contrast, the two other authorizing committees (House Committee on Energy and Commerce and the Senate Committee on Labor and Human Resources) review approximately 70% of all federal health program legislation, but they directly affect only 15% of total health dollars spent.[114]

Once considered stable legislative bodies, with long tenure for members and a committee seniority system that ensured enduring power to multiterm members (especially committee chairs), the House and Senate in recent years have been plagued by high membership and staff turnover, overlapping jurisdictions, and changes in rules that have significantly increased the independence of individual members at the expense of party discipline, diffused institutional accountability, and heightened legislative paralysis or "gridlock."

Along with HHS, the Congress has much to do with agenda-setting and alternative specification. The political stream is the domain of the Congress. Changes in the partisan nature or the ideological bend of the Congress dramatically influence what is brought to the policy agenda, regardless of the wishes of the President. Re-election campaigns, the influence of interest groups on campaign funding, keeping the mood of the representatives electorate in mind, all conspire to shape the dynamic political stream in which congressional members decide on policy issues. Many prominent members of Congress, especially the chairmen of key committees, can set agendas, and, much more often than the President, they act as policy entrepreneurs when policy windows open. These chairmen have seniority that allows them to get bills through Congress, they have expertise in the issue to know what alternative within the policy stream has the best hope of success given the political stream at that point in time, and they have the staff to produce the indicators and the program feedback that can make a condition into a problem.

The congressional staffers are critical to alternative specification. They are usually the final common pathway for all hidden participants because they often write the legislation and they are the closest to the congressional member who functions as the visible participant and agenda-setter. Academics, interest groups, members of think tanks, and staffers from executive branch offices all try to convince congressional staffers that their view of and solution for a given policy issue is the most prudent. Some of the most important recombinations of policy issues that can make or break an issue occur through congressional staff.

The Role of Interest Groups

The efforts of organized interest groups to influence government policy in the U.S. are an inherent part of the political process, and they rest on First Amendment guarantees of free speech and the people's right to petition the government for a redress of grievances. The increase in the role of government in the everyday lives of its citizens has tended to heighten such organizational activity as part of the political process. Thus, as power has moved toward the federal government, there has been a proliferation in interest group activity, in both number and variety, at the national level. In 1974, there were 608 political action committees (PACs) in the U.S., whereas in 1992, there were 4,221 PACs.[115] Each year, interest groups attempt to wield, and often do, considerable influence over government policy through campaign fund donations and informational discussions with members of Congress and their staffers. The health care lobby has increased in numbers, and the funding flowing into and out of PACs has increased dramatically since health care reform re-entered public awareness during the 1992 presidential campaign. The American Medical Association (AMA) PAC spent $4.7 million in 1990, which ranked fourth in PAC spending in 1990. Half of these dollars were contributions to the campaign funds of federal candidates; this figure ranked second in the nation for all PACs. During the last two years, these dollar amounts have almost doubled as the AMA attempted at first to block and then to modify to its liking the Clinton health reform initiative. Other influential health interest groups include the Health Insurance Association of America (HIAA), the American Hospital Association (AHA), the Pharmaceutical Manufacturers Association (PMA), and the American Association of Retired Person (AARP), which has approximately 40 million members.

Interest groups have the greatest effect on alternative specification. This influence occurs mostly at the subcommittee or committee level, where hearings about certain bills are heard, and at agency hearings where legislation is implemented.

The Adventures of a Bill

Figure 7.6 illustrates the process by which a bill becomes a law. Note that there are numerous opportunities for interest groups, congressional members, staffers, and other participants to alter the bill before it is enacted.

The Failure of the Clinton Health Security Act

During the 1992 presidential campaign, Bill Clinton was able to make health care reform one of the campaign's most divisive and decisive issues. He ran on a platform of domestic policy action using the promise of deficit reduction, health care reform, a national crime bill, and a jobs bill to defeat a domestically weak George Bush. Clinton was a visible participant in the political stream who promised to raise health care reform to the decision agenda if elected President. He was a policy entrepreneur who linked a problem to the political stream. He saw a policy window opened by problem identification and by a changing political scene that he hoped he could exploit to get the most significant national health legislation passed since the 1960s. What seemed like a real opportunity at reform, however, did not come to fruition. What went wrong is as follows.

◆ **The policy window was open for only a short time.** In his inaugural address, President Clinton promised a health bill reform before Congress in 100

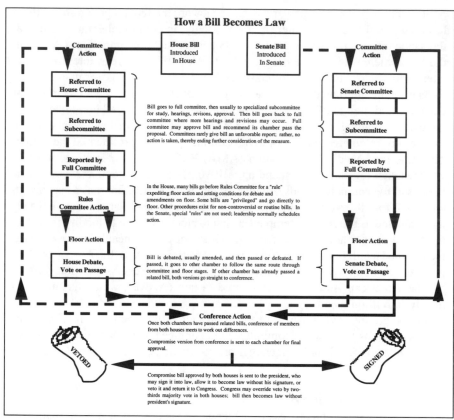

How a Bill Becomes Law

Committee Action

House Bill Introduced In House

Senate Bill Introduced In Senate

Committee Action

Referred to House Committee

Referred to Senate Committee

Bill goes to full committee, then usually to specialized subcommittee for study, hearings, revisons, approval. Then bill goes back to full committee where more hearings and revisions may occur. Full commitee may approve bill and recommend its chamber pass the proposal. Committees rarely give bill an unfavorable report; rather, no action is taken, thereby ending further consideration of the measure.

Referred to Subcommittee

Referred to Subcommittee

Reported by Full Committee

Reported by Full Committee

Rules Commitee Action

In the House, many bills go before Rules Committee for a "rule" expediting floor action and setting conditions for debate and amendments on floor. Some bills are "privileged" and go directly to floor. Other procedures exist for non-controversial or routine bills. In the Senate, special "rules" are not used; leadership normally schedules action.

Floor Action

Floor Action

House Debate, Vote on Passage

Bill is debated, usually amended, and then passed or defeated. If passed, it goes to other chamber to follow the same route through committee and floor stages. If other chamber has already passed a related bill, both versions go straight to conference.

Senate Debate, Vote on Passage

Conference Action

Once both chambers have passed related bills, conference of members from both houses meets to work out differences.

Compromise version from conference is sent to each chamber for final approval.

VETOED

SIGNED

Compromise bill approved by both houses is sent to the president, who may sign it into law, allow it to become law without his signature, or veto it and return it to Congress. Congress may override veto by two-thirds majority vote in both houses; bill then becomes law without president's signature.

Figure 7.6 Adapted from the Congressional Quarterly Guide to Current American Government, Congressional Quarterly, Inc., Washington, D.C., 1992, p. 118.

days, which would have been April 30th. The Clinton Health Security Act did not reach Congress until October 27, 1993. This delay resulted in letting the health care reform bill fall off the decision agenda and letting other issues reach the decision agenda, and it also allowed opposition forces to mobilize. The most glaring example of this were the Harry and Louise commercials run by the HIAA in September 1993. Between January 1993 and May 1994, the AMA, the AHA, the HIAA, and various drug companies, all of which were resolutely against the Clinton proposal, contributed $26 million to members of Congress in an attempt to block the bill or to reduce it to an insurance reform bill at best.[116] At the time of the inauguration, there were few persons who opposed some form of health care reform, but by the time the 1,342-page Clinton Health Security Act had finally come out, it was difficult to find any supporters, and it was easy to find ardent opposition.

✧   **Other domestic and foreign policy issues moved health care off the decision agenda while it was languishing in the health care task force and committees in Congress.** Examples include situations in North Korea, Somalia, Bosnia, and Haiti, as well as two pieces of legislation, the North American Free Trade Agreement and the national crime bill. The crime bill was especially exasperating because Senate republicans held the bill up to further put off the health care debate, sensing they had already killed any chance at comprehensive health reform.

✧   **The policy stream was divided during the election, and it still is two years later, with regard to what reforms are necessary to contain costs, to increase access, and to maintain the choice and quality of health care most Americans enjoy.** Although the Clinton plan reached the five Congressional subcommittees responsible for health care reform legislation by October 1993, markup of the President's bill was not done in three of the five committees until June 1994. The House Committee on Energy and Commerce was hopelessly deadlocked over employer mandates, and it took no action on the President's bill. The critical Senate Finance Committee adopted a bill without employer mandates that aimed to reach only 95% coverage by 2002. The President's plan had championed employer mandates and universal coverage.

✧   **The methods used by the Clinton Administration to write legislation and to enlist support for the measure ended up alienating Congressional supporters, and they diminished the positive political stream the Administration had experienced early on.** The appointments of Hillary Rodham Clinton, the First Lady, and Ira Magaziner, a personal friend to the President, to head up the Health Care Reform Task Force hurt the favorable political stream. Both were looked at as Washington outsiders, and they incurred a great deal of circumspection from congressional democrats, many of whom had been working on health care reform for more than a decade. Both were accused of meeting with staffers on Capitol Hill and various interest groups and not listening to the political exigencies being discussed. The deep secrecy used by the task force to conduct their business further alienated key democrats in Congress. Also, as many on the task force have admitted, political concerns were not adequately considered when drawing up the grand plan, which led to problems in committee deliberations in Congress later.

✧   **Overestimation of election mandate and the strength of the political stream.** Bill Clinton received only 43% of the popular vote in the 1992 election. Perhaps he overestimated his political support in Congress and among the American people. Some believe he misinterpreted what Americans wanted. Bob Blendon's studies showed that what Americans really wanted was portability of health insurance and less cost, but not overarching reform. The political stream also disintegrated as time went on.

✧   Senate democrat John Breaux and House democrat Jim Cooper introduced their own health reform bills in Congress.

✧   Dan Rostenkowski, a Clinton supporter, was indicted on 17 criminal charges, and he had to relinquish his chairmanship of the Ways and Means Committee in the House of Representatives, further weakening the President's position.

✧   Senate democrat Daniel Patrick Moynihan, Chairman of the vital Senate Finance Committee, was at best a lukewarm Clinton supporter, and he had his committee write its own bill, which ignored the most important planks in the Clinton plan, such as employer mandates and universal coverage, and he called financial numbers provided by the Clinton Administration "fantasy" when the Health Security Act was unveiled in October 1993.

In conclusion, President Clinton attempted to be a policy entrepreneur, and he did link a problem to a favorable political stream at the time of his election. What he did not realize was the short duration of this window of opportunity, the lack of consensus in the policy stream, and the changeability of the political stream. The Clinton Health Security Act did not succeed because there was only partial coupling of the streams with a policy window that was open for perhaps the first six months of the Clinton presidency.

EVOLUTION OF THE ROLE OF STATE
AND LOCAL GOVERNMENTS ❖

Broadly speaking, the health-related activities of state and local government are the following.[117]

+ Traditional public health, including health monitoring, sanitation, and disease control.
+ Financing and delivery of personal health services, including Medicaid, mental health, and direct delivery through public hospitals and health departments.
+ Environmental protection, including protection against man-made environmental and occupational hazards.
+ Regulation of the providers of medical care through certificate-of-need and state rate setting, as well as licensing and other functions.

State and local government involvement in public health began with the great epidemics of cholera, smallpox, and yellow fever in the late 1700s and early 1800s. Government responded to these epidemics by instituting quarantine measures and efforts to improve community sanitation. Generally, these efforts were directed by physicians appointed by the state government. At the local level in the early 1800s, local health Boards began employing persons to serve as their agents, which was the first step in the formation of local health departments. Health departments were established in Baltimore in 1798, Charleston in 1815, Philadelphia in 1818, and Providence in 1832.[117]

Despite these early efforts, public health as we know it did not begin to evolve until the latter half of the 1800s. During this period, two major events took place. The first was publication of the Shattuck Report by the Massachusetts Sanitation Commission in 1850, which recommended establishment of state health departments and local Boards of Health in each town. Soon after, Massachusetts established the first state Board of Health, and by the end of the century, 38 other states followed suit.[117] The other significant development, which was really a series of related developments, involved breakthroughs in microbiology. By the late 1800s, the discoveries of Pasteur and others had built a foundation of knowledge that led to dramatic progress in the control of infectious diseases. Armed with this new science, health authorities began to act with greater discrimination with regard to quarantine and environmental sanitation techniques. This maturation continued into the 1930s, and it was substantially augmented by the development of antibiotics and subsequent use of antimicrobial therapy in the delivery of health care services. State and local health departments became the major vehicle by which these advances in both microbial science and environmental sanitation were made available to the public.

As state and local health departments began to direct their attention to the causes of death and morbidity, they broadened and redefined their activities. The earliest efforts at preventive services began with programs aimed at those considered at risk for contracting disease, especially women and children. The states also began licensing physicians in an attempt to regulate the quality of care their citizens received. As the nation suffered through the Great Depression and the benefits of governmental intervention through Roosevelt's "New Deal" became clear, traditional American ambivalence toward government interference gave way to a desire for the benefits that government could provide to the public through sanitation, control of communicable diseases, and other traditional public health activities.

At the same time, state and local governments had an increasingly important role in the delivery of personal health services. The poorhouses of the 1700s and 1800s, which were more concerned with providing welfare than medical services, evolved by the late 1800s into city hospitals whose primary purpose was to deliver medical services. In the early 1900s, these hospitals became affiliated with medical schools, and they acquired full-time staffs. Starting in the late 1800s, state and local governments also began taking financial responsibility for the burgeoning psychiatric population. The inpatient population of state mental institutions grew to a peak of 560,000 in 1955. Currently, as a result of the deinstitutionalization movement of the last 25 years, there are approximately 150,000 persons in state mental hospitals.[117]

State and local government involvement in environmental issues began at the local level during the industrial revolution as a result of the "smoke nuisance" found in most industrial cities of the 1800s.[117] Air pollution problems first reached the local agenda, then the state and finally the federal level. Slowly, the environmental concerns of state and local governments have expanded to include air and water pollution, radiation control, hazardous waste, and occupational health and safety, although state and local governments did not always have formal responsibility for these problems.

The federal health programs of the 1960s dramatically increased public expenditures for health care for the poor by two methods that would profoundly affect both the role and the fiscal responsibilities of state and local government in health. The first strategy, Medicaid, was intended to provide insurance coverage so that eligible low income persons could purchase medical services from private hospitals and physicians. State governments were asked to administer the program and to pay 50% of the cost of the program. The second strategy was to directly increase federal support for the delivery of services by public hospitals and local health departments. The federal government, through the local health departments, directly subsidized medical services to the poor through the development of community and mental health centers, rural and migrant health centers, and other community-based delivery organizations not connected to hospitals.

By the 1980s, state and local governments were heavily involved both in traditional public health activities and in the delivery of personal medical care services, particularly to the poor through Medicaid and aid to public hospitals. The election of President Reagan and his "New Federalism," the deep recession of the late 1970s and early 1980s, and spiraling Medicaid costs made the 1980s a difficult period for state and local government health budgets. The goals of New Federalism were to substantially reduce the size of the federal budget through reductions in nondefense spending and to dramatically increase the fiscal and the administrative role of the states in the domestic arena. This approach translated into sharp reductions in health aid to state and local governments at a time when state tax revenues were decreasing due to the recession and Medicaid costs were increasing at an alarming rate. The New Federalism consolidated 21 health programs into four block grants. Although the original intent of the block grants was to allow states flexibility to shift funds both among the blocks and between them, the opposite occurred due to statutory "strings" placed on the grants by Congress. Predictably, conflicts arose between the legislative and the executive branches of state government over control of the block grants, and between state and local governments. A study conducted by the U.S. Conference of Mayors reported that almost three fourths of the nation's cities believed they had been adversely affected by the block grants and had not been adequately represented in the block grant allocation process.[117]

Since 1980, the state share of Medicaid has increased at a rate more than 2.5 times that of state revenues and reserves, and it has been increasing faster than any other major component of state budgets.[117] As a result, health care cost containment has been the active word in state legislatures around the country, and state demonstration projects that contain costs have been indispensable to health policy makers.

As the 1990s dawned, state and local governments found themselves spending more money than ever before on Medicaid, which consumed an ever-increasing percentage of health dollars in state and local budgets. Due to the increasing funds dedicated to Medicaid, less money was available for public health measures, public hospitals, and other health program expenditures.

ROLE OF STATE GOVERNMENTS ❖
State Expenditures on Health Care

In 1991, total state government expenditures were $628 billion, 10.5% of which was spent on Medicaid and 9.5% of which were spent on health and hospitals.[118] Of the $125 billion spent on health, which represents 20% of the total state budget, 53% was spent on Medicaid, 35% on hospitals, and 12% on public health.[117] Only education, which consumes 35% of state budgets, was a bigger expenditure item.

In contrast to the federal government, whose influence over health stems from its enormous fiscal power, the states derive their control over health issues from their broad, comprehensive legal authority for a wide variety of programs. As a result, their role in health has taken a number of forms.

+ Financial support for care and treatment of the poor and chronically disabled, including primary responsibility for administration of the Medicaid program.
+ Quality assurance and oversight of health care practitioners and facilities (e.g., state licensing and regulation).
+ Regulation of health care costs and insurance carriers.
+ Provision of the major share of costs for training health care professionals.
+ Authorization of local government health services.
+ Provision of laboratory services, either directly or by contract.

The two most pivotal functions that state governments fulfill is administration of the Medicaid program and willingness to experiment with innovative financing and delivery systems. For a thorough discussion of the Medicaid program, including history, eligibility criteria, benefits, financing, and problems, see Chapter 6. Many of the ideas currently being discussed on the federal level with regard to national health reform have been tried in some form at the state level. The states have long functioned as test sites and demonstration projects for health reformers.

Chapter 13 evaluates a broad cross-section of financing and delivery reform proposals that have been implemented at the state level.

States have organized in different ways to provide public health services. Not all state level public health services are provided by the state health department, nor are all state health departments found in the same place on the organization charts of state governments. A survey of the 50 state, six territorial, and one district state health agencies (SHAs) shows that 35 are organized as independent agencies responsible to the Governor or a Board of Health, and 22 are a component of a larger agency.[117]

The responsibilities of state health departments vary as well: 45 were designated the State Crippled Children Agency, 15 were designated the State Mental Health Authority, 10 were designated the Medicaid Single State Agency, 33 were designated State Health Planning and Development Agency, 17 were designated the Lead Environmental Agency, and 24 operated hospitals or other health care institutions.[117]

Seventy-four percent of the total expenditures by state health agencies is spent on personal health services, which include services for handicapped children, maternal and child care, chronic disease care, dental health, purchase or direct provision of inpatient care and mental health, programs dealing with communicable diseases, and provision of public health nursing, nutrition, health education, and health screening services.[117]

ROLE OF LOCAL GOVERNMENTS ❖
Local Expenditures on Health Care

In 1991, total local government expenditures were $623 billion, 11.5% of which was spent on health and hospitals.[118] Currently, the core of our "public" delivery system is the nation's 90 urban public hospitals, owned by city or county government, and 45 state-owned university hospitals. These 135 hospitals represent roughly two thirds of the total public hospital beds in the U.S. The other 1,800 hospitals serve primarily as community hospitals, and they admit predominantly private patients. Although Medicaid and Medicare do enable large numbers of poor to purchase care from private hospitals and physicians, the size and scope of state Medicaid programs varies tremendously. As a result, in many large cities these public and private teaching hospitals continue to have a vital role in delivering personal health services to the poor, as well as other special population groups, including alcohol and drug abusers, victims of violence, and chronically mentally ill patients. Nationally, public hospitals in the nation's 100 largest cities provide four times as much care for the poor (as a proportion of the total care they deliver) as private hospitals in the same cities.[117]

In general, local health departments have at least one full-time public health professional: a health officer, a public health nurse, or a sanitarian. Services usually provided by local health agencies include public health nursing, sanitation, communicable disease control, epidemiology, health statistics and records, school health services, and home health care. Many of the larger local health departments also provide dental care, emergency medical services, animal control, alcohol and drug abuse prevention and control, laboratory services, and maternal and child health care.

❖ Suggested Reading ❖

U.S. Government Manual 1993/94. Washington, DC: Office of the Federal Registrar, National Archives and Records Administration, 1993:294.
  The source for defining the mission and the functions of the government.
Kingdon JW. Agendas, alternatives, and public policies. Boston: Little, Brown, 1984.
  Should be read by anyone working in government or having contact with government in any way. Explains how public policy is made.
Litman TJ, Robins LS. Health politics and policy. New York: Wiley Medical Publications, 1984.
  Although somewhat dated, this text gives excellent insights into the forces that influence health care policy.
Statistical Abstracts of the United States 1993, 113th ed. Austin, TX: The Reference Press Inc., 1994.
  The best source for dollar figures on all areas of health spending in the United States.

Challenges

Cost

Colin Baker and Joseph Newhouse

Of all the challenges facing the United States (U.S.) health care system, none has generated more interest than the problem of increasing health care costs. Although there are many other aspects to what we call health reform—the uninsured, quality, and the ratio of primary care physicians to specialists—most would agree that the motivating issue of the health care crisis is that of runaway costs. Consumers fear being bankrupted by major illnesses that will not be covered by their insurance, if they have it at all. Employers fear losing out in global competition due to high premiums they must pay. Governors fear growing Medicaid budgets that eat up much needed funds for other programs. Finally, the federal government sees controlling health expenditures as the only way to begin to attack the budget deficit.

In this chapter, we look closely at the issue of health care costs. We begin by looking at how much we spend, how we spend it, and how we compare to other industrialized nations in this regard. Next we turn to explaining some of the trends we see: why do we spend more than other countries, why do high costs matter, and why are costs increasing so fast? Using what we learn about the causes of increasing high costs, we turn to a general discussion of several policy options that may be used to control these costs, and we end with a brief look at what may be the only long-term solution to rising costs: rationing care.

HEALTH COSTS IN CONTEXT ❖
Historical Background

The amount of money we spend on health care in the U.S. has been steadily increasing for the past several decades, and it is currently more than six times its 1960 level, measured in inflation-adjusted terms. Figure 8.1 and Table 8.1 show the dramatic increase in total national health care spending, the growth of real health care expenditures, and the percentage of gross national product (GNP) by decade. During this period, health spending grew at an average annual rate of more than 6% per year. For the increases in spending during this time to continue and accelerate as they did, there had to be enough hospitals and enough physicians to provide the care, there had to be enough people with medical insurance to demand more medical services, and there had to be an expansion of medical technology and practice to treat wide ranges of previously untreatable illnesses. In the past several decades, all these pieces fell together.

The poor health of many wartime recruits in the 1940s highlighted the dearth of effective health services in many regions of then-rural America, and Congress later responded with programs like the Hill-Burton Hospital Construction Act, which encouraged rapid building of hospitals across the country. Federal aid to medical schools encouraged expansion of medical programs, and increasing numbers of young people entered the field of medicine. In 1965, for example, there were 139 physicians per 100,000 U.S. civilians; by 1990, this figure had increased to 237.[119] Increasing availability of health insurance and general increases in wealth led to leaps in the demand for health services; as incomes increased in the

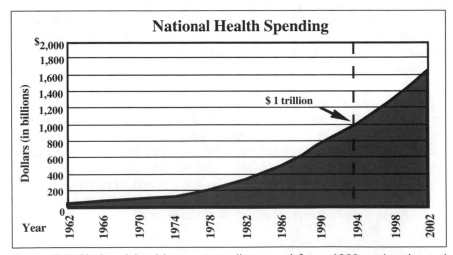

Figure 8.1 National health care spending trend from 1962 and estimated through the year 2002. (Source: HCFA, CBO Forecasts. Adapted from White House Domestic Policy Council 1993, the President's Health Security Plan.)

Table 8.1 Growth in Real Health Care Expenditures and GNP, by Decade

	Growth in real health care dollars, per capita	Growth in real GNP per capita	Health care share of GNP at end of period
1929–1940	1.4%	0.0%	4.0%
1940–1950	4.0%	3.1%	4.5%
1950–1960	3.6%	1.5%	5.3%
1960–1970	6.5%	2.5%	7.3%
1970–1980	3.8%	1.7%	9.1%
1980–1990	4.4%	1.7%	12.2%

Adapted from Newhouse, Health Affairs Supplement 1993.

postwar period, we purchased more of everything, but disproportionately more in the area of health services. Introduction of the Medicare and Medicaid programs in the 1960s contributed to increases in spending because millions who had lacked coverage were now able to visit the doctor or the hospital. The elderly, who prior to establishment of the Medicare program were disproportionately poor and lacking in coverage, were given access to a generous set of medical benefits, and they took advantage. Medicaid, a state-administered program for the poor and certain others with costly illnesses, provided services to many more who would have otherwise not been able to obtain care.

How the Money Is Spent

In 1991, the latest year for which official figures are available, Americans spent $752 billion on health care and related services, of which slightly less than 90% was spent on actual health services.[120] For this year, spending comprised more than 13% of the *gross domestic product* (GDP), and it represented approximately $2,900 spent per capita. One third of the total amount was paid for through private health insurance, and another 23% was paid for by out-of-pocket sources or other private funding. Government programs financed the remainder: Medicare paid 16%, and Medicaid paid 13%.

Table 8.2 provides a breakdown of how the $752 billion health bill was spent, by category of service. Spending on hospital services was by far the largest single component; it comprised 38% of total spending. Nearly all hospital costs were paid by insurance or other third-party financing, such as government programs: Private insurance financed 35%, Medicare and Medicaid financed 56%, and the rest came from out-of-pocket spending or philanthropic sources. Short-term acute-care community hospital services comprised the bulk of hospital spending (86%). Inpatient services accounted for 75% of community hospital costs, which is a lower proportion than that seen previously, because services continued a shift toward the outpatient sector.

Table 8.2 U.S. National Health Expenditures 1991

Spending Category	Billions of 1991 Dollars	% of Total Spending	Annual Rate of Growth 1986–91
Total Health Expenditures	752	100	11
Hospital Care	289	38	10
Physician Services	142	19	12
Drugs and Medical Non-Durables	61	8	8
Nursing Home Care	60	8	10
Dental Services	37	5	8
Other Professional Services	36	5	14
Program Adm. and Insurance	44	6	12
Govt. Public Health Activities	25	3	13
Research and Construction	23	3	8
Other Personal Health Care	14	2	15
Vision Products & Medical Durables	12	2	9
Home Health Care	10	1	20

Source: HCFA Office of the Actuary, National Health Expenditures 1991.

Physician services were the next largest component (19% of overall spending). Sources of funding for physician services differed in this sector from the hospital sector: Private insurance and out-of-pocket financing represented 65%, whereas public financing represented only 35%. Also, out-of-pocket spending is a much more substantial factor in physician services than in hospitals: $26 billion, or 18%.

Pharmaceuticals and nursing home care services, both much-discussed components of national health spending, each represented 8% of total spending. Approximately 60% of spending on pharmaceuticals is for prescriptions; the remainder is spent on over-the-counter medications and other items, such as first-aid products.

Smaller components of national spending included the services of such professionals as chiropractors, podiatrists, and other licensed nonphysicians (see Table 8-2; Other Professional Services, a category also including independent outpatient health clinics), which accounted for 5% of the total. Dentists accounted for 5%. Home health care services, a rapidly growing segment of spending, still amounted in 1991 to only 1% of the total health bill (excluding hospital-based home health care agencies). Other personal health care services, a category consisting mainly of public spending on such things as school health clinics, was 2%.

Components of the national health bill not involving actual health care services included administration and insurance, public health spending, and research and construction. The first consists of the costs incurred by third-party reimbursement of claims; it does not include the costs to providers of processing these claims (such costs show up in the respective provider category).

Table 8.3 Total Health Expenditure as a Percent of Gross Domestic Product and Per Capita Health Spending, Select Countries 1990

Country	Percent of Gross Domestic Product	Per Capita Spending in U.S. Dollars
United States	12.1	2,566
Canada	9.3	1,770
France	8.8	1,532
Germany	8.1	1,486
Japan	6.5	1,171
Great Britain	6.2	972

Source: Schieber et al, Health Care Financing Review, 1992.

Every category of spending has undergone rapid growth. All sectors of health spending have consistently grown at rates exceeding the general rate of inflation, which is approximately 3% per year.

International Comparisons

By any measure, whether it be per capita health spending, total spending, or the proportion of national income spent on health services, the amount spent by Americans greatly exceeds that of any other advanced industrialized nation. Table 8.3 compares U.S. health spending to that of several other wealthy countries in 1990. The high relative spending levels in the U.S. are immediately apparent: more than 12% of GDP in the U.S., compared with approximately 9% for the two next-highest nations, Canada and France, respectively. This disparity, although striking, masks much of the difference in patterns of spending due to the relatively high level of GDP in the U.S. A more telling comparison is seen in the level of per capita spending: $2,566 in the U.S. in 1990, compared with $1,770 in Canada and $1,532 in France (all figures are expressed in 1990 dollars).

Moreover, recent rates of increase in spending have been greater in the U.S. than in other wealthy nations, measured either as a fraction of GDP or in per capita terms. From 1980 to 1990, the U.S. had the largest rate of increase in per capita spending among the industrialized nations (annual average, 9.2%) (Figure 8.2).[121]

EXPLAINING THE TRENDS ❖
Why Do We Spend More Than Other Countries?

Why are there such stark differences in health spending between the U.S. and other industrial nations? First, comparisons drawn between nations in terms such as per capita health spending or the proportion of GDP devoted to health services

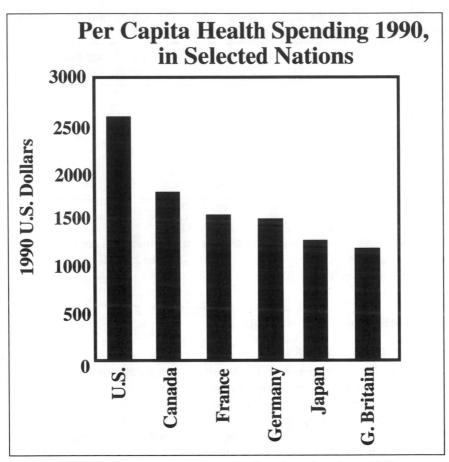

Figure 8.2 Per capita health care spending in selected nations, 1990. (Source: Schieber et al., Health Care Financing Review, 1992.)

are for many reasons not perfect measures of real differences in health spending patterns. Difficulties as mundane as converting currencies over fluctuating exchange rates can make the results hard to interpret, but the disparity between the U.S. and every other nation nonetheless appears substantial. What are the reasons for this disparity?

Differences in the age distribution of a population can be important in explaining differing spending levels. The U.S., for example, has a higher proportion of elderly persons than Canada; we might therefore expect the U.S. to spend more simply because older persons are known to incur greater costs. Also, differences in the price of care due to varying income levels of physicians could account for much of the disparity, because physicians in the U.S. earn more than their counterparts in most other nations.

Another important reason offered by many for the relatively high level of spending in the U.S. is the simple fact that the U.S. is the richest country in the world.

The amount of health services demanded by individuals increases with greater incomes, by a factor greater than the actual increase in income. It should be expected that the U.S., with the highest per capita income in the world, should spend at least somewhat more than other nations.

Perhaps the most consequential factor in the apparently high relative spending in the U.S. is its greater intensity of services. Extensive use and rapid expansion of new medical technologies seen in the U.S. is unique in the world, and it can certainly be expected to result in high costs. American citizens, at least those with insurance, enjoy much easier access to and make far greater use of advanced diagnostic and therapeutic procedures than citizens of other nations, across the gamut of clinical medicine. For example, there are nearly eight times as many magnetic resonance imaging (MRI) units per person in the U.S. as in Canada, as well as more than three times the number of cardiac catheterization facilities.[122] The U.S., unlike any other nation, also has an extensive and costly commitment to financing the ongoing treatment of end-stage renal disease.

Why Are High Costs Important?

The next obvious question to ask is, does it matter that we are spending so much on health care? After all, expenditures on computers and software, for instance, are high and increasing rapidly as well, and yet no one is calling for drastic reform in these markets.

The reason economists believe high health costs are not good for the economy is that this spending is not efficient. Put another way, some of the money spent on health care could be spent for better effect elsewhere in the economy.

Why is this so? The main reason is because, in health care, *typical consumers do not face the true cost of what they consume at the time of consumption.* This reality causes consumers to spend more on health care than they should, and they also get less benefit from this money spent on health care than if the money was spent elsewhere.

Thus, the presence of medical insurance prevents the market for health services from functioning like those for other goods. Insurance, usually paid directly out of one's paycheck before the fact, entitles one to health services when needed; once needed, there is little reason from the consumer's point of view not to consume every last service that might be of any benefit. When an insured person becomes sick and there is some costly treatment that might benefit them at all, they generally get it regardless of cost, perhaps without much consideration given to the likelihood of medical benefit versus dollar cost. They may incur a bill of tens of thousands of dollars on treatments that were never thought likely to be of much help.

No one pays a premium permitting them to consume any amount of computer services for which they should suddenly develop the need; we decide how much to buy based on our willingness to pay, even if our basic needs remain unfulfilled.

But for fully insured individuals, the only incentive at the point of illness (for patients or physicians) is to keep using more services until the point of absolute worthlessness is reached.

Imagine what would occur if instead of the current standard health insurance, we had coverage that simply gave us a lump sum of money on illness, and we then paid in cash for each service provided, pocketing the remainder. Under such a scheme, we would expect that for many illnesses, people would forego much of the treatment now commonly rendered because they would value the benefits of alternative consumption heavily relative to, for example, a very small chance of locating a treatable illness using MRI. A patient on a limited budget, hospitalized for a rapid heart rhythm, would likely pick and choose among those tests or treatments which, on a physician's advice, offered the highest probability of yielding useful information or care, rather than indulging in every procedure that could be of some small benefit.

With insurance, however, patients face no such incentive to economize, and everything is already paid for. The presence of insurance means that more health care services are bought than would be if a patient actually had to forego alternative consumption to pay for each service; in other words, the incremental benefit of the last unit of service purchased might be less in value to the consumer than the cost to them and society of providing it. The delivery of that unit of care represents a social welfare loss, because those resources could have been spent to greater benefit in another manner. With insurance, however, that unit is provided nonetheless.

Economists call this perverse set of incentives the ***moral hazard*** of health insurance, and it is the basis of the common remark that we spend "too much" on health care. Decisions made by consumers in other markets about how much is enough are not made in the same way for health services. Copayments and deductibles are targeted precisely at this problem, and they have been shown to substantially reduce the amount of care consumed without a tremendous loss in terms of medical outcomes.[123] In general, however, we do not face the same kind of economic choice with health care that we do with other goods, and our incentive is usually to consume more than we would absent insurance.

To exaggerate matters, federal tax treatment of income spent on health insurance premiums adds further to the incentives to spend on health care, because the portion of any worker's wages devoted to health premiums in a given year is currently not subject to taxation. Assume that taxation removes one fourth of a worker's gross income; it now takes $1.33 of income to purchase one dollar's worth of stereo equipment, beer, or automobiles. But one dollar of income buys one dollar of health care, and it therefore makes sense to spend more than we otherwise might.

Why do economists not approve? After all, the tax exemption helps people obtain good coverage. Like the moral hazard problem, the tax-exempt status of health spending skews an individual's incentives to direct their spending toward goods that provide the highest benefit for the money spent. Without the tax exemption, people would likely spend less on health services, which suggests that in their valuation, alternative consumption would yield greater benefit.

Why Are Costs Rising?

Most agree that the result of the special tax treatment and moral hazard is a higher level of spending on health services. Levels of health care spending are not simply high, however; they are rapidly increasing. Although high, stagnant levels of spending might bother us; they would be unlikely to cause the clamor currently seen in the health care debate. What interests us about health spending is that it just seems to keep growing. What are the sources of the continued increases in spending?

Table 8.4 shows estimates calculated by the Office of National Health Statistics of the relative importance of particular factors behind the increases in medical spending over recent years. *General inflation* in the economy as a whole explains a large percentage of the increase in health care costs, and *sector-specific inflation* (i.e., increasing prices of health care goods) explains a little more. *Population growth* accounts for 11% of the increase in spending due to inpatient hospital care, as well as 9% of the increase in spending due to physician services during the 1980 to 1990 period. *Aging of the population* has generated much discussion, and it is often said to be a large contributor to increases in health spending, although its substantial contribution is sometimes overstated. The aging of America has us spending more, and it will continue to do so. Research has shown that the increasing proportion of elderly in the population accounts for approximately 7% of per capita medical care cost increases,[124] although many expect the contribution of aging to cost increases to diminish in the future.[125]

Utilization, or per-capita visits to the doctor or days in the hospital, is the factor most under the control of employers, the health care industry, and policy makers, and its pattern in Table 8.4 reflects the efforts of these groups. The 1980s saw introduction of several policies designed to slow the rate of increasing hospital spending, mainly by targeting the number of inpatient hospital days. Hospital cost-control measures such as the shift toward prepaid *health maintenance organizations* (HMOs), which utilize fewer hospital days, and establishment of *diagnosis-related groups* (DRGs) for reimbursement of Medicare providers helped reduce the number of hospital days during the 1980s. Indeed, the number of inpatient hospital days was reduced by as much as 28% during this time.[126] Although inpatient days decreased, however, outpatient expenses increased because services were shifted to this cheaper setting.

It is striking that although inpatient hospital days underwent such a drastic diminution in the 1980s, overall health costs slowed only somewhat. Some analysts pointed out that although the efficiencies in hospital inpatient days were being achieved, their effect was offset by the continuing upward pressure on costs resulting from diffusion of new medical technologies. *Intensity* is a measure of

Table 8.4 Factors Accounting for Growth in Expenditures for Selected Categories of National Health Expenditures

Category of Service	General Inflation[a]	Population Growth	Utilization[b]	Intensity[c]	Sector-Specific Inflation
Physician Services					
1970–1980	64.3	7.8	2.6	18.3	7.0
1980–1990	41.3	9.0	3.6	19.8	26.1
Inpatient Hospital					
1970–1980	52.9	6.4	3.6	30.0	7.1
1980–1990	51.1	11.1	−34.3	52.2	20.0
Outpatient Hospital					
1970–1980	42.0	5.1	21.6	25.6	5.7
1980–1990	28.4	6.2	19.1	35.2	11.1
Drugs & Medical Non-Durables					
1970–1980	78.7	9.6	NA	35.1	−23.4
1980–1990	48.9	10.6	NA	1.1	39.4

[a]General inflation is measured by the gross domestic product implicit price deflator
[b]Per capita visits or days
[c]Real services per day or visit
Source: Health Care Financing Administration, Office of the Actuary. Data from the Office of National Health Statistics.

the diffusion of new technological services to patients. An inpatient receiving an angiogram, for example, is subject to more "intensive" treatment than one subjected to a radiograph. The intensity of treatment for most major pathologies is currently far greater than that even just a few years ago, and the result is, most agree, constant upward pressure on costs. Technology certainly does appear to have had a large role in the increase in health spending in recent years, and it will likely continue to put tremendous pressure on spending in the future.[127] The most notable part of Table 8.4 is the "intensity" column. Indeed, from 1980 to 1990, 52% of the increase in spending on inpatient hospital care and 35% of the increase in spending on outpatient hospital services was attributed to increases in the intensity of care.

There are myriad medical treatments currently available that were unheard of just 10 or 15 years ago, treatments that add to length or quality of life—at great cost. Some examples help illustrate the point. Transplantation of heart, liver, kidney and bone marrow, once unheard of, is occurring at an ever-increasing rate, and it is resulting in longer, costlier lives for patients. Pharmaceuticals have made huge strides in recent years in both medical value and cost (e.g., monoclonal antibodies, erythropoietin), and advances in biological research promise much more. Noninvasive diagnostic imaging has undergone its own revolution with mainstream use of MRI, computed tomography (CT) scans, and positron emission tomography (PET); each year, these technologies become more sophisticated and are used in broader sets of clinical circumstances.

Although technological advances may reduce costs for selected patients, their aggregate effect is usually to increase costs. Consider the case of a patient with a difficult-to-diagnose clinical presentation whose diagnosis in the past would have required costly, risky invasive surgery. Although MRI is probably cheaper than that surgery, it is so risk-free that there is little reason for the physician not to order one, and it will be performed far more than the old method. The diagnosis could lead to costly treatment that was itself unavailable prior to the development of MRI. Although delivery of any particular unit of care is made cheaper by advances in technology, the high-technology package of care includes many more aggressive diagnostic and therapeutic procedures, all of which will involve an added cost.

Furthermore, many costly surgical procedures once confined to narrow clinical situations are performed for ever-larger clinical populations. Liver transplantation, which at one time excluded alcoholics, and heart transplantations, which were once not done on the elderly or for those suffering from additional illness, are now performed much more frequently due to liberalization of eligibility criteria, decreased procedural risk, and decreased cost. Such treatments are currently commonplace at most large teaching hospitals, and as expertise continues to develop for these procedures, they will be deemed safe for even broader populations. All these forces put tremendous pressure on health costs and premiums.

POLICY OPTIONS FOR COST CONTAINMENT ❖

Many analysts have said that *the key to understanding health care costs and how to reduce them lies in the distinction between the level of current spending and its rate of growth.*[128] At any moment in time, the amount or level of spending includes some fixed amount of waste that could be eliminated for greater efficiency, but in general, the bulk of the rate of increase in spending is attributable to advances in technology that provide real benefits to patients. Keeping costs down over time would involve not only elimination of wasteful spending, but also denial of many benefits of some costly medical technologies. Were every last bit of wasteful spending expunged from our system, the resultant savings would shortly be wiped out as the continued stream of medical advances provided ever-more beneficial services.

We next turn to describing some general policy approaches for containing health care costs. Note especially for each whether it seems to address the level of costs or the rate of increase. A good example is provided by the widespread calls for more people to be enrolled in HMOs or other prepaid managed care plans. At any moment in time, the average costs incurred by an enrollee in an HMO are low relative to those in traditional fee-for-service plans, but these costs tend to increase each year at about the same rate. Shifting more Americans into HMOs saves money, but only in the sense of bailing water from the canoe without plugging the leak. The underlying rate of increase, resulting from introduction and utilization of new technologies and the other factors mentioned, are unaffected by this financing arrangement. Unless patterns of care are altered so that costly new technologies are rationed, managed care is likely to do only so much to keep costs down over time.[129]

Tort Reform

The area of physician malpractice is frequently discussed in the purview of cost containment. Fear of litigation appears often as a cost culprit, because many say it compels physicians to order more tests and services for patients than they would absent the threat of legal action. Such "defensive medicine" results in large amounts of wasteful spending by many accounts, and caps on the level of malpractice awards are offered as a cost-reducing option. The actual effects on health costs of malpractice, however, are difficult to measure.

Analysts at the American Medical Association report that defensive medicine imposed additional costs to physician services of $13.7 and $15.1 billion in 1984 and 1989, respectively.[130] This is a large amount, but total spending on health services during this period increased from $390 billion to $603 billion, meaning that defensive medicine by these estimates could have contributed only marginally to the growth in expenditures during this period. Notably, the average physician's malpractice insurance premiums are currently higher than 10 years ago, but they represent about the same proportion of income.[131] For more on tort reform and malpractice issues in general, see Chapter 15.

Reducing Administrative Costs

The area of *administrative costs* (i.e., processing insurance claims) is another in which many say there are large potential savings to be achieved. Recall that the $44 billion under the heading of insurance in Table 8.2 does not include the costs to hospitals and physicians themselves associated with processing claims; these costs, and there is no small controversy over how large these costs are, show up in the category for the provider's services. Those who favor a single-payer, Canadian-style financing system argue that the presence of an insurance industry and the Byzantine system of reimbursement that currently exists in the U.S. greatly adds to overall health costs. With only one insurer, there is no issue of determining eligibility, and much of the red tape of the current system would be done away with. Even if reducing administrative costs could reduce the level of costs, however, it would be hard to argue that this reduction would have any effect on the growth in spending.

Reducing the Number of Hospital Beds

Many have observed that there is an apparently high number of empty beds in the nation's hospitals at most points in time, and low-occupancy hospitals are frequently mentioned as a source of potential savings. Although it is true that many hospitals have a low average census with chronically empty beds, it is difficult to determine what is waste when confounding factors such as allowances for seasonal variations are considered. More important, however, is the fact that empty beds tend to impose little in the way of costs to hospitals, because the overwhelming bulk of a hospital's expenses are in the area of labor and supplies. Shutting down low-occupancy hospitals is likely at any rate to simply force patients and their costs to move on to the next hospital; therefore, it is hard to say what sort of savings we could achieve in this area.

Prepaid Group Practices

HMOs and other managed care arrangements are a key component of many cost-containment proposals. What characterizes the disparate variety of such organizations is an attempt to remove the incentives for overutilization of medical resources through some internalization of delivery and financing of care. In the simplest case of the traditional fee-for-service arrangement, insurers simply reimburse providers for any services delivered; providers therefore have little motive for efficient delivery. An HMO, however, combines the functions of insurance and delivery of care, and the profit-maximizing incentive at any premium level is to provide medical services as cheaply and efficiently as possible. As noted earlier, HMOs have been shown to cost less than their fee-for-service counterparts. Many point out, however, that those enrolled in these programs tend to be healthier people with less medical risk, people who should be expected to incur lesser costs. HMO enrollees, for example, are disproportionately young. See Chapter 5 for a more in-depth look at managed care and how it may or may not save money.

Competitive Markets

In a competitive market, suppliers of goods or services compete with each other to offer their product to consumers at the lowest cost, and consumers base purchasing decisions on the attributes of the product and its comparative price. If a producer believes they can offer a comparable product at a price lower than that of their competitors, they will do so, thus stealing their business. The result of market competition, economists tell us, is an efficient allocation of resources with prices as low as appropriate given the demand and the costs of delivering the service.

Prepaid health plans, with their emphasis on efficient delivery, are popular among advocates of free-market competition. Many such advocates go a step further, and their ideas might be as follows. Purchasers of health care, for the reasons discussed earlier, do not face the true cost of their health plans. Moreover, they have difficulty choosing health plans on the basis of price because different plans offer different kinds of benefits. If competitors offered identical low-cost basic benefits packages, and if the employer contribution to the costs of this package were uniform and the tax exemption was eliminated or reduced, then the consumer would face the full cost of their choice of plans if they chose one more expensive than the basic benefits package. Consumers would then be able to base their judgments on the price and value of the product, just as they do in the markets for other goods, and producers would keep prices low to beat out competitors. The rate of increase in premium costs and overall spending would likely be slowed; if it did continue to increase, it would reflect real cost-benefit judgments by consumers, and it would therefore not cause the worry to policy makers seen in the current market.

These are some of the important aspects of managed competition, which is the basis for many proposals for health reform. See Chapter 14 for more on federal proposals that include these ideas.

Single-Payer Financing

A universal coverage system financed exclusively by government is an old and enduring idea for reform, although it appears to have been left out of the Clinton Administration's Health Security Bill. Its proponents offer arguments based on issues of fairness and equity, as well as costs. Canada and several European nations have health systems that fit this broad description, and they certainly maintain lower levels of spending per capita than the U.S. As noted earlier, one of the principal arguments as to why this difference is true has to do with administration; with only one source of payment and universal eligibility, much of the costly and tedious process of filing, verifying, and processing claims is obviated. Exactly how much could be saved is a source of much dispute.

Perhaps more important in terms of cost containment is such a scheme's relative advantage in controlling the diffusion of costly medical technologies. Canada and European nations serve as good examples of how such government-financed arrangements can inhibit the kind of rapid technological diffusion that drives cost increases. Oversight of central and regional government bodies with regard to purchasing health care facilities and capital investment can help keep total levels of spending down.

An obvious criticism of the single-payer approach is that it invariably leads to denial of medical services of great value to many people. Great Britain, for example, enjoys very low levels of spending, but it is famous for its chronic shortages of facilities and long queues for procedures, such as hip replacements. The very fact of low levels of spending means that less care is being purchased, and the very same phenomenon occurs in Canada and other nations with such financing arrangements, which spend far less on health than the U.S. The popularity of these health systems in Great Britain and Canada probably reflects a simple difference in values between citizens of these nations and Americans, and many argue that Americans would have far less tolerance for a system that frequently placed ill people on waiting lists for much-needed services. Others, however, believe the rationing carried out under single-payer systems may be the only way to reduce cost growth in the long run. Chapter 12 describes in more detail the single-payer systems of Canada and Great Britain.

Price Regulation

Many argue that the medical marketplace should be regulated to ensure that suppliers of goods and services are unable to increase prices above levels viewed as fair or equitable. This argument has been made with particular reference to the pharmaceutical industry, because it is often perceived as having inflated the prices of many drugs to levels high above the actual cost of production. Such advocates point to the profit margins of many firms in the pharmaceutical business, which are frequently among the highest of any firms in the country. Some members of Congress have long advocated that price controls be placed on certain pharmaceutical products to make them more affordable to patients, and others make similar arguments regarding physician services in general. Needless to say, the industry is a vociferous opponent of such ideas, and it points out that revenues from its products help cover the costs of research and development. Without such research, the industry argues, many beneficial drugs could not be developed and made available, and without the incentive of high potential profits, there is less reason for entrepreneurial firms to experiment with new technologies.

Global Budgeting

Although *global budgeting* is usually associated with single-payer systems, it can be implemented with or without such a financing scheme. With a global budget, the government would simply set overall limits on the amount of national health spending in an effort to control the rate of growth of health spending. A proposal forwarded by the Clinton Administration would establish a national Board that would set such limits for the entire health care system. Additional mechanisms would be established to set limits for states, districts, and individual providers. A hospital, for example, would not be permitted to receive reimbursement from payers in excess of the level established for it under the budget cap.

Many believe a global budget combined with managed competition is the best solution. A budget cap is necessary with managed competition, some argue, for the following reasons.

✧   Managed competition might not actually succeed in substantially slowing the rate of increase in spending, or it might not do so for a number of years, because, among other reasons, people still might not understand the incentive to shift to low-cost programs.

✧   Providers would continue to compete to attract the best physicians through procuring all the latest medical technologies, thus increasing costs. A capped budget for providers would be the only way to force these institutions to spend less.

Critics of the budget cap approach point out that hospitals and other provider institutions have been adept at shifting costs to avoid such budget limits. For example, to avoid the effect of a budget constraint, a hospital might simply increase the services taking place in remote, outpatient settings. The cap is avoided, yet the health system still bears the cost. The difficulties associated with making a budget cap work could be tremendous.

RATIONING HEALTH SERVICES ❖

We have seen that although targeting areas such as physician malpractice and administration might lower the level of health expenditures, it will likely have little effect on the rate of growth. The major proposals to regulate this growth, such as global budgeting, all are based on the premise that the dilemma of increasing health care costs is essentially one of controlling diffusion of costly medical technologies. Modern medicine can and will provide far more in the way of valuable treatments than we as a society can finance under any kind of arrangement.

Assuming for a moment that some kind of overall budget limit is put in place, with either managed competition or a Canadian-style single-payer system, the amount of health care purchased in the country will depend on the size of the budget, and, at some point, physicians will have to start saying no. The decision of the budget-setting Board as to the proper amount for total spending is obviously a political one, but assuming that society does not want to permit rapid cost increases to continue indefinitely, rationing of some health services will invariably be necessary. Difficult ethical, economic, and political decisions will have to be made as to what kinds of services will be provided or denied to whom. How might such decisions be made?

A fundamental result from economics holds that a consumer, faced with a limited budget and a wide range of needs and wants, will most efficiently allocate their budget so that the last dollar spent on each kind of good provides no less benefit than any possible alternative; in an efficient state, this last dollar cannot be spent in any other manner to yield greater benefit. The added benefits of any good are not constant over increased amounts. For example, starting from zero, the first unit of food one consumes is of tremendous value, the second less so, and so on. Eventually, the added benefits from more food (or higher-quality food) will diminish. Before reaching the point at which these added benefits disappear, however, one is likely to divert funds to areas in which the added benefits are greater (i.e., heating oil or clothing).

This concept has implications for how a hospital might be forced to operate under a limited budget in the event that health reform imposes such a constraint. Assume for a moment that a budget cap is set on hospitals and they may not exceed its limit on spending without penalty. Administrators would have to make decisions about what sorts of services to provide and what not to provide. They will likely find themselves unable to permit physicians the freedom to order costly diagnostic tests whenever these tests might be expected to have some value. They might not be able to offer costly therapies for some patients who are unlikely to survive or benefit appreciably. Administrators would hopefully optimize a hospital's patterns of care under a budget cap so that its resources could not be rearranged to provide much larger benefits. Therefore, the lowest-valued, although still positively valued, uses of many treatments and procedures would be truncated.

Consider the hospital's dilemma. Nonionic contrast media, a fairly recent innovation that enhances diagnostic imaging while posing less health risk than the old media, is valuable, but it costs several times more than the old material; to use it under a limited budget, the hospital must forego other valuable possibilities. Bone marrow transplantations have been shown to have positive effects on women with breast cancer. How widely should this treatment be used for this patient population, given that these small health benefits come at a very high cost? If a periodic flexible sigmoidoscopy for men over 40 years has been shown to reduce deaths from colon cancer, should it become routine when this approach would involve tremendous added costs?

Treatments and procedures that are costly yet unlikely to yield substantial benefits will have to be denied to patients. At some level, clinical thresholds for medical intervention will have to be established that will demand, for example, substantial clinical abnormalities to exist before a physician could order a costly diagnostic procedure, such as MRI.

This discussion leaves out the nettlesome question of whose services are to be rationed. Will a hospital budget cap mean that services could be denied even to those with extensive insurance or to those willing and able to pay cash? Or will such limits apply only to persons with limited coverage or those on government-financed health programs? Oregon has already started to grapple with such issues in its Medicaid program (see Chapter 13), but it seems inevitable that all of us will soon face these same hard questions. We believe it will be imperative that physicians and other clinicians take an active role in such debates, and we hope you will feel comfortable enough with the issues to participate.

❖ Suggested Reading ❖

Aaron HJ. Serious and unstable condition: financing America's health care. Washington, DC: Brookings, 1991.

An excellent review of U.S. health care finance, with a good overall discussion of health care costs.

Newhouse JP. An iconoclastic view of health cost containment. Health Affairs 1993;12 (suppl):152–171.

A systematic look at why health costs are increasing, which concludes that the real reason is improving technology, and that increasing health costs may not be as bad as some feel.

Schwartz WB. The inevitable failure of current cost-containment strategies: why they can provide only temporary relief. JAMA 1987;257:220–224.

An argument for why rationing may be the only real way to slow the growth of health costs.

Access

Tamara L. Callahan and Ronald David

Many people feel that the most pressing problem facing the United States (U.S.) health care system is the lack of access to health care for many residents. Currently, 37 million Americans are uninsured, and millions more are underinsured. However, health insurance coverage is only one of several factors that influence access to health care.

This chapter provides an overview of the access issue, as well as the cultural, social, and political issues surrounding the access debate. It also identifies the barriers to access, the people most affected by those barriers, as well as the consequences of inadequate health care services for these underserved populations. Finally, we discuss several proposals for increasing health care access.

OVERVIEW OF ACCESS IN THE U.S. ❖

Unequal access to care and the disparate health status of disenfranchised communities has been a central theme in public health and policy debates for some time. Despite technological advances and annual expenditures of more than $900 billion, the U.S. still lags behind most industrialized nations in providing health insurance for all its citizens (Figure 9.1). In fact, the U.S. is one of the only major industrialized nations that does not guarantee health insurance for all its residents.[132]

Many have come to associate the term *access* with the availability of health insurance, doctors, and health care facilities. However, the availability of these resources does not guarantee that people who need care will receive it. Therefore,

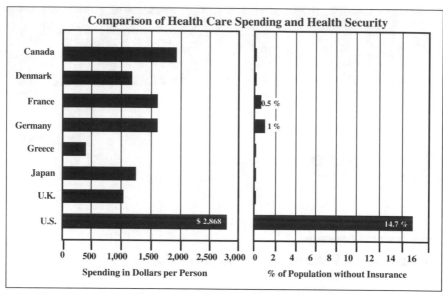

Figure 9.1 Comparison of health care spending per person in each of eight countries and percentage of the insured population within each of those countries. The U.S. ranks 19th in infant mortality rates, 21st in life expectancy for men, and 16th in life expectancy for women. Data source: Organization of Economic Cooperation and Development; Department of Health and Human Resources. (Adapted from The White House Domestic Policy Council, 1993. The President's Health Security Plan.)

for the purposes of this chapter, access to health care services will be defined as the set of factors that affect the potential and the actual ability of an individual or a group to acquire timely and appropriate health care services.[133] Lack of access, by extension, is likely to exist when there are systematic differences between groups in the utilization of health care resources or health status.

Traditionally, access to health care services has been limited on the bases of race, gender, age, and class. Vulnerable groups have included women and children, people of color, the poor, and the elderly.[134] These populations have had poorer health outcomes despite, in many cases, a greater expenditure of resources for emergency and intensive care services due to delays in the seeking of health care.[135] Although not discussed herein, additional populations at risk of inadequate access are the chronically ill, the mentally ill, persons with the acquired immunodeficiency syndrome (AIDS), substance abusers, homeless individuals, immigrants, survivors of abuse, and high-risk mothers and infants.[136]

Currently, however, access to health care is no longer a concern only among the disadvantaged. Public opinion polls reveal that most Americans are concerned that their access to health care is increasingly limited, especially as it is affected by cost. Coupled with confidence that medical care is effective in improving health and the quality of life, there is a shared belief that no citizen should be without ba-

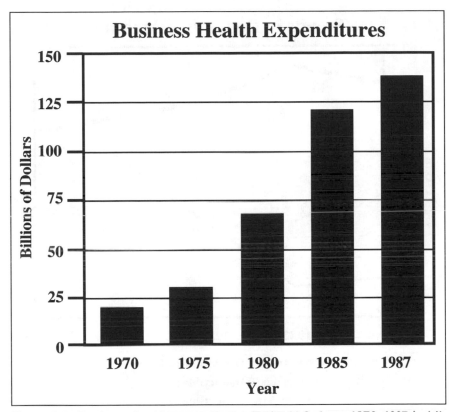

Figure 9.2 Business health expenditures in the U.S. from 1970–1987 in billions of dollars. Source: Health Care Financing Administration, Office of the Actuary. (Adapted from U.S. Surgeon General Accounting Office, 1990.)

sic services.[137] However, Americans are much further from consensus when it comes to defining which services should be considered basic and, more importantly, determining how (and by whom) those services will be paid. Paul Starr succinctly argues that " . . . the issue of universal health insurance is on the agenda, not so much because of the continuing failure to provide care for the excluded, but because of the economic impact of uncontrolled health costs and the increased jeopardy of the middle class."[138]

Many proposals have been set forth in an effort to address the multifaceted problem of obtaining access to health care. The range of proposals is as varied as the many barriers that block access to care. These proposals range in approach and breadth from universal health plans to expanding employer-based insurance to training more minority physicians to support for individualized transformation to counter institutionalized racism, sexism, and social class ostracism. No matter what the approach, increasing access is on the national agenda, and national health reform will likely focus on it.

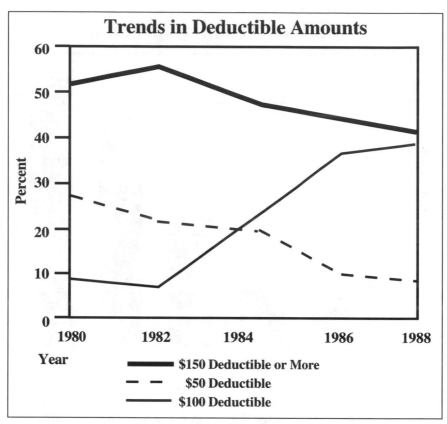

Figure 9.3 Trends in deductible amounts in medical plans with deductible, in medium-size and large firms from 1980 to 1988. (Source: BLS. Adapted from U.S. Surgeon General Accounting Office, 1990.)

WHO ARE THE UNINSURED AND THE UNDERINSURED? ❖

Much of the attention centered on the lack of access to health care has focused on the problem of the uninsured. We start by looking first at who exactly are the uninsured, and the underinsured, and why, and then we turn to a broader discussion of other barriers to access.

The Effects of Poverty

As health care reform has moved to the national agenda, America's middle class has grown more concerned that efforts to increase access to the poor will, on average, result in fewer choices and services for them. This belief is rooted in the

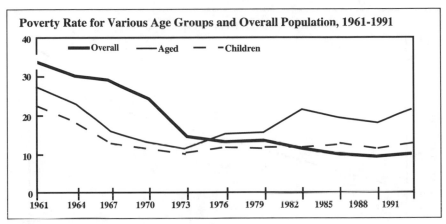

Figure 9.4 Poverty rates of aged, children, and the overall population from 1961 to 1991. (Source: U.S. Bureau of the Census. Adapted from Subcommittee on Human Resources, 1993.)

misperception that the uninsured are composed solely of indigent people. This belief ignores the multifactorial determinants of insurance coverage, such as age, sex, race, family type, geography, and employment status. Although economic status is an important indicator of insurance status, the ranks of the uninsured are by no means limited to the poor, the unemployed, or those on public aid.[139]

There is no doubt, however, that the poor and the disenfranchised have been hardest hit by the attempted measures to control escalating health care costs. Since 1978, there has been a slow but substantial increase in the number of United States residents living in households with incomes below the poverty level (Figure 9.4)[140] Although the ranks of the poor have continued to increase, the number of people without private insurance has also dramatically increased by 47% from 1980 to 1985 (Figure 9.5).[141] Nationally, since 1978 there has been a 40% increase in the number of uninsured, which topped more than 35 million in 1991,[142] including 9.5 million children under 18 (14.6% of all children).[143] Changes in state Medicaid eligibility requirements are partially responsible for a decrease in the proportion of poor families covered by Medicaid, from 66.0% in 1979 to only 46% in 1985.[144]

Employment Status

Despite stereotypes to the contrary, 85% of the uninsured live in families headed by full-time or part-time workers in 1991 (Figure 9.6). Some of these workers chose not to purchase insurance or could not afford it, but many of the working uninsured are never offered insurance by their employers.[145] In fact, 13.5% of all employed individuals were uninsured in 1991, and the percentage continues to increase.[146] Table 9.1 shows that child and adult dependents of workers comprised 31.3% (11.4 million) of the total uninsured in 1991, whereas workers themselves

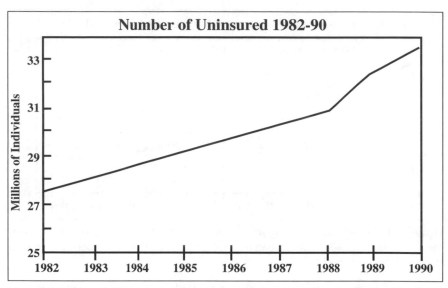

Figure 9.5 Graph illustrates the increase in the number of uninsured individuals in the U.S. from 1982 to 1990. Note the years 1982 through 1987 are estimates. (Source: Health Care Financing Administration, Office of the Actuary. Adapted from U.S. Surgeon General Accounting Office, 1990.)

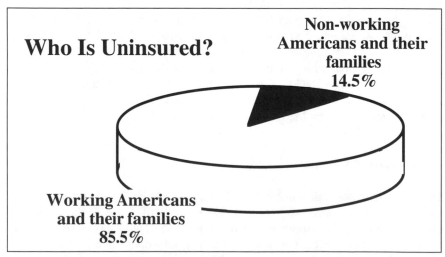

Figure 9.6 Source: 1990 data, Employee Benefits Research Institute, 1992. Adapted from White House Domestic Policy Council 1993.

Table 9.1   Dependent Coverage by Employment Status of Head of Family

Family Head	Number without Health Insurance (Millions)	Percentage of Total without Health Insurance
Worker (full time/full year)	9.7	26.6%
Adult dependents	2.1	5.9%
Children	5.5	15.0%
Others workers	10.8	29.8%
Adult dependents	1.0	2.6%
Children	2.8	7.8%
Non-worker	2.0	5.6%
Adult dependents	1.2	3.2%
Children	1.2	3.4%
TOTAL	36.3	100.0%

Source: Employee Benefit Research Institute, Issue Brief #133, 1993.

comprised 56.4% of the total. Clearly, when health insurance is not offered as a benefit of employment, the impact affects not only the worker, but their dependents as well.

Geographic Distribution

There is a wide variation among states in the proportion of the population without insurance or those who are underinsured (Figure 9.7). The District of Columbia, for example, had the highest proportion of uninsured in 1991 (30.3%), followed by Texas (25.3%), New Mexico (24.5%), and Florida (23.5%). Connecticut had the smallest percentage of uninsured in 1991 (8.8%), followed by Hawaii (9.0%), North Dakota (9.2%), and Pennsylvania (9.4%). These state-by-state differences reflect not only different employment and economic conditions and demographic profiles, but also variation in state funding of public insurance programs, such as Medicaid.

The Underinsured

Just as the number of uninsured has increased dramatically, so has the number of underinsured—the segment of the U.S. population that has health insurance that may be inadequate in the event of serious illness. The Congressional Budget Office defines the underinsured as any person with out-of-pocket expenditures for health care that exceed 10% of income.[147] Bodenheimer maintains

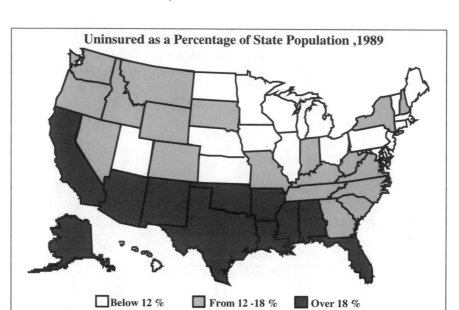

Uninsured as a Percentage of State Population ,1989

☐ Below 12 %　　■ From 12 -18 %　　■ Over 18 %

Figure 9.7 Graphic representation of the uninsured population by percentage of each state's population (1989). (Source: Current Population Survey, Bureau of the Census (3/1990). Adapted from U.S. Surgeon General Accounting Office, 1990.)

that there are six major causes of high out-of-pocket expenditures in the U.S. health system.[148]

✦　Lack of adequate coverage for catastrophic medical expenses due to dollar limits on lifetime medical benefits.

✦　Exclusion from coverage or long waiting periods (mean = 9 mos) for coverage of pre-existing conditions when new coverage is obtained (most commonly at a new job).

✦　Certain benefits (vaccinations, well-baby care, and routine physical examinations) are often not covered by private insurance.

✦　Widespread and increasing use of deductibles and coinsurance payments by employment-based group health plans.

✦　Medicare, even when supplemented by Medigap (i.e., optional coverage purchased to supplement Medicare benefits) fails to provide complete coverage for medical expenses.

✦　The high cost and virtual nonexistence of any coverage for long-term care (97% is out-of-pocket expenditures).

These stark statistics aptly demonstrate how changes in the structure and financing of health care have adversely impacted middle America as well as business, medical, and insurance communities. In short, access to health care in the 1990s is no longer an issue germane only to the poor and the disenfranchised.

BARRIERS TO ACCESS ❖

In addition to the lack of adequate insurance, there are many other reasons why many in the population do not have good access to health care. Barriers to access may be grouped into three broad categories: the inability to pay, sociocultural obstacles to care, and organizational problems with the structure of the health care delivery system.

Inability to Pay

Inability to pay most commonly results from lack of or insufficient insurance coverage or inadequate provider reimbursement rates, which result in fewer physicians caring for patients.

Lack of or Insufficient Insurance Coverage

We have already discussed the reason why so many Americans are either uninsured or underinsured. Even Americans who are fortunate enough to receive some health insurance through their employment have been faced with increasing premiums compounded by decreasing benefits. Others are seeing higher copayments and deductibles. For many, changing jobs represents a risk because it is difficult to obtain similar or adequate coverage with a new employer. Likewise, patients considered as "high risk" due to pre-existing medical conditions fear having their policies canceled and losing coverage altogether.[149] The phenomenon of remaining with a current employer because of the fear of losing current health insurance benefits when switching jobs is known as *job lock*.

Inadequate Provider Reimbursement Rates

One means the government has employed to control health care expenditures is to limit the amount of provider reimbursement for Medicaid patients. Because Medicaid reimbursement is often significantly less than the customary charge for services, providers have become less willing to care for Medicaid patients. As a result, patients with Medicaid as a primary source of health insurance have had a difficult time finding private physicians who will care for them, and they are often forced to rely on treatment from public facilities.[150]

Sociocultural Barriers

Sociocultural barriers are increasingly being recognized as important deterrents to access. In fact, these barriers, which are separate from financial barriers, may be responsible for much of the persistent racial disparities in health outcomes.

Provider/Staff Attitudes

Many authors have documented the difficult relationships and communication failures that occur between health care providers and low income patients.[151] These difficulties include poor communication about procedures, failure to answer questions, and hurried or otherwise impersonal caregiving. This relationship is fostered by organizational strategies that place a premium on seeing large volumes of patients. The result is often hurried visits, lack of continuity of care, long clinic waits, and poor patient-doctor communication. Likewise, differences in the socioeconomic and cultural backgrounds of providers and patients may greatly contribute to communications problems.[152]

Language Incompatibility

Adding to these difficulties are language incompatibilities between providers and patients. With the exception of relatively large communities where a single, non-English language is spoken, most facilities are ill-equipped to handle language barriers. Ad hoc solutions, such as using a patient's child or relative as an interpreter or utilizing auxiliary clinic staff (who have full-time duties in other capacities), still leave much to be desired.[153] Even though patient compliance and satisfaction with the care rendered are greatly improved by having providers and staff members who are bilingual, the curriculum committees of medical schools and residency training programs have not embraced the idea of offering language training, even on a voluntary basis.

Cultural Preferences

In addition to language barriers, health care providers seem unwilling or unable to accommodate different cultural beliefs of their patients. Although it is not reasonable to think that every cultural belief can be incorporated into a physician's caregiving plan, little has been done to sensitize providers to the cultural beliefs of their patients and the need to accommodate them when possible. Unfortunately, in traditional patient-doctor relationships, fear of physician disapproval or ridicule prevents many patients from revealing their beliefs about certain medications, surgery, alternative healers, and cultural therapies. For example, in some Hispanic and Asian cultures, it is unacceptable to have a pelvic examination performed by a man. However, if these women insist on only being seen by female physicians or nurses, they may be labeled as difficult or ungrateful by providers and staff.[154]

Fear of Deportation

Another factor that influences health care utilization by many minority and low income individuals is their illegal alien status, which leaves them in constant fear of deportation by the Immigration and Naturalization Service. As such, many illegal immigrants do not seek traditional forms of health care, and they may delay care for themselves and their children nearly to the point of death. This practice results in unacceptable excesses in morbidity and mortality for these families, as well as dramatic increases in treatment-intensive health care expenditures.[155]

Organizational Barriers

Many of the difficulties in gaining access to health care result from the structure of the health care delivery system, including availability or organization of services or problems with quantity and quality of resources. In his work on barriers to prenatal care, Brown divides the barriers innate in the delivery system into inadequate organizational capacity and problems with the organization and atmosphere of delivery systems.[156]

Inadequate Capacity

Traditionally, health care services for the uninsured have been provided outside the private office system, in community health centers, hospital outpatient departments, and public health departments. Unfortunately, the structure of these often poorly funded delivery systems poses barriers to access, including an inadequate number of clinics, an inadequate number of appointment slots, and long waiting periods for appointments.

Capacity issues also include a shortage of health care providers in some regions due to an uneven distribution of physicians nationally. In fact, despite the growing number of physicians in the U.S. (Table 9.2), many rural and inner-city communities still have difficulty recruiting and maintaining health care providers, or they have no available providers at all.[157]

Table 9.2   Decade-by-Decade Growth in Numbers of Physicians per Person (Annual Rate of Increase)

Year	% Change
1930–1940	0.6
1940–1950	−0.6
1950–1960	−0.1
1960–1970	1.1
1970–1980	2.4
1980–1990	2.0

Source: Health, United States, 1989. (Table 85). The figure for 1990 is a projection. 1930 and 1940 figures from Physicians for a Growing America: Report of the Surgeon General's Consultant Group on Medical Education, F. Bane, Chrm., Table 1.

Problems with Organization and Atmosphere of Delivery Systems

Brown identifies four major barriers in organization and delivery of health care services that limit access for the poor and the disenfranchised, including lack of coordination of services, difficulties in obtaining Medicaid coverage, difficulties securing transportation, and child care coupled with inconvenient clinic hours and long waits, as well as other personal factors.

Lack of Coordination of Services

In addition to health care services, the poor are often in need of additional services to assist with housing, education, Medicaid, nutrition, and the plethora of other human service agencies. Problems in organizing these services for patients limit their ability to obtain comprehensive care. Because of funding limitations for many of these organizations, there are relatively few formalized linkages between groups. As such, a patient, particularly one with little money or knowledge of the system, can become easily overwhelmed and unnecessarily taxed by a system that is unable to coordinate all of the needed services in one area.[158]

Problems Securing Medicaid Coverage

Another major obstacle in the structure of the health care delivery system is the complex process of securing Medicaid coverage, which is the major source of payment for poor patients. Because Medicaid programs rarely publicize their benefits or enrollment procedures, many people are simply unaware of the services, their eligibility, or how to apply. Even for those that know about available Medicaid coverage, many find additional barriers in the application process, which is fraught with lengthy applications (averaging 14 pages and 80–100 questions), extensive documentation requirements, and long delays between time of application, notification of eligibility, and receipt of the Medicaid card. Combined with the vast variation in benefits and eligibility requirements from state to state, the complexity of the Medicaid application process can be a major deterrent to health care accessibility.[159]

Transportation Barriers

Lack of transportation for most patients is very closely associated with poverty; as such, it can be an obstacle to securing health care. For instance, many individuals with limited incomes are forced to travel long distances by public transportation to reach available health care services, many others cannot afford the cost of public transportation, and still others live in areas where mass transportation is limited or nonexistent. In each case, lack of available or affordable transportation poses a major barrier to health care access.[160]

Child Care Barrier

Similarly, for women with children, the availability of affordable, convenient child care can be a major determinant in utilization of health care services. When these services are unavailable or unaffordable, a mother may be forced to bring all her children to appointments. For a mother dealing with long clinic waiting lines in small reception areas, the burden of bringing children to an appointment may outweigh the benefits of keeping the appointment for that family, particularly for a well visit.[161]

Clinic Hours and Waiting Periods
Likewise, inconvenient office hours (usually 9 to 5 at many neighborhood health centers) can limit a person's ability to obtain health care if the person works or attends school. For individuals who work from 9 to 5, the only option for obtaining care is during the lunch hour; unfortunately, many clinics do not see patients at this time. Therefore, for individuals who work or attend school, taking time for a medical visit can mean lost time from work or school, lost wages, or increased expenses for child care.[162] This problem is exacerbated by long waits before being seen, which can be routine in publicly financed clinics.[163]

Personal Factors
Many other personal factors are likely to influence utilization of health care services, such as the patient's perception of what constitutes a health problem for them and their dependents. Conflicts between the patient's and the provider's interpretation of the seriousness of an illness or the necessity of a particular treatment can vary widely and can result in decreased utilization of services when the disparities are too wide. Similarly, an individual's fear of hospitals, doctors, or procedures can be a primary reason for not seeking care or for perceiving health care services and personnel as inaccessible.[164]

CONSEQUENCES OF POOR ACCESS ❖
Poor Health Outcomes

Lack of health care, real or perceived, is a major contributor to excess morbidity and mortality in the U.S.[165] The lack of adequate coverage has resulted in poorer health care outcomes and inefficient use of resources for traditionally underserved groups—the working poor, people of color, and women and children. Lack of access to health care has differentially affected the health care outcomes of the most vulnerable populations. Although it would be impossible to describe the full impact of inadequate access to health care services on health outcomes, the following briefly describes the general influence of lack of access on vulnerable groups.

The Uninsured
Lurie and colleagues compared health outcomes for two groups of low income individuals originally covered by Medi-Cal (the California Medicaid program). One

group retained coverage and another was dropped by Medi-Cal. Lurie found that the prevalence of uncontrolled diabetes and hypertension was significantly increased in the group dropped from coverage compared with the other group.[166]

Similarly, in 1991, Hadley, Steinberg, and Feder used hospital discharge data to examine the utilization and mortality rates for the uninsured. They found that the uninsured were 29 to 75% less likely to get specialized services (i.e., high cost or high-discretion procedures), and they were 1.2 to 3.2 times more likely to die while hospitalized, compared with privately insured patients of similar health status. These findings support previous studies that show the amount and type of health care provided to an individual in the U.S. is directly related to whether the individual has insurance.[167]

Minorities

In 1987, Baquet and Ringen used National Cancer Institute data to investigate the incidence and mortality of cervical cancer for black and white women. Their findings showed that, although the mortality rate of cervical cancer had declined for both groups between 1975 and 1984, black women continued to show mortality two to three times higher than white women. The American Cancer Society found that survival rates for cancer of the uterus in white women has increased over the past 13 years, but the survival rate for black women actually decreased in 1987.[168] Similarly, an American Cancer Society study on breast cancer (the number one cause of cancer death in black women) revealed that, although black women are less likely to get breast cancer than white women, black women are more likely to die from the disease.[169] The major reason for these findings, according to Baquet and Ringen, were inequalities in the distribution of health resources, not genetic or biological factors.

Some critics argue that the interplay of poverty, insurance, and race make it impossible to ascertain the true cause of racial discrepancies in health care outcomes. Investigating this issue, Whittle and co-workers performed a retrospective analysis of the use of cardiovascular procedures among black and white veterans discharged from Veterans Administration (VA) hospitals with the primary diagnosis of cardiovascular disease or chest pain during fiscal years 1987 to 1991.[170] After adjusting for potential confounders, they found that white veterans are more likely to receive cardiac catherization, angioplasty, and coronary artery bypass surgery than black veterans with comparable clinical profiles (Table 9.3). Their finding suggests that *even in the absence of financial incentives,* social or clinical factors influence the use of life-saving procedures in white and black patients.

Children

In his 1985 study of health care utilization impact on children's health status, Rosenbach found that low income children without private insurance or Medicaid

Table 9.3   Relative Risk for the Use of Procedures Among
Whites as Compared with Blacks with Cardiovascular
Diagnoses, Adjusted for Potential Confounders

Diagnosis Group	Cardiac Catheterization	PTCA	CABG
All patients	1.38 (1.34–1.42)	1.50 (1.38–1.64)	2.22 (2.09–2.36)
Unstable angina	1.55 (1.43–1.67)	1.62 (1.34–1.96)	2.30 (2.01–2.64)
Chronic ischemia	1.26 (1.18–1.36)	1.13 (0.96–1.32)	1.75 (1.58–1.94)
Myocardial infarction	1.13 (1.05–1.21	1.55 (1.33–1.82)	1.90 (1.64–2.20)
Angina	1.33 (1.21–1.46)	1.52 (1.13–2.06)	2.67 (2.16–3.31)
All ischemic diagnosis	1.30 (1.25–1.35)	1.41 (1.29–1.55)	2.03 (1.90–2.17)
All ischemic diagnosis, NSC	1.32 (1.26–1.39)	1.38 (1.22–1.55)	2.01 (1.85–2.19)

Figures adjusted for primary diagnosis, age, coexisting morbidity, region, CABG center, year and
VA eligibility status. Digits in parentheses represent 95% confidence interval. NSC-non-service connected category A eligibility. (Adapted from Whittle, 1993.)

coverage were more likely to go without physician care (36%) than children with
private insurance (4%) or children covered by Medicaid (25%). Studies have
shown that Medicaid is an important factor in improving health care access for
children, but only 30% of poor children are covered by these services.[171] Furthermore, cutbacks in state and federal Medicaid funding has further curtailed children's access to health care.[172]

Incredibly, the immunization rate of children in the U.S. has significantly
deteriorated over the past decade, leading to a resurgence of otherwise preventable childhood diseases, such as measles and mumps. Despite the fact that
laws in every state require full immunization of children by the time they enter
school, an estimated 1.2 million children under the age of 2 have not been immunized against vaccine-preventable diseases, a record far worse than most developed nations.[173]

Emergent and Delayed Care

Currently, lack of access to adequate health care services forces many in this underserved population to seek emergency services that are much more costly than
ambulatory care and that do not have the added possible benefit of the preventive
and comprehensive services offered by a primary care provider. Even more concerning is that members of these underserved populations are also much more
likely to delay seeking medical care for various reasons, including inadequate
finances, as well as less obvious sociocultural forms of inaccessibility, including
incongruities in patient-doctor expectations, language barriers, cultural insensi-
tivities, and fear of deportation.[174]

Cost Shifting

The increased costs associated with emergency care and delayed care are usually absorbed by the hospital and result in internal *cost shifting* (i.e., hospitals that provide free care pass the costs on by inflating charges to the insurance companies of patients who are able to afford care). To avoid the costs of providing free care or of receiving inadequate reimbursement by Medicaid, many hospitals have begun refusing to admit patients with no insurance or Medicaid; instead, they send them to county hospitals, a practice known in the late 1980s as "dumping."[175]

These studies suggest a need for improvement in the delivery of services, the distribution of resources, and the quality of services through programs that target specific populations and barriers to access. Rectifying these discrepancies will require intensive examination and transformation of attitudes and practices of medical educator, health care providers, and health policy legislators.

POLICY PROPOSALS FOR IMPROVING ACCESS ❖

The issues that must be considered when designing a plan to improve access are the targeted population; the effect on providers, insurers, and employers; concerns over implementation; political support; sources of funding; and the quality and effectiveness of care.[176]

Addressing the Delivery System's Organizational Barriers
Strengthen Community and Migrant Health Centers

Since their inception in 1965, numerous studies have documented the effectiveness of the nation's 800 *community health centers* (CHC) in providing comprehensive, effective, culturally sensitive health services in underserved areas.[177] Nearly 70% of CHC patients are minorities, more than 60% have family incomes below the federal poverty line, and approximately 50% are uninsured.[178]

The major problems that prevent further development and improvement of CHCs are lack of adequate funding, high operating costs, unavailability of malpractice coverage, lack of access to capital for equipment and physical plant upgrades, and difficulties in recruiting and retaining staff. CHCs have had serious problems with recruiting and maintaining staff physicians because of an inability to offer competitive salaries, the difficult work atmosphere physicians face, limited resources and capital, and a needy patient population. On average, the annual salary of physicians working in CHCs is $30,000 less than salaries for physicians in the same specialty and geographic region.[179]

This lack of adequate funding exists at a time when demands placed on these health centers are being increased by homelessness, worsening poverty, AIDS, and the crack epidemic.[180]

Strengthen the National Health Services Corps

The *National Health Services Corps* (*NHSC*) scholarship was established by Congress in 1972 to increase the number of medical personnel in underserved areas. The scholarship provided one year of a medical student's tuition and living expenses for each year that the newly trained physician agreed to work in a medically underserved area chosen by the NHSC. At its peak in 1981, the NHSC, with its $80 million budget, awarded more than 6,400 scholarships to medical students. However, by 1990, only 50 additional scholarships were awarded, while more than 400 physicians complete their obligation each year.[181] In 1990, only 2,000 recipients were fulfilling their obligations.[182]

Despite its successful attempts to distribute the nation's physicians more equitably, the NHSC has not been able to recruit and retain enough personnel to alleviate this problem. Continuing shortages of primary care providers, including non-MD providers such as midwives, nurse practitioners, and physicians assistants, make the struggle all the more difficult. To address these concerns, a three-pronged approach has been suggested to revitalize the NHSC and to promote placement of physicians in medically underserved areas: recruitment programs, financial support, and retention efforts. These approaches would involve attracting new people, particularly minority students, to rural and inner-city areas by linking up with them early in their education (i.e., junior or senior high school) and offering mentoring, guidance, and financial support throughout.[183]

Increase the Number of Minority Physicians

Studies have shown that minority physicians are more likely to treat patients of their own racial or ethnic group and practice more frequently in areas where there are shortages of physicians.[184] More innovative strategies are needed to recruit and retain health care providers in underserved areas, which can be achieved both by focusing on providing competitive incentives for providers to remain in underserved areas and by focusing on the training of more minority physicians. Similarly, providing positive experiences for nonminority medical students and residents to observe and to provide care in medically underserved areas, particularly in urban areas, could be a powerful incentive to attract physicians to practice in these areas. These objectives cannot be achieved, however, without also strengthening financial support for such efforts, such as the loan repayment program established by Congress in 1987 and other means of countering large educational debt.[185]

Train More Primary Care Physicians

There has been a national movement toward training more primary care physicians, not only as a means of addressing the need for increased access to health care services, but also as a means of reducing national health care costs. Factors that make primary care a less attractive choice for young physicians include relatively low salaries and reimbursement compared with specialists.

Moreover, most academic medical centers have failed to focus on the training of general physicians, even though national studies conducted over the past 30 years have recommended that they do so. This neglect has resulted in a disproportionately high number of specialists relative to primary care physicians (Figure 9.8). Boufford suggests that both community health centers and academic medical areas can better meet the challenges of a changing medical milieu by forming collaborations.[186] These relationships would increase access to patients in underserved areas by increasing recruitment and retention of staff and by promoting medical student and resident exposure to primary care medicine.

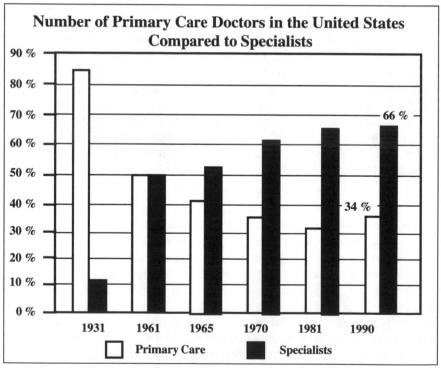

Figure 9.8 Number of primary care doctors, compared to specialists, in the United States. (Source: Council on Graduate Medical Education, Oct. 1992. Adapted from The White House Domestic Policy Council, 1993. The President's Health Security Plan.)

Addressing Sociocultural Barriers

Countering racism, sexism, social class ostracism, and cultural chauvinism must take place through legislative and administrative reform and redress, as well as through personal transformation.

Organized medicine has been derelict in its responsibility for self-policing, and it has been resistant to external oversight or control. However, the persistence and impact of racism and sexism has been well documented, and they must be dealt with forthrightly.[187] Civil rights legislation must be vigorously applied, and state health agencies must be involved in discovering and monitoring patterns of discrimination, as well as exercising their authority to rescind licenses and other privileges to practice on discovery of discrimination.

Personal transformation is far more difficult, but no less critical, to achieve. Katz presents an alternative model of healer education that stresses commitment to service in the community.[188]

Addressing Financial Barriers

The next section of this book discusses several proposals at various levels to address the financial barriers to health care in the U.S. Specifically, we look at what private companies, states, the federal government, and other countries are doing to improve access, as well as to reduce the cost of health care. Two initiatives specifically aimed at improving financial access are creation of uncompensated care pools and expansion of Medicaid.

Uncompensated Care Pools

Rather than totally redesigning the current medical care system, some have suggested a more conservative approach to dealing with the access issue, including establishment of funding sources to supplement providers for uncompensated care given to the uninsured and the underinsured. This approach is based on the premise that access to the uninsured and continued financial health of providers can be best ensured by providing funds to hospitals that currently provide uncompensated care. A variety of program designs have been proposed, including giving direct state and federal subsidies to hospitals, establishing *uncompensated care pools,* and all-payer systems (i.e., hospital rates are set by a state agency that calculates uncompensated care into the budget).

The advantages of these types of plans is that they increase access, maintain costs, ensure that all providers share the cost of uncompensated care, and lower the risk of hospitals closing from the burden of uncompensated care. However, a major disadvantage is that the programs still rely on the willingness of the provider to accept patients without insurance. Because these systems are primarily directed at hospital care rather than direct support to private physicians, much of the care given will be costly care through hospital emergency rooms, inpatient services, and ambulatory centers. Little will be provided in the way of continuity of care, well-patient visits, preventive care, prescription medications, and primary care.

Expansion of Medicaid or General Assistance Medical Benefits

Another means of improving access for the uninsured is to expand Medicaid and General Assistance eligibility to include the majority of the uninsured by income, age, or social circumstance. In this proposal, the majority of cost would be assumed by the state directly or through additional funds collected from income taxes, excise taxes, or similar sources. The advantage of these programs is that they rely on existing programs, and they would therefore involve very few administrative, financing, or provider changes. By providing eligibility to all the unemployed uninsured, these programs would drastically reduce the amount of uncompensated care needed. In contrast, a major disadvantage of these programs is that they place an additional financial burden on the states. Similar to uncompensated care pools, these designs rely on the provider being willing to accept these people as patients.

CONCLUSION ❖

An attempt has been made to summarize the history and the current issues in the health care access debate, to delineate the characteristics of the uninsured, and to identify the barriers and the possible solutions to the American access crisis. Health providers, consumers, politicians, and policy makers must focus their energies on the multitude of potential solutions, which address each of the very different barriers to access, be they financial, structural, personal, or attitudinal, at the federal, state, local, or organizational levels. Those involved in the delivery of health care will hopefully be willing to change medical education, health care delivery, and the patient-doctor interaction to break down these barriers to access.

❖ Suggested Reading ❖

Aday L. At risk in America: the health and health care needs of vulnerable populations in the United States. San Francisco: Jossey-Bass, Inc., 1993.

Provides a comprehensive guide to the populations most vulnerable to being without health care access, including high-risk mothers and infants, people with AIDS, the chronically ill and disabled, substance abusers, and the homeless, among others. Lays out the framework for understanding cost, quality, and access issues for each of these groups, and suggests appropriate social and health policies to decrease their risk of vulnerability in America.

Blendon RJ, et al. Access to health care for the medically indigent: a resource document for state and local officials. Washington, DC: Academy for State and Local Government, 1985.

Provides a broad overview of the state of health care access for the medically indigent, devoting great care to delineating the critical role of state and local governments in improving access for its residents. Although some of the data are now outdated, the vision and insight of this report are well worth the read.

Millman ML. Access to health care in America. Institute of Medicine (US). Committee on Monitoring Access to Personal Health Care Services. Washington, DC: National Academy Press, 1993.

A text prepared by a 17-member national committee charged with developing a set of national indicators for monitoring access to personal health services over time. Concentrates on five specific objectives: increasing successful birth outcomes, reducing preventable diseases, early detection and diagnosis of treatable disease, reducing the effect of chronic illness, and prolonging life.

Rogers DE, Ginzberg E, eds. Medical care and the health care of the poor. Boulder, CO: Westview Press, 1993.

Offers a provocative perspective of the access debate by examining the role of poverty, race, age, and class in the determination of health care access, and by raising ethical concerns about inequalities in the delivery of health care services. It goes on to offer a frank discussion of future policy options for addressing barriers to access in the American health care system.

10

Quality

Linda G. Greenberg and Lisa I. Iezzoni

Change in the health care delivery system is inevitable, driven primarily by concerns about escalating costs. In many locales around the country, this change is already well under way, accompanied by an emphasis on competition, "managing" care, networks of "preferred" providers, and "gatekeeper" physicians as conduits to services. A common element of many of these initiatives is the realization that Americans will no longer enjoy unquestioned, unfettered access to whatever specific services they wish—a scary scenario for persons accustomed to freedom and choice. Quality concerns are therefore a nervous and increasing undercurrent to these changes. As New York State Health Commissioner Mark R. Chassin observed, quality heretofore has been the "missing ingredient" in health care reform: "Very little attention has been paid to how quality of care will be assured and improved, to how the health of the public will be protected in the headlong rush to control costs."[189]

Despite these growing concerns, "quality of care" is difficult to debate in an informed, objective fashion; it is an elusive concept, often defined in the eye of the beholder. In addition, the methodological complexities of measuring quality hamper meaningful presentation in 30-second sound bites. The discourse on quality therefore frequently resorts to emotional appeals and stories of tragic failures in the health care delivery system, anecdotes that resonate with most people. As change proceeds, however, this discussion must be raised to a more objective, informed plane to answer real and troubling questions: Can quality of care be ensured in a competitive environment as health plans try to keep costs low? Will care of equal quality be provided to all? How will health plans be held accountable for quality of care?

This chapter introduces selected considerations central to the discourse on quality of care. First, we present various definitions of quality. Second, we highlight the differing perspectives of the stakeholders in this arena—purchasers, providers, and patients. Third, we describe briefly major methods and initiatives in quality measurement. Finally, we discuss the policy and practical issues involved in measuring and maintaining quality of care. Given the brevity of this chapter, we can mention only a few topics from the large and expanding literature on quality of care. References cited at the end of the chapter provide valuable sources of additional information.

DEFINING QUALITY OF CARE ❖

The term "quality" is difficult to define, especially in health care. One reason for this difficulty may be that "health" itself is an intimate, personal concern, about which each individual has his or her own private expectations. Nevertheless, defining quality is an essential first step toward its measurement. Even though a single definition may not satisfy all parties, there is a growing consensus that it is possible to define the quality (or qualities) of health care.

The End Results of Care

An early definition of quality came from Ernest Amory Codman (1869–1940), a Boston surgeon who aimed to quantify his patients' "end results."[190] Codman's interest in patients' results started when he and his Harvard Medical School classmate Harvey Cushing served together as clerks at the Massachusetts General Hospital.[190] Medical students were required to provide anesthesia to surgical patients; after being anesthetized, Cushing's first patient vomited and died. This event upset Cushing, but the senior surgeon was unconcerned, observing that such deaths were fairly frequent. Cushing and Codman challenged each other to compare their patients' outcomes during the remainder of the clerkship.

Throughout his career, Codman continued to look at the outcomes of surgical care, often to the discomfiture of his Massachusetts General Hospital colleagues. He was not afraid to compare his results with those of others, acknowledging that, "Comparisons are odious, but comparison is necessary in science. Until we freely make therapeutic comparisons, we cannot claim that a given hospital is efficient, for efficiency implies that the results have been looked into."[191] Codman's unique contribution was his effort to link patient treatment to outcome—a straightforward perspective on quality of care. He labeled this perspective the "End Results Idea,"

. . . which was merely the common-sense notion that every hospital should follow *every* patient it treats, long enough to determine whether or not the treatment has been successful, and then to inquire "if not, why not" with a view to preventing similar failures in the future.[191]

For surgical patients, this could require monitoring them for years following the operation.

Structure, Process, and Outcomes

Decades later, Avedis Donabedian formulated a three-pronged framework for evaluating quality, focusing on structure, process, and outcome. **Structure** relates to the characteristics of the care setting, such as the attributes of the hospital or health center environment (e.g., physical plant, available technology, staffing pattern, provider credentialing procedures). **Process** involves all aspects of providing or receiving care services—what is done to the patient. Processes of care can be both technical and interpersonal (see below), ranging from what therapies were administered to how the physician elicited information about preferences for care from the patient. **Outcomes** indicate the effect (or "end results") of care on a patient's health status; outcome measures can include death, complications, physical functioning, psychological functioning, knowledge, and sense of well-being.[192] Changes in health status, either positively or negatively, cannot be attributed to the care provided until all other possible causes have been eliminated. These three dimensions are intertwined: the underlying assumption of quality assessment is that ". . . good structure increases the likelihood of good process, and good process increases the likelihood of a good outcome."[192] Depending on how narrowly or broadly one defines "health," the definition of "quality" changes, likewise.[192]

Over time, students of health care quality have tended to gravitate either to process or outcome measures. As Donabedian observed:

> . . . There seems to be a curious dualism that attracts people to either one or the other of the two camps—the one that has pledged allegiance to process, or the other that accepts no master other than outcome. It is my impression that the more traditional clinicians are to be found in the first group, whereas the second group harbors the nihilists and the iconoclasts who either delight in, or are weighed down by, what they believe to be the uselessness of a great deal of what constitutes contemporary medicine. Also to be found in the second camp are many health planners, policy makers, and administrators, who fear that the emphasis on process will increase costs without producing corresponding improvements in health. And, finally, there are those who have turned to outcomes because they have been disappointed by the imprecision and the costliness of the assessments of process.[193]

Illuminating the relationship between processes and outcomes of medical care has been problematic and puzzling. Few accepted medical practices have solid evidence from well-controlled studies to establish the relationship between the technical process of care and clinical outcome. Outcome measurement is an indirect means of assessing the effectiveness of medical practices. In measuring health care outcomes, improvement or deterioration in health status must be adjusted for other intervening factors before they can be *attributed to* medical care. This leads to the question of "attributional validity," defined by Donabedian as follows:

> The presence of a valid causal linkage between specified processes and outcomes signifies only that it is possible to achieve certain outcomes under specified conditions. It does not mean that the outcomes observed in any given situation have been actually produced by the antecedent processes . . . This means that when outcomes are used to make inferences about the quality of care, it is necessary first to establish that the outcomes can, in fact, be attributed to that care. We may call this the problem of "attribution," and its satisfactory solution may be said to confirm "attributional validity." Note that this kind of validity depends on the prior establishment of a causal linkage between process and outcome on scientific grounds.[193]

John W. Williamson observed that when confronted with this complexity, early investigators of quality in health care often gave up. He suggested starting initially with outcome measures to see whether they met expectations or acceptable standards. Only in situations where outcomes were suboptimal would one return to try to link process of care to outcomes. He recommended further focusing only on process measures that could actually be improved. Williamson's encouragement to take a practical view of quality measurement was echoed years later by Lohr of the Institute of Medicine, who observed, "When outcomes are poorly linked to specific medical practices . . . they offer little guidance for improving quality of care, which militates against their use in quality assessment and assurance."[194]

Technical and Interpersonal Care

A related definition of "quality" focuses on two broad dimensions:

- ✧ **Technical** aspects of care (e.g., how well a medical procedure was performed, diagnostic precision, the effectiveness of an intervention); and
- ✧ **Interpersonal** aspects of care (e.g., the personal interactions with the health care system and providers; respect for patients' preferences).[192]

One common example relating to poor access to care clarifies this distinction.

Many persons, especially those in heavily populated inner-cities, do not have ready access to primary care and often use emergency departments as their primary source of care.[195] The emergency room is a very expensive and inappropriate setting for delivering routine care; it is neither organized nor equipped to offer the continuity of care or the preventive services that are the centerpiece of good primary care. Emergency room visits by patients with primary care needs are generally triaged behind patients with life threatening or urgent needs. Hours can elapse in congested waiting rooms before they are seen by harried emergency personnel.

For such patients, while the quality of care for their specific complaint may be *technically* adequate, their overall care suffers, in that it is neither comprehensive nor longitudinal. The *interpersonal* aspect of care is also often compromised, by brief encounters focused on a single complaint and busy providers geared to handle more emergent needs. In the debate about health care change, the rhetoric of opponents often focuses on the interpersonal perspective, with warnings that medicine will be run with the "efficiency of the Postal Service or the warmth of the I.R.S."[196]

It is a curious paradox that much of what is considered "great" about American medicine—the technological advances, the sophistication of services, and subspecialization—may also erode the interpersonal dimension. As patients seek care from ever-more-specialized providers wielding ever-more-sophisticated diagnostic and therapeutic tools, some complain that care is impersonal and focused on diseases, not patients. Yet, when asked what is best about American medicine, people often emphasize the sophistication of our medical technology and techniques. With few exceptions (e.g., the discoveries of antibiotics, immunizations for polio and smallpox), most new medical approaches are costly although their ultimate impact on "health" is sometimes unclear. They frequently represent "halfway" technologies—interventions effective in redressing the effects of diseases, that do not absolutely cure or prevent disease (e.g., coronary artery bypass graft surgery, kidney dialysis, many cancer chemotherapies). As physician-writer Lewis Thomas observed, halfway technology is tremendously expensive.[197] But for many, this sophisticated technology is the very essence of what Americans perceive as "high quality" medicine.

Thus, Americans are quick to praise technological prowess and have typically assumed that ready access to new approaches is both desirable and a "right." As Thomas noted, "modern medicine has left in the public mind the conviction that we know almost everything about everything."[197] However, the effectiveness and clinical merit of many procedures or treatments—both new and old—is often unproven by rigorous scientific studies. Nevertheless, physicians have considerable discretion about use of such services. In the fee-for-service sector, there are powerful financial incentives for physicians to provide more care. This has led to worrisome findings of excessive and inappropriate use of services (see below).

New technologies also lead to thorny ethical questions. An excellent example is the ability of medical technology to allow post-menopausal women to give birth using ova donated (or purchased) from younger women. At the other end of life there are concerns about the use of costly intensive services for elderly persons who have little chance of meaningful recovery. Does the provision of high quality care mean that everyone who wants it should be allowed unrestricted access to all that the medical armamentarium offers? What would be the impact on health care costs of such freedom?

Appropriateness of Medical Care

Others have approached defining quality from a slightly different but inter-related perspective by looking at the appropriateness of services—that is, whether care was clinically indicated. This perspective acknowledges that there are two broad types of potential errors:

◆   Errors of *omission*—not doing something that is necessary.
◆   Errors of *commission*—doing things that are unnecessary.

Errors of omission occur when physicians are not well-informed about current diagnostic, therapeutic, or preventive care modalities and indications. Omissions also arise when providers fail to correctly evaluate patients' clinical presentations. Increasingly, errors of omission may relate to whether a payer is willing to reimburse providers for particular medical services (many insurers are limiting access to highly expensive, and sometimes experimental, treatments for illness and disease). Patients may also refuse medically reasonable interventions; for example, a Jehovah's Witness may refuse a blood transfusion judged to be clinically indicated. When medical indications contradict patients' preferences, however, the term "error of omission" seems inappropriate.

Errors of commission can arise due to a number of causes, such as financial motivation of providers, lack of understanding about appropriate indications for services, failure to critically appraise the patient's clinical presentation, fear of malpractice ("defensive" medicine), and pressure from patients. The problem with errors of commission is that almost everything in medicine has a potential cost: both economic costs and a cost in terms of risks of morbidity for the patient (e.g., even something as simple as taking aspirin presents a risk of gastrointestinal hemorrhage for some patients). A judgment about the appropriateness of particular interventions in certain clinical situations implicitly involves weighing these costs versus potential benefits. Will patients fare better or worse from a particular medical treatment? How much better? Providers and patients must decide whether the potential benefits of a medical treatment outweigh possible risks and costs.

The appropriateness perspective on quality was fueled by studies such as the 1973 report by John Wennberg and Alan Gittelsohn of large variations across small geographic areas in the use of certain medical procedures. They found that in largely rural, epidemiologically homogeneous Vermont, age-adjusted utilization rates varied dramatically from one region to another. For example, tonsillectomies per 10,000 residents ranged from 13 to 151 in the lowest to highest rate areas; for women, dilatation and curettage procedures ranged from 30 to 141 per 10,000 in the lowest to highest rate areas.[198] These general findings were replicated innumerable times in the ensuing years, in other regions, and for a range of medical services.[199] In addition, several studies have found inappropriate use of health care services.[200] This evidence suggests that the care patients receive depends not only on the region of the country in which they live, but also on the doctor who is treating them.

One important study found that Medicare beneficiaries are hospitalized at higher rates in Boston compared to counterparts in New Haven.[201] However, overall death rates (adjusted for age, sex, and race) between the two cities did not vary. Studies that reveal variations in the use of surgical and diagnostic procedures beg the inevitable question: "Which rate is right?"[202] An answer to this question requires one to determine whether it is "appropriate" to perform a given service—an exercise that is similarly compromised by the absence of compelling scientific evidence about what constitutes excellent care in medicine.

It has been a short leap from developing criteria about appropriateness of services to devising clinical practice "guidelines" (i.e., specifying when interventions are indicated). Therefore, a relatively recent emphasis of quality-of-care investigations has been examining the departure of actual practices from specified guidelines. Determinations of clinical efficacy are addressed by the following queries: "When is it appropriate to use one operation instead of another? When is it appropriate to use a medical, rather than a surgical, approach or simply to watch and wait?"[202]

Although focusing on medical necessity has a slightly different emphasis than the classic structure-process-outcome triad, both strategies underlie a multidimensional definition of quality. For example, Philip Caper blends these perspectives in his "working consensus" definition of quality, comprised of three parts: efficacy, appropriateness, and the caring function of medicine.[203] This multidimensional approach may also reflect the way many patients think about health care quality. According to quality-of-care expert Robert Brook, three things are important to patients concerning the quality of health services: "First, if you need it, you want it, but if it will hurt you without improving your health, you don't want it; second, you want it done well; and third, you want to be treated like a human being."[204] However, as suggested in the next section, the "stakeholders" in the health policy debate (purchasers, providers, and patients) may sometimes have very different perspectives on how quality should be defined and measured.

STAKEHOLDERS' PERSPECTIVES ON QUALITY OF CARE ❖

In the current health care delivery environment, there are three major groups of stakeholders—purchasers (those who pay the bills), providers (those who provide care, such as hospitals, physicians, and nurses), and patients (those who receive care). Not surprisingly, these three groups have somewhat different perspectives on the debate about health care quality.

Purchasers' Perspectives

Purchasers—businesses and government—are universally motivated by concerns about cost. Although purchasers do not speak with one voice about how to balance cost and quality, they often share common themes. For example, most purchasers agree that performance data comparing providers are absolutely essential. Many payers view their function in strictly business terms; they see medicine as comparable to any other business that can be motivated (e.g., to improve, to cut costs). They believe that the quality of medicine can be defined and measured in the same way that the quality of manufacturing inputs, such as steel and chemicals, can be defined and measured. Purchasers (businesses and government) rarely argue that the data on provider performance are perfect. While they concede that there are flaws in the data, most argue that some data are better than none.

Contrary to the prior era, when health care delivery was viewed as an untouchable, sacrosanct world, the huge cost burden and growing number of providers has demystified this system. Purchasers often now have the upper hand. Some wield it towards providers in an explicitly directive fashion, requiring that providers meet certain standards to get their business (i.e., access to their employees as potential patients). Some purchasers also require that providers accept routine oversight, such as concurrent, "pre-certification" programs (i.e., external review of the appropriateness and necessity of services ordered by physicians before the service would be reimbursed). Many purchasers emphasize the concept of *value*—a blend of cost and quality or "getting the best quality at the best price." Purchasers also increasingly advocate public dissemination of information about providers' quality and price. For example, business coalitions are behind many of the state and regional initiatives to publish performance data on quality of care (see below).

Providers' Perspectives

Having their clinical performance publicly displayed and their practices questioned is a new, often uncomfortable experience for health care providers. Not surprisingly, providers are concerned that externally imposed monitoring may yield results that do not provide a complete and accurate picture about the provider's performance. This response, however, is not uniform: some providers proactively monitor and publicize their performance, aiming to get the edge in a competitive marketplace. One such example involves a network of high volume cardiac surgeons located in 40 cities who are marketing, directly to big companies, standardized services at lower cost but comparable quality.[205] The dynamics are different, however, when the quality evaluation comes from outside and there is a presumption that performance information will be used punitively. One of the problems is the seriousness of the stakes—providers feeling their livelihoods at risk, while purchasers (such as third-party payers) emphasize that their financial viability is jeopardized by escalating health care costs. While providers are increasingly coming to terms with these data, several common themes typify their concerns.

A major concern has to do with the methods employed to measure or maintain quality. Insurance company efforts to ensure that services are appropriate (e.g., utilization review) often involve non-physicians implicitly or explicitly question-ing physicians' judgments. When comparisons of patient outcomes are used, a typ-ical criticism is that the patients being contrasted are clinically different. For example, a physician whose patients had a higher-than-expected mortality rate might argue, "But my patients were sicker than those of other doctors." Even if these outcomes are adjusted for patient risk or severity, physicians are often sus-picious of such statistical approaches. As one physician observed, "Practicing medicine is not a science; it's an art. You cannot practice by numbers; you cannot use an average approach to treat all patients because every patient is different."[206] Nonetheless, efforts to mandate appropriateness guidelines based on medical ef-fectiveness of particular interventions are emerging.

Many providers view findings from health care outcome studies as a screening tool to suggest areas requiring more detailed investigation, generally by the providers themselves. Anecdotal evidence suggests that when such information is used internally by hospitals to "screen" for areas to be examined in greater depth, provider acceptance increases. However, viewing these data only as a screen may be distinctly different from what purchasers want, resulting in an inherent conflict. In addition, the question about whether information should be made public is often a stumbling block. Often there are reservations about the quality of the data and many providers are concerned by what they perceive as sensational reporting of the results, without appropriate emphasis on the limitations of the data. For ex-ample, even President Clinton in his 22 September 1993 address on health care re-form cited an example from Pennsylvania:

> We have evidence that more efficient delivery of health care doesn't decrease quality. In fact, it may enhance it. Let me just give you one example of one commonly performed procedure, the coronary bypass operation. Pennsylvania discovered that patients who were charged $21,000 for this surgery received as good or better care as patients who were charged $84,000 for the same procedure in the same state. High prices simply don't always equal good quality.[207]

On face value, these figures illustrate wide cost differences. However, they do not reflect adjustments for differences in patients' severity of illness. In addition, the "quality" measure was limited to in-hospital morality—certainly a critical concern but hardly a complete picture of health care quality. As J. William Thomas, Uni-versity of Michigan professor and expert in severity systems, observed, "The un-fortunate thing is that after these figures are published in the newspaper, all of the cautions that may be incorporated in the original document are usually cast aside and the numbers are taken as facts."[208]

Another concern is that business leaders are increasingly explicit about in-tending to affiliate with providers based on their performance information. This may save money for purchasers, but some providers are concerned about clarify-ing their own specific goals and those of payers. Many providers feel that cost containment—not maintaining quality—is the primary aim of purchasers. An example is "physician profiling" activities, such as Washington state's King County Medical Blue Shield insurance plan, which dropped several hundred doctors from their list of preferred providers because they were viewed as too costly.[209] An insurance representative claimed that the plan would curb "unnecessary and marginal care" to patients. Yet, the plan does not actually correlate cost and quality—the data upon which the decision was made did not include measures for health outcomes for patients or the technical or interpersonal quality of care.

For performance data to be accepted fully, they must be perceived as fair and nonpunitive—or at least providing "due process" for those contesting any findings. For example, Berwick and Wald surveyed the opinions of leaders at 195 hospitals across the country about the annual release by the Health Care Financing Administration (HCFA) of hospitals' risk-adjusted mortality rates (see below).[210] Eighty percent of the respondents viewed the data as a fair to poor indicator of hospital performance, and 95 percent also rated its usefulness to hospitals in improving quality as fair to poor. The researchers concluded:

> . . . These survey results likely reflect the degree of fear abroad in the hospital community today—fear that overwhelms more constructive possible responses to these mortality data. This is a tough time to run a hospital; the executives facing the HCFA data may be thinking first of the fragility of their organizations and not of their long-range improvement. Their concerns about public reaction forestall the more subtle enterprise of using the data.[210]

Historically, the argument that "quality" is an intangible concept has been used by providers to thwart its examination altogether. Tomorrow's doctors and health professionals will need to confront the serious issues central to quality of care, especially transcending the tension between self-interest and altruism central to modern medicine.[211] In addition, pressures to contain rising health care costs while simultaneously ensuring high-quality care are occurring in a setting of rapid change. A strong professional tradition of service is challenged because of both internal and external cost concerns. In 1927, Francis Weld Peabody told Harvard Medical School students:

> The good physician knows his patients through and through, and his knowledge is bought dearly. Time, empathy, and understanding must be lavishly dispensed, but the reward is to be found in that personal bond which forms the greatest satisfaction of the practice of medicine. One of the essential qualities of the clinician is interest in humanity, for the secret of the care of the patient is in caring for the patient.[212]

Given current external exigencies, whether this caring tradition will prevail is a critical challenge to modern American medicine.

Patients' Perspective

Historically, the physician-patient relationship was based on a paternalistic model,[213] with an unequal decision-making balance-of-power. Physicians often ignore patients' concerns, focusing on the more technical aspects of medicine. Increasingly, however, better understanding of the patient's perspective has attracted attention.[214] As Reiser wrote, the interest in outcomes of care is increasingly giving a voice to the patient:

> The modern outcomes movement, which developed in the 1980s and made the consequences of a medical intervention to its recipient a major criterion of determining its value, further enhanced the authenticity and authority of the patient's perspective . . . The objective biological standards of evidence, which had formed the foundation of 20th-century medicine, were found to depict the effects of a medical procedure inadequately. Thus, the medical ethics and outcomes movements both drew their strength from the significance they gave to the patient's view of illness and therapy.[215]

Patients have a unique perception of the quality of care they experience. They are a rich source of information about health care processes, as "eyewitness to hundreds of human interactions."[216]

Patients have different attitudes and preferences for medical interventions. Some patients seek more aggressive medical interventions than others in hope of delaying death or disability. Because of the nature of these aggressive interventions, however, these patients are more likely to suffer iatrogenic complications. This may result in an inherent conflict for the provider whose performance measures are being externally monitored. For example, physicians who treat a disproportionate fraction of patients requesting aggressive interventions may exhibit higher complication rates and higher costs per case.

There is relatively little evidence about whether the outcomes information is being used by individual consumers to choose health care providers. However, anecdotal evidence suggests that some providers may avoid high-risk patients who could suffer poor outcomes. For example, several months after *Newsday* published surgeon-specific mortality rates in New York, an Op-Ed piece appeared in the *New York Times* by a woman whose mother had had a heart attack and who apparently needed coronary artery bypass graft surgery to survive. The essay documented a five-day struggle to enlist the services of a cardiothoracic surgeon willing to accept a high-risk case.

> We learned that in New York State the Department of Health scrutinizes a cardiac surgeon's rate of failure and success. A high incidence of mortality produces poor records. This information is then shared with the public. The state rating takes into account the degree of risk of patients going into surgery. But the public disclosure of a surgeon's record seems to have created skittishness to downright paranoia among doctors.
>
> "Don't you think that the chief of surgery would love to do this operation?" one doctor said. "He's a great surgeon but he's taken too many high-risk cases lately and has

too many black marks on his name." Black mark is the doctor's code phrase for death. While the surgeons worried about black marks, my mother lay dying 20 feet down the hall in need of an operation that no one would perform.[217]

The mother eventually did receive surgery and survived.

Nevertheless, patients should be provided with information and knowledge to become more active in making decisions about their treatment plan. As proper questions for patients to ask after a medical treatment, quality expert Jacqueline Kosecoff suggests: "Is the quality of your life better? Do you have more symptom-free days? Is your physical, mental and social functioning what it should be?"[204] Traditionally, patients have not been in a position to make clinical decisions about their treatment options. Norman Cousins has appealed to physicians to be more sensitive, caring, and compassionate of patient's needs and values toward different treatment options. To ensure care of high quality requires listening and learning from patients' experiences with the care they receive.

TRENDS IN MEASURING QUALITY OF CARE ❖

In this brief presentation, it is not possible to cover fully all methodologies and initiatives for measuring quality of care. Methods for monitoring quality of care have stirred much controversy.[218] This field has burgeoned tremendously in the last decade, fostering its own arcane argot—such as "outcomes management," "physician profiling," "continuous quality improvement" or CQI, "benchmarking," "practice guidelines," "critical paths," "indicators," "severity measurement," "appropriateness," and "total quality management" or TQM. Given that costs are heaviest in the inpatient setting, much of this development has focused on hospital care. Increasingly, however, the emphasis is shifting to an outpatient setting, such as ambulatory care.[219] This section reviews several of the major activities in this field, organized around structure, process, and outcomes.

Structure

Structural characteristics are a "rather blunt instrument in quality assessment."[192] Nonetheless, especially in prior years, "quality assessment . . . is, primarily, an administrative device used to monitor performance to determine whether it continues to remain within acceptable bounds."[192] Such have been the goals of the Joint Commission on Accreditation of Healthcare Organizations (JCAHO), a professional organization that voluntarily accredits hospitals and other health care organizations around the country. JCAHO has a long history of accrediting hospitals based on their structural characteristics, such as board certification and medical staff credentialing, and clinical standards and processes to ensure quality care.

In the mid-1980s, however, JCAHO shifted its approach from the long-standing interest in structural measures to a focus on outcomes. The so-called "Agenda for Change" is due to be instituted nationwide in the mid- to late-1990s, with the goal "to make continuous improvement in patient outcomes and organizational performance the central and explicit objective of Joint Commission accreditation activities."[220] JCAHO has created "indicators" or quantitative measures to evaluate the quality and appropriateness of care for specialties and clinical departments, including obstetrics and anesthesia. Indicators may include measures for the process and outcomes of patient care.[221] For example, the indicators for trauma care include the efficiency of emergency medical services, the monitoring of trauma patients, airway management of comatose trauma patients, and timeliness of diagnostic testing and surgical interventions.[221] Other sets of indicators are being developed in oncology, cardiovascular care, medication use, infection control, and home infusion therapy.

It is unlikely that structural measures will ever vanish altogether. For example, it will always be important that health care facilities meet stipulations regarding building fire codes, handicapped access, staffing levels and training, and equipment testing and maintenance. However, most would agree that the current emphasis has shifted away from structural concerns.

Process
Traditional Peer Review

Cutting across the process and outcomes dimensions is traditional "peer" review. The assumption underlying this approach is that only physicians, namely "peers,"—have the requisite knowledge to judge quality of care. This review is generally retrospective and involves examining records of care (e.g., the medical chart) for selected patients. Typically these physician reviews are *implicit*—based on the reviewer's clinical judgment, rather than on *explicit* indicators of quality.

Although implicit peer review is the traditional approach toward evaluating quality of care for individual patient encounters, this process has significant limitations. Perhaps most important are questionable reliability and the possibility that the "reviewer's knowledge of the outcomes of care clouds the assessment of the process."[222] Although it is the "most widely accepted approach," retrospective reviews of medical records may be a "hopelessly flawed observation technique."[223] A review of 12 studies of the inter-observer reliability of peer reviews concluded, "Overall, physician agreement regarding quality of care is only slightly better than the level expected by chance."[224] The subjective nature of medicine is illustrated by Brook and Appel, who found that in 16% of cases physicians changed their minds about the process of care during a subsequent review.[225]

As suggested by Donabedian, one key to improving inter-observer reliability involves structuring the review to examine specific aspects of care.[226] This was the tactic adopted at RAND in their examination of quality of care of Medicare beneficiaries.[227] To explore how well state peer review organizations(PROs) judge the quality of hospital care, one study examined one highly respected PRO in depth. The study found that the initial screening process of the PRO failed to detect nearly two of every three records that were considered "below standard."[228] It also found that PRO physicians referred more records for quality review than considered necessary: only one in five were judged to have quality problems. Also, "two of every three records that PRO physicians judged to be quality problems were judged standard or above," according to the study's standards.[228] In 1990, the Institute of Medicine conducted a comprehensive investigation of quality assurance in Medicare.[229]

Total Quality Management

Health care has traditionally focused on two approaches to improve quality of care: a retrospective review to ferret out the "bad apples" and deficiencies in the system of care or a prospective, concurrent review to anticipate quality problems and resolve them in a cooperative fashion. Donald Berwick, a quality improvement advocate, observes that the "Theory of Bad Apples"—the search for "discovering bad apples and removing them from the lot"—is inadequate to deal with quality problems because it pursues deterrence and putative measures to the neglect of improvement.[230] Physicians may react defensively to queries of quality control strategies that involve inspection and disciplinary actions. Unique among health professionals, physicians typically view themselves as single "agents of success or failure," not as participants in complex processes in the delivery systems.[230] However, the advent of managed care and new provider networks and hospital collaborations has fostered CQI strategies that recommend a fundamental change in the way work is structured and production processes maintained.

American industries have jumped on the bandwagon of quality management strategies that have gained international recognition. Pioneers in quality improvement, theorists W. Edward Deming and Joseph M. Juran, have been influential in improving industry abroad, especially in Japan. Deming's total quality management (TQM) strategies are based on the notion that customers have a central role in identifying deficiencies with a good or service and may assist suppliers in designing strategies to improve their product. Total quality management strategies, also known as continuous quality improvement (CQI), are philosophies focusing on the organization's production processes and resources to meet the needs of its clients. CQI aims to reduce wide variations in the provision of services by establishing rules of routine procedures. Statements of purpose and formulas for achieving particular objectives are essential to quality improvement activities.

During the 1980s, competitive pressures to gain market share and reduce costs mounted, forcing many health plans to become more efficient in delivering care. Although initially resistant to learn from outside industries, many health plans have incorporated quality performance strategies to improve processes of production. The underlying principle of quality improvement is to construct the system based on need. Another core concept involves trying to understand sources of variation and to eliminate variations. Wide variations observed in medical practice, such as the frequency of use of certain diagnostic procedures, are targets for intervention under the rubric of continuous quality improvement and clinical guidelines. Increasingly, hospitals are interested in "benchmarking," comparing their patterns of care with other hospitals that have better results of care.[231] Hospitals may learn from others' experience how best to refine their practices.

Even the giant Medicare program is getting into this arena. In 1992, Medicare introduced the Peer Review Organization (PRO) Health Care Quality Improvement Initiative (HCQII) with the following objective: "To develop and share with the health care community information on patterns of care and patterns of outcomes that will lead to measurable improvements in care and outcomes for Medicare beneficiaries."[232] The HCQII shifts the generally state-based PROs from their traditional concentration on finding individual clinical errors to monitoring practice patterns and assisting providers to improve their outcomes. The HCQII aims to facilitate local initiatives between PROs and provider groups to analyze regional outcomes and improve care quality. Although many hurdles are acknowledged, "The role of the PROs in the HCQII is to work with hospital administrative and medical staffs . . . Pattern analysis, variation analysis, and improved feedback and focusing techniques are to be used to identify and resolve quality problems."[232] The Health Care Financing Administration encouraged PROs to examine "provider-specific distribution of important variables such as admissions, readmission, transfers, and a provider-specific average length of stay for specific DRGs."[232]

Practice Guidelines and Critical Paths

Most recently, decision-making about treatment options for certain conditions, including coronary artery disease, have been guided by medical effectiveness research. Critical paths map processes of care that are appropriate or indicated during the patient's clinical course of care. According to medical society representatives, the primary motive of guideline development is to improve quality of care.[233] Clinical practice guidelines may serve as educational tools for physicians and patients to understand better the effectiveness of certain medical interventions. New interest in improving quality of care and the appropriateness of medical procedures has spurred the federal Agency of Health Care Policy and Research (AHCPR) to create clinical practice guidelines, which aim to outline the optimal care practices and therapeutic approaches to treat certain medical conditions. Practice guidelines are also intended to eliminate care that is perhaps unnecessary, inappropriate, or marginally effective. Physicians, however, have been characteristically resistant to follow clinical guidelines, or algorithms, because of notions that it threatens professional autonomy and transforms them into "robots who do not think."[234] They equate clinical guidelines with "cookbook medicine," which prescribes certain strategies to diagnose and treat illnesses.[235] The issuance of guidelines themselves may determine whether certain services are reimbursed by payers, thus, influencing physicians to provide those specified services. In theory, financial incentives to provide appropriate services will provide better care and ultimately reduce excess care and inefficiencies in the health care system.

In the last several years, a variety of guidelines have been developed, including those devised by federal agencies and professional societies. To date, AHCPR has convened panels of experts to review studies on clinical procedures to evaluate the medical effectiveness of various treatments for certain illnesses (including urinary incontinence, arthritis, heart attack, cancer pain, and pain management following surgery) and to recommend guidelines to improve clinical practice and, ultimately, patient outcomes. In 1992, the AHCPR released guidelines to detect and treat urinary incontinence and pain management for trauma and certain diagnostic procedures. The guidelines for urinary incontinence recommend physicians ask all patients about urine control problems, examine and test those with complaints of incontinence, and begin therapies that are least invasive, including medication, bladder retraining, and pelvic muscle exercises.[236] The pain management guidelines recommend the use of morphine as a first order measure, rather than commonly used meperidine or Demerol, because continuous dosing is easier with morphine than with other drugs.[236] The AHCPR guidelines are voluntary, similar to those of the federal Centers for Disease Control on childhood immunizations and panels of the National Institutes of Health on cancer treatment.

Appropriateness Measurement

Appropriateness of care stems from concern that patients should receive the proper diagnostic tests and treatments for particular ailments. Concern about unnecessary services is appropriate because all medical interventions involve some amount of risk, which may cause a harmful side effect. Patients and providers need to decide whether medical procedures that are likely to yield marginal effects ought to be performed.

There are two distinct approaches to evaluating whether care is appropriate and medically necessary:

+ **Retrospective review** of medical records; and
+ **Concurrent review** of medical procedures (e.g., **precertification**).

Joseph Restuccia and colleagues developed an instrument, the Appropriateness Evaluation Protocol (AEP), to compare hospital services against guidelines of appropriateness of care.[237] A patient's condition was deemed unstable if certain clinical criteria were met. Thus, hospitalization was required for patients due to various clinical factors, including transfusion due to blood loss, ventricular fibrillation or electrocardiogram (ECG) evidence of acute ischemia, and coma, which was defined as unresponsiveness for at least one hour.[237] The AEP shows that a significant proportion of hospital care is inappropriate. For example, a review of 8,031 hospital records of patients in 41 Massachusetts hospitals suggests that inappropriateness of care was found among nearly one-third (32.2%) of the medical patients and one-quarter (24.3%) of the surgical patients.[237]

An example of the concurrent approach to determine the appropriateness of care is the work of Jacqueline Kosecoff and colleagues, who developed computer software programs to help insurers decide whether certain medical procedures, such as tonsillectomies, should be reimbursed services.[238] Before medical and surgical procedures are performed, third-party payers often require patients to seek prior approval and a second surgical opinion after an operation has been recommended. Insurers often pose queries to both patient and physician on key clinical indicators to ensure that algorithms are followed for the treatment of medical conditions. Otherwise, insurers may deny reimbursement for services that have not been preapproved. Physicians who disagree with the insurer's judgment whether to approve the service may appeal to the insurance company or ask the patient to pay for the service. Such preauthorization practices have created serious administrative problems among physicians and patients; insured patients sometimes suffer delayed care while appeals are made to the insurance company for a medical procedure deemed "medically necessary" and appropriate. Too often, the onus is on the patient to implore the insurer to pay for physician-ordered services. Some physicians argue that such precertification practices interfere with the practice of medicine, one that often has no preordained formula of set procedures.[238]

Physician Profiling

In recent years, profiling physician performance has emerged as an opportunity to assess quality of care. Physician profiling involves analyzing physician practice patterns rather than individual clinical decisions, to evaluate the nature and even appropriateness of physician services.[239] Profiling methods typically rely on large administrative data bases to examine patterns of care.[240] Concerns about cost containment are driving insurers' efforts to use new sophisticated computer software programs to profile physician services. As the previous example of Washington state illustrates, insurers may increasingly use this type of information to dismiss doctors from their list of participating providers. Profiling physicians' practices has the potential to:

◆ Provide comparative data to physicians on practice patterns in relation to their peers
◆ Determine whether physicians follow practice guidelines
◆ Measure the quality of care by physician group practices.[241]

While physician profiling is the subject of recent attention, it presents challenges for data collection methods (e.g., Who shall collect the data? What type of data should be collected?). "The public has a right to know about the quality of its doctors, yet . . . it is irresponsible to release information that is of questionable validity, subject to alternative interpretations, or too technical for a layperson to comprehend."[242]

Patient-Centered Care

The long-standing presumption that patients are unable to judge the quality of care they receive is increasingly discredited. While it is true that patients generally lack the requisite knowledge and the technical expertise to judge clinical aspects of care, they are able to distinguish quality care from their personal experiences. Adapting the guidelines Supreme Court Justice Stewart employed in identifying obscenity, persons typically "know 'quality' when they see it." Patients judge the quality of their care based on how they are treated: whether they had long waiting times for the hospital staff to meet their needs, whether hospital staff were respectful and courteous, whether family and friends were involved in decision making about treatment options. In particular, patients are the only ones who are really equipped to judge definitively the interpersonal quality of care.

Patient-centered care is concerned with the human interactions and the personal aspects of caring that patients experience during their hospitalization. The Picker/Commonwealth Program for Patient-Centered Care has enumerated seven dimensions of patient-centered care, as defined through patients' experiences of illness and health care, including:

✦ Respect for patients' values, preferences, and expressed needs
✦ Coordination and integration of care
✦ Information, communication, and education
✦ Physical comfort
✦ Emotional support and alleviation of fear and anxiety
✦ Involvement of family and friends
✦ Transition and continuity of care.[243]

A 1989 national survey, conducted by the Picker/Commonwealth program, found that health status strongly predicts the likelihood of whether a patient experiences problems with quality of care.[244] Patients who rated their health status as "fair" or "poor" had experienced the most problems with the quality of care they received. The study suggests that the number of problems the patient reports is a good predictor of patient satisfaction. While most patients are generally satisfied with the quality of care they receive during a hospital stay, when specifically asked about various aspects of interpersonal care, patients are more likely to provide specific examples of dissatisfaction. An important finding from the Picker/Commonwealth program is that patients are very concerned about issues central to making the transition from hospital to home. While 84% of discharged hospital patients received prescriptions for medication, one-third of these patients reported receiving no information on the potential side effects of such medications.[245]

Additional innovations in patient outcomes research aim to assist clinicians and patients decide about different treatment options. Wennberg and colleagues have developed educational materials, including an interactive video, to provide patients with information to assist them in making decisions among alternative treatment options for specific illnesses, including prostate cancer, breast cancer, back pain, and others. The aim is to permit patients to be informed consumers of health care services, to choose those interventions that reflect their goals and preferences.

Outcomes

Monitoring outcomes has become the mantra for those interested in quantifying what is being purchased with the health care dollar. To date, outcomes measurement has relied on large computerized databases to identify outcomes and track costs and service use. Large administrative data bases are typically created in the process of paying for services (i.e., the information contained in them is derived from claims or bills submitted by providers); they are now commonly used in quality assessment and medical effectiveness research.[246] "Perhaps the most important effect of the outcomes movement has been a broadening of our focus to include a wider range of outcomes . . . including functional status, emotional health, social interaction, cognitive function, degree of disability, and so forth."[247] Outcomes research has found great variation in the use and cost effectiveness of certain medical interventions. A variety of state and federal initiatives have adopted this perspective.

Federal Hospital Mortality Reports

One of the first outcomes to be examined was death, primarily because it is easily defined and the information is readily available. For example, in the mid-1980s HCFA was compelled by reporters' demands under the federal Freedom of Information Act to publicly release figures on mortality rates of Medicare beneficiaries. Unfortunately, a furor accompanied this initial dissemination in March 1986. According to governmental predictions, 142 hospitals had significantly higher death rates than predicted, while 127 had significantly lower rates. Because the data did not adjust adequately for severity of illness, the most aberrant experience (with 87.6% of Medicare patients dying, compared to a predicted 22.5%) was at a hospice caring for terminally ill patients.[248] This early HCFA model did not adequately capture severity of illness.[249]

The HCFA algorithms have improved since then, although they are bound by the fixed limitations of administrative data. Despite these methodological advances, it is still not known whether the Medicare hospital mortality figures provide useful information about quality of hospital care. Although initial publications of HCFA's mortality figures provoked avid press interest and front page newspaper coverage, more recent releases have generated muted attention. It is also not obvious that the public has used this information widely to choose among hospitals.[249] In June 1993, newly appointed HCFA administrator Bruce Vladeck halted dissemination of the most recent Medicare hospital mortality report, claiming that the data may unfairly penalize inner-city public facilities. Vladeck noted that because the mortality figures appeared to be quality "scores," the information "has had more importance attached to it than I think was justified."[250] When asked if he believed the data were valid for large tertiary institutions, Vladeck responded, "My answer is quite literally that we don't know."[250]

State and Regional Outcomes Initiatives

States and regions are increasingly examining patient outcomes that have been adjusted for differences in severity of illness. Initiatives to use risk-adjusted outcome measures vary from state to state and locale to locale. The business community is prompting providers to develop quality performance strategies, a mechanism to ensure accountability among providers for the cost and quality of health care services. Purchasers of care are increasingly comparing providers to negotiate the most for their health care dollar: high quality care for the best-cost providers. More and more hospitals have been collecting reams of data to determine how well they are treating patients based on risk-adjusted health care outcomes and comparative data on hospital costs. Ranking providers according to survival rates, or grading physicians on specific quality performance measures, has sparked intense national debate. As more health plans increasingly compete on price and quality, lessons learned from state initiatives may be very instructive. The following three case studies illustrate the dynamic relationship between purchasers and providers in ensuring cost efficiency and quality performance.

❖ CASE STUDY 1 ❖

In 1989, a coalition of Cleveland-area businesses, hospitals, and physicians joined forces to control health care costs and improve quality of care. The goal of the partnership, the Cleveland Health Quality Choice (CHQC) project, was to improve quality of care regionally by measuring and comparing data on clinical outcomes at 30 local hospitals. The CHQC developed risk-adjusted outcome measures to examine intensive care unit (ICU) care, general medical and surgical care, and obstetrical care. Indicators also evaluated patient satisfaction with hospital services. The comparative data that ranks hospital services are not intended to be released to the public. The information is designed to assist businesses in directing employees to cost-effective, high-quality care services. Hospitals will use the information to compare their services to services at other hospitals.❖

✦ CASE STUDY 2 ✦

In 1986, Pennsylvania became the first state to mandate the use of performance data to compare risk-adjusted outcomes. Hospital-specific data on costs and patient outcomes was collected by the Pennsylvania Health Care Cost Containment Council. The business community exerted pressure on the state to require all hospitals to implement a specific severity measurement system, MedisGroups, which requires detailed abstraction of clinical data from medical records. In 1992, the Council published comparative data on providers' (hospitals and heart surgeons) cost and mortality rates as a way to help consumers make informed decisions. Pennsylvania may be considered a trailblazer in developing an initiative to evaluate the cost-effectiveness and quality of care. A few states have followed Pennsylvania's lead with new data gathering mandates, while others have selected less ambitious approaches using existing administrative data bases.✧

✦ CASE STUDY 3 ✦

New York has sparked a near revolution in health care by providing consumers with information on hospital- and physician-specific mortality rates. Since the late 1980s, New York's Department of Health (DOH) has collected data on risk-adjusted outcomes for coronary artery bypass (CABG) surgery. In an unprecedented move, it made such information available to the public. The course of publicly releasing data on hospital- and physician-specific mortality rates has not been without challenges. In 1990, the hospital mortality rates were initially published in the *Journal of the American Medical Association.*[251] A Freedom of Information Act request was filed by a New York newspaper, *Newsday,* to obtain access to the physician-specific mortality data. In 1991, the New York State Supreme Court ordered hospitals to make such information on CABG mortality rates available to the public. On 18 December 1991, *Newsday* first published information on physician-specific mortality rates for CABG surgery.[252] New York's DOH report, *Cardiac Surgery in New York State,* released in December 1993, serves as a consumer guide to select hospitals based on mortality rates of cardiac surgery. Over the last several years, death rates from CABG surgery have declined to 2.51% in 1992 from 3.53% in 1990.[253]✧

CHALLENGES AHEAD ❖

As stated at the outset, as changes unfold in the health care delivery system, it is necessary to raise the discussion about quality to a more objective, informed plane to answer a number of important questions. As Mark Chassin wrote, "We have a long way to go before . . . quality measures routinely work to improve outcomes for patients across a wide spectrum of conditions and procedures. Physicians, hospitals, employers, and government should be equally enthusiastic about working together to achieve this goal."[254]

Nevertheless, while this goal to improve quality of care obviously is laudable, it is difficult to design a road map about how exactly to attain such achievements. Collecting quality of care data may itself incur a significant cost, contributing to high administrative expenses.[255] A major question remains: "What is the *minimum information* needed to monitor quality of care *in a feasible and cost-effective manner across a range of populations and types of services?*"[256] In addition, the fundamental question remains: "How do we make the intellectual leap of faith from data assembly to a change in physician behavior?"[257]

While tools for measuring quality are gaining increasing recognition and experience, perceptions of their credibility may still lag, especially in the provider community. For example, the literature addressing the relationship of hospital mortality rates and quality of care for adult patients yields inconsistent conclusions. Several reports link higher-than-expected mortality rates to substandard care,[258] while some do not[259] and others provide equivocal conclusions.[260] Despite this, other aspects of health care reform are asking much from quality measurement—basically, that mechanisms be put in place to guarantee quality in the face of increasing cost constraints. Such quality measures must have not only the imprimatur of objectivity and validity from the clinical community, but they also must address wariness among the public about the impact of changes in the health care system.

The worrisome sensation of "too-little-time-too-much-to-do" pervades medicine and ultimately affects human interactions and personal relationships between physicians and patients. As pressures to contain health care costs mount, many are concerned with whether providers always act in "the best interest" of the patient. Is the manner in which health care is financed changing the ethos of medicine? Are financial incentives and cost containment strategies limiting access to certain medical interventions more than others?

President Clinton's Health Security Act proposed national quality performance standards including measures on appropriateness of health care services provided to consumers. The most controversial aspect of monitoring quality performance is the notion of provider "report cards."[261] It is too early to determine the exact content of these report cards and the impact that they will have on the medical profession. As stated previously, providers are likely to perceive the report cards as a blunt measure of quality performance and an ultimate threat to professional autonomy. Some physicians fear that the "[p]ublic release of information about quality at the physician level will dramatically change the way we practice."[262] However, a recent study proposed that "scorecards" on clinical outcomes could lead to improvements in the quality of care.[263]

Provider report cards have become a controversial topic of health policy debates. The National Committee on Quality Assurance, a Washington, D.C.-based nonprofit organization that accredits managed care plans, is already developing quality indicators of HMO performance, the so-called Health Plan Employer Data and Information Set 2.0 (HEDIS) report card. Also, HCFA has funded research on provider "report cards" for the Medicare population that may explore non-clinical variables, including multidisciplinary aspects of care.[264] Ware and Berwick suggest that report cards should be multidimensional, measuring various dimensions of care including nursing and daily care; hospital environment and ancillary staff; medical care; information; admissions; and discharge and billing.[265]

As the debate about health system change continues, political leadership must ultimately ensure that health care security for all Americans includes guarantees for high quality health care.

❖ Acknowledgments ❖

The authors gratefully acknowledge the helpful comments of Deborah W. Garnick, The Heller School, Brandeis University, and Patty Delaney Klafehn, Office of the Associate Commissioner for AIDS and Special Health Issues, the Food and Drug Administration.

❖ Suggested Reading ❖

Berwick DM, Godfrey AB, Roessner J. Curing health care: new strategies for quality improvement San Francisco, CA: Jossey-Bass Publishers, 1990.
A report on the lessons learned from the National Demonstration Project on Quality Improvement in Health Care. Describes well the methods of the continuous quality improvement process.

Donabedian A. Explorations in quality assessment and monitoring. Volume I. The definition of quality and approaches to its assessment. Ann Arbor, MI: Health Administration Press, 1980.
Provides a conceptual framework for defining quality of care and describing approaches to assess it. The basic approach to quality assessment, focusing on structure, process, and outcome is explored in detail. The other two volumes in this series as well provide an excellent foundation on quality of care issues.

Goldfield N, Nash DB, eds. Providing quality care: the challenge to clinicians. Philadelphia, PA: American College of Physicians, 1989.
A series of quality of care experts explore concepts central to the definition, measurement, and assessment of quality care, including terms such as utilization review, mortality measures, and severity of illness.

Iezzoni LI, ed. Risk adjustment for measuring health care outcomes Ann Arbor, MI: Health Administration Press, 1994.
A collection of articles describing the concept of risk adjustment and exploring how to design and evaluate risk- adjustment systems.

Health Care Reform

Private Initiatives

Rushika J. Fernandopulle and David Chin

My years at HEW, and six more outside government, lead me to believe that the great hope of containing health care costs lies in an aroused private sector . . . Our best hope to change the health care system rests in an awakened, competitive world of business purchasers demanding and bargaining for high-quality care from a variety of producers at a much lower cost.

Joseph Califano Jr, former Secretary HEW[266]

Most of the debate in the United States (U.S.) about how to fix the health care system revolves around the role of the government. The next three chapters of this section detail efforts by foreign countries, various states, and the U.S. federal government to address the problems of cost, access, and quality in health care.

There are many, however, such as Joseph Califano (quoted), who believe that the true responses to these challenges can come from the private sector, not the public sector. Indeed, one can argue that many of the problems facing us today are not solely market failures, but government failures due to the unforeseen consequences of often well-meaning government policies. Examples can be found throughout this book, including the *ERISA* legislation discussed more fully in Chapter 13, the *Hill Burton Act* (Chapter 2), and the tax deductibility of insurance (Chapter 1). Thus, perhaps the solution to the problems of the health system lie not with the government, but with the market.

In this chapter, we look at what the private sector is doing to address the problems with the U.S. health care system. We start by discussing why some argue the private sector is better equipped than the government to address some of these issues, and we then turn to examples of what different players in the private sector are actually doing. We look first at efforts by individual employers to lower health costs, and then at coalitions of employers in various cities and regions. Next, we turn to some initiatives by providers, such as hospitals, insurers, and others, not only to become more efficient, but also to improve quality and access. Finally, we address the question of whether any of these initiatives actually work to solve the problems facing the U.S. health care system.

WHY THE PRIVATE SECTOR? ❖

Although it is obvious that some sort of government action is needed to address the problems of cost, access, and quality discussed in the previous three chapters, there are many reasons why it may be easier and perhaps preferable to leave much of this task to the private sector. Clark Havighurst, a professor at Duke University, suggests at least three such reasons.[267]

❖ Private companies are not subject to the same political pressures as governments. Health care is a huge and powerful industry, as discussed in the first chapter. More than 9.1 million people currently work in the health sector,[268] and more than 1/6 of new jobs in the country are in health care.[269] There are countless examples of governments trying to close local hospitals for economic reasons, but they are thwarted because of political opposition caused by the potential loss of jobs and community pride.

❖ Allowing the private sector to try to solve these problems is a much less risky proposition, because the market will determine which strategies work and which do not. Government programs, although usually well meaning, are rarely self-correcting, and, as we have seen, they often develop unforeseen complications that are difficult to fix.

❖ Market mechanisms allow for more individual variation in consumption. Although some societies pride themselves on consistency and uniformity, we value individuality and freedom. Different people have different needs and desires of the health system; government solutions tend to impose uniform standards rather than allow for diversity.

Finally, to many in the private sector, government solutions have not been coming fast enough. Harry Truman first suggested major health care reform in the 1940s, yet little structural reform has taken place due to lack of government action, except for passage of Medicare and Medicaid (Chapter 6). Due to this frustration, many private players are taking matters into their own hands.

EMPLOYER INITIATIVES ❖
Employers: Why Should They Care?

American business has long been involved in health care. As discussed in Chapter 4, due to wage freezes during World War II, employers started offering health benefits as incentives to their workers. After the war, health care was cheap, and the economy was booming, so companies continued to expand their health commitments to their employees. Currently, more than 92% of medium and large employers provide health insurance to their workers, and approximately two-thirds of all Americans get their insurance through their employer.[270]

Why do employers care about health care? The first reason is that it simply costs so much. In 1991, employers spent an average of more than $3,573 per employee on health benefits, which works out to a total of more than $180 billion each year.[271] Employers frequently state that this figure represents 55% of pretax profits, or more than 98% of post-tax profits (this is a somewhat misleading figure, however, because health costs are really counted as expenses, and it is not very useful to compare them to profits).

The second reason for concern is that these costs are increasing so rapidly. In 1965, health benefits constituted 2.2% of the total spent on salaries and benefits; in 1989, it was 8.3%. In 1965, businesses paid for 17% of all the health care consumed in this country; in 1989, this figure had increased to more than 30%.[272] Between 1970 and 1989, employer spending in real dollars (taking into account inflation) for salaries and wages cumulatively increased only 1% and retirement benefits increased 32%, whereas health benefits increased a staggering 163%.[273]

These cost concerns suggest the third reason for business action in the health sector: fear of loss of global competitiveness. Lee Iacocca testified in Congress that health benefits added $700 to the price of a new Chrysler, whereas they cost less than $200 per car for the Japanese.[274] Uwe Reinhardt, a Princeton economist, however, disputes this reasoning; he believes that what really affects competitiveness is not just health benefits, but total compensation packages given to workers. Thus, he argues that although the U.S. has greatly increased health benefits, we have compensated for this by holding wages down (remember the 1% growth in real salaries over 20 years).

Finally, these increasing health care costs have led to much friction between business and labor over the past few years. Businesses are trying to increase the percent of costs borne by workers (partly as a method of cost control), but labor has been loathe to give up these hard-won benefits, which they have gotten frequently at the expense of higher wages. Indeed, in 1989, more than 78% of the strikes that involved more than 1,000 employees concerned health benefits, leading to more than $1.1 billion in lost wages and productivity.[274]

Employers, therefore, have many motivations to act on health care, specifically to reduce costs. A poll of 1,000 CEOs of Fortune 500 service and industrial companies showed that 35% rated health costs as a top concern, whereas 60% rated it as a major concern, relative to other costs of doing business.[275]

In contrast, employers believe that only government action can solve the real problems. More than 15% of their costs, for example, are really due to cost shifting from uninsured patients,[276] something they have little control over. Thus, in the same survey of CEOs, 91% said that fundamental changes or a complete rebuilding of the U.S. health system was needed, and only 12.7% believed their company would be able to bring costs mostly under control in the next year or two.

However, the problems of health care costs are so large that most employers believe they have no choice but to try and do what they can.

Initiatives by Individual Employers

A study by a benefits consulting group called the Wyatt company found that 97% of the 1,115 firms surveyed had made some changes in their health plans to try to slow their increasing health costs.[277] Initiatives by individual companies include the following.

✧   Increasing *cost-sharing* in their plans (i.e., putting a larger burden of payment, in the form of higher premiums, copayments, or deductibles, onto their employees). A 1990 survey conducted by another benefits consulting group found that less than 18% of employers offer 100% reimbursement for health costs, not only to directly shift some cost onto workers, but also to make them more cost-conscious consumers of health care. As discussed in Chapter 4, the Rand study showed fairly conclusively that increasing copayments reduces health spending, with no measurable decrease in health outcomes.

✧   Providing incentives for employees to join *managed care* plans rather than traditional indemnity plans. A Foster Higgins study in 1990 showed the average health maintenance organization (HMO) cost employers $2,683 per employee per year, whereas a PPO cost $2,952 and an indemnity plan cost $3,214. See Chapter 5 for a detailed discussion of the different types of managed care plans and why they may save money.

✧   *Self-insuring.* As discussed more fully in Chapter 13, self-insuring (i.e., taking on the financial risk of insurance yourself rather than passing it onto an insurance company) allows a company much more flexibility in benefit design, because ERISA exempts self-insured companies from state-mandated benefits. These benefits include (in many states) in vitro fertilization for infertility, mental health and substance abuse benefits, and more. In 1989, 37% of employers with less than 1,000 employees and more than 82% of those with more than 10,000 employees were self-insured.[278]

✧   Using *case-management* to concentrate on their sickest employees who end up incurring most of the costs. The Rand study found that the sickest 1% of the population generate 28% of the health care costs, and the sickest 10% generate more than 70%. Thus, many companies employ case managers to individualize treatments and options for these few sick employees. As far back as 1983, some companies reported saving an average of more than $41,000 a case using these techniques, and in some cases, more than $100,000.[279]

♦ Requiring *preadmission testing,* mandatory *second opinions,* and *ambulatory care* facilities for elective surgery wherever possible.

♦ Using *extended care* facilities, such as rehabilitation hospitals, nursing homes, hospices, or home health care, when appropriate rather than keeping patients in a hospital.

♦ Providing annual *physicals, wellness programs,* and *financial incentives* for healthy lifestyles.

Specific companies have individualized these approaches to fit their own corporate missions and cultures. John Deere, for instance, has created its own integrated health system, and it is currently marketing it to other employers. Delta Airlines has identified centers of excellence where it can obtain high quality and low cost on big ticket items, such as coronary artery bypass graft surgery, and it flies its employees to these centers for free, even across the country.

Employer Coalitions

Although most employers are trying various things to reduce health care costs, most believe they cannot do it alone. Indeed, a survey in *Modern Healthcare* in 1991 reported that 46% of businesses believed they could not significantly control their health costs alone, and the figure was much higher for smaller employers. One of the most popular and successful responses to this dilemma has been formation of health care coalitions in the U.S. The same survey showed that more than 10% of businesses already belonged to such a coalition, and many more were considering joining or starting one.[280]

The first business groups founded exclusively to deal with health care became prominent in the 1970s, when health costs again were at the forefront of the nation's agenda. The two most prominent groups at the time were the Dunlop Group of Six and the Washington Business Group on Health (WBGH). The Dunlop group was named after the then Secretary of Labor, John Dunlop, and it was comprised of representatives from labor, business, providers, insurers, hospitals, and Blue Cross/Blue Shield. WBGH represented the interests of many large U.S. corporations, and by 1990, it counted more than 180 of the Fortune 500 as its members. These groups were engaged in discussions on the future of the U.S. health system, government lobbying, and formation of purchaser coalitions around the country.[281]

Health care coalitions are a collection of local employers who band together to try and affect their health care costs. Their actions can range from finding and publishing data on providers, negotiating group rates with hospitals, to pressuring governments for favorable health care legislation.

Rochester, New York, is perhaps the most successful model of employer involvement in lowering health costs. Since the 1970s, area employers led by Kodak and Xerox have been involved in community planning of health services. They have imposed community rating on all insurers, set up a network of community-based clinics, and coordinated reimbursement to hospitals. A Rochester area Hospital Council required all providers to submit for their approval any plans for expansion and to justify these plans on the basis of community need. Any hospital acting without approval was simply refused payment by the employer coalition.[282]

These actions have led to some spectacular results. The cost per employee of health insurance was $2,378 in 1992, which is less than two thirds of the national average ($3,573) and only 55% of the New York state average ($4,361). Only 6% of the population was uninsured (compared with 14% nationally), and 84% of the population was satisfied with their health system (compared with 71% nationally). All this progress was accomplished with no measurable differences in health outcomes.[283]

Employers in many other markets are trying to accomplish similar results in their cities. Some specific examples include the following.

❖ In Columbus Ohio, a group of employers, along with Blue Cross/Blue Shield, published a buyers guide to health care and distributed it to all their employees. This guide listed the average charges and length of stay for the 25 most common diagnostic groups in each of 40 local hospitals.[284]

❖ The Los Angeles (L.A.) Employers Health Care Coalition, comprised of the 30 largest employers in L.A., is tracking utilization and quality data on local providers, as well as insurance plans and HMOs. They realize that national data, such as on cesarean section rates, mean little in a local context due to large geographic practice variations (see Chapter 2), they therefore hope such local data can enable them to make more informed health purchases.[285]

❖ The Cleveland Health Quality Choice Program, sponsored by 150 corporations and more than 8,500 small businesses, is measuring cost and quality data, including customer satisfaction measures, for 30 local hospitals. They are also attempting to generate a list of which providers offer the best services at the lowest prices.[286]

Table 11.1 shows some other examples of health care coalitions around the country, although it is by no means complete.

PROVIDER INITIATIVES ❖
Initiatives by Hospitals

Partly due to pressure from employers, many providers are changing their behaviors not only to decrease costs, but also to improve access and quality of health care. Hospitals, because they comprise the biggest portion (38%) of health care

Table 11.1 Examples of Business Groups Scrutinizing Hospitals in Quality and Price Issues

Group	City	Date Started	People Covered	No. of Hospitals	Price/Cost Studies	Quality Surveys	Direct Contracts
The Alliance	Denver	1984					
Midwest Business Group on Health	Chicago	1987	represents 140 employers in 9 Midwest states		√1	√1	√
Central Iowa Quality Health Services Purchasing Demonstration	Des Moines	1991	100,000		√2	√2	
Business Coalition on Health	New Orleans	1991		63	√	√	
Prospective Pricing Initiative	St. Louis	1988	500,000	2	√		
Greater Cleveland Health Quality Choice	Cleveland	1989	300,000	30	√	√	
Lehigh Valley Business Conference on Healthcare	Bethlehem, PA	1990	80,000		√		√3
Memphis Business Group on Health	Memphis, TN	1985	200,000	15	√		√
Buyers Healthcare Cooperative	Nashville, TN	1983	140,000	20	√	√	√
Foundation for Healthcare Quality	Seattle	1988	covers population, providers statewide		√4	√4	
Alliance Purchasing Initiative	Madison, WI	1990	50,000	3	√	√5	√
Healthcare Network of Greater Milwaukee	Milwaukee	1986	150,000	13	√	√6	√

Adapted from Modern Healthcare, July 29, 1991. 1-Total quality management demonstration projects underway in Chicago, Milwaukee, and Kingsport, TN. 2-Studying cardiac care, maternity & child health, mental health, & substance abuse. 3-Contracts for prescription drugs, lab services. 4-Studies on lower-back pain and obstetrics care in conjunction with the University of Washington. 5-Studies on administrative services and clinical care. 6-Participant in total quality management demonstration project sponsored by Midwest Business Group on Health.

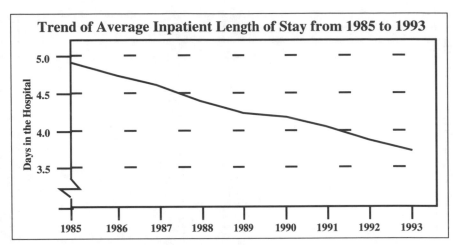

Figure 11.1 Average length of stay expressed as the median number of days for 5,000 general acute-care institutions, 1985–1993. (Data source: American Hospital Association, HCIA, Inc.)

spending, have faced the most concentrated pressures from the market to become more efficient. Over the past several years, average lengths of stay have declined dramatically, from approximately 5 days in 1985 to approximately 3.7 days in 1993 (Figure 11.1).[287] Many illnesses once treated in the hospital are being taken care of in doctors' offices; as a result of the advent of laparoscopic surgery, operations that once required days of in-patient recuperation are currently done as out-patient procedures. Because of these forces, many hospitals are losing money: In 1988, less than half of hospitals covered their expenses,[288] and many community hospitals have been forced to close down.

Hospitals have responded to these pressures in several ways.

✦ ***Horizontal integration*** refers to merging enterprises doing essentially the same thing to gain a larger market share or efficiencies of scale. One such way to integrate is for hospitals to form ***large purchasing groups.*** Experts estimate that by 1995, 90% of hospitals will be part of some sort of alliance or purchasing group. Forming larger networks also makes these hospitals more attractive to purchasers, because they need to contract with fewer entities to provide care for their customers.

✦ ***Consolidation.*** A second horizontal strategy is employed by Columbia Hospital corporation, which ***buys multiple hospitals*** in a given market and then ***closes the least productive ones,*** thus consolidating services. This strategy not only improves efficiency, but also makes Columbia a significant employer in the market, thus giving it additional political influence if necessary. Many local governments would like to do what Columbia is doing (i.e., closing nonproductive hospitals), but they cannot for political reasons.

✧ *Vertical integration* refers to the process of combining entities involved in different levels of the same industry to achieve efficiencies of production. Thus, a car maker such as Ford may try to buy a tire manufacturer, a steel company, and a glass company in an attempt at vertical integration. Similarly, many hospitals are trying to establish themselves throughout the continuum of care to compensate for their loss of inpatient revenue. Many hospitals are setting up networks of primary care clinics, entering into joint ventures with physicians, or buying medical practices to increase referrals to their hospitals. Others have tried to start their own insurance plans, but these attempts have been unsuccessful due to conflicting interest between the insurance and the delivery sides of the organization.

✧ The most ambitious plans try to *integrate all aspects of care,* including primary care doctors, acute and tertiary care hospitals, rehabilitation, home health, nursing homes, and financing. The Henry Ford Health System in southeastern Michigan is a good example of such a system, although some believe that such complete vertical integration is difficult because of the varied management skills needed to run such a diverse group of entities.[289] Figure 11.2 summarizes the operations of the Henry Ford Health System.

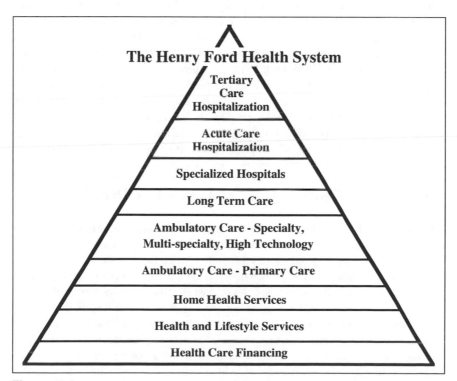

Figure 11.2 Adapted from HFHS/Integrated Health Systems.

Other Providers

Hospitals are not the only providers affected by pressures of the market. The entire HMO movement, started by Kaiser Permanente (see Chapter 5), was a private initiative to control cost. Currently, traditional indemnity insurers, such as Cigna and Aetna, are also jumping on the bandwagon by buying up physician practices and establishing their own staff model HMOs. Smaller insurers are banding together to form larger networks to become more attractive to larger customers. Private Healthcare Systems of Lexington, Massachusetts, is a good example of such a venture.

Providers are also trying new things to cut costs and to improve quality and access. One opportunity is to step into niches in the market that are well compensated but poorly served. Some physicians, for instance, are opening ambulatory clinics in shopping malls, with extended hours for customers who work during the day. Other companies are starting "focused factories," bringing multiple specialties related to a single illness under one roof. Salick Health Company's Breast Centers are a good example; they allow patients to coordinate their care with oncologists, radiologists, surgeons, nurses, and social workers, all in one location. Finally, groups such as Planetree are opening patient-centered hospital units, where nursing stations are abolished and patients have access to their own charts and are encouraged to add their own perceptions of their progress each day.

Finally, many free-standing companies have been set up to sell reduced cost or improved quality health care. Caremark and Phycor are examples of publicly traded companies that, employing a strategy somewhat similar to Columbia Hospitals, enter small markets with low HMO market penetration and buy up a significant percentage of physician practices. This approach gives them market clout to negotiate contracts with HMOs or directly with payers for the provision of health services. Finally, some companies concentrate on quality measurements, such as United Health Care, which publishes HMO report cards.

ARE THESE PRIVATE INITIATIVES WORKING?   ❖

The range of private initiatives in health care, as we have seen, is huge. The obvious question is, are these initiatives working? We have shown many specific cases where initiatives have saved money for individual payers or providers. The real public policy question, however, is whether these savings affect society at large, or whether they are simply more examples of cost shifting from one part of the economy to another. Put simply, are these initiatives lowering health costs overall?

In January 1994, a *Washington Post* lead story reported "There is more and more evidence that health care cost increases are slowing dramatically—thanks to market forces."[290] Labor Department statistics showed that health costs increased only 5.5% in 1993, the lowest rate of increase since 1973, and the U.S. Chamber of Commerce reported that the average premium cost to employers actually decreased from \$2,811 per worker in 1991 to \$2,754 in 1992. These changes happened while no major government-initiated changes in health care were actually taking place, although the debates over Clinton's managed care proposals were heating up in Congress.

It is hard to tell if this slowing of health cost increases is due to real structural changes, or if it is simply a result of potential government action. Social scientists are familiar with what is called the *Hawthorne effect,* which says that by merely by observing a system you can change its output. It originates from an experiment at a GE factory, where managers increased the wattage of light bulbs in the factory, and productivity rose dramatically. However, a later experiment showed that by reducing the wattage, they got the exact same result. Thus, it is unclear whether the changes reported in the *Post* article reflect real change, or merely the Hawthorne effect. In any case, the initiatives described are continuing, and they illustrate that the government may not be the only or even the best source of solutions for the problems that face our health system.

❖ **Suggested Reading** ❖

Bergthold L. Purchasing power in health. New Brunswick, NJ: Rutgers, 1991.
An in-depth, historical look at the involvement of business in health care.
Jaeger J. Private sector coalitions: a fourth party in health. Durham, NC: Duke, 1982.
An early look at employer coalitions, but still applicable today.
McArdle F. The changing health care market. Washington, DC: Employee Benefit Research Institute, 1987.
Although a little dated, this book contains many important discussions about how employers can reduce health costs.

12

Foreign Models

Bradley S. Marino and William Hsiao

The problems of containing cost inflation, maximizing access, and maintaining or improving quality are challenges faced by all nations, and each nation addresses these problems through a system distinctly their own. Examination of the health care systems of other industrialized nations offers useful insights that may prove helpful to United States (U.S.) health policy makers as they struggle with the issues of cost, access, and quality. This discussion outlines a framework for creating the optimal health care system for a nation and how to evaluate that health care system; we then use this framework to analyze the health care systems in Britain, Canada, and Germany. Once readers are familiar with the different methods of health care financing and delivery, they will accompany a hypothetical patient named John Smith through each health care system to view the system from the patient's perspective.

CREATING THE OPTIMAL HEALTH SYSTEM ❖
Fundamental Questions

Each health care system must address four fundamental questions.

+ What proportion of a nation's total resources are to be spent on health care, and who determines this proportion?
+ What are the sources of funding?

✦ How and by whom are scarce health resources to be allocated?

✦ How will the system obtain maximum efficiency in the production of health services, or put another way, how will the system get the most bang for its buck?

Factors that determine a system's efficiency include the nature of ownership, organization, and management of its health facilities, as well as its incentive structure, which comprises the method of physician and hospital compensation.

To address these fundamental questions, a nation must choose a macroscopic theoretical framework, usually either a demand-side or a supply-side approach. Such a policy choice reflects a nation's historical antecedents, culture, social values, and the balance of political power among the stakeholders in health affairs. This macroscopic choice impacts greatly on the operational structure of that system, which includes financing, organization, and incentives. More specifically, adopting either the supply-side or the demand-side approach determines the system's financing structure, as well as which stakeholders have fiscal control to determine the budget constraint for the system, the funding sources, and the allocation of resources within the system (answers the first three questions posed) as well as the system's organization and incentives that attempt to maximize efficiency (answers the fourth question posed).

Financing Structure
The Demand-Side Approach

The demand-side approach asserts that health care is like any other good in the marketplace in that consumers decide on what goods to buy and at what price. The basic tenets of the demand-side approach include that purchasers and providers have the same information, providers have little ability to induce patient demand or the market power to set prices, allocation of resources is based on consumer willingness to pay, and organizations that provide health care should be privately owned. Demand-siders believe that competition for consumer dollars forces providers to produce services efficiently; in the long run, production occurs at the lowest average cost. The total level of health care spending is not important to the demand-side school because it assumes that expenditure decisions are the direct result of consumer utility maximization.

The demand-side approach results in a financial structure in which the private sector is utilized to finance health care; consumers decide whether to buy insurance or to pay directly at the point of delivery; and, due to consumer independence, the government cannot mandate insurance, regulate a benefits package, or set premium rates. The result of this approach is multiple insurance plans competing in the marketplace and selecting the risks they want to insure. The U.S. system adheres to this approach; consequently, it has neither mandated coverage nor a minimum benefit standard, which results in many U.S. health services being rationed by price, according to a patient's ability and willingness to pay.

The Supply-side Approach

The supply-side approach believes that health care is a right and that everyone is entitled to access to health care, regardless of their ability to pay. The supply-side school believes that market failure in the health sector has resulted from three market forces.

- ✦ The existence of insurance, which reduces both consumers' and providers' sensitivity to price (moral hazard).
- ✦ The tendency of high-risk individuals to buy insurance (adverse selection) and the selection of favorable risks by insurers (risk selection), both of which impair competition in insurance markets.
- ✦ Information asymmetry between the physician and the patient, which leads to physician dominance over medical decisions and enables physicians and hospitals to induce demand and to set prices.

To correct these market failures, supply-siders advocate placing fiscal power in public or quasipublic agencies, which use a political or bargaining process rather than the flawed market to determine a total budget constraint for the given health care system. Government also has an important role, both in allocating resources to regions and programs, and in maximizing efficiency through system organization and incentives built into provider compensation mechanisms.

The supply-side approach has resulted in four distinct financing structures, all of which provide universal access.

✧   Central or provincial government finances health care and determines the proportion of total tax revenue to be spent by weighing the benefits of health expenditures against other claims on total tax revenues. The government either provides health services directly through the public sector or facilitates private sector provision of services (i.e., Britain and Canada).

✧   Local government finances health care and determines the proportion of total local revenues to be spent by weighing the benefits of health expenditures against the benefits of other local services (i.e., Sweden).

✧   Health care is financed by a separate tax, such as the Social Security payroll tax. Health expenditures do not have to compete directly against other claims on total tax revenue.

✧   Health care is paid by health insurance, which is provided by a mixture of public and private plans that are extensively regulated by the government. Interventions include mandating universal coverage, regulating risk selection, and defining a minimum benefits package. Under this structure, representatives of both payers and providers negotiate a total budget with a single channel for paying providers. This global budget limits expenditures for the following year. The single channel of payment allows the insurers to identify which providers abuse the system for higher revenues (i.e., Germany).[291]

Almost all large industrialized nations, except for the U.S., use a supply-side approach to finance their health care, in the form of either a national health service or compulsory health insurance coverage.

Cost-containment Strategies

Cost-containment may be sought on either the supply side or the demand side of the health care economy, and it may be sought with either macromanagement or micromanagement of that economy. Choosing a given macroscopic approach does not preclude use of the other approach on a microscopic level. In fact, most of the financing measures used in industrialized countries are a conglomeration of both, although one generally predominates. A compact summary of the various strategies used in modern health economies to contain costs is shown in Table 12.1.[292]

Table 12.1 Alternative Cost-Containment Strategies in Health Care

Target	Micromanagement	Macromanagement
Supply-side strategies	✦ Encouragement of efficiency in the production of medical treatments through economic incentives, for example, diagnosis-related groups or capitation. ✦ Legal constraints on the ownership of health care facilities.	✦ Regional planning designed to limit the physical capacity of the health system and to ensure its desired distribution among regions and social classes.
Demand-side strategies	✦ Conversion of patients to consumers through cost sharing. ✦ Hands-on supervision of decisions of doctors and their patients—managed care.	✦ Predetermined global budgets for hospitals and expenditure caps for physicians.
Strategies aimed at the market as a whole		✦ Price controls.

Adapted from Reinhart, U.; Princeton U., NJ, 1989.

Flow Diagrams of Goods, Services, and Resources

When examining a health system, it is critical to be able to identify the flow of goods, services, and resources that occurs during the delivery of health care. This flow can be seen in the abstract as three distinct nexi (Figure 12.1).

In nexus A, a third-party payer, which is either a private insurance carrier or a government, shoulders the financial risks of illness the patient would otherwise face in exchange for a transfer of money. This transfer can take the form of either insurance premiums that reflect the insured's own health status as best as can be determined by the insurer, or taxes or premiums that are totally divorced from the insured's health status and based on ability to pay.

In nexus B, the third-party payer transfers money to providers under a variety of compensation methods. These methods may take the form of piece-work payment or prepaid compensation in the form of capitation or salaries for the physicians or global budgets for inpatient facilities.

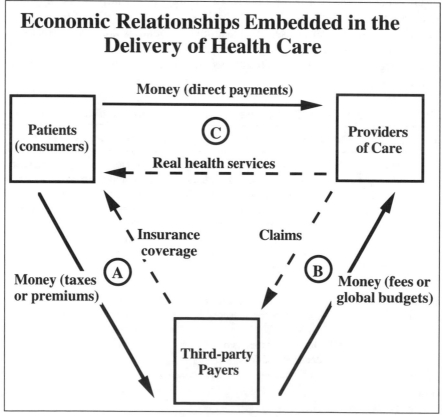

Figure 12.1 Economic relationships embedded in the delivery of health care. (Adapted from Reinhart U.: Princeton, NJ, 1989.)

Finally, in nexus C, health services and supplies are transferred from individual providers of health care to individual patients.[293]

Obstacles

For many nations, developing an optimal structure for their health care system has proved to be an elusive task for three reasons. In the abstract, most nations embrace three goals for their health care system: universal access to quality health care, control of health care costs to a reasonable level, and effective use of resources. The first reason optimal health systems have not been found is the fact that nations cannot reach consensus on the relative importance of these goals. The relative importance of each goal depends on socioeconomic, historical, and political imperatives facing each nation. Sometimes these goals are mutually exclusive, and to maximize one imperative, another must be given less importance. Trade-offs exist in that cost-containment can result in diminished quality, and improved access or quality can result in increased cost. The second reason the development of optimal health care systems has proved to be elusive concerns the ideological debate between those who support cost-containment from the supply-side and those who support cost-containment from the demand-side. This debate has resulted in health systems that change slowly and vacillate between the two approaches. Finally, optimal health systems have been slow to develop because of insufficient empirical data. Little is known about the performance of the many varied types of health systems and the key dynamic forces that influence outcomes.

Although many experts engage in comparative research and believe useful insights can be learned from other countries, others warn of the difficulties of transferring a specific approach across national boundaries. Therefore, the goal should not be to duplicate another nation's system, but to understand better the key factors that affect one's own health system and to adapt lessons from other systems to address these key issues.

Evaluating Health Care Systems

Evaluation of a health care system requires examination of health expenditures and outcomes through health status indices, public satisfaction, and utilization rates.

Health expenditures are a reliable indicator of resource utilization. When comparing health care expenditures between nations, the expenditures are usually expressed on a per capita basis and as a percent of gross national product. One cannot say, based on these two measurements, whether a nation spends too much or too little on its health care. The "right" amount of spending is determined either by the market, if the nation ascribes to a demand-side approach to financing, or politically, if the nation ascribes to a supply-side approach to financing. The usefulness of these measurements is not to compare across nations but to see which systems over time have been able to contain expenditures and how that containment affected access and quality.

Health status is a useful measure of outcomes; unfortunately, measures of health status are difficult to find and crude at best. The most common indices used to measure health status are infant mortality and life expectancy. A multitude of factors affect both of these measures of health status, and health care most likely has a small if not a minimal impact on both. Despite this fact, infant mortality and life expectancy are frequently the chosen measures of health status.

Consumers derive satisfaction from both tangible and intangible benefits of health services. Public satisfaction is a key indicator to ascertain how well a nation's health system is meeting the needs and the expectations of its consumers. To measure public satisfaction, health care consumers are usually asked if they are satisfied with their own health care and if they are satisfied with their nation's health care system.

Health care is not only used to cure disease, but also to quell anxiety and to provide comfort and assurance for patients. Therefore, access to care has value intrinsically. The utilization rates of visits per year per capita and admission rate per 100 persons provide instructive measures of access to care.

FOREIGN MODELS EXAMINATION ❖

We now turn to reviewing the health care systems of Great Britain, Canada, and Germany. These three nations were chosen because all are industrialized nations with large populations whose health care systems represent a broad cross-section of how nations finance and produce health services. Their systems provide a basis of comparison to the health system of the U.S., and their experiences may prove helpful as the U.S. attempts to reform its own health system.

Before examining differences among these three health systems in detail, we compare them broadly and place them into a conceptual framework. Table 12.2, which categorizes health systems by how each system finances and delivers health care, illustrates the position of each system in the health care spectrum. In the ***British*** system, the government operates the production of health care, and it provides financing. This type of health care has often been termed *socialized medicine*. The ***Canadian*** system combines government financing with a pluralistic, partly private and partly public delivery system. This type of system has often been called a *single-payer* or an *all-payer system*. The ***German*** system combines both pluralistic financing and a delivery system (although both facets are tightly regulated by the federal government). The U.S. system, like Germany's, combines both pluralistic financing and a delivery system, but neither is regulated by the government.[294]

Table 12.2 Alternative Mixes of Health Insurance and Health-Care Delivery

Production and Delivery	Indirect Financing of Health Care			Direct Financing
	Government Financed Insurance	Private Health Insurance		Out of Pocket by Patients at Point of Service
		Within a Statutory Framework	Within an Unregulated Market	
Purely Government Owed	A	D	G	J
Private Not-for-Profit Entities	B	E	H	K
Private For-Private Entities	C	F	I	L
	The Canadian Health System	The West German Health System	The U.S. Health System	

Cell B represents the British system of health, also referred to as socialized medicine. The Canadian system is often called a single-payer or all-payer system and occupies cells A, B, and C. The West German system, cells D, E, and F, is both a pluralistic financing and delivery system. Cells G, H, I, J, K, and L combine unregulated pluralistic financing and delivery systems in the U.S. health system. (Adapted from Reinhart, U.; Princeton U., Princeton, NJ, 1989.)

As we look at each of the three systems, we will examine its:

✦ *Theoretical framework.* Defines the economic approach taken (supply-side or demand-side) and places the system in the health care spectrum based on how the nation finances and delivers health care.
✦ *Financing structure.* Defines how the national health care expenditure is determined, funding sources, and how resources are allocated.
✦ *Efficiency maximization.* Accomplished by the organization of the health system and its incentive structure.

In addition we will look at:

✦ Diagrammatic flow of goods, services, and resources
✦ Cost-containment strategies
✦ Access
✦ Quality
✦ Strengths and weaknesses

British Model
Theoretical Framework

Socialized medicine, supply-side approach, in which the federal government finances and produces health care. The National Health Service (NHS) operates the health care system.

Financing Structure
Health Care Expenditure Determination
The governmental health care expenditure is determined by the Prime Minister and his or her cabinet through a political process in which available funds are allocated among the various governmental departments. This determination is done in consultation with the Department of Health and Social Security. See Figure 12.2 for a comparison of health care expenditures per capita between the U.S., Britain, Canada, and Germany.

Funding Sources
Ninety-five percent of the total health care expenditure is funded by the federal government, and 5% is funded by the private sector.[295] Ninety-eight percent of governmental health care funding results from government taxation, and 2% results from charges for certain services, including prescriptions, dental work, ophthalmological services, and private beds in NHS hospitals.[295]

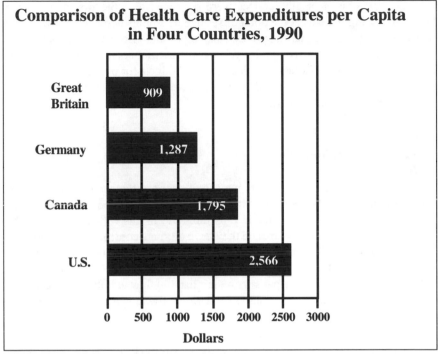

Comparison of Health Care Expenditures per Capita in Four Countries, 1990

Great Britain: 909
Germany: 1,287
Canada: 1,795
U.S.: 2,566

Dollars

Figure 12.2 Comparison of health care expenditures per capita in four countries, 1990. Shown in U.S.$ with conversions made using Purchasing Power Parity. (Data source: OECD, 1991. Adapted from Hsaio, Journal of Health Politics, Policy and Law, 1992.)

Resource Allocation

Resources are explicitly rationed through the NHS. The Department of Health and Social Security allocates the decided on expenditure through the NHS to Regional Health Authorities (RHAs), who then allocate their funding to District Health Authorities (DHAs). RHAs are responsible for strategic planning and resource allocation for each geographic area, whereas DHAs have operational responsibility for each geographic area. There are approximately 15 regions and 200 districts. There are approximately 3 million people in each region and 500,000 people in each district.[295] Until 1991, each hospital within each district received a prospective global budget lump-sum payment to cover all its operating expenses for the year. Likewise, each Family Practitioner Committee (FPC) within each district received a prospective lump-sum payment to compensate general practitioners for primary care services provided. Hospitals then allocated resources to hospital-based physicians through a flat salary, which was set by the hospital based on training level. Funds were allocated to general practitioners through capitation payments that were set by the FPC within each district.

In 1991, in an attempt to create competition on the district level and to give patients more choice, the NHS began phasing in internal markets in which financing and the provision of health services were separated. For the first time, money began following patients at the point of service. Hospitals began contracting with districts based on real costs and prices. Hospitals could also opt out of district control and become NHS trusts. Similarly, general practitioners in big group practices could become "budget-holders" with control of budgets for both primary and hospital care. As of 1994, all hospitals became independent trusts that ceased receiving prospective global budgets.

Efficiency Maximization
Organization
Choice of Provider   Consumers may freely choose their general practitioner (GP), but they can only see a specialist, in Britain called a "consultant," or be admitted to a hospital if they are referred by their GP. In this way, the British GP is the "gatekeeper" of their system, and they have ultimate control over consumption of health resources. GPs handle 90% of cases without the assistance of a consultant[295]; 98% of the British population is registered with a GP.[295] A GP has the right to decide whether to accept a patient on their list, but they are obliged to give necessary treatment to any person asking for treatment who is not on any other GP's list or who needs emergent treatment.

Ownership and Management of Hospitals   Until 1991, almost all hospitals were government-owned and operated, but due to reforms, nearly all are currently NHS trusts. Private beds in NHS hospitals account for less than 1% of total beds.[295] There are a few private hospitals that handle predominantly nonacute patients who need chronic care. The majority of private hospitals are nursing homes that care for elderly, mentally challenged, or chronically ill patients. The private hospitals are not in competition with the NHS; they function as a complementary parallel system that fills gaps in the NHS system.

Incentives
Physician Compensation   Seventy percent of GPs receive capitated fees from the FPC with whom they are contracted, which account for 50% of their income. The other 50% of the GP's income is derived from obstetrical services, contraceptive advice, and immunizations.[295] Thirty percent of GPs are "budget-holders" (i.e., physicians cannot bill above the rigid fee schedule set by the FPC). Physicians in hospitals work for the NHS, and they receive a flat salary from the hospital's prospective budget.

Hospital Compensation   Hospital trusts are compensated for services provided to each patient. Figure 12.3 illustrates the diagrammatic flow of goods, services, and resources.

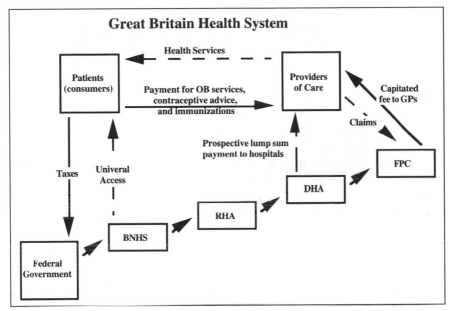

Figure 12.3 Schematic model of the British health system. BNHS = British National Health Service; RHA = Regional Health Authority; DHA = District Health Authority; FPC = Family Practitioner Committee; GP = General Practitioner; OB = obstetrics.

Cost-Containment Strategies

❖ *Macromanagement/supply-side.* Health expenditure competes directly with all other government programs; thus, resources are constrained by total tax revenues and the political process involved in expenditure determination. Also, regional planning is designed to limit the physical capacity of the health system and to ensure its desired distribution among regions and social classes.

❖ *Macromanagement/demand-side.* Prospective negotiated global budgets for hospitals and physicians within a given region.

❖ *Micromanagement/supply-side.* Legal constraint on the formation of NHS hospital trusts and general practitioner group practices.

❖ *Strategies aimed at market as a whole.* Price controls on the pharmaceutical industry based on pharmaceutical corporation profits.

Access

NHS is the sole insurer, and it provides universal access. The private insurance sector is very small, and private insurance is usually obtained to cover hospitalization for the private NHS, nonhospital dental work, eyeglasses, hearing aids, or long-term or chronic care.

Quality

See Figures 12.4, 12.5, and 12.6 for some measures of health care quality seen in the British system as compared with those in Canada, the U.S., and Germany.

Strengths

+ Universal access with effective cost-containment.
+ Stable health care system in which consumers need not worry about coverage or loss of benefits.
+ Free choice of GP, with no out-of-pocket costs, copayments, or deductibles.
+ Relative to the U.S., British health care is much cheaper.
+ Because it is a single-payer system, government is the sole payer, and administrative costs are much lower than in the U.S.
+ Gatekeeper role of GPs ensures universal primary care, decreased hospitalization rates, and results in better containment of costs.
+ Because physicians are paid on a capitated basis (GP) or with a flat salary (Hospital Consultants), there is no incentive to overprovide services.
+ Subsidized drug prices for poor and elderly.

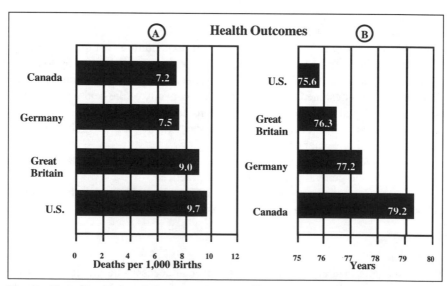

Figure 12.4 Panel A = infant mortality rates in four countries, 1989. Data on Canada and Great Britain is for 1988. Panel B = life expectancy in four countries, 1990. (Data source: OECD, 1991. Adapted from Hsaio, Journal of Health Politics, Policy and Law, 1992.)

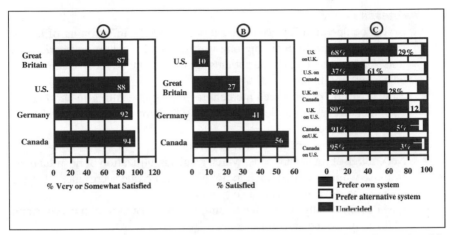

Figure 12.5 Panels A and B measure public satisfaction with their own health care, in each of four countries. Panel A data source: Harvard Community Health Plan, 1990. Panel B data source: Blendon et al., 1990. Both adapted from Hsaio, Journal of Health Politics, Policy and Law, 1992. Panel C measures public preference for an alternative health system of another country compared to the health system in their own country. Data source: Harris poll, 1988. (Adapted from Terris, Technology Review, 1990.)

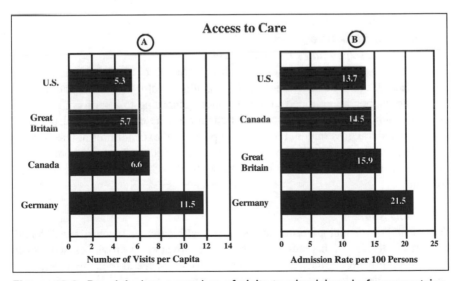

Figure 12.6 Panel A shows number of visits to physicians in four countries, 1989. Note data on Germany and Canada are for 1988. Panel B shows rates of admission for inpatient care in four countries, 1989. Note data on Canada and Great Britain are for 1988. (Data source: OECD, 1991. Adapted from Hsaio, Journal of Health Politics, Policy and Law, 1992.)

Weaknesses

✦ Severe competition for tax-financed budget results in rationing of health care. Patients must remain on long waiting lists for elective surgeries and tests. Due to rationing, some patients are not eligible to receive care based on age or condition.

✦ Slow diffusion of advanced medical technology, resulting in shortage of equipment in certain regions and waiting lists for certain advanced technological procedures.

✦ Variable coverage for long-term or chronic care.

✦ Not enough chronic care beds, which results in utilization of hospital beds by those who are well enough to not be there. Private sector has filled the void of chronic care beds to a certain degree.

✦ Low density of physicians due to emigration to the U.S. in the 1960s and 1970s in post-Medicare era.

✦ Low medical staff morale and the perception of the "best and brightest" not going into medicine anymore.

Canadian Model
Theoretical Framework

Single-payer system, supply-side approach in which the province is the sole insurer, and health care is provided by both publicly and privately owned sources.

Financing Structure
Health Care Expenditure Determination
The federal Department of National Health and Welfare determines the proportion of federal dollars that will be spent on national health insurance, and this total amount is then apportioned to the provinces according to a set formula. Each province then supplements the federal budget with its own provincial tax revenue. The federal government requires that provincial expenditures at least match the federal allocation given to each province. See Figure 12.2 for a comparison of health care expenditures per capita between the U.S., Britain, Canada, and Germany.

Funding Sources
Federal and provincial governments finance health care; each contributes 45 and 55%, respectively.[296] This ratio varies slightly for the poorer provinces, which get slightly more from the federal government. Provinces spend their own funds on the margin, thus the province has total control of the NHS budget for each province. Of the 55% put forward by the provinces, anywhere from 0 to 20% is obtained by employer payment.[297] The health resources provided by the federal government and the provinces are for the most part obtained through progressive taxation.

Resource Allocation

The provincial budgets are then allocated by the province through negotiations with each provincial medical association and each hospital within that province. The global budget for physician services negotiated by the medical association negotiators is then divided among the medical specialties as the association sees fit to create the provincial fee schedule. Each hospital receives a prospective global budget lump sum payment to cover all its operating expenses for the year, based on the expected number of patient days of care. Capital funds for new facilities, major renovations, or new equipment and technology are not part of a hospital's global budget; these funds are allocated based on hospital requests and provincial planning goals.

Efficiency Maximization

Organization

Choice of Provider Consumers have free choice of both physicians and hospitals. The majority of physicians are in private practice, and they have hospital admitting privileges wherever they choose.

Ownership and Management of Hospitals The large majority of hospitals are private nonprofit institutions.

Incentives

Physician Compensation Physicians are paid on a fee-for-service basis by each province; the fee schedule is determined by the provincial medical association. Physicians cannot bill above the negotiated fee schedule. Physicians are not employees of the hospital.

Hospital Compensation Hospitals are given one lump sum prospectively, which is based on expected patient days of care. Institutions receive more if they produce more patient care days than expected. Thus, there is an incentive for hospitals to keep patients in the hospital. Figure 12.7 illustrates the diagrammatic flow of goods, services, and resources.

Cost-Containment Strategies

♦ *Macromanagement/supply-side.* Regional planning designed to limit the physical capacity of the health system and to ensure its desired distribution among regions and social classes.

♦ *Macromanagement/demand-side.* Prospective negotiated global budgets for hospitals and physicians within a given province.

♦ *Micromanagement/demand-side.* Conversion of patients to consumers through cost sharing via premiums in some provinces.

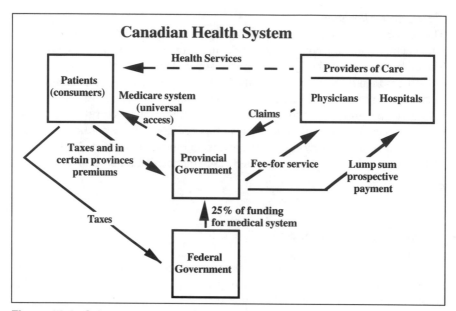

Figure 12.7 Schematic model of the Canadian health care system.

Access

The provincial Medicare system is the sole insurer, and it provides universal access. By law, private insurers that operate in Canada are prohibited from offering benefits that are financed through provincial plans. As a result, private insurance is very limited in scope, and it only covers hospitalization for a private or semiprivate room, nonhospital dental work, eyeglasses, hearing aids, or long-term chronic care.

Quality

Once again, see Figures 12.4, 12.5, and 12.6 for some comparative indices of quality.

Strengths

- ✦ Universal access with effective cost-containment.
- ✦ Stable health care system in which consumers need not worry about coverage or loss of benefits.
- ✦ Free choice of providers, both physician and hospital, with no out-of-pocket costs, copayments, or deductibles.
- ✦ Relative to the U.S., Canadian health care is cheaper, and, for the most part, it is of equal quality.
- ✦ Because it is a single-payer system, administrative costs are much lower than in the U.S., which has a multitude of third-party payers.

Weaknesses

+ Fee-for-service compensation for physicians along with a rigid fee schedule creates incentive for physicians to render a greater number of services in an attempt to increase their revenue, and it generates pressure from physicians to increase fees. Government response to these pressures in some provinces has been regulations that limit total payment pool and caps on physician income.

+ Slow diffusion of advanced medical technology, resulting in shortage of equipment in certain regions and waiting lists for certain advanced technological procedures, elective surgeries, and tests. Waiting lists were a temporary phenomenon that existed in 1990 to 1992, but this factor has largely been remedied. Currently, the problem is very minor in Canada relative to Britain.

+ Variable coverage for long-term or chronic care.

+ Not enough chronic care beds, which results in utilization of hospital beds by those who are well enough to not be there.

+ Some delays in service and treatment, but these delays are minor relative to the British model.

German Model
Theoretical Framework

Highly structured, regulated private insurance system, supply-side approach in which both financing and delivery of health care are accomplished through multiple parties in the private sector. Key features include the following.

◇ Ninety percent of persons covered by statutory health insurance system and 10% covered by private commercial insurance carriers.[292]

◇ The statutory health insurance system consists of 1,200 fiscally independent, self-governing, not-for-profit "sickness funds." Each fund serves small geographical areas (local sickness funds), workers of a particular firm, or members of a particular trade or craft. These three types of sickness funds have traditionally provided health financing for blue-collar workers.[292] Also 15 substitute funds are housed within the statutory health insurance system, which cover white-collar workers predominantly and are nationwide.[297]

◇ Government statutes dictate a catalogue of basic benefits that each fund must offer to their members, governance of funds, and fiscal regulatory relationships with providers.

◇ Every German is entitled to join the statutory health insurance system. An individual's membership in a statutory sickness fund automatically covers all of the member's dependent family members.

✧   Membership in the statutory system is compulsory for all employees with incomes less than $30,000 and for retired persons who had belonged to the system during their work life. Currently, 75% of the 90% of the population insured by the statutory system are compulsory members; the remainder have joined the system voluntarily.[297]

✧   Those persons who choose not to join the statutory system in favor of a private insurance carrier lose the right to ever return to the statutory system. Think of the statutory health insurance system as the private-sector extension of the government's will.

Financing Structure
Health Care Expenditure Determination

The national health care expenditure is determined by an annual assembly of all the stakeholders in the country's health care system. The current Congress has met since 1977, and it is mandated to meet by law.[292] Participants of the convention include providers (physician associations and hospitals); statutory and private health insurance carriers; representatives of the pharmaceutical industry, major unions, and associations of employers; and representatives of state and local governments. The goal of the annual meeting is to arrive at broad national health care expenditure guidelines. It is intended by government to be a consensus-building device. The convention has no formal governmental powers, and its guidelines are not legally binding for any of the parties. The guidelines serve as a benchmark for negotiation of fees, prices, and per diem compensation for health services that take place between associations of insurers and providers. See Figure 12.2 for a comparison of health care expenditures per capita between the U.S., Britain, Canada, and Germany.

Funding Sources

Sources of health care financing break down as follows: statutory health insurance system, 73%; federal government, 13%; private insurance, 7%; and private household funding, 7%.[292] The statutory health insurance system is financed by equal payments by employers and employees that total 8 to 16% of the employees' income.[298] Unemployed persons have their premiums paid by the federal unemployment insurance fund. Retiree health insurance premiums, which are by law paid by their pension fund, equal a percentage of their pension payment. This percentage is on average 13%.[298]

Resource Allocation

Within a region (state or substate), statutory sickness funds join together in associations to negotiate with counterpart associations of physicians' fee schedules, which must be accepted by the individual physician as payment in full. Since 1985, physicians have agreed to an overall expenditure cap for their services.[294] The expenditure cap is negotiated annually as so many deutsche marks (DM) per insured person (adjusted for age and sex). Once this amount is set by the sickness funds and physician associations, the physician associations disburse moneys to its members on a fee-for-service basis. Funds with a particularly heavy load of retired members receive compensating contributions from a national reserve fund. The objective of the contributions is to equalize the financial burden imposed by the aged on working members across various sickness funds. In some states, sickness funds in particular distress receive cross-subsidies from more financially sound funds.

Efficiency Maximization
Organization
Choice of Provider   The distinction between ambulatory and hospital-based physicians is important because ambulatory physicians do not follow their patients into the hospital after they have referred a patient there, as is customary in the U.S. Forty-five percent of German physicians are private practitioners, whereas 55% are hospital-based.[294] Patients may freely choose their ambulatory physician, hospital-based physician, and the hospital in which they want to be cared for.

Ownership and Management of Hospitals   Hospitals are both privately and publicly owned: 52% are publicly owned, 35% are private non-profit institutions, and 15% are private for-profit institutions.[294]

Incentives
Physician Compensation   To receive compensation, ambulatory physicians must be part of a regional physician association. Ambulatory physicians are paid on fee-for-service basis. A binding fee schedule is arrived at by negotiation between regional physician associations and regional sickness funds. The expenditure cap for ambulatory physicians results in policing of the physician associations to make sure that particular members are not receiving more compensation than they should. Hospital-based physicians are employees of their hospital, and they are paid a flat salary. This salary is based on specialty and seniority. Private insurance plans compensate ambulatory physicians based on a rigid fee schedule negotiated between the federal government and an insurance carrier; this fee schedule is similar to those negotiated between physician associations and sickness funds, but it is on average 2 times greater. For example, if an office visit costs 20 DM and an appendectomy costs 400 DM according to the sickness fund fee schedule, it will cost 40 DM and 800 DM according to the private insurance fee schedule.

Hospital Compensation   Hospitals are compensated for each patient on a prospective per diem basis from the sickness fund and private insurers. Per diem compensation from private insurers is less than that of the sickness fund. A prospective per diem payment schedule is determined by negotiations between

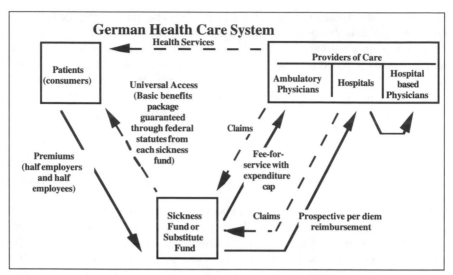

Figure 12.8   Schematic diagram of German health care system.

hospitals and regional associations of sickness funds and private insurers. Hospital budget caps furnished by state governments are based on regional planning. Figure 12.8 illustrates the diagrammatic flow of goods, services, and resources.

Cost-Containment Strategies
  ◆ *Macromanagement/supply-side.* Regional planning designed to limit the physical capacity of the health system and to ensure its desired distribution among regions and social classes.
  ◆ *Macromanagement/demand-side.* Prospective negotiated global budgets for hospitals and expenditure caps for physicians.

Access
Ninety-nine percent of the German population have comprehensive coverage. Minimum benefits include ambulatory physician care, inpatient care, prescription drugs, dental care, and medical supplies/appliances (e.g., braces, optical wear).

Quality
See Figures 12.4, 12.5, and 12.6 for comparative performance data on the German health care system.

Strengths
  ◆ Universal access with effective cost-containment.

✦ Stable health care system in which large majority of consumers need not worry about coverage or loss of benefits.

✦ Free choice of provider and no out-of-pocket costs, copayments, or deductibles.

✦ Relative to the U.S., German health care is cheaper.

✦ Tight regulation of the insurance market has eliminated adverse selection, exclusion of high-risk individuals, and job lock, as seen in unregulated multiple third-party systems.

✦ Hospital budgets and physician expenditure caps have not resulted in rationing of care.

✦ High utilization rates of patient visits/year.

Weaknesses

✦ Per diem reimbursement results in average length of stay in hospitals that is three times greater than in U.S. This approach is an effort to increase revenues. If a prospective DRG system was used, such as in the U.S., average length of stay would likely decrease. Although high average length of stay increases revenue, it also increases cost to the hospital, which has resulted in low staffing intensity in hospitals in an attempt to control costs.

✦ Variable coverage for long-term or chronic care.

✦ Not enough long-term/chronic care beds, which results in utilization of hospital beds by those who are well enough to not be there.

✦ Some delays in service and treatment, but they are minor relative to British and Canadian systems.

JOHN SMITH ❖

We have focused on the health care systems of Britain, Canada, and Germany from a macromanagement perspective. In this section, we shift to the micromanagement level and follow John Smith through the health care systems of the U.S., Britain, Canada, and Germany to see what each system is like from the perspective of the patient. We have given Mr. Smith heart disease because it is prevalent in all four countries.

John Smith Is Cared for in the United States

The U.S. health care system is a pluralistic system with wide variations in coverage depending on your ability to pay for insurance or your membership in a group, such as the elderly, poor, or veterans. Due to the wide variation in coverage, we have chosen two scenarios for Mr. Smith. In the first scenario, Mr. Smith is a middle-income person with insurance provided by his employer. In the second sce-

Table 12.3 International Comparison at a Glance

	United States	Great Britain	Canada	Germany
Financing	unregulated insurance industry	government	government	regulated insurance industry
Delivery	public/private	government	public/private	public/private
Financing Structure	demand-side	supply-side	supply-side	supply-side
Health Expenditure Determination	determined by market	Prime Minister, Cabinet, & Dept. of Health & Social Welfare	Dept. of Natl. Health and Welfare, and Provincial Ministers of Health	annual health care congress
Resource Allocation	determined by market	National Health Service through RHAs, DHAs, and FPCs	provinces through negotiations with hospitals & physician assocs.	within region sickness fund assoc.'s negotiate with physician assoc.'s & hospital assoc.'s
Choice of Provider	amount of free choice dependent on coverage	free choice of GP, must be referred to a consultant	free choice of primary care and specialist physicians	free choice of primary care and specialist physicians, primary care physician does not follow care of patient in hospital as in U.S., U.K., Canada

Table 12.3. (continued)

Ownership & Management of Hospitals	most private, non-profit	all hospitals government owned and operated	most private, non-profit	50% publicly owned 35% private non-profit 15% private for-profit
Physician Compensation	mix of fee-for-service, capitated fees, flat salaries	GPs receive capitated fee from FPCs plus income derived from obstetrical services, contraceptive advice and immunizations; hospital-based physicians receive a flat salary	rigid fee schedule determined by provincial medical assoc.	ambulatory physicians paid fee-for-service, rigid fee schedule determined through negotiations between regional physician & sickness fund assocs., expenditure caps for reimbursement of ambulatory physicians in place; hospital physicians receive a flat salary
Hospital Compensation	DRG prospective payment, third party payment	lump-sum prospective budget	lump-sum prospective payment	compensated for each patient on per diem basis by sickness fund
Access	15% uninsured 15% underinsured	universal access	universal access	99% total access, 90% covered by statutory system, 9% covered private carrier

nario, Mr. Smith works for a small business that does not provide insurance, and, because of his low income, Mr. Smith cannot afford health insurance for himself or his family. The first scenario was chosen because it represents the majority of the U.S. population. The second scenario was chosen because it represents 75% of the 37 million uninsured persons in the U.S.

Scenario 1

Mr. Smith is a 55 year-old man who is covered by insurance provided by his employer. Mr. Smith has both hospital coverage and physician coverage. When Mr. Smith consumes health services, the providers submit documentation to his insurer for reimbursement.

Mr. Smith has a one-year history of exertional angina, which has been followed by his primary care physician and his cardiologist. Mr. Smith chose his physician and cardiologist. Mr. Smith pays a $50 deductible and 10% of the fee amount to see his internist or cardiologist. In the U.S., the deductible and the percentage of the fee that the patient is responsible for varies from plan to plan, depending on its comprehensiveness. The internist, in conjunction with the cardiologist, prescribed a beta-blocker b.i.d. and sublingual trinitroglycerine p.r.n. for episodes of chest pain. Mr. Smith does have pharmaceutical coverage included in his insurance; therefore, he does not bear the brunt of the high cost of his drugs each month.

When unstable angina developed, a coronary angiogram was performed without delay. Unlike other countries, he did not have to be put on a waiting list. Pending the results of the coronary angiogram, Mr. Smith, if needed, would be scheduled for a coronary artery bypass graft (CABG) operation. Mr. Smith would not have to be put on a list for a CABG. The majority of the cost for both these procedures would be paid for by his insurer, although Mr. Smith would have to pay a $500 deductible for the first 60 days of care in the hospital. Mr. Smith's cardiologist and cardiac surgeon would be paid by the insurer based on the negotiated fee-for-service schedule the insurer has with the physician. Mr. Smith's hospital care would be paid for by his insurer through a prospective payment. If services to Mr. Smith cost more than the prospective payment the hospital has received for his care, the hospital loses money.

Scenario 2

Mr. Smith is a 55 year-old man who works for a small business that does not provide health insurance, and he cannot afford to purchase it for himself or his family. When Mr. Smith consumes health services, he must either pay out-of-pocket for services or demonstrate that he is an emergency case and hope the hospital provides him with charity care.

Mr. Smith has a one-year history of exertional angina. The condition was diagnosed in the emergency room, because Mr. Smith does not have a primary care physician. The emergency room services were paid for by Mr. Smith out-of-pocket. Mr. Smith's angina has been worsening over the course of the year, but he has been slow to go to a physician because of the cost of a visit and any medications the physician might prescribe. Finally, after urging from his family, he went to see a physician at the walk-in clinic at the local hospital. The internist prescribed a beta-blocker b.i.d. and sublingual trinitroglycerine p.r.n. for episodes of chest pain. Mr. Smith, due to his lack of pharmaceutical coverage, must bear the brunt of the high cost of his drugs each month.

When unstable angina developed, Mr. Smith went to the emergency room again, was admitted, and was scheduled for a coronary angiogram without delay. Pending the results of the coronary angiogram, Mr. Smith, if needed, would be scheduled for a coronary artery bypass graft (CABG) operation. Mr. Smith would not have to be put on a list for a CABG. Although Mr. Smith does not have to wait for the angiogram or the CABG, he is unable to pay for either procedure or the hospital costs associated with them. The hospital in which Mr. Smith is treated would have to write-off all the services he consumed as charity care. Obviously, hospitals that have large charity care loads and who service many patients like Mr. Smith would have trouble being financially viable. Mr. Smith's cardiologist and cardiac surgeon would be paid by the hospital based on the negotiated fee-for-service schedule the hospital has with the physician for charity care.

John Smith Is Cared for in Great Britain

Mr. Smith is a 55 year-old man who is cared for by the NHS. Mr. Smith does not pay for anything other than his private insurance for use of a private or semiprivate bed in an NHS hospital.

Mr. Smith has a one-year history of exertional angina, which has followed by his GP and a cardiologist that his GP chose and referred him to. Mr. Smith freely chose his GP, and he has had the same GP for 20 years. Mr. Smith does not pay a fee, a copayment, or a deductible to see his GP, who receives a capitated fee from the district FPC with which the GP has contracted. Mr. Smith does not pay a fee, a copayment, or a deductible to see his cardiologist, who is salaried by the hospital where he practices. The GP prescribed a beta-blocker b.i.d. and sublingual trinitroglycerine p.r.n. for episodes of chest pain. Mr. Smith pays a small amount for his medication because they are heavily subsidized by the government.

Mr. Smith has been on a list for a coronary angiogram for approximately nine months. According to NHS rules, Mr. Smith is not eligible for a CABG operation because of his age, and Mr. Smith is a retired laborer who does not have enough money to pay for it himself. It is hoped that a balloon angioplasty will be able to ameliorate his angina, but once he has his coronary artery angiogram, he will need to go on another list for balloon angioplasty. While he is waiting, there is a substantial risk that he could have a fatal or a further debilitating heart attack.

John Smith Is Cared for in Canada

Mr. Smith is a 55 year-old man who is covered by his provincial Medicare plan. To receive care, all Mr. Smith has to do is show his provincial card; he pays for nothing other than a small annual premium to the province.

Mr. Smith has a one-year history of exertional angina, which has been followed by his primary care physician and his cardiologist. Mr. Smith chose his physician and his cardiologist. Mr. Smith does not pay a fee, a copayment, or a deductible to see his internist or cardiologist. His internist and cardiologist receive a capitated fee from the province, which is the sole insurer in the province. The internist, in conjunction with the cardiologist, prescribed a beta-blocker b.i.d. and sublingual trinitroglycerine p.r.n. for episodes of chest pain. Mr. Smith pays a small amount for his medication because they are heavily subsidized by the government.

When unstable angina develops, Mr. Smith is put on a list for a coronary angiogram for approximately one week. Pending the results of the coronary angiogram, Mr. Smith might then go on either a list for balloon angioplasty or a list for a CABG operation, both of which could be as long as one month, depending on the province. An important difference between Mr. Smith's experience in Canada relative to the U.S. is that Canadian physicians practice more conservative medicine; for moderate heart disease, they would be less likely to do a coronary angiogram, balloon angioplasty, or CABG. Both procedures would be paid in full by the province. Mr. Smith's cardiologist and cardiac surgeon would be paid by the province according to the rigid fee schedule negotiated by the provincial medical association and the province.

John Smith Is Cared for in Germany

Mr. Smith is a 55 year-old man who is covered by his local sickness fund. Both Mr. Smith and his employer each pay 6.5% of his annual salary to Mr. Smith's sickness fund (total, 13% of Mr. Smith's annual income). Mr. Smith joined his sickness fund because his profession has traditionally been a member of that particular fund and most of his fellow workers belong to the fund.

Mr. Smith has a one-year history of exertional angina, which has been followed by his primary care physician and his cardiologist, who is hospital-based. Mr. Smith chose his physician and his cardiologist. If Mr. Smith needed hospitalization, his internist would not follow him in the hospital because the division between ambulatory physicians and hospital-based physicians is distinct. Mr. Smith does not pay a fee, a copayment, or a deductible to see his internist or cardiologist. When Mr. Smith receives care, he fills out a form for the ambulatory physician or hospital that they submit to the sickness fund for payment. The hospital-based cardiologist is an employee of the hospital and is paid a flat salary. The fee that Mr. Smith's internist receives from the local sickness fund has been negotiated by the region's physicians medical association and the region's association of sickness funds. The hospital is paid by the sickness fund on a per diem basis. This per diem amount was negotiated by the region's hospital association and the region's sickness fund association.

The internist prescribed a beta-blocker b.i.d. and sublingual trinitroglycerine p.r.n. for episodes of chest pain. Mr. Smith pays a small amount for his medication because they are heavily subsidized by the government.

When unstable angina develops, Mr. Smith has a coronary angiogram performed without delay. Pending the results of the coronary angiogram, Mr. Smith might then be scheduled for a balloon angioplasty or a CABG operation. He would not be placed on a list for either procedure. Both procedures would be paid in full by Mr. Smith's sickness fund. The hospital at which Mr. Smith's cardiologist and cardiac surgeon did the procedure would be paid by the sickness fund according to the rigid per diem fee schedule negotiated by the region's hospital association and the region's association of sickness funds.

❖ Suggested Reading ❖

Blendon R, Humphrey T. Views on health care: public opinion in three nations. Health Affairs 1989; 149–159.
The premier source on public satisfaction with health care in the United States, Britain, and Canada.

Hsiao WC. Comparing health care systems: what nations can learn from one another. J Health, Politics, and Law 1992; 17:613–645.
Excellent framework for creating and evaluating health care systems.

Reinhardt UE. What can Americans learn from Europeans? Health Care Financing Rev 1989; (suppl) 97–103.
Defines the economic relationships embedded in the delivery of health care. Source of the diagrammatic flow of goods, services, and resources.

Reinhardt UE. West Germany's health-care and health-insurance system: combining universal access with cost control. Report Prepared for the U.S. Bipartisan Commission on Comprehensive Health Care, June 1990, p. 3–16.
Short, complete overview and analysis of the West German system.

Roemer MI. Canada. In: National health systems of the world. New York: Oxford University Press, 1991: 161–170.
Short, complete overview and analysis of the Canadian health system.

13

State Initiatives

Rushika J. Fernandopulle and Penny Feldman

In his book, *Democracy in America,* written in the late nineteenth century, Alexis de Tocqueville observed that the states were the "laboratories of democracy." In no area of public policy is this more true today than in health reform. Faced with the challenges of containing costs, providing access, and ensuring quality, and frustrated with the lack of federal actions to address these issues, many states are attempting to take matters into their own hands. Indeed, in 1993 alone, all but two states debated some form of health reform, and seven actually passed legislation making significant changes in their health care system.

In this chapter, we look first at the advantages and the disadvantages of state-level reforms, and we then give a broad overview of the types of initiatives being tried by the various states. We then turn to discussing specific actions by eight states to control costs, improve access, or both, and we end by looking at some lessons learned from these states, both in terms of policies as well as politics.

The specific details of what each state has done are not important, but the general principles and conceptual frameworks they use to grapple with the challenges facing their health system are important. Although specific plans may come and go, the basic ideas discussed in this chapter will be very much applicable for many years to come.

ADVANTAGES AND DISADVANTAGES OF STATE INITIATIVES ❖

There are several reasons why it is both good and bad for states to undertake health reform, as opposed to the federal government. Advantages to state reform include the following.

❖ *Local fit.* States can tailor their own proposals to fit local conditions. Not all states are alike, and we will see how different demographics, histories, and politics have led to very different policies in different states. It is not clear that a mandated, uniform federal plan could capture such diversity.

❖ *Easier coalition building.* It is easier to build support for health reform at the state level than at the national level. States are generally more homogeneous than the entire nation, and the political dynamic is different at the state level. It may be easier to achieve coalitions between political parties and between the executive and the legislative branches at the state level than at the federal level. This advantage especially applies to small states, such as Vermont.

❖ *Pilot projects.* Finally, state proposals could be used to test ideas before they are implemented at a national level. Managed competition, for instance, the basis of Bill Clinton's original health plan, is being tried in Washington and Florida, and this experience will be invaluable to evaluate the feasibility of applying these concepts to the nation as a whole.

In addition to these advantages to state-level reform, however, are many disadvantages and barriers.

❖ *ERISA.* The major barriers to state reform are federal statutes that prohibit state action. By far the most important of these statutes is the Employee Retirement Income Security Act of 1974, otherwise known as *ERISA,* which prohibits states from regulating self-insured employer health plans (i.e., plans in which the employer takes on the financial risk of the insurance) (see Chapter 4 for more details). ERISA was passed by the United States (U.S.) Congress to address problems in the solvency of employer-funded pension plans, but it also applies to all self-funded benefits.

Although ERISA was passed in 1974, when very few firms self-insured, currently more than half of U.S. workers are covered by self-insurance. ERISA prevents states from mandating benefits, taxing premiums, or otherwise regulating self-insured companies. Thus, although it allows large employers to offer the same benefits to employees in different states, ERISA has prevented much state action on health reform. Only Hawaii, which passed an employer mandate before ERISA, has an exemption from this law.

In addition to ERISA constraints, states are also constrained by Medicare and Medicaid rules if they wish to receive federal funding. To implement many plans, especially those that address questions of access for the poor, states need apply for a waiver from the federal *Health Care Financing Administration* (HCFA). This constraint held up Oregon's health reform plans for many years.

✧   *Mobility of businesses and consumers.* It is easy for both people and businesses to move into and out of states. Thus, states fear imposing too high a burden on employers, because they may leave the state, taking their jobs with them. States also fear giving too generous benefits for fear of attracting sick people from neighboring states. Although there are little data to show either of these scenarios actually occur because of health reform, fear of them affects the decisions of many state decision-makers.

✧   *Equity concerns.* Different state proposals make it harder for national companies to do business. This factor was one reason ERISA was passed, and a patchwork of plans brings up many questions of equity between states.

✧   *Lack of funding.* States lack the financial resources of the federal government. Most plans to expand access require large amounts of state funding, at least in the short run. State economies are more subject to economic cycles than the national economy is; thus, state-imposed taxes cannot provide as stable a revenue base. Also, many states must by law balance their budgets each year, and unlike the federal government, they cannot simply print more money. Thus, for financial reasons, state reform is difficult.

The bottom line is that states are facing real problems with their health systems. Costs are increasing, and many states spend up to 20% of their budgets on health care. In addition, almost all states face a large problem with uninsured persons; some states have uninsured rates of more than 25% (Figure 13.1).[299] Thus, regardless of the barriers, many states feel they have no choice but to pursue health reform. In addition, many feel they will be in a better position for national health reform if they already have their own programs implemented when the federal government finally gets a proposal passed.

OVERVIEW OF INITIATIVES   ❖

In general, *proposals by states can be seen primarily as trying to either increase access or reduce costs.* Proposals affect the financing or the delivery of health care, are either voluntary or compulsory, and make either incremental or radical changes. In this section, we give an overview of the different approaches states have taken to increase access, reduce cost, and provide financing.

Expanding Access

States have undertaken a variety of initiatives to improve access to health care, particularly by reducing financial barriers.

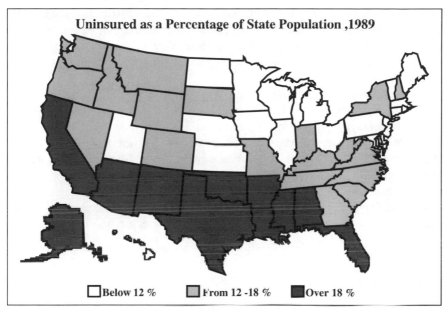

Figure 13.1 Graphic representation of the uninsured population by percentage of each state's population (1989). Source: Current Population Survey, Bureau of the Census (3/1990). Adapted from *U.S. General Accounting Office, 1992.*

❖ *Expanding Medicaid.* Many states have tried to improve access by adding to their Medicaid programs. Vermont's Dr. Dynasaur program and Minnesota's Children's Health Plan, for example, provide basic insurance to uninsured children and pregnant women.[300] Many states have proposed providing state-subsidized health insurance to people who are too poor to buy it on their own, but not poor enough to be categorically eligible for Medicaid. (As discussed in Chapter 6, far from all the poor are eligible for Medicaid.) Some believe the way to achieve universal access is by adding one group at a time to guaranteed coverage.

❖ *High-risk pools.* Many states have established **high-risk pools** to insure people too sick to purchase private insurance. These pools are usually funded through a tax on premiums paid by those who are not employed by a self-insuring business. The number of people uninsured because of high risk, however, is quite small (many think less than 1%); therefore, subsidizing insurance for high-risk individuals does not make a large dent in the number of uninsured as a whole.[301]

❖ *Uncompensated care pools.* Some states have created monetary funds to compensate providers, usually hospitals, for providing **uncompensated care.** We look at the many problems associated with this approach, and why it alone cannot be a solution to the problems of access.

❖ *Helping small business.* As discussed in Chapter 9, a large portion of the uninsured are actually employed, or they are dependents of people who are employed. Many of these people are employed by small businesses who have trouble purchasing insurance (see chapters 4 and 9). As a result, many states implemented insurance reforms or provided subsidies to make it easier for small companies to insure their workers. There is little evidence, however, that offering such plans will make it more likely for a significant number of employers to actually provide coverage.

✧ *Mandates.* Many believe the only way to truly achieve universal coverage is through mandates of some kind—either that all individuals purchase insurance or that all employers provide insurance. Hawaii is the only example of a state with an *employer mandate,* and Massachusetts passed but has not implemented a variation of this mandate, known as *"play or pay."* Chapter 14 contains a more detailed discussion of mandates, because they are the controversial centerpiece of many federal proposals.

✧ *Single payer.* Finally, some states, such as Vermont, are exploring the possibility of implementing a single-payer system, such as the one in Canada (see Chapter 12) to guarantee universal coverage.

Reducing Costs

Although most states are very concerned about the plight of the uninsured, cost control has really been driving most of them in their attempts at health reform. There are a number of strategies being tried to reduce health care costs (see also Chapter 8 for an overview of strategies to control costs).

✧ *Rate setting.* Some states, such as Maryland and New Jersey, have established regulatory systems applying to all payers in the state to set prices for health care services.

✧ *Competition.* Other states, such as Massachusetts, have tried to deregulate the health industry, hoping competition between payers will drive down health costs. Oklahoma has proposed letting citizens establish tax-free health accounts to pay for health insurance and expenses, letting them keep the remainder for other consumption. Finally, some states, such as Florida and Washington, are trying forms of managed competition similar to Bill Clinton's original health plan to keep costs down.

✧ *Uniform billing.* Maryland and New York are both trying to reduce high administrative costs by establishing uniform billing procedures and electronic filing of claims.

✧ *Certificate of need (CON) programs.* Most states have in place some sort of mechanism to review all new major capital spending on health care. These attempts, usually called CON programs, however, have not led to as much cost savings as had been expected, mainly due to political pressures to approve many unnecessary projects.

✧ *Expenditure targets.* Some states believe the only way to guarantee a slowdown in health expenditures is to set explicit limits on spending, a concept known by many names, including expenditure targets and global budgeting. Minnesota, Washington, and Vermont have all considered implementing such proposals, and many federal plans also include such targets.

✧ *Rationing.* Many health policy analysts agree that the real underlying cause of cost growth in health care is the use of new technology. Therefore, the only real way to slow this growth may be to ration care. Oregon has embarked on a bold attempt to prioritize different medical interventions, in an attempt to pay for only those that are most beneficial.

Financing Health Reform

Finally, no matter how one tries to expand access and to reduce cost, most health reform proposals end up costing money, at least in the short run. How are states proposing to fund these programs, especially given the financial constraints discussed in the previous section?

✧ *Sin taxes.* A politically popular way to fund health reform is through taxing goods such as cigarettes and alcohol. In theory, this approach will not only raise revenue, but also save health costs by reducing unhealthy behaviors. Compared with many other countries, our taxes on goods such as cigarettes and alcohol are quite low, and there is usually less political opposition to this option than others.

✧ *Provider taxes.* One way to raise revenues for health reform are to tax providers. Thus, many states add surcharges to hospital bills, or they tax physicians and other providers. In reality, economists say that these taxes eventually get passed on to the consumer anyway, but they may be politically easier to implement than direct consumer taxation.

✧ *Employer taxes.* Some proposals impose a tax on employers, similar to Social Security or Medicare levies. Again, these taxes eventually get passed on to workers in the form of lower wages, but they may also be politically easier to pass. States worry about placing too high a burden on employers for fear they will leave the state.

✧ *General revenue.* Finally, some states have floated proposals to fund health reform out of general revenues (i.e., from sales or income taxes). None of these proposals have passed, however, and in a climate of budget deficits and economic slowdowns, these proposals are not at all popular with the public. Thus, although many people agree we should provide health care to the uninsured, few would be willing to pay higher taxes.

SPECIFIC STATE PLANS ❖

With this overview as a background, we look at eight different states that have addressed the problems facing the health care system in different ways. The important factors are not the specifics of what each state did, but rather the general policy approaches that have been taken, as well as the general lessons we can learn from each state in terms of policy and politics.

Hawaii: Employer Mandates

Hawaii was the first state to pass significant legislation to address the problem of the uninsured, and it is the only state close to having universal access. In the early 1970s, Hawaii had an uninsurance rate of 12% to 17%, which was very similar to the rest of the nation. Spurred mainly by the labor unions, in 1974, the state legislature passed the Prepaid Health Care Act, which contained both an employer mandate and significant insurance reform.[302] This law required all employers to provide insurance for their workers who worked more than 20 hours each week, to pay at least half the cost, and capped the employee contribution at 1.5% of their wage. The minimum plan that could be offered was set equal to the plan that had the most number of subscribers, and community rating was established for all other plans. In addition, a strong focus was established on primary and preventive care.

In 1989, the state created the State Health Insurance Program (SHIP) to address the needs of the "gap group," which was not covered by the employer mandate. This program provided a bare bones, government-subsidized insurance plan that covered all primary and preventive care, but it covered only 5 days, or $2,500, of hospital care each year. This plan could be purchased by those earning less than 300% of the federal poverty level, with a sliding-scale premium (i.e., the higher your income, the higher percent of the actual premium you had to pay).

These efforts have led to some spectacular results. A recent survey of states by Northwest National Life Insurance Company ranked Hawaii number one among all 50 states in disease prevention, lifestyle, access to health care, and life expectancy. Indeed, Hawaii's life expectancy of 84 years for women and 80 years for men tops even Japan. Another poll showed that 82% of Hawaiians were very or somewhat satisfied with their health care, compared with 71% in the nation. Less than 5% of Hawaiians are uninsured, and only 17% reported that they put off seeking health care at some time last year for financial reasons, as compared with 30% nationally. This reform has been done at a cost significantly lower than the national average. The U.S. Office of Personnel Management reported in 1992 that the average monthly premium for a family was only $381 in Hawaii, compared with $649 nationally. Thus, Hawaii spends only 8% per capita GDP on health care, not the 14% seen in the rest of the country.[303]

It is true that Hawaii is very different than the rest of the country. Its major industries are tourism and agriculture, which are both much healthier than many industries found on the mainland. Its people are healthier to begin with (except for the Polynesian population), and Hawaii has the highest concentration of physicians of any state. Also, Hawaii is the only state that has been able to impose an employer mandate, because its efforts predated ERISA. Finally, because it is a group of islands, businesses have a harder time relocating, and sick people have a harder time coming into the state to seek health care.

Regardless of these caveats, Hawaii does show that near universal coverage can be reached, and that it might even save money in the long run. Unfortunately, however, Hawaii also points out that although universal access and primary care may lower the level of costs, they do not necessarily reduce the rate of growth of these costs (see Chapter 8). Hawaii also faced double-digit rates of health care inflation like the rest of the country, and it is planning to implement a managed competition plan to try to reduce costs while maintaining access for most of the population.

Massachusetts: "Play or Pay"

In 1988, the governor of Massachusetts, Michael Dukakis, was the very popular Democratic nominee for President of the U.S. In this context, the Massachusetts legislature passed its attempt to achieve universal access. Prevented by ERISA from imposing an employer mandate, like Hawaii had, Massachusetts used its taxing powers to enact what was known as a "pay or play" statute. This statute imposed a payroll tax on all employers with 6 or more employees, which went directly into an insurance fund. If a company provided adequate health insurance for its employees, it could deduct this cost from its tax. The government would then purchase insurance for the uninsured by using the insurance fund. In essence, employers had a choice: they could "play" (i.e., insure their workers) or "pay" the state to do so for them.

Soon after enactment of this legislation, however, the political climate changed dramatically in Massachusetts and the economy soured. Governor Dukakis lost the presidential election, and a new Republican governor replaced him in the State House. Although the "play or pay" legislation was not repealed, its implementation was delayed for many years, and most believed the delay would continue indefinitely. Many lawsuits were also being prepared to challenge the "pay or play" legislation on the grounds that it violated at the least the spirit of ERISA. Whatever the eventual outcome, Massachusetts illustrates not only another approach to universal access, but also the political fragility of such proposals.

Vermont: Single Payer

Vermont has also been moving toward universal access. Led by its Governor Howard Dean, who was a practicing internist until he took office, Vermont has implemented several pieces of health reform already, and it may become the first state to try a single-payer plan.

In 1987, Vermont's Health Insurance Planning Board recommended the state enact a "pay or play" statute, as well as establish a subsidized basic benefit plan for the poor. This proposal did not go very far in the legislature, but out of the debates came the Dr. Dynasaur program discussed earlier, which provided health care to more poor children and pregnant women than were covered by Medicaid at the time. In 1991, Vermont applied community rating to the small group market (see Chapter 4 for a discussion of community rating), and, in the spring of 1992, a comprehensive package called the Vermont Health Care Act was passed. This act set out to do several things.

✧ Establish uniform claims forms for administrative simplicity.

✧ Create purchasing pools of employees of the state, public universities, and municipalities.

✧ Expand Dr. Dynasaur to cover children up to the age of 18 years from poorer families.

✧ Expand community rating to include individual policies, as well as small group policies.

✧ Most importantly, establish the Vermont Health Care Authority (HCA). This three-person group, appointed by the Governor, was chartered to make two specific proposals to the state legislature for comprehensive health reform: one using a single payer, the other with multiple competing payers. Both plans would include a uniform package of benefits, and both would establish a state-wide global budget. After more than one year of expert testimony and public meetings, the HCA made its proposals by the end of 1993 for the legislature to consider.

Regardless of the final outcome, the efforts of the Vermont HCA have placed Vermont among the vanguard in development and implementation of health reform.

New Jersey: Uncompensated Care

New Jersey was one of the leaders in the area of cost control; it was the first to establish a prospective fee schedule for hospital payment. Chapter 3 contains a discussion of this fee schedule, called DRGs, and how they may help cut costs. We concentrate on New Jersey's efforts to use this fee schedule and other techniques to pay for uncompensated care.

In 1982, New Jersey extended its hospital fee schedule to all payers; each hospital, however, was allowed to add a surcharge to its regular fee to cover uncompensated care. Soon, a vicious cycle developed. Hospitals that served many indigent patients had to add a huge surcharge to cover their costs (up to 25% for some inner city hospitals). This scenario caused fewer paying patients to go to these hospitals, causing the surcharge to get even higher.

To respond to this problem, New Jersey established an uncompensated care trust fund in 1987. All hospitals had a uniform surcharge, and each received money from the fund proportional to the amount of uncompensated care they gave. This system also started to rapidly break down. First, the fund only paid for hospital care. Thus, there were incentives for poor people to seek care in a hospital, rather than in a much cheaper ambulatory facility. New Jersey's uninsured used 30% more hospital days than the insured did, which is a huge contrast to the national average (the uninsured used 47% fewer days than the insured).

Second, there was no distinction made between truly charity care and care that simply wasn't paid for (bad debt). In 1989, more than 80% of the uncompensated care in New Jersey was bad debt, rather than care for those who were uninsured. For both reasons, even the uniform surcharge began to increase, until it reached 19%.[304]

In 1989, Medicare pulled out of the all-payer system, and it started to pay New Jersey hospitals at the national rate, without any surcharge. In May 1992, Judge Alfred Wolin of the federal district court ruled that the now huge surcharges could not be applied to self-insurance plans because of ERISA. With Medicare and self-insurers out of the mix, the uncompensated care system broke down yet again.

On November 30, 1992, the New Jersey legislature passed the Health Care Reform Act of 1992. This act used the $500 million unemployment trust fund to pay for uncompensated care in the short term, and it would phase out all such subsidies in a few years. These efforts in New Jersey point out both the difficulty in paying for uncompensated care, and the complexities inherent in reforming a fragmented, multiple-payer system.[305]

Minnesota: The Gang of Seven

Minnesota is an important example, not so much for what it enacted in terms of health reform, but for how it did so. In 1991, after three years of study by a Health Access Commission, the Minnesota legislature passed House File 2, a bill guaranteeing universal access funded through general revenues, with no cost-control measures. The bill, however, was vetoed by the governor, and many realized that the pressing problem facing the state was not access but cost. Average family health spending increased in Minnesota from $2,936 in 1980 to $7,220 in 1991. Public spending for health also increased to more than 41% in the 5 years between 1985 and 1990.[306]

To address these issues, a group of seven top legislators and executive officials began to meet regularly, and they soon became known as the "Gang of Seven." They agreed on some interesting ground rules.

+ If they reached an agreement, no individual member or party would take credit for it.
+ Once the group agreed on a proposal, they would all support the entire package, not just the parts they agreed with.
+ They instructed their staff not to discuss their work with the media, lobbyists, or even other legislators.

This strategy worked. In March 1992, the "Gang of Seven" released their proposal; in less than 6 weeks it was passed in both houses of the legislature, and it was signed into law. The plan set up a 25-member Health Care Commission comprised of representatives of physicians, chiropractors, labor union representatives, employers, consumers, insurers, hospitals, and the government. This Commission would set expenditure targets to lower health cost growth by 10% each year for 5 years relative to 1991, and it would do so by limiting new technology, conducting outcomes research, establishing centers of excellence for complex procedures, determining minimum volume standards for physicians, and conducting public information campaigns about taking personal responsibility for health.

In addition, the plan included a subsidized minimal benefit plan for low income families, as well as insurance reform, such as broader community rating and a reduced allowable scope of pre-existing conditions. The new subsidies were to be funded by a 2% provider tax, as well as a 5-cent increase in the cigarette tax and a $400 increase in physicians' annual licensing fees. These provider measures were not seen as taxes, but, as state senator Diane Benson put it, "recycling excess money in the health care system."[307]

The "Gang of Seven" in Minnesota exemplifies how nonpartisanship and commitment to change can result in health reform.

Maryland: Regulation

Maryland, more so than the other states discussed, has relied on a regulatory approach to cost control. Maryland has a long history of regulation in the health industry; indeed, Maryland has more mandated benefits (32) than any other state. Like New Jersey, Maryland has had a strong all-payer system of hospital financing since the late 1970s. Although this system has controlled cost per admission, it has had less clear success in keeping down overall hospital expenditures.

In 1993, Maryland moved to expand this all-payer regulation to physicians as well as hospitals. The Governor appointed a Health Care Access and Cost Commission and charged it with several tasks, including standardization of billing across the state to reduce administrative cost and establishment of a fee schedule for physician payment. This schedule would be similar to the Resource-based Relative Value Scale (RBRVS) used by Medicare (see Chapter 2), and it would include three components for each payment.

✦ A provider-specific component, which would take into account a particular provider's experience, malpractice costs, overhead, and other expenses.
✦ A procedure-specific component, which would compensate for the time and the intensity spent doing a particular task.
✦ A conversion modifier to convert these relative values into a real dollar amount.

The Commission would have the power to determine if one group of providers was earning too much under this system, and it could adjust the fee schedule accordingly.

In addition to this fee schedule, Maryland passed a series of insurance reforms. By 1994, all insurers in the state had to offer a standard benefits package to small businesses; by 1995, preexisting conditions could not be used to exclude coverage, and all insurers would have to use community rating formula to set premiums, adjusting only for age and geographical location. A unique part of Maryland's proposal is to cap the price of the standard package at 12% of the average state wage. If the cost increased above this limit, the Commission would re-evaluate the standard package and scale it down.

Depending on Maryland's success in implementing broad-based payment and price regulations, it may serve as the only working model for other states interested in payment regulation as a vehicle of health reform.

Washington: Managed Competition

On the other coast, Washington has decided not to use a regulatory system like Maryland's, but instead to use market forces through a voluntary form of managed competition. Washington has had a long history of managed care, and its oldest health maintenance organization (HMO), Group Health of Puget Sound, has been in existence since 1947. By 1989, HMOs covered 15.6% of the state's residents, and PPOs covered 22% (see Chapter 5 for more on the different types of managed care).

In 1987, based on the proposal of the McPhadden Commission, which was made up of legislators, providers, employers, and consumers, the Washington legislature passed a bill that expanded Medicaid, created a high risk pool, and gave grants to hospitals that provided a large amount of uncompensated care. In addition, they set up a 5-year demonstration program called the Basic Health Plan (BHP), which would enroll 30,000 people in each district who were less than 65 years old and earned less than 200% of the federal poverty limit in one of several managed programs that had contracted with the state. The enrollees would pay a subsidized premium based on their income, and they would otherwise be treated just like the other members of the managed care plans.

At the end of the 5-year period, several lessons were learned. Providers did participate in the program, and many low income people did enroll. Indeed, many said they preferred the program to Medicaid because it did not have the same stigma associated with it. In 1993, Washington passed the Health Services Act to expand the BHP concept throughout the state. This act created a Health Services Commission, which would oversee a state-wide managed competition program. The Commission was to develop a uniform package of benefits, set a maximum premium for this plan, and develop a mechanism for risk adjustment to minimize risk selection by insurers.

The state was broken into four regions, each of which was covered by a Health Insurance Purchasing Cooperative (HIPC). These HIPCs would offer a menu of several Certified Health Plans (CHPs), which could be either traditional insurers or managed care plans that followed certain guidelines. All plans would be community-rated, and there could be no consideration of pre-existing conditions. Employers had to offer their workers a choice among at least three CHPs, and they had to contribute at least half the cost of the cheapest. Business could still self-insure, but their plans had to follow the same rules as were applied to the CHPs.

The Health Services Commission would set a premium cap, and it would implement a phased reduction in the maximum allowable premium for the community-rated standard benefit package. To guarantee access, an individual mandate would be in place by 1999, and an employer mandate would be phased in starting in 1995 for those that employed more than 500 workers, and ending in 1999, when all employers would have to cover their workers.

This plan is extremely complex and ambitious. It looks a lot like Bill Clinton's original managed competition proposal, and it could be a good test of the feasibility of such a plan to control costs and to expand access. Full implementation, however, has to wait for a federal ERISA waiver.

Oregon: Rationing by Priority List

Oregon's priority list for the rationing of services may well be the most controversial state initiative. In contrast, there are those who think that Oregon is actually ahead of its time, and that the issues Oregon has grappled with over the past few years will return to face the nation in the near future.

The idea of prioritizing treatments first arose in 1987, when the state faced a $20 million shortfall in Medicaid funding. Many at the time felt the public would be better served by providing basic services to a large number of people, rather than by spending huge sums arbitrarily on a few. Thus, with surprisingly little debate, the legislature decided to discontinue Medicaid funding for major organ transplantations and to use the money saved for prenatal care and new enrollees. This effort was short-lived, however, because the negative press of people being denied transplantations caused the legislature to rescind their decision.

This was not the end of Oregon's attempts at determining what should be paid for and what should not; rather, it was just the beginning. For the next several years, the Oregon Medicaid Priority Setting Project, founded by the Senate president John Kitzhaber, MD, worked on coming up with a more sophisticated priority list. In August 1989, the Health Services Commission was established, consisting of five MDs, four consumers, one social worker, and one public health nurse. This group conducted public hearings, held provider meetings, and conducted telephone surveys. They first defined a list of condition treatment pairs (e.g., acute myocardial infarction and angioplasty). They then ranked these pairs using two criteria: (1) net medical benefit as determined by expert testimony, and

(2) the social values of these outcomes as determined by a phone survey. The Commission then adjusted the list based on "common sense." Note that cost of procedures did not explicitly enter into this ranking.

This priority list was incorporated into law as SB 27 in 1991. However, like most of the proposals mentioned, it required a federal waiver to be implemented. The Bush administration refused to give such a waiver, claiming finally that the scheme violated the Americans with Disability Act, because public weighing of outcomes gave more weight to a life without disability than to one with a disability. Oregon went back and reordered its list, and it downplayed functional status after treatment.

In March 1993, the new Clinton Administration approved the new list and granted the Medicaid waiver. The plan as approved had 699 treatment pairs, of which Medicaid would fund the first 565. By 1995, an employer mandate would be phased in, making all employers either provide a basic package similar to the Medicaid one, or pay into an uninsurance pool.

Although the waiver has been granted, the rationing plan has faced renewed opposition both within and outside the state. Although some only criticize the methodology of making the list, others are bothered by the fact that services are only being rationed to the Medicaid population and not to everyone else. Still others question the cost-containment aspects of the rationing scheme because it does not address the problem of excess utilization within the approved treatment pairs. The future of the Oregon list is uncertain, but the concept of prioritizing interventions is one that will probably face many other states in the near future.

LESSONS ❖

What can we learn from the efforts of these and other states to reform the health care system? We can break these lessons into two groups: those concerning policy and those concerning politics.

Policy

We can see clearly from these examples that each state is very different from each other, and that these differences require different policy solutions. As discussed earlier, different populations, ideologies, histories, and politics make it unlikely that the same solution will work in different states, which brings into question the feasibility of a uniform national health reform plan.

ERISA is a major barrier to state attempts to address the problems facing their health systems. Almost every proposal mentioned requires a federal waiver before it is implemented. The writers of ERISA clearly did not intend the law to constrain state action in the way it currently does; thus, it needs to be changed to allow more flexibility.

Efforts that focus on just one part of the health system do not work, because the problems just crop up somewhere else. New Jersey's efforts to improve access by funding uncompensated care to hospitals is a good example.

Politics

Closed door meetings and secrecy may have their place in implementing health reform. Minnesota shows us what can be accomplished by using such unorthodox tactics. This approach, however, can backfire, as the Clinton administration found out in its unpopular, health reform task force deliberations.

Task forces and commissions are useful ways to allow public debate on an issue and to bring items onto the public agenda.

Finally, strong leadership is needed to pass health reform, as well as a good working relationship between the executive and the legislative branches. It is also probably not a coincidence that many of the states that have passed health reform have had powerful physicians who are elected officials leading the charge.

❖ Suggested Reading ❖

Government Accounting Office. Access to health care: states respond to growing crisis. GAO/HRD 92–70.

Might be hard to find, but a good overview of state proposals up to 1992.

Health Affairs, Summer 1993 issue.

An entire issue dedicated to state initiatives.

Federal Proposals

Atul Gawande and David Blumenthal

The growing problems of cost and access for families, businesses, and government (described in Chapters 8 and 9), as well as Bill Clinton's election to the White House following a campaign that made health reform a top priority, prompted an outpouring of health policy proposals from Washington. In addition to President Clinton's own Health Care Security Act, more than one dozen different plans to reform the American health care system were filed in Congress from across the political spectrum during the Administration's first year. These plans were not static. The plans under consideration have changed enormously, and new bills have been introduced during the evolving debate and legislative process.

Despite their variety, however, federal solutions for reforming the health system attempt to address the same core issues and draw from a limited set of major options for doing so.

We explain these central issues and policy options, and we describe the policies included in the major proposals before Congress in 1994.

ISSUES AND OPTIONS ❖
Improvement in Coverage and Benefits
The Problem

As noted in Chapter 9, 39 million Americans were uninsured in 1991, an additional 100,000 Americans are added to that group every month, and an additional population roughly equal in size has inadequate coverage for a serious illness. For the

273

uninsured and the underinsured, two principal barriers stand in the way of obtaining good coverage: affordability and discriminatory insurance practices.

Affordability

Low-income families do not have enough income to pay the full costs of health care coverage. Those without good employer benefits or assistance from Medicaid or other programs simply go without insurance. As described in Chapter 9, superinflationary increases in insurance premiums have exacerbated the problem by putting individual insurance out of reach even for families well above the poverty line and causing employers to reduce or drop benefits.

Discriminatory Insurance Practices

Under current practices, insurers commonly exclude from coverage precisely those individuals who need coverage most. They do so through a variety of means permitted in most states.

❖ *Pre-existing condition exclusions.* Refusing coverage for individuals with a pre-existing condition (i.e., diabetes, heart disease, pregnancy) who are seeking new coverage (e.g., when they change or lose jobs, when retired, self-employed, or in a job without benefits).

❖ *Termination.* Cutting off or refusing to renew policies for people with high medical costs.

❖ *Experience rating.* Charging substantially higher rates, sometimes astronomically higher, for older people, women, and individuals who become ill or have previous illnesses, family risk history, or other health risks, or for companies that have such people.

❖ *Selective marketing.* Engaging in a number of practices that make it difficult or unlikely for individuals with higher health risks to enroll in coverage. This approach includes refusing to sell coverage to individuals or small businesses or in particular communities, and designing benefit packages and advertising that discourages unwanted customers (e.g., offering free health club memberships with enrollment).

Options for Expanding Coverage and Benefits

The fundamental step in reducing the number of people without adequate health coverage is not deciding what programs and policies are needed to address the causes of uninsurance, but defining what the goal for reforms to expand coverage is. The goal then determines, or at least limits, the programmatic approach. Federal proposals can be divided into two basic categories: proposals emphasizing insurance reform that does not seek universal health care, and reforms to provide health coverage for all.

Option 1: Insurance Reform

The main goal of reform for backers of federal proposals for insurance reform alone is to open access to insurance to any American regardless of their health condition. Therefore, they would put in place new federal laws and regulations to eliminate at least the most egregious discriminatory insurance practices that deny coverage to Americans with health risks. These policies include, at minimum; the following.

✧   Banning exclusion of coverage for pre-existing conditions. If everyone is required to buy coverage, proposals typically ban exclusions outright. However, if coverage is voluntary, people may wait until they need care to buy coverage and drop coverage while they are healthy. Thus, reforms that keep a voluntary system often allow exclusions for a pre-existing condition for a certain period (e.g., six months) if an individual was not insured prior to applying for coverage.

✧   Guaranteed renewal. This reform outlaws insurer termination of policies and guarantees that people are able to renew their coverage without being turned away by insurers.

✧   Regulation of premium rates: community-rating or rate banding. Such regulations restrict insurers from charging higher prices on the basis of health status. Insurers must charge everyone in a community the same rates for coverage (i.e., *community rating*) or limit the differential in charges among consumers in a community (i.e., *rate banding*).

Proposals may go further to standardize benefits so that insurers cannot gain benefit packages to attract one group of people and discourage another, and to regulate their service areas so they do not **"redline"** particular communities.

Advantages   Proponents argue that achieving open access to insurance would eliminate the most odious and detested aspects of our health care system without massive changes that could jeopardize quality. Furthermore, this approach avoids creating an expansive new entitlement program, adding to the federal deficit, or raising taxes in a lackluster economy. For several decades, the city of Rochester, New York, has maintained a similar, successful system with community-rating and no pre-existing conditions, as well as local cost-containment measures that have slowed inflation in insurance costs. The result has been that only 6% of residents are uninsured (compared with more than 15% nationwide) despite having no additional subsidy programs.[308]

Disadvantages   Insurance reform alone does not seek to substantially reduce the financial barriers that prevent the majority of the uninsured from having access to coverage. These reform proposals may offer modest increases in spending through existing programs, such as Medicaid, or through limited subsidization of insurance premiums for the very poor. However, they do not intend to offer sufficient subsidies to make coverage financially accessible for all families, nor do they offer policies that contain runaway inflation in health care costs. Therefore, a main root of current coverage problems would remain unaddressed, and a vast majority of uninsured will remain behind.

Option 2: Universal Health Care

The aim of universal health security is to have a system in which, regardless of how little a person earns, no one should fear being unable to afford coverage for medical needs or having it taken away. Achieving this goal depends on having financing and insurance polices that expand adequate coverage to everyone, as well as having an effective means to contain costs over time. Cost-containment is needed to keep a new entitlement to health coverage from bankrupting those paying for it. As odd as it may sound, covering everyone is the easy part in formulating policy (coming up with the money to pay for it is the hard part politically). One simply needs insurance reforms that open coverage for an adequate benefit package to everyone without discrimination and subsidies that provide assistance to families without enough money to buy coverage on their own.

Reforming Insurance   Just as with more limited reform, a plan for universal access or for mandatory coverage requires policies that end insurance discrimination against sick, elderly, or high-risk individuals. Whether offered by private insurance companies or through a public insurance program, reforms would make insurance available across all communities, guaranteed renewable, without exclusions for pre-existing conditions, and without major price differentials based on health risk. They would also require that insurers offer a package of benefits that include at least preventive and primary care and hospital and physician services for acute care, and that would limit the deductibles and copayments an insurer could charge.

Making Coverage Affordable   Reform to create universal health care would ensure everyone can afford coverage. Policies must subsidize the cost of coverage for people of modest means so that it does not consume an unacceptably large proportion of income. There are an enormous variety of ways of financing health care coverage, and there is great disagreement on what constitutes an "unacceptably large" proportion of income. Figure 14.1 illustrates three basic approaches.

✧   *Flat premium* is a simplified version of the current private insurance system in which families pay (with assistance from employers) a flat premium, which does not vary with income, and no subsidies are provided. Figure 14.1B shows that low income families who do not have employee benefits or coverage from Medicare, Medicaid, or other programs must devote a very high proportion of their earnings to health care to buy a typical $5,000 family insurance policy.

✧   *Flat income cap* is a subsidy program that provides government payment to cover insurance costs that exceed a fixed percentage of income. Figures 14.1A and 14.1B show an approach that protects families from paying more than 13.3%

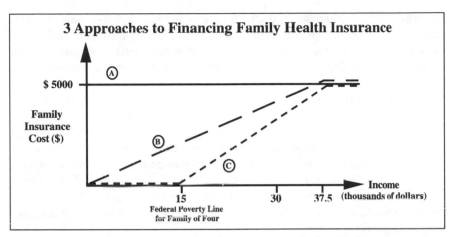

Figure 14.1A Three approaches to financing family health insurance. A = Flat premium of $5000; B = 13.3% of income cap on family costs; C = Free coverage below poverty line, partial subsidy up to 250% of poverty.

of income for basic coverage by subsidizing all families that earn less than 250% of the federal poverty line (≈$37,500 for a family of four in 1994).

✦ *Progressive subsidy.* Subsidies can be customized to provide greater assistance to the poorest families, while steeply reducing assistance for near-poor families to avoid higher program costs. Figure 14.1A shows what individuals at different incomes pay if subsidies cover all the costs of basic coverage for anyone earning below the poverty line, as well as a scaled portion of costs for those earning between 100 and 250% of poverty. As Figure 14.1B illustrates, subsidy design greatly affects the percentage of income a family must devote to health care. Backers of a progressive subsidy argue that the poorest should get the most protection because the relatively fixed costs of food and shelter make each 1% of income mean

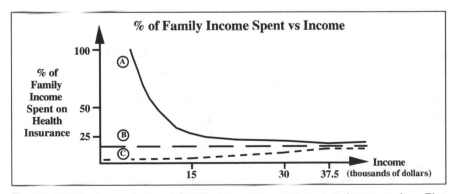

Figure 14.1B Percentage of family income spent versus income. A = Flat premium of $5000; B = 13.3% of income cap on family costs; C = Free coverage below poverty line, partial subsidy up to 250% of poverty.

far more to someone earning $5,000 than someone earning $25,000. However, critics argue that working Americans just barely out of poverty should not be left paying the highest percentage, and everyone should be expected to pay something, or else the system will reward those who do not work in preference to those who do.

In addition to the basic subsidy design, one must consider the income cut-off for subsidies in assessing the fairness of different approaches. Some proposals cut subsidies off at twice the poverty line—leaving a family with a $30,000 income paying a full $5,000 premium (16.7% of income). Others seek more generous subsidies, but at substantial cost because (1) health costs currently consume more than 14% of national income, growing to 19% by 2000 if unchecked; and (2) increasing assistance to cover costs that exceed 10% of income, for example, subsidizes families earning up to $50,000, a huge proportion of the population, because median family income is less than $30,000.

Advantages   There are a number of reasons proponents favor universal coverage over proposals for insurance reform without sufficient subsidies to make coverage affordable to everyone. Many argue it is fundamentally unethical that the citizens of a wealthy industrialized nation should find that access to care for their basic health needs depends on how much they earn. Indeed, American public opinion generally holds that, like a basic education, basic health care should be available regardless of income. Having a healthy populace with access to appropriate preventive and acute care, like an educated populace, is required to build a strong, productive nation with a high standard of living. Indeed, some argue that when one takes into account the health costs and the lost productivity of uninsured Americans with untreated and unprevented disease, the current system is more costly than a universal one. Furthermore, cost-containment efforts in a nonuniversal system will likely lead insurers and hospitals to turn more people away, which is much easier than increasing efficiency, to keep their day-to-day costs down.

Disadvantages   Few opponents of universal coverage disagree with these arguments. However, most believe we simply cannot afford anything more than insurance reform and limited subsidies targeted to assist only the poor. They argue that imposing taxes or mandates required to cover the costs of generous insurance for all would harm growth and jobs in an economy with unemployment that is already too high and growth that is already too slow. For evidence, they point to the high taxes and unemployment, increasing health costs, and slow economic growth of European countries with national health insurance. Critics also argue that universal coverage makes inevitable far greater government intrusion into patient care than we already have. If the government is paying the health care bills for a large part of the country, it will quickly become involved in regulating physicians and their care of patients, even to the point of rationing, sacrificing quality, and increasing bureaucracy to limit budgetary costs.

Defining Benefits

Under any strategy to improve coverage, an additional issue deserving greater discussion is the question of what benefits government will provide (or require to be provided). In reality, the topic of benefits covers many different issues, each with their own controversies. Should coverage pay for treatments provided as part of clinical trials? Treatments that are not proven clinically effective? Emergency room visits that are not emergencies? Mammograms for women under age 50? Elective abortion? Unlimited psychotherapy visits? Home health aides? Hospice? Smoking cessation programs? Weight loss programs? Fitness programs? Drug addiction counseling and treatment? Nursing home care? Should insurers be required to offer a single standard package, a minimum package they can add to, or whatever they want? Should government regulate the deductibles and the copayments insurers charge, and if so, what should the cost-sharing be? Should Congress, a national commission of experts, or a panel representing all various interests set the benefits package? Should benefits be removed if costs increase too fast?

Designing a benefits package raises fundamental questions of what does and does not constitute "health care," how much regulation is acceptable, and how expensive the program will be. There is substantial literature on these issues, and a book could be written about benefits alone. Briefly, however, health reform plans tend to fall into three different categories of benefits packages.

✧ ***Comprehensive coverage.*** Benefits are relatively broad, covering not only physician and hospital acute care services, but also broad preventive benefits, primary care visits, hospice and home health care, mental health services, drug treatment, and, in some proposals, even long-term and chronic care. Cost-sharing expected of patients is generally limited (e.g., $10/visit), and it is subsidized for the poor if required at all.

✧ ***Catastrophic coverage.*** Benefits are more limited to keep costs down. Usually, they cover physician and hospital acute care services and a few preventive benefits, but not mental health and drug treatment. Furthermore, patients are expected to pay large deductibles ($1000–$3600/year, depending on the proposal) and 20 to 50% of medical bills, without an upper limit.

✧ ***Benefits to be specified by an independent commission.*** Some proposals do not specify a benefit package, instead instructing an independent commission to develop the package of services and cost-sharing insurers must offer. This approach is hoped to avert Congressional gridlock on highly contentious benefits issues.

Paying for Universal Care

Although the bottom line remains that universal health care requires insurance reforms that open access to coverage to everyone and subsidies that make coverage affordable for everyone, someone has to pay the bills. In the current system, individuals, business, and government each pay roughly one third of total costs, although some individuals pay far more than others, some businesses pay nothing at all, and government assistance is fairly idiosyncratic (i.e., it covers elderly regardless of income, but it helps a poor married couple with a 10-year old child hardly at all). There are three different approaches to financing costs in a new universal health care system, distinguished by how they distribute costs among these three actors. Reforms may require individuals, employers, or government to pay for the bulk of costs.

The three options are distinguished more by politics than policy. As economists point out, under any approach, individuals always end up paying because they pay the taxes that government spends on subsidies, and they sacrifice wages that businesses cut to pay any mandated benefits. Depending on how the taxes and the subsidies are designed, a fully government-financed health system and one that relies on a combination of individual, employer, and government payments may have an identical impact on individuals of different incomes. The political impact of each approach, however, could not be more different.

Option 1: Individual Premiums with Public Subsidies

As is currently the case, individuals are responsible for purchasing coverage from insurers, and employers may provide worker health benefits to assist with these costs. However, in a universal system, new subsidies provide generous assistance for low income individuals, through an income cap on, or progressive subsidization of, insurance payments. The costs of the subsidies must be paid through cuts in other programs or new taxes (e.g., sin taxes, payroll taxes), the combination of which greatly affects the impact of reform on different individuals.

Advantages

These subsidies shift the costs of coverage for low wage workers from individuals and business to government. Thus, it would not only assist families that cannot afford coverage, but also relieve employers with low wage workers, often small businesses, of responsibility for the high cost of health benefits.

Disadvantages

Federal budget costs increase substantially, in part shifting to taxpayers costs currently borne by businesses. The government ends up paying not only for the low income uninsured, but also for currently insured low wage workers because businesses will have an incentive to drop health benefits.

Option 2: Employer Mandate with Public Subsidies

Employers are required to pay for a set percentage of a basic insurance plan for all employees and their dependents. Individual subsidies are still required to assist nonworkers who have no employer coverage and low income workers with the portion they must pay. Furthermore, proponents often include subsidies for businesses with low wage workers to avoid imposing costs that would lead them to lay off workers or cut wages too far. These subsidies are then paid for through budget cuts or new taxes.

Advantages

Advocates argue that this approach avoids unnecessary shifts in the financing of health care for the vast majority of insured Americans and their employers, and it minimizes direct government expenditures. Employers currently pay on average roughly 80% of insurance costs for 85% of American workers. Instead of allowing employers to shift a large bulk of these costs to the government, as the other approaches would, employers pick up costs for the remaining 15% of workers who are uninsured. Unlike today, this option also makes a level playing field for competing businesses because no firm can escape responsibility for worker health costs. Backers also deny deleterious economic effects, pointing to evidence that far larger increases in the minimum wage have not increased unemployment at all and the thriving small business community of Hawaii, where an employer mandate has been in place since 1974.

Disadvantages

Critics argue that economic models suggest employer mandates lead to layoffs, particularly of minimum wage workers, whose wages cannot be adjusted to offset the new costs. They also hold that the employer mandate creates an unworkably complex financing system. The payment requirements must fairly distribute costs among multiple employers in a family with dual workers or a member working in more than one job. Payments for part-time workers must be adjusted. Subsidies and employer payments must be adjusted with job changes, as well. As a consequence, the costs of coverage for any given individual may come from myriad sources (e.g., family members, all employers, an individual subsidy program, a business subsidy program), each of which must be tracked, reconciled, and accounted for.

Option 3: Tax Financing of All Health Costs

Instead of individuals and employers paying premiums to insurers, taxes are paid to the government. The government then either pays insurers to provide coverage or pays for health costs directly. Taxes could be assessed as a head tax (i.e., a flat premium), as a payroll tax (analogous to a flat income cap), as a progressive income tax, or as a combination of different taxes, depending on the type of subsidization desired.

Advantages

A system of public financing collects all payments in the simplest, most straightforward manner, particularly if it relies on payroll or income taxes that are already collected. This approach would provide substantial administrative savings. Furthermore, policymakers can design taxes to be far more equitable than premiums that do not require the wealthy to pay more than the costs of their own care.

Disadvantages

The major political downside is that by having the government pick up health costs, freeing employers and individuals of direct responsibility, large taxes are required. Furthermore, in simplifying payments, this approach is highly redistributive, making enormous changes in what currently insured individuals and employers already providing coverage must pay. (Of note, taxes could be adjusted to avoid redistribution [e.g., families can pay higher rates than singles, rates can be adjusted regionally], but simplicity is sacrificed.) Finally, it makes it difficult to operate a competitive system in which individuals pay the additional costs of more expensive health coverage.

Reform to Contain Costs
The Problem

As described in more detail in Chapter 8, the superinflationary growth in health care costs underlies the concerns of families, business, and government, and the causes of the cost explosion are intrinsically connected with the financing and delivery of American health care.

Put simply, the market for health care services has failed. In other parts of the economy, a well-functioning market prevents runaway costs. For example, car buyers keenly compare price, quality, and other factors. Car companies have an incentive to keep price down and quality up, because buyers may choose another car or delay purchasing altogether. When it comes to medical care, however, financial incentives are skewed in ways that fuel inflation.

✧ *Doctors control both the supply and the demand for services.* Buying medical care is not like buying a car. As one economist has said, it is more like having a car break down on a desert highway at 2 AM. When a tow truck comes, you take what they offer and you pay what they charge. In health care, patients are in a poor position to exercise choice. To know what is needed to diagnose and treat one's ailment and what the costs are requires the expertise of a physician. The last thing anyone is able to do when sick and in a hospital is shop around. People turn to doctors as professionals, not salesmen, who can tell them what needs to be done.

✧ *Insurance insulates providers and patients from costs.* People buy health insurance to protect themselves from the costs of a catastrophic illness and, increasingly, to cover the costs of routine care. However, the result is that doctors and patients decide what needs to be done without any cost consideration, because a third party is paying the bill.

✧ *Fee-for-service payment increases costs.* Insurers generally pay providers a fee for each service, which means the more services ordered, the more money made. Fear of malpractice litigation further bolsters doctors' incentives to order tests and services. As a result, public and private insurers have found that cutting fees by one dollar saves only 50 cents because providers increase the volume of services they order to maintain income. As George Bernard Shaw put it, somewhat caustically, "any sane nation, having observed that you could provide for the supply of bread by giving baker a pecuniary interest in baking for you, that gives a surgeon a pecuniary interest in cutting off your leg is enough to make one despair of political humanity." Consequently, many insurers are turning to capitation (i.e., a set payment per patient or diagnosis) or salarying doctors to change current incentives.

✧ *Market rules protect insurers from competition.* Unlike medical care, there is nothing intrinsic to health insurance that should prevent people from comparison shopping (i.e., competition to attract consumers should force insurers to act more effectively to contain the costs of health care delivery, maintain quality, and improve consumer satisfaction with them). Several factors, however, undermine competition and accountability to consumers. Most Americans have few if any insurance choices, because 85% of small and medium-sized employers offer just one plan, few affordable nongroup plans are available, and pre-existing conditions exclusions and experience rating lock people out of plans. For those with choice, it is hard to do a real cost comparison when insurers vary benefits in so many ways. Finally, many workers have little reason to consider price because employers often pay extra when workers choose a more expensive plan, because any spending on benefits is excluded from taxes. Consequently, it has been easier for insurers to raise premiums and to exclude poor health risks than to take difficult steps to contain costs.

Options

The current health system is largely based on a combination of public and private insurance with private health care delivery. Among the insured, public insurance programs (Medicaid and Medicare) cover low income, elderly, and disabled people, whereas private insurance covers the others. They all pay for services delivered through hospitals and clinics that are operated by the private sector, not the government, and through physicians who are self-employed or privately employed. There are several options for addressing cost problems by transforming this structure of insurance and health care delivery or by reforming within it.

Option 1: Government Insurance and Health Care Delivery

This option transforms our system into one not unlike the public school system—the government pays the costs and manages the delivery system. A public insurance program covers every American for their basic health care needs, and the services are provided through hospitals and clinics operated by, and physicians employed by, the government. The costs are financed through taxes.

Advantages   Proponents argue that this approach directly attacks the problems in the health care market. By operating hospitals and clinics, directly employing doctors, and putting them on a public budget, government removes profit from medicine, discourages unnecessary services, and encourages efforts to economize. The option provides the greatest leverage over costs, and it creates full public accountability in medicine.

Disadvantages   Opponents argue that this option takes a sledgehammer to health care. Although it is straightforward, it only replaces the problems of the private market with the larger problems of nationalization of one seventh of the economy. The government has neither the personnel nor the ability to take over and manage hospitals, clinics, and physician care across the country. Government's accountability is weak because the ballot box only allows the public to indicate its opinion of the general direction of the system, public management tends to be unresponsive to consumers' needs, and interest groups tend to veto needed changes. As a consequence, opponents argue that quality and innovation suffer.

Examples of government insurance and health delivery include the Veterans Administration, the Indian Health Service, and the National Health Service in the United Kingdom.

Option 2: Government Insurance and Regulation of
Private Health Care Delivery

Under this option, a tax-financed public insurance program covers any American for basic health care services, but delivery of health care remains private. As under Medicare, the government pays directly for services through private hospitals and physicians, or even through HMOs. To control costs, the government sets the fees it pays providers according to a national health budget. Furthermore, it takes steps to regulate the increasing volume of services physicians order, such as DRG-based payment (i.e., fixed payment for total care based on diagnosis), requirements to obtain government authorization before major procedures, and other utilization review measures.

Advantages   Backers of this single-payer option argue that by cutting out private insurance—with its profiteering, advertising, and insurance agents—and replacing premiums with a simple, equitable financing structure (i.e., taxes), the plan would reap substantial administrative savings. There is considerable experience with such systems, including Medicare and Canada, which show operating costs are lower and implementation is feasible. People in these systems have also reported far higher satisfaction with their care and coverage than those seeking private insurance coverage.

Disadvantages   Critics argue that this approach does little to correct the intrinsic problems driving costs up. Simpler paperwork produced only one-time savings, and, under current proposals, incentives to do more tests and procedures under fee-for-service medicine remain. The only tools a government insurer has to contain private hospital and physician costs are the crude, centralized methods of fee cuts, DRG-based payment, and utilization review, which have not succeeded (Medicare and Canadian health care costs continue to far outstrip inflation).

To some, the key problem is that a government insurance system provides no incentives for changes in private delivery, which may have more far-reaching effects on cost (e.g., consolidating local hospitals and practices to eliminate duplication in technologies and improve economies of scale, diverting patients from specialists to primary care gatekeepers, increasing the role of nurse practitioners, or experimenting with different forms of physician payment, such as salaries). Indeed, government insurance may make innovation unlikely because of the veto power held by special interest groups. Also, shifting from premiums to taxes forces insured middle-income workers to pay much more because families with two workers must pay twice, singles receive no discount, and their payments must also cover poor people. To backers of a public system, the primary problem is not with government insurance, but with private health care— they argue that costs cannot be contained if there is any profit in medicine.

Examples of government insurance and regulation of private health care delivery include Medicare, Medicaid, and the provincial health system in Canada.

Option 3: Federal Regulation of Private Insurance and Private Health Care Costs

This option extends private insurance and health care services to all Americans through insurance reforms that provide equal access to coverage and government subsidies that pay all or part of the cost of a basic plan, depending on one's income. If desired, this approach can be coupled with an employer mandate to pay for a portion of the premiums. To control costs, it establishes a national health budget, which is enforced through any of a number of strategies.

◇ *Rate regulation.* The government regulates payments to doctors and hospitals, and it requires insurers to pay providers according to a fee schedule set to hold costs within the national budget. Because managed care plans do not pay through a typical fee-for-service arrangement (e.g., plans may pay physicians a salary or may own a hospital and simply give it a budget for all services), they are usually exempted.

◇ *Premium caps.* The government sets a maximum for the average insurance premium charged in a given area. In typical proposals, fee-for-service insurance pays providers according to a federally regulated fee schedule, and managed care plans are free to use alternative payment arrangements for providers. However, the average premium must remain within the cap. Because insurance pays for hospital and physician services, insurers are under pressure to contain not only fees but also the volume of unnecessary services ordered.

✧   *Technology controls.* To supplement these approaches, the government regulates new technology and capital investment, requiring that sufficient need or efficacy be shown before a new scanner or a hospital wing is set up.

Advantages   Backers argue that this type of reform directly addresses the problems of our system without up-ending those aspects that work well or discouraging the changes in health care delivery needed to bring costs under control. Insurance reform removes the pre-existing condition exclusions and discriminatory pricing that threaten coverage for even well-insured families. Premium subsidies or an employer mandate removes the financial barriers low income Americans face. Rate and premium controls attack all the sources of runaway costs. At the same time, the reforms preserve private health care delivery and consumer choice among health plans. Competition among insurers encourages them to attempt innovations in health care delivery, which attract patients while meeting budget targets. Some localities with rate regulation currently have had lower health care inflation and intense activity in hospital consolidation and managed care innovation. Finally, backers note that premium-based financing avoids the greater redistribution (i.e., changes in what currently insured Americans pay) of tax-based financing.

Disadvantages   Single-payer advocates hold that preserving premiums, multiple insurers, employer payments, and private health care delivery maintains profit and layers of costly complexity in the system. They argue that waste and bureaucracy will continue unless most if not all of these factors are eliminated. For example, where a simple tax automatically scales payments to income, under this option an enormous new agency is needed just to process and to determine premium subsidies for the millions of low income and business applicants needing assistance.

Critics favoring greater competition agree with maintaining private insurance and private health care. However, they argue that this option creates regulation that is both ineffective and counterproductive, while failing to create genuine competition among plans. Government regulation does not stem doctors' incentives to order more services to offset cuts in the fee per service, and it has not consistently curtailed costs, particularly for ambulatory services. A premium cap may limit total costs, but it has the government decide what the appropriate trade-off between cost and quality is for every American community, something it does not have the knowledge or experience to do. The greatest danger is that, if the cap is set too low and insurers do not have enough leverage over providers to meet the cap, they will go bankrupt, thus endangering coverage for entire communities. Finally, these opponents argue that this option fails to correct the problems that protect insurers from consumer choice and competition.

Regulatory approaches to cost control have been attempted in the city of Rochester, New York, and in the states of Maryland, New Jersey, and Massachusetts (i.e., hospital rate regulation plus technology controls).

Option 4: Federal Regulation of Private Insurance with Market Constraints on Private Health Care Costs

As in the previous option, this option maintains private insurance and health care services. Instead of relying on regulation of health payments, it would rely on creating a functioning market to contain costs. Government's role would be to enforce insurance market rules that encourage families to make cost-conscious health care choices. The two main market-oriented reform strategies are "managed competition" and "Medisave."

The more prominent proposal of the two, managed competition, aims to encourage price-conscious choice among competing health plans for individuals the way that big businesses have choice and leverage over plans. In the current market, individuals and workers in small businesses have few if any plans available. Under managed competition, they are among hundreds of thousands joined together in a regional health alliance, which bargains with plans for fair premiums and offers members a menu of health plans that offer a standardized, federal benefits package. The alliance provides comparative price and quality information, and individuals can change plans annually. Pre-existing condition exclusions and experience rating are banned, so people can switch freely. Also, proposals often cap tax deductibility for employer-paid health benefits, or they require that employer health benefits are paid as a fixed dollar amount, so workers pay the full cost of taking more expensive plans. These policies encourage individuals to weigh price with quality, convenience, and other factors when choosing a health plan, just as they would when buying the family car. Although managed competition backers often believe HMOs will win in this competition, it is by no means clear that consumers will not decide it is worth it to pay more for traditional, fee-for-service plans.

Rather than create competition among plans as managed competition attempts, Medisave and similar reform plans put a higher financial burden on consumers to create competition among care providers. Medisave requires health plans to carry a large deductible (e.g., $2,000). When families need care, they would pay for services with cash held in tax-free, Medisave bank accounts. The government assists low income families by depositing up to the full deductible amount in a family's account. Employers can pay into the accounts as well. The theory is that patients paying cash will choose treatments carefully, bargain shop among providers, and push costs down.

Advantages   Backers of a consumer choice option argue that it avoids undermining the innovation, choice, and quality people value in the private system of health care and coverage. Unlike option 3, however, they argue that it is preferable and more effective to reform health care so consumers—not government, providers, or insurers—decide what the appropriate trade-off between cost and quality is.

Proponents of managed competition argue that competition forces health plans to be far more accountable to consumers than government-operated or regulated plans would be. To attract enrollees, a successful plan must drive hard bargains with doctors and hospitals and make innovative changes in private health care to hold costs down (e.g., consolidate hospitals and duplicate services, provide more primary care). But it must do so in ways that keep physicians satisfied and maintain quality, or it will drive patients (and doctors) away to other plans. Backers argue that the government has not demonstrated this kind of innovation and accountability to individuals, yet these attributes are needed to bring costs in line. Furthermore, health alliances provide consumers with a bargaining agent on their side and thousands of small businesses with much lower administrative costs through a single, consolidated employee benefits operation. Corporations and public employee organizations that have adopted managed competition principles have reported substantial reductions in costs, and they have spurred many innovations in private health delivery.

Those who favor Medisave argue that making consumers pay cash for basic medical services takes not only government but also private insurers out of the physician-patient relationship. Yet, it controls costs because patients will think twice before going to the emergency room for the sniffles, and they will ask tough questions before submitting to expensive, invasive treatment.

Disadvantages   Single-payer advocates feel no differently about competition among insurers than about regulation of insurers (i.e., it maintains the complexity and profiteering of private insurance middlemen, as well as the financial convolutions of government subsidies, employer payments, and individual payments, all scaled to individual income and changing with job status). Some of these opponents likewise view private physicians and hospitals as keeping profiteering in medicine.

Those favoring regulation over competition argue that these reforms are an enormous gamble based on policies that have been attempted only on a small scale. Relying on incentives alone carries no guarantee that inflation will be controlled. It would be no surprise if consumers, forced to make Hobson's choice between quality and cost, opt for quality everytime in this all important arena. As imperfect as government must be, it is the only entity that can enforce cost-containment. Furthermore, this policy is incompatible with reforms that mandate universal health care, because it is bad policy to mandate that individuals buy coverage and yet fail to guarantee that the costs of that coverage are under control.

Critics of managed competition also argue that its regional health alliances are just a new government bureaucracy; that it will spur the growth of HMOs, which only increase intrusion into physicians' practices; and that taxing employee benefits as income will make families feel less, not more, financially secure about their coverage. They also argue that for some groups, competition is inappropriate—rural areas cannot sustain competition among multiple plans when it is difficult enough to find multiple doctors or a single hospital, and many poor people cannot be expected to make informed choices in the market.

Critics of reforms, such as Medisave, which is based on catastrophic coverage, argue that even in theoretical terms, this approach will not control costs. Most medical spending is for acute or chronic illnesses, or even an uncomplicated pregnancy, the costs of which greatly exceed even a large deductible. The Medisave plan does nothing to contain the costs of care for the 5% of the population who account for 58% of spending. As a result, the premiums of a catastrophic policy are not low enough to make up for its high deductibles when compared with typical insurance policies (which is why catastrophic policies sell very poorly). Finally, critics argue that without physician advice, patients are in a poor position to decide what treatment and tests they need; paying cash saves little money, while discouraging preventive care and turning physicians into salesmen.

Examples of **managed competition** include the public employee systems in California and Wisconsin, some large corporations (e.g., Alcoa, Xerox), and the states of Florida and Washington (reforms under way). Nine states have sponsored catastrophic plans, including Kansas, Illinois, and Florida.

Option 5: Combination Approach

The current system consists of a combination of starkly different approaches (compare Medicare, Medicaid, the VA system, and private insurance). A reformed system may proceed no differently. Indeed, many federal proposals leave Medicare, the Indian Health Service, or the veterans system unchanged while restructuring health care for the private insurance market.

Advantages   Advocates argue that this approach makes fundamental changes in health care for the large population of people with inadequate coverage and the highest costs without undermining comparatively successful programs with broad support, such as Medicare. Furthermore, it avoids turning the beneficiaries of popular programs against reform.

Disadvantages   Critics argue that health costs cannot be contained without a unified system. Multiple systems maintain extra layers of administration and complexity and leave large programs in which health care costs can continue to escape control.

Maintenance and Improvement of Quality

Although people are generally satisfied with the quality of American health care, many have concerns that health care reform that attempts to extend care to all while reducing health care inflation will end up sacrificing quality in the process. It is certainly plausible that quality may suffer when shifting from a system in which cost is no object to one in which physicians face the limits of a national health budget or pressure to reduce costs from insurers under stiff competition.

Others, however, point out that quality monitoring in medicine is already weak by comparison with other enterprises. Few physicians keep careful data on quality in their own practices, and there is even less data available that allow physicians to compare their results with others. It should be no surprise then that studies indicate patients receive more than $100 billion worth of unnecessary procedures and tests (including surgery, drugs, and other potential harmful treatments) in a given year.

Options

There are two core options for a more sophisticated quality improvement system: quality regulation or quality incentives. With either approach, however, improvement begins with information. In a medical practice, one needs a database with, for example, history and diagnosis of patients, treatment attempted, whether and when symptoms improved, and how satisfied patients are with treatment and care, among others. For health plans, data may show how satisfied enrollees are with their plan; how long a standard visit is; how many enrollees receive their immunizations, mammograms, and other screenings; and other such information. Without such data, it is impossible for physicians to have a reliable sense of how effective their treatments are, how satisfied patients are, or how to improve care, and it is impossible for hospitals, health plans, and others to know how they are doing. Standardizing data collection also makes it possible to aggregate information from hundreds of providers, thus allowing comparison of treatment modalities and issuance of detailed guidelines for treatment of particular diagnoses. It even enables comparison of physicians, hospitals, laboratories, and health plans. Clearly, the data must be appropriate to the comparison, and what constitutes quality must be clearly defined. Such measurement is in its infancy, and data collection will need to be perfected over time. Once this information is gathered, however, the question is how to use it. The answer depends on the option chosen for improving quality.

Option 1: Quality Regulation

A regulatory strategy relies on having government set goals and standards and assess whether they are met. If appropriate, data are collected, which allows measurement of the level of quality produced. Regulations can then set standards for performance in medical care (i.e., attempt to control results directly). For example, health plans could be required to show that a specific percentage of enrolled children are immunized, and that their enrollees report a high level of satisfaction with care and services, among others. Standards and goals could also be set for medical procedures and other aspects of care. However, few of these data are currently collected, and it is not often done.

The more common type of regulation applies to the inputs for quality care (i.e., it controls processes and products that affect quality). For example, federal law requires government approval of drugs and medical devices, and it sets rules for personnel and facilities for every laboratory test (e.g., Pap smears can only be read by pathologists who read a specified number per year). Similarly, regulations could set standards for specific medical services and procedures to assure that a basic level of quality care is the result.

To be effective, quality regulations must be enforced, but policy makers may choose from a range of powers. Government power can be limited by relying on peer enforcement, in which providers, through their organizations, establish the regulations and monitor and enforce them. Alternatively, government can provide the central role in enforcement by monitoring adherence to regulations through audits, surveys and certification, and suspending ability to practice for those who fall short.

Advantages Those who favor quality regulation argue that this approach has been employed with great success in maintaining the quality and the reliability of pharmaceuticals and medical devices. Using new data measuring performance and applying these same techniques to medical procedures, the practices of health insurers and other aspects of health care would achieve the same result—assurance to the American public that our system continues to provide quality care. Furthermore, under particular types of health reform (i.e., a single-payer system with public health care), there is no other alternative.

Disadvantages Critics argue that regulations are a crude, ineffective, and costly approach to maintaining quality. They are crude in that rules permit only a simplistic conception of quality. Rules do not encourage the excellence Americans value, only competence at best. At worst, providers focus on meeting regulations, not on quality care. Regulations are static and have little subtlety. They are not easily adapted to changes in medical care and patient concerns. However, quality improvement requires that providers constantly monitor and seek feedback, adjust standards, and make even minor changes, a process regulations cannot capture. Furthermore, critics argue that setting standards and regulations for major medical procedures and facilities intrudes on patient care, takes enormous time and money, and goes beyond the capacity and expertise of government bureaucrats. Finally, the quality data we have today are crude—often wrong, misleading, or biased and, therefore, worse than useless for people who use it to make decisions.

Examples include Medicare and Medicaid quality regulations, FDA drug and device approval, the Clinical Laboratory Improvement Act, and state certification of insurers.

Option 2: Quality Incentives
This option seeks to encourage quality improvement primarily through the incentives that competition creates. To a large extent, the level of quality in the current system is the result of competition. For the most part, people choose their physicians and hospitals, and quality is a key factor in that choice. Providers who do not

maintain excellent skills, or who fail to be responsive and humane to patients, risk losing their patient base to others. This kind of patient choice tends to reward providers who do more than the minimum, make subtle efforts to do better, and go the extra mile to improve quality. In the current system, the incentives for quality are, nonetheless, unsophisticated. Patients have little information for comparing doctors or hospitals beyond the anecdotes they hear and advertising. "Quality" care is simply a provider with a good word-of-mouth reputation who escapes malpractice litigation.

To improve quality through competition, better information on doctors, hospitals, and insurers is needed. If appropriate data are collected as described, a report card could be constructed with a variety of information. People could compare levels of satisfaction of patients with different providers or different insurers, as well as measures of convenience (e.g., waiting times, average length of visit). If data were sophisticated and accurate enough, even practitioners' success with particular procedures could be illustrated. Better comparative information should compel providers to ensure their care is not only subjectively satisfactory but also objectively effective. For example, it may encourage a reduction in unnecessary tests or changes in technique that affect a patient's impression of the care very little, while improving quality greatly.

Advantages   Advocates argue this approach to improving quality is better than quality regulation for a number of reasons. It builds on the competitive framework of American care, which already encourages excellence in care. It leaves greater autonomy to professionals who know best how to care for patients, rather than constraining their judgment and flexibility with regulations. Informed consumer choice encourages providers to respond to patients, not regulators, and to make quality a constant concern. It requires far less government spending and intrusion, and it may make many regulations unnecessary. Finally, only this approach holds hope of continuing to promote excellence in care.

Disadvantages   Critics argue that there are too many circumstances in which an incentive approach will fail to make it the centerpiece of a quality improvement effort. Many patients have no choices about the providers they see. Many have only one doctor available, especially if they are rural residents or if they need a specialist, and it is not uncommon to have just one hospital in an area. Provider information without provider regulation tells them when they have poor quality care without doing anything about it. Furthermore, critics argue that patients often cannot or do not choose what is best. Even with widespread information, patients still smoke and drive without seatbelts. Similarly, reasons of convenience, ignorance, or information overload or misuse will lead patients to low quality providers, and government's role is to ensure quality is always there.

FIVE MAJOR FEDERAL PROPOSALS ❖

Policymakers choose among the basic options just outlined to construct reform plans. During the health reform debate in Congress in 1994, five widely different approaches came to prominence that are excellent examples of how the issues of cost-containment, lack of access, and quality improvement can be addressed (Table 14.1).

+ President Clinton's Health Security Act.
+ Single-payer Plan (of Sen. Paul Wellstone and Rep. Jim McDermott).
+ Conservative Democratic Plan (of Rep. Jim Cooper and Sen. John Breaux).
+ The Senate Republican Plan (offered by Sen. John Chafee).
+ The House Republican Plan (offered by Rep. Robert Michel).

Although health care reform was not enacted in 1994, the debate over how to improve the U.S. health care system is far from over as costs continue to escalate, access remains elusive to 15% of the populace and this number continues to grow, and issues of quality improvement persist.

The specific details of the five proposals outlined below are less important than the conceptual framework they use. These five plans illustrate the types of proposals Congress will be choosing from in the future. The summaries that follow provide more detailed information for comparing the proposals, including the following.

+ How coverage and benefits are improved.
+ How coverage is financed.
+ How costs are contained.
+ How quality is maintained.

President Clinton's Health Security Act

The President sought to achieve mandatory coverage and cost-containment in a system of reformed private insurance and private health care delivery. Individuals are mandated to purchase coverage for a standard set of benefits, and they receive assistance from employers, who must contribute 80% of an average premium for each worker, and government, which covers all or part of premiums for low income families and early retirees. Reforms based on managed competition are

Table 14.1 Five Major Federal Proposals in Congress at a Glance

	Coverage/Benefits	Who Pays What?	Cost Containment	Quality
Clinton Plan	Insurance reforms (open access for all) – ban on pre-existing exclusions – community rating Alliances guarantee choice of plans Comprehensive benefits: – basic care + mental health, dental, preventive – plans may be HMO, PPO, or fee-for-service	Employer mandate: – firms pay 80% – individuals pay rest – nonworkers pay 100% Govt. subsidies to ensure universality: – people pay no more than 3.9% of income – firms pay no more than 3.5–7.9% of payroll	Managed competition + cap on health costs: – alliances provide choice health plans to con- sumers, forcing plans to compete – national health budget limits Medicare, Med- icaid, and insurance costs to grow no faster than GDP	Quality incentives: – report cards will compare quality of plans and providers for people choosing among them Increased research spending
McDermott/ Wellstone Plan— Single Payer	Public coverage open to all (private insurance eliminated) Comprehensive benefits: – Clinton benefits + long term care – no deductibles/copays	Tax financing – 4–8.4% payroll tax + 2.1% income tax – states finance the remain- ing costs	Public regulation of private health services: – global budget limits state health spending	Current policy
Cooper Plan— Managed Competition	Insurance reforms (open access for all): – ban on pre-existing exclusions – community rating Alliances provide choice of plans Nat'l. board sets benefits and cost sharing requirements	Individuals responsible for premiums, but employers may provide benefits Subsidies pay for: – 100% of least cost plan for people below poverty line – varying % of such plan for those at 100–200% of poverty	Managed competition – alliances provide choice of health plans to con- sumers, forcing plans to compete – limits employer tax de- ductions for employee plan costs; thus, workers pay the difference when choosing more expensive plans, stiffening competition	Quality incentives: – report cards will compare quality of plans and providers for people choosing among them

Table 14.1 (continued)

	Coverage/Benefits	Who Pays What?	Cost Containment	Quality
Chafee Plan	Insurance reforms (better access): – ban pre-existing exclusions – rate-banding Benefits set by commission: – 2 types cost sharing: "standard" vs. high deductible "catastrophic"	Individuals mandated to buy coverage, but employers may provide benefits Low income help: – premiums on a sliding scale for those <240% of poverty line (in year 2005)	Medisave and limited tax deductibility increase cost consciousness: – "catastrophic" plan has people pay cash for routine care – tax deductibility capped so workers buying high cost plans pay the extra costs, not employers	Current policy
Michel Plan	Limited insurance reforms: – can exclude an illness starting <3 months before coverage – rate-banding Outside group sets basic benefits: – 2 types cost sharing: "standard" vs. "catastrophic: with $1800/$3600 deductible	People pay as under current system (no new subsidies)	Efficiency measures: – standardized insurance forms – electronic billing systems – anti-fraud measures	Current policy

proposed to contain costs; caps on premiums and regulation of providers' fees, if competition is not enough to slow medical inflation, are also proposed to contain costs. Medicare remains the coverage for the elderly and the disabled, although the new plan replaces Medicaid.

Coverage and Benefits   Universal, Mandatory Coverage Under Private Insurance

Insurance Reform

Discrimination by health status is outlawed. Reforms ban pre-existing condition exclusions, and they require renewability and portability. Plans must charge community rates (i.e., all alliance members enrolling in a given plan pay the same premium without variation for health status, age, gender, or other factors).

Choice of Coverage

Legal residents under 65 years old are required to purchase one of several private health plans offered through a state-designated, regional health alliance. Subsidies are provided to low income families. Large companies (>5,000 workers) can create their own purchasing alliance. Alliances must offer at least three plans, including one fee-for-service plan that does not restrict choice of providers. Those who do not join are assigned a plan when they show up for treatment, and they will be assessed back premiums and penalties.

Standardized Comprehensive Benefits

All plans must offer a standard package, with benefits and cost-sharing set by law and modified by a National Health Board over time. The package includes preventive care, acute care, intermediate care facilities, home health and hospice care, prescription drugs, vision, hearing, dental, and substance abuse and mental health services (initially limited, but made unlimited in 2000). Children of low income families are entitled to additional medical and social services through a new federal program. Health plans must use one of three styles of cost-sharing.

✦ *HMO style:* $10 copayment, no deductible for care by HMO's providers; $200 deductible, 40% copayment for care by outside providers.

✦ *PPO style:* $10 copayment for preferred providers; $200 deductible, 20% copayment for care by outside providers; $3,000 annual out-of-pocket limit.

✦ *Indemnity style:* $200 deductible, 20% copayment, $3,000 annual out-of-pocket limit for care by any provider.

Future of Medicare and Medicaid

Medicaid is eliminated; however, Medicare remains, with prescription drug coverage added for elderly and disabled. States may request permission to include these beneficiaries in alliances, and people enrolled in a plan through an alliance may stay with it when they turn 65.

Who Pays What   *Employer Mandate, Public Subsidies, and Individual Payments*

Reforms require employers to pay 80% of an average premium for workers and their dependents, thus covering the bulk of costs. Individuals pay the rest, which varies depending on the cost of the plan they choose. To assist low income working and nonworking families, government subsidies cover any costs that exceed 3.9% of income (care is free for the unemployed and others with no income). The government pays 80% of an average premium for retirees aged 55 to 64, who are ineligible for Medicare, so their costs are no different from workers'. To limit expenses for firms, the government also covers costs that exceed 3.5 to 7.9% of payroll (depending on size and average wage). Some of the federal subsidy costs are paid for by tobacco taxes and a 1% payroll tax on self-insured companies ($89 billion). The bulk of the revenues, however, are generated by constraining private and public health costs to grow no faster than the economy. This approach produces revenue gains from companies with lower health benefit costs ($71 billion in increased tax payments) and from reduced growth in Medicare ($124 billion), Medicaid ($65 billion), and other federal programs ($41 billion).

Cost-Containment   *Combination of Managed Competition and Regulation of Private Costs*

The pooling of purchasing power; adoption of standard, simplified forms; and fewer plans produce substantial administrative savings while retaining private insurance and private health care delivery. To contain costs over time, the policy relies on both competition and regulation.

Managed Competition

Health alliances, insurance reforms, and financing policy are designed to have consumers choose from a menu of plans with varying prices. Generally, those who opt for higher cost plans pay the extra costs, thus encouraging competitive plans to hold premiums down, reform private health delivery, and maintain quality. (Note: the Clinton plan keeps current policies that allow employers to pay the extra cost of expensive plans and not count it as taxable income to workers).

Health Budgeting

To contain Medicare and Medicaid costs and to ensure private costs are constrained if competition falls short, a National Health Board limits federal health spending and private premium costs to grow no faster than the gross domestic product by 1998. The Board sets a schedule of fees for doctors, hospitals, and other providers, which plans may follow to meet the premium target. If a health plan pays according to this schedule, providers may not bill the patients for more.

Quality   *Incentive-based Quality Improvement*

Individuals choosing plans will receive report cards comparing the care received in different plans according to convenience, quality, and other measures. Ongoing surveys and a uniform, national database with improved data on patient care will allow improvements in this report card over time and may allow comparison of individual providers in the future. Funding for basic and clinical research is increased.

Single-payer Plan (Sen. Paul Wellstone and Rep. Jim McDermott)

These liberal Democrats seek mandatory coverage and cost-containment through public insurance and regulation of private health costs in a plan very similar to Canada's system. Individuals automatically receive acute and long-term care coverage in a public insurance program run by their state and financed through new federal payroll taxes and state tax revenues. Private insurance, Medicare, and Medicaid are abolished. The federal government sets a global budget that states must meet, and states determine the fees to be paid to providers according to the budget.

Coverage and Benefits   Universal, Mandatory Coverage Under Federal Insurance

Public Coverage

Legal residents are automatically enrolled by their states in a state government–run plan at birth or at time of immigration. Eliminates Medicaid, Medicare, the VA system, and private insurance.

Comprehensive Benefits

The package includes preventive care, acute care, intermediate care facilities, long-term care (including nursing home care), home health and hospice care, prescription drugs, vision, hearing, dental, and substance abuse and mental health services. There are no copayments or deductibles, and patients may see any provider.

Who Pays What   *Tax-Financing*

All health costs currently borne by individuals and employers are shifted to the government. Thus, taxes are the sole source of financing. The plan relies primarily on a 4 to 8.4% payroll tax plus a 2.1% income tax, which are expected to cover 81 to 91% of states' health costs. Costs beyond this are a state's responsibility.

Cost-Containment   *Public Regulation of Private Health Care Costs*
The federal government sets a global budget. States are allocated a portion, and they set physician fees and hospital budgets to meet their state budgets. States are wholly responsible for costs that exceed the budget. Providers are banned from collecting additional payments from patients.

Quality
Current policy remains in effect.

Conservative Democratic Plan (Rep. Jim Cooper and Sen. John Breaux)

The congressional conservative Democrats aim for universal health care and cost containment in a voluntary, private insurance system with private health care delivery. Neither individuals nor employers are mandated to pay for insurance. To achieve universal access to coverage, the government must pay the full premium for people with family incomes below the poverty line, as well as pay part of the premium for near-poor families. Medicare remains, but Medicaid is replaced by the new system. Reforms based on managed competition give individuals a choice of plans offering standard benefits with no pre-existing condition exclusions, and they foster competition among plans to contain costs, such as under the Clinton proposal. Unlike the President, however, these Democrats oppose the regulatory cost controls involved in national health budgeting.

Coverage and Benefits   Subsidized Access to Private Insurance

Insurance Reform
Discrimination by health status is outlawed. Reforms ban pre-existing condition exclusions and require renewability and portability. Plans must charge community rates (i.e., all alliance members enrolling in a given plan pay the same premium without variation for health status, age, gender, or other factors).

Choice of Coverage
State-designated, regional health alliances offer a menu of health plans at different prices to individuals who are not in Medicare or who work in a large business

(defined as having more than 100–500 workers, depending on the state). Individuals are not required to purchase coverage.

Standard Benefits Set by Commission
An independent national commission will set a standard package of benefits, including standard cost-sharing requirements. Preventive services will be included, with no cost-sharing required.

Medicaid/Medicare
Medicaid recipients are covered through alliances. Medicare beneficiaries remain in Medicare.

Who Pays What   *Individual Payments and Public Subsidies*
Individuals pay the premium of the plan they choose. Employers may pay for employee benefits. However, employer contributions in excess of the cost of the least expensive plan in a worker's alliance are not tax-deductible. The federal government pays the cost of the least expensive health plan for people with income below 100% of the poverty level, and they subsidize on a sliding scale that cost for people between 100 and 200% of poverty. Cost-sharing is also subsidized. Tax revenues are generated by limiting the tax deductibility to the price of the lowest cost health plan. Additional savings result from reductions in the growth of Medicare spending.

Cost-Containment   *Managed Competition*
Pooling of purchasing power; adoption of standard, simplified forms; and fewer plans produce substantial administrative savings while retaining private insurance and private health care delivery. To contain costs over time, however, the policy relies on managed competition.

Managed Competition
Health alliances, insurance reforms, and financing policy are designed to have consumers choose from a menu of plans with varying prices. Those who opt for higher cost plans pay the extra costs, thus encouraging competitive plans to hold premiums down, reform private health delivery, and maintain quality.

Quality   *Incentive-based Quality Improvement*
Individuals choosing plans will receive report cards comparing the care received in different plans according to convenience, quality, and other measures.

The Senate Republican Plan (Offered by Sen. John Chafee)

The moderate Republicans in the Senate also seek universal coverage and cost-containment in a system of private insurance and private health care. Their plan requires that individuals buy private insurance, and it provides some form of subsidies for low income families to assist with the costs. It does not require businesses to provide employee benefits. To contain costs, the plan includes a limited form of managed competition, and it offers a Medisave plan that individuals may choose. Medicare and Medicaid remain in place.

Coverage and Benefits   Universal, Mandatory Coverage by Private Insurance

Insurance Reforms
Limits on discrimination. Reforms ban pre-existing condition exclusions and require renewability and portability. Premiums may vary for health status, age, gender, or other factors, but states must establish rating bands (i.e., upper and lower limits for premium variation).

Individual Mandate
Individuals are required to purchase coverage under a private health plan. Small businesses (<100 workers), people with no insurance, and the self-employed have the option to purchase coverage through a state-designated, regional purchasing cooperative (same as a health alliance).

Benefits Set by Commission
A national benefits commission will propose a standard package of benefits, which must include preventive care, prescription drugs, substance abuse coverage, and "severe" mental health services. The commission will propose two types of cost-sharing: a "standard" policy and a "catastrophic" policy with a high deductible and the option of a medical savings account.

Medicare/Medicaid
States may cover Medicaid recipients through plans offered by alliances. Medicare beneficiaries remain in Medicare.

Who Pays What   *Individual Payments and Public Subsidies*
Individuals pay the premium of the plan they choose. Employers may pay for employee benefits. However, the total tax deductibility of employer contributions cannot exceed the average of the lowest priced one third of plans offered by a

worker's alliance. By the year 2005, the federal government will provide income-linked subsidies to families with incomes below 240% of poverty. These subsidies pay for all or part of the cost of coverage under a plan with a premium in the lowest third of plans.

Cost-Containment   *Medisave and Limited Tax Deductibility*

Those choosing a catastrophic plan with a Medisave account will pay cash for routine health costs, thus encouraging them to be cost-conscious consumers of medical care. The plan also limits tax deductibility so that workers who buy higher cost plans pay the extra costs, thus encouraging competitive plans to hold premiums down, reform private health delivery, and maintain quality. However, states need not establish a purchasing cooperative, and businesses are not required to join. Growth in Medicaid and Medicare is reduced from 12 to 7% over six years through increased beneficiary payments, reduced payments for uncompensated care and providers with a disproportionate share of public patients, and encouraged managed care. Finally, medical malpractice reforms, including caps on damages, are expected to produce savings.

Quality

Current policy remains in effect.

The House Republican Plan (Offered by Rep. Robert Michel)

The more conservative House Republicans propose limited insurance reforms, including a Medisave option to be available to workers in small businesses and other nongroup purchasers, and they oppose greater structural changes in the existing health care system. Insurance reforms set minimum benefit standards, place limits on rate variations based on health status and other risks, and restrict pre-existing condition exclusions.

Coverage and Benefits   Insurance Reform to Expand Access

Insurance Reform
Limits on discrimination. Reforms limit pre-existing condition exclusions to illnesses beginning less than 3 months before coverage; exclusions are limited to 6 months after coverage (pregnancy cannot be excluded). Renewability and portability of employer plans are required. Plans may vary premiums for health status,

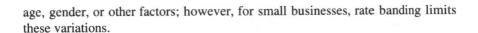

age, gender, or other factors; however, for small businesses, rate banding limits these variations.

Obtaining Coverage
Current system of coverage remains, including Medicaid and Medicare. Health plans operate under reformed insurance rules, including requirements for the benefits they offer.

Catastrophic Benefits Guaranteed
The National Association of Insurance Commissioners sets minimum benefit standards. Insurers for small businesses and individuals must offer two types of cost-sharing: a "standard" policy (defined by the insurer) and a catastrophic policy with a deductible of at least $1,800/individual, $3,600/family, as well as the option of a Medisave account.

Who Pays What *Premium Payments Continue as in the*
Current System
Individuals obtain coverage and make premium payments. Employers may offer health benefits, but they are not required to do so. Deposits to Medisave accounts are tax-deductible.

Cost-Containment
Standardized insurance forms, electronic billing, and antifraud provisions are intended to reap savings.

Quality
Current policy remains in effect.

These proposals have a wider scope than described herein, because they include policies on changing the medical malpractice system, training medical professionals, providing long-term care, changing coverage for veterans and the military, and more. However, these summaries offer a close comparison of five federal solutions that encapsulate the major options and issues Congress faces as it attempts to address the central problems of cost, coverage, and quality in the American health care system.

❖ Suggested Reading ❖

President Bill Clinton. Health Security Act. Summarized in: Health security: the President's report to the American people. Simon and Schuster, 1993. Introduced as Bill H. R. 3600 by Rep. Richard Gephardt, D-MO.
President Bill Clinton describes his health care plan and its rationale.

Enthoven AC. The history and principles of managed competition. Health Affairs, 1993; (suppl). 24–48.

The architect of managed competition explains how it would work and why it is preferable to other proposals.

Starr P. The logic of health-care reform. Whittle Direct Books, 1992.

The Pulitzer Prize–winning sociologist describes the policy and the political benefits of a proposal melding of managed competition and single-payer financing.

Himmelstein D, Woolhandler S. The national health program book. Common Courage Press, 1994.

The founders of Physicians for a National Health Plan explain and argue for Canadian-style single-payer health reform.

Other Health Policy Issues

Medical Malpractice

Jill Horwitz and Troyen Brennan

The topic of medical malpractice has provoked more emotional, polemical debate than perhaps any other health reform issue. Most Americans believe that greed and waste on the part of lawyers, doctors, or insurers have caused increasing health care costs. In fact, "[a]lmost half the public (46%) includes malpractice lawyers among the one or two groups most to blame for rising health-care costs . . . [while only] slightly more than one-in-three Americans lays blame on the doorstep of doctors and insurance companies."[309] Not only laymen, but also physicians, the media, and others with a direct interest in the malpractice realm often refer to the "malpractice crisis." In response, President Clinton's national health plan, as well as every competing plan introduced in Congress in recent years, contained provisions for medical malpractice reform.

This chapter provides an introduction to medical malpractice, a health care topic that has been central to health reform discussions. It begins with a discussion of why this is such a hot topic, then moves on to a description of the current medical malpractice legal system, analyzes its strengths and weaknesses, and surveys proposals for incremental and radical reforms.

WHY MALPRACTICE IS IMPORTANT ❖

The prevalence of malpractice liability in health care reform discussions may be warranted despite the fact that even the most successful reform would have an imperceptible affect on health care costs and expenditures; malpractice premiums

307

add up to only 1% of total health care spending.[310] And, "the total cost of mal-practice insurance—the most generous estimate is about $9 billion—is only a tiny fraction of the nation's $130 billion in tort liability expenditures . . . and of its $190 billion total liability bill."[311] Even the highest estimates of the total mal-practice system costs constitute "between 3% to 7% of total annual health care spending."[312] Still, legislatures in almost every one of the United States (U.S.) have passed some variety of medical malpractice reform. In all likelihood, mal-practice reform will continue to share center stage with more fiscally significant aspects of health care reform, such as intensity of care and excessive utilization due to moral hazard (see Chapter 8).

Yet, health care providers and policy makers should focus on improving the malpractice system to improve care for patients and equity for physicians and communities that pay the costs of medical injuries. Medical interventions cause serious injuries at an alarming rate: Out of every 100 hospitalizations, one patient receives a disabling injury, 25% of which are caused by negligence.[313] Consumers also need an effective and efficient system that reduces their risks of harm through negligence and that compensates them when they are harmed.

Physician concerns regarding the high cost of medical malpractice insurance also need attention. A dramatic increase in insurance prices during the 1980s made liability insurance inaccessible to many physicians, and it caused others to pass higher costs through to patients. Whereas U.S. physicians spent an average of $14,805, or more than 5% of all practice costs, for malpractice insurance in 1988, specialists spent significantly more.[314] By 1990, obstetrician-gynecologists spent an average of $37,808 in premiums[315]; in some regions of the country, the figures were more dramatic. In 1991, mean cost of coverage for obstetrician-gynecologists in New York reached almost $70,000 per year.[316] Obstetricians in Dade County, Florida, report liability insurance costs of more than $100,000 per year for 1994. Table 15.1 shows the national mean costs per physician and the av-erage net earning by specialty.

These concerns, among others, have caused patients, physicians, hospital risk managers, lawyers, and others to question the efficacy and efficiency of the med-ical malpractice system.

THE TORT SYSTEM ❖

In the U.S., malpractice litigation proceeds through what is known as the *tort sys-tem*. A **tort** is an act that results in injury when someone fails to use reasonable care in dealing with others. The obligations assigned by tort law are not based on an exchange of things or services, but, instead, on a less easily articulated respon-sibility to behave carefully. The responsibility of the acting party varies according to circumstances that mitigate or aggravate the offense. The tort system is meant to provide compensation to an injured party, to penalize the negligent party, and to deter negligence in the future.

Product liability cases provide a familiar example of how the tort system functions. When a company produces a faulty product, it has some responsibility for the harm the product causes. For example, the manufacturer of flame-retardant sleepwear holds a duty to make sure that fabric will not ignite. If it does, a court would determine the extent of the manufacturer's responsibility and order it to pay the burn victim. However, the company's responsibility may be limited if the consumer has unreasonably tested the power of the flame retardant. For example, if someone leans over an open flame while wearing clothing and it ignites, the company may not have the entire responsibility of compensating the consumer. Similarly, the court examines medical malpractice cases to assign blame when physicians fail to act with a reasonable duty of care while stopping short of forcing physicians to guarantee the results of their art.

What Is Negligence?

Although medical negligence is difficult to define, courts will generally decide in favor of a patient when certain conditions are met. Under the tort model, there are 4 conditions.

First, the defendant, usually the attending physician, but often the hospital, nurse, or other provider, must owe the patient a duty of care. The duty to give care, in legal terms known as "continuing attention," to a patient is based on the existence of a physician-patient relationship. Usually that relationship is established when a patient seeks care from a doctor for a particular problem and the doctor agrees to treat the patient. "In general, the law respects the physician's freedom to choose those with whom to establish a professional relationship. There is thus, for physicians, no analog to the public-utility-like duties imposed on hospitals to render at least emergency care to patients seeking it."[31] But courts have found the duty of care in referral situations and others in which the patient did not schedule an appointment to see a particular doctor. Doctors, however, do not have a legal responsibility to treat every sick or injured person. And, even if a medical professional does treat someone, the doctor-patient relationship may not exist. For example, when a physician attempts an emergency rescue, Good Samaritan laws protect physicians from negligence claims because the doctor-patient relationship is not established.

Second, once the patient-doctor relationship is established, it must be proved that the physician's services did not conform to the appropriate standard of care. Historically, medical malpractice cases defined the appropriate standard of care based on the locality rule, which held that it would be unreasonable to demand that all physicians, regardless of circumstance, be held to the same standard. For example, a rural physician, without resources, supplying care to a disadvantaged population should not be held to the same standard as a physician working at a well-funded, technologically advanced, urban teaching institution. Over time, the courts, recognizing the national nature of medical training and certification, as

Table 15.1 Mean Costs per Physician and Average Net Earnings, by Specialty: 1988

Specialty	Physician Earnings	Non-physician Employee Earnings	Office Space Costs	Medical Equipment Costs	Malpractice Costs	Medical Supply	Other Costs
All Physicians	$163,114 (1,917)	$ 52,111 (867)	$ 20,187 (309)	$ 4,955 (173)	$ 14,805 (261)	$ 11,457 (262)	$ 20,219 (361)
Medical Specialties							
General and Family Practice	105,339 (3,207)	51,559 (1,931)	19,794 (728)	4,926 (353)	8,639 (316)	14,085 (674)	15,218 (770)
Internal Medicine	121,320 (3,586)	49,746 (1,749)	19,381 (592)	5,204 (358)	8,019 (306)	12,941 (771)	19,182 (1,031)
Cardiovascular Disease	237,655 (16,876)	59,919 (5,131)	24,108 (1,694)	7,673 (988)	11,911 (741)	9,289 (991)	23,326 (2,161)
Gastroenterology	188,497 (7,893)	54,680 (3,649)	21,549 (1,094)	5,956 (633)	10,234 (530)	10,169 (917)	20,040 (1,454)
Other Medical Specialties	137,703 (4,975)	51,646 (2,572)	19,845 (910)	3,351 (351)	7,669 (326)	15,199 (982)	18,365 (1,200)
Surgical Specialties							
General Surgery	178,027 (6,806)	41,571 (2,017)	19,227 (875)	3,479 (315)	24,993 (1,010)	7,062 (562)	17,760 (975)
Cardiothoracic Surgery	329,903 (19,629)	60,132 (4,255)	21,258 (1,499)	5,511 (757)	33,930 (1,558)	4,743 (803)	27,907 (2,365)
Orthopedic	261,699 (12,644)	94,992 (4,820)	35,405 (2,419)	7,310 (707)	31,704 (1,405)	18,183 (1,252)	25,545 (1,674)
Ophthalmology	205,888 (10,443)	82,483 (5,120)	31,053 (1,688)	11,958 (1,270)	10,398 (384)	15,874 (2,280)	28,924 (2,289)

Table 15.1 (continued)

Specialty	Physician Earnings	Non-physician Employee Earnings	Office Space Costs	Medical Equipment Costs	Malpractice Costs	Medical Supply	Other Costs
Urologic Surgery	167,238	43,283	21,601	5,780	16,267	11,708	20,629
	(5,476)	(1,979)	(1,000)	(623)	(685)	(725)	(1,486)
Obstetrics and	179,706	6,392	23,570	4,184	35,735	15,028	25,184
Gynecology	(4,950)	(2,378)	(961)	(347)	(1,278)	(878)	(1,493)
Other Surgical	197,519	68,057	31,185	6,546	22,452	12,459	25,090
Specialties	(9,075)	(4,430)	(1,766)	(661)	(951)	(1,173)	(1,648)
Other Specialties							
Psychiatry	119,641	20,753	13,420	627	3,925	1,090	14,897
	(3,857)	(3,760)	(733)	(114)	(179)	(160)	(1,203)
Anesthesiology	212,951	37,013	4,684	1,060	23,168	838	19,625
	(6,565)	(5,347)	(689)	(322)	(999)	(223)	(1,366)
Radiology	213,017	39,684	12,543	11,555	11,201	10,686	23,392
	(8,431)	(4,051)	(1,612)	(2,585)	(613)	(1,354)	(1,883)
Other Specialties	161,259	33,554	11,135	2,943	8,049	5,687	20,650
	(6,852)	(6,852)	(1,248)	(520)	(597)	(1,090)	(1,930)

Notes: Cost shares were calculated at the practice level. Mean costs are reported per physician to facilitate comparisons across specialties. Standard errors are in parentheses. Data were trimmed to exclude cost values more than 4 standard deviations from the arithmetic mean. Data are for self-employed physicians. (Source: Health Care Financing Administration, Office of Research and Demonstrations: Data are from the 1988 physicians' practice costs and income survey. Adapted from Health Care Financing Review/Spring 1993.)

well as the universal nature of illness, replaced the locality rule with national standards. Accordingly, the courts now demand that physicians act in a way that reflects "medical knowledge as is commonly possessed or reasonably available to
minimally competent physicians in the same specialty or general field of practice
throughout the United States, to have a realistic understanding of the limitations
on his or her knowledge or competence, and, in general, to exercise minimally adequate medical judgment."[318] The locality rule has not disappeared entirely: The
national standard is still tempered, but not subsumed, by local custom and limits
on resources.

*Third, it must be shown that the failure to act in accordance with the duty of
care was the proximate cause of the patient's harm.* This concept, although theoretically simple, is not always easy to apply. Perhaps a surgeon neglected to remove one remnant of a bullet while operating on a patient. After a lengthy illness,
the patient died. Was the surgeon's oversight necessarily the cause of the death?
What if the patient was ill before being shot and, had they been healthier, they
would have been better able to resist the infection? More complicated determinations of causation arise when the patient is obese or a smoker.

*Finally, it is not enough if the physician owed the patient care and deviated
from practice standards if the patient did not suffer a "physically objective and
ascertainable" injury.*[319] Courts and legislatures have used several definitions of
the word "injury," including "(1) the alleged negligent act or omission; (2) the
physical damage or manifestation resulting from the act or omission; or (3) the legal injury, i.e., all the essential elements of a claim for medical malpractice,"
which includes physical harm suffered.[320] Exceptions to the requirement that a
physical injury exist arise when "the nature of the relationship between the parties
is such that there arises a duty to exercise ordinary care to avoid causing emotional
harm."[321] Accordingly, an obstetrician would have a duty to present information
regarding the necessity of performing an emergency cesarean section with a degree of gentleness not required in a discussion with a less vulnerable patient under less extreme circumstances.

Other factors, such as the patient's understanding of procedural risk, consent
to undergo treatment, resource constraints, use of clinical innovations, and contributory fault of the patient all color the decision of whether negligence caused
the injury.

The Process

The tort system involves a long process, from discovery of the injury through resolution of the case. Claims are not usually brought until more than one year has
passed since infliction of the injury. On average, claims take between 25 and 30
months, and they can require more than a decade to be resolved.[322]

Usually, once the patient (plaintiff) identifies the problem, they seek the advice
of an attorney, who takes a narrative summary of the events, obtains permission

from the patient for release of all relevant medical records, and retains a physician to review the substance of the case. In some states, the attorney must file the case with a screening board, which rules on the reasonableness of the case and gives the plaintiff permission to move forward with the charge against the defendant. In some instances, if the screening panel does not grant permission and the plaintiff proceeds with the claim and loses, they pay a substantial penalty.

Having made the decision to proceed with the case, the plaintiff and the defendant file various documents with the court and each other. First, the plaintiff files a complaint that puts the defendant on notice about a claim against them and they in turn issue a response. Second, the court defines a period known as discovery, in which both sides demand each other to produce relevant documents, ask key witnesses questions in meetings known as depositions, and build records on which the case is argued.

Throughout this process, both sides generally file documents with the court known as testing motions. In these documents, the parties ask the court to rule on the controversy immediately either because the complaint has no legal merit or because the facts agreed to by both parties are sufficient for a final judgment. Also, throughout this time, the parties negotiate settlement terms. More than 90% of cases settle before trial, and the closer the trial, the more likely there will be a settlement.

If and when the parties go to trial, only those questions of fact and law unsettled through the process of exchanging documents are addressed. Eventually the judge or the jury make a decision. If the case is found for the plaintiff, an award, consisting of economic damages for medical expenses and lost wages, as well as pain-and-suffering damages for the less concrete effects of the injury, is granted to the plaintiff. The party that loses the case may appeal the decision to a higher court, but the appeal is usually limited to complaints about bad interpretations of law, not the facts of the case.

DOES THE TORT SYSTEM WORK? ❖

This tort system was conceived with a dual purpose: deterrence and compensation. In theory, the threat of economic loss through a lost suit deters the physician from acting negligently. Furthermore, harmed patients are compensated for their injuries. There seems to be widespread agreement that the tort system, at least as it currently functions, is not working well. Every state in the country has enacted some kind of plan to reform the tort system. Tort critics point to claims rates, compensation trends, and the monetary and quality costs of tort as failings of the system. Although trends in these areas are certainly of interest to those studying reform, they are incomplete indicators of the accuracy and efficacy of the tort model; approximately 80% of all cases are settled through private negotiations with physicians' insurers and the plaintiff, and information regarding the settlements is impossible to collect.

Table 15.2   Annual Malpractice Claims per 100 Physicians

	Year						Average Annual Rate of Change, 1985–1990
	1985	**1986**	**1987**	**1988**	**1989**	**1990**	
National	10.2	9.2	6.7	6.4	7.4	7.7	− 8.9%
By Region							
New England	7.6	10.1	4.0	8.4	4.0	2.4	−31.9
Middle Atlantic	13.9	12.7	7.8	7.1	7.5	9.6	−11.6
East North Central	13.2	10.1	10.5	7.5	10.8	9.5	−10.4
West North Central	9.6	8.6	3.9	4.0	5.9	5.8	−15.5
South Atlantic	7.0	7.5	5.6	4.7	4.8	5.7	− 6.6
East South Central	5.5	7.3	9.2	6.4	9.0	5.6	0.6
West South Central	12.4	8.6	6.3	10.4	10.7	11.4	− 2.8
Mountain	6.2	9.0	4.1	5.0	5.6	8.8	12.4
Pacific	9.3	7.5	5.4	4.4	6.1	7.0	− 9.0

Table represents national and regional data. (Source: AMA). Socioeconomic Characteristics of Medical Practice 1992. M Gonzalez ed. Chicago, IL: AMA 1992.

Claim Rates

The number of medical malpractice claims has increased over the past several decades. One study shows that filed claims ratios, measured by number per 100 physicians, "rose from about 1 per 100 doctors around 1960 to an estimated high of 17 per 100 doctors by the mid-eighties before settling around 13 per 100 at the end of the eighties."[323] Although there is conflicting evidence, it seems that the number of claims has stabilized since the late 1980s. Table 15.2 shows annual malpractice claims per 100 physician, both regionally and nationally, from 1985 to 1990.

Claims do not affect physicians of all specialties equally. There is wide variation according to type and geographic area of practice. Traditionally, surgeons, radiologists, and obstetrician-gynecologists are most likely to be sued. A recent American College of Obstetricians and Gynecologists survey found that 79.4% of surveyed obstetrician-gynecologists were defendants in at least one filed professional liability suit.[324]

Patient Compensation

The Harvard Medical Malpractice Study, which was conducted in New York in 1990 by a team of Harvard researchers and remains a widely cited study because of its comprehensive nature and large scale, showed that patients harmed by negligent medical practice are seldom compensated.[325] Often, injured patients do not even initiate claims. Study investigators maintain that there are 7.6 patients harmed by negligent medical interventions for every filed claim. There are many plausible explanations for this deficiency in claims: It may be difficult for a patient to determine the source of their injury, many patients believe the illness or injury that brought them to the hospital caused the subsequent adverse outcome, whereas others may be reluctant to sue a physician with whom they have a long-standing, trusting relationship. "Because about one in two patient claims is ultimately paid, this means that the tort litigation/insurance system paid one claim for every 15 tort incidents."[326]

Deterrence

According to malpractice tort theory, not only should patients be compensated for harm, but physicians should be deterred from practicing medicine negligently. The threat of a lawsuit and expensive judgment, according to the theory, encourages providers to reduce bad practice because they will not risk the economic loss associated with malpractice litigation. Under the current system, however, physicians do not absorb that economic loss; malpractice insurance shields physicians from the direct economic costs of their actions because they pay for their medical malpractice insurance and not the penalties of negligent care. Furthermore, most insurers do not experience-rate: premiums are not based on a physician's individual likelihood of committing malpractice. Instead, they are based on the likelihood of a physician of given specialty in a given region being successfully sued for malpractice. In many states, physicians can effectively shield their assets from claims. As the links between the bad care and the individual physician become more tenuous, the deterrent effects of the malpractice system dissolve. Some argue, however, that where the physicians lose responsibility and the hospitals or health maintenance organizations for which they work pay the costs of insurance or suits, the entities can effectively regulate the quality of physician care.

Assigning Blame

As the delivery of medical care becomes more complex, doctors may have less control over the care they deliver. It may not be fair, therefore, for them to shoulder the burden of paying all the costs of injuries. If faulty equipment caused the accident, maybe the hospital technician or some other party should have spotted the problem. Perhaps the hospital or health maintenance organization should have offered more thorough training to its staff when the new equipment was purchased. In response to some of the ambiguity posed by the changing health care environment, many health care policy makers are advocating that institutions, rather than individuals, bear the burden of malpractice costs under a system known as "enterprise liability."

Finally, whether physicians or institutions pay for malpractice insurance, deterrent effects are still limited. Costs of insurance can be passed on, through higher service charges, to those parties who pay for patient care.

Direct Costs of Medical Malpractice
Payments on Claims

Researchers have found significant increases in average jury verdicts over the past several decades. According to one estimate, "the average verdict (in constant 1987 dollars) increased from $501,000 in 1980 to $1.3 million in 1985."[327] When juries believe there was negligent care, they award large sums compared with other kinds of tort cases. For example, the average malpractice verdict is three times the size of motor vehicle verdicts.[328] Table 15.3 describes the average awards, their range, and their percentage change between 1980 and 1987.

Insurance Costs
During the 1970s and 1980s, as the number of claims and payments on those claims grew, medical malpractice insurance costs skyrocketed. Several private insurers, unable or unwilling to bear the increasing loss experiences, left the insurance market altogether. In some specialties, physicians found the costs of insurance prohibitive, and they either went without it or left their practices.

While average costs increased, the malpractice cost disparity among specialties and the likelihood of being sued grew as well. Obstetrician-gynecologists were among the hardest hit. An American College of Obstetricians and Gynecologists report showed that, on average, obstetricians are sued three times over the course of their career.[329] Furthermore, one of eight surveyed obstetricians stopped delivering babies because of the threat of a malpractice suit.[330]

Table 15.3   United States Verdict Averages and Ranges

Year	Average ($)	% Change	Range ($)
1980	404,725	—	1,708–6.8 million
1981	850,396	110.1	3,500–10.0 million
1982	962,253	13.2	531–29.0 million
1983	887,938	−7.7	1,500–25.0 million
1984	640,619	−27.9	1,000–27.6 million
1985	1,179,095	84.1	5,000–12.7 million
1986	1,478,028	25.4	2,500–15.8 million
1987	924,416	−37.5	340–13.0 million
1988	732,445	−20.8	300–8.1 million
1980–1987		12.5	

Data source: Financial Times, Nov. 24, 1989—Jury Verdict Research.

Conditions have improved since the mid-1980s. As the number of claims filed decreased, insurers began to re-enter the market, and premium growth slowed. The stabilization of claims, and subsequently the market, can be explained by a number of factors. First, as more physicians opened their own insurance companies, they dismissed those physicians most prone to cause negligent injuries. Second, judges appointed by Reagan and Bush and juries, reflecting more conservative times, may have been less sympathetic to injured patients and encouraged insurers back to the market. Finally, reform programs and attention to the issues may have led to improved insurance conditions. However, before taking comfort in the improved insurance situation, readers should keep in mind the fact that fewer injured patients may be being compensated.

Administration Costs
The medical malpractice system is not only expensive, but inefficient. If the flow of money is any indication, lawyers are often rewarded more than patients are compensated. Although estimates vary, most sources agree that more than half of medical malpractice premiums are paid to administration of the system, particularly lawyers' fees.

The lawyers themselves are not necessarily the cause of the high administrative costs. The nature of malpractice cases tends to make the battles long and, as a result, expensive. Unlike many cases of product liability, in which companies do not suffer extreme losses under litigation, physicians have special incentives to fight litigation as long as possible. Medical practices rise and fall on reputation; a lost medical malpractice case can destroy a career overnight. Therefore, cases that may have ended quickly and efficiently in another context may take significantly more time and financial resources to resolve.

Staffing Costs
The litigious climate has motivated providers to employ legal consultants or staff departments to develop and manage practice protocol and to prevent suits. These costs are difficult to estimate, and any estimate must be balanced against the benefit of better quality of care and the deterrent effect of the malpractice system.

Indirect Costs of Medical Malpractice

Although careful study may lead to dollar estimates of the costs of the medical malpractice system, it is more difficult to measure indirect costs.

Defensive Medicine
Fear of expensive litigation may encourage physicians to provide more care than necessary, which, in turn, increases the total cost of medical care and health

Table 15.4   Practice Changes in Response
to Increasing Professional Liability Risk

Activity	% of Physicians Making Change		Average % Change per Physician in 1984[a,b]	Cost of Change per Physician in 1984, $[a,b]
	Prior to 1984	1984[a]		
Increased record keeping	56.9	31.0	2.9	900
Prescription of more tests or treatment procedures	43.0	20.0	3.2	*
Increased time spent with patients	35.9	17.0	2.4	1800
Increased follow-up visits	NA	17.0	2.6	1900
% of physicians with at least one listed practice change	70.0	41.8	—	—
Average Total Cost per Physician of Listed Practice Changes in 1984	—	—	—	4600

[a]Figures reflect only new or increased practice changes in 1984. Physicians making practice changes in 1984 and the amount of these changes made prior to 1984 in response to liability risks are not reflected in these figures.
[b]Calculations includes zeros for physicians who did not make any practice change in 1984.
*Lack of data on the average cost of an additional test or treatment procedure make it impossible to fill in this item.
NA, not available.
Source: third quarter 1983 and fourth quarter 1984 American Medical Association's Socioeconomic Monitoring System surveys.

insurance. Although scholars differ on the extent and effects of *defensive medicine,* the American Medical Association reported that between 1983 and 1984, "physicians reported changes in their medical practices that were worth an additional $4600 per physician per year . . . [an] increase in defensive medicine costs [which] was more than 3.5 times the concomitant $1800 in premiums."[331] Table 15.4 delineates the costs associated with practice changes in response to increasing professional liability risk.

If the threat of having to pay large claims because of negligence leads to more expensive care, that additional care may not be excessive. Perhaps additional tests, more complete record keeping, and careful provision of services prevents accidents. Health care economists disagree on the usefulness of defensive medicine.

Quality of Care
Quality medical care involves more than the provision of a technical service. Effective physicians must engender the trust and the cooperation of their patients.

The very nature of the tort system, one based on competing claims and the proving of negligence, positions the physician and patient as adversaries. If the trusting relationship is compromised by the possibility of future legal action, the quality of care is compromised.

Furthermore, poor medical care may be the result of systematic flaws in structure and not individual negligence. Malpractice cases do not seem to focus on a few, particularly negligent physicians. For example, the New York Department of Health found that, from 1980 through 1983, only 131 doctors, most of whom were high-risk specialists, of the state's 35,552 practicing physicians had paid on more than two claims. These doctors accounted for less than 10% of all paid claims in New York. A later study shows that the number of individuals with more than two claims changes over a four-year period.[332]

Excessively High Standards

Although many professionals are held to high standards, the tort system, in theory, holds physicians uniquely accountable for their work. If the physician has a small lapse, it can lead to devastating consequences for both the patient and the physician. The small error, if caught and prosecuted successfully, can end a career. Although physicians should take all possible precautions, it may not be fair to hold them liable for any imperfect behavior.

These very high standards, promulgated to protect patients and to punish negligence, may have had exactly the opposite effect. The high standards, and the perception that they may be too strict, may, in part, explain why physicians are reluctant to report the negligent behavior of their colleagues and why members of peer review boards seldom fulfill their responsibilities to discipline negligent doctors.

TORT REFORM ❖

Recognizing its limits, policy makers have designed, proposed, tested, and adopted changes to the tort system. The proposals range from minor tinkering with the current system to complete replacement of the tort system. Table 15.5 describes state tort reform efforts as of 1993.

Incremental Reforms
Reforms to Limit Claims
Statutes of Limitations

One of the major difficulties of malpractice insurance, not posed by other types of insurance, is a characteristic known as the *long tail*. This term refers to the special difficulty of predicting the necessary funds to pay for claims over time because insurance payments made today will not be paid out on claims for several years. The

Table 15.5 States' Approaches and Experience with Malpractice Reform

State	Medical Malpractice Arbitration Provisions[a]	Attorney Fee Limits[b]	Caps on Damages	Collateral Source Offset	Periodic Payment of Awards	Pretrial Screening Panels
New York	x	x		M	D	
North Carolina						
North Dakota			O	D/O	D	
Ohio	x		O	M	M	
Oklahoma		x				
Oregon			x	D	D	
Pennsylvania		O		O		O
Rhode Island				M	D	O
South Carolina					D	
South Dakota	x		x	D	M	
Tennessee	x	x		M		M
Texas			O			
Utah	x	x	x	M	M	M
Vermont						M
Virginia	x	x	x			V
Washington		x	O		M	
West Virginia			x			
Wisconsin		x	x			

[a]An "x" indicates states with voluntary, binding arbitration provisions that are designed specifically for medical malpractice cases. Voluntary, binding arbitration is an option in *every* state under general arbitration statutes. In Hawaii the provision applies to mandatory non-binding arbitration.

[b]An "x" means the statutory provision limits attorney fees to a specific % of award. In a few states the courts are given the authority to determine or approve attorney fees.

M = mandatory, D = discretionary, V = voluntary, O = malpractice provision overturned by court. In certain states, the legislature corrected the constitutional deficiency.

Source: Office of Technology Assessment, 1993.

GAO reports that "[t]he average length of time from the injury to claim filing was about 16 months for all claims."[333] The long time line makes it difficult for insurers to invest and to produce the funds necessary to cover claims. These uncertain insurance conditions drive up the cost of medical malpractice insurance.

Physicians, whose vulnerability grows as the evidence for defense disappears over the years, also need protection from the long tail. As patient, witness, and physician memories dull, justice may be compromised. Also, as technology changes, juries and judges find it difficult to remember and to determine what the standard of care should have been. To address these concerns, each state has a law, known as a statute of limitation, that limits the length of time in which an injured patient may bring a claim.

Shortening the statute of limitations too much may harm patients with legitimate reasons for not filing early claims. A patient may not discover the injury until significant time has passed. Accordingly, discovery provisions, incorporated in the statutes of all but 11 states,[334] provide exemptions for injuries discovered beyond the statute of limitations. Also, the power relationship between patients and physicians may provide reason for giving the patient leeway in filing a suit. For example, the patient may be under anesthesia during the negligent incident and, thus, have no way of determining the cause of an injury; it may be unfair to limit their ability to pursue action when more information arises.

Capping Attorney Fees

Critics of waste in the tort system have pointed to attorney's fees as the aspect most ripe for reform. Although estimates vary, 33% is a widely cited estimate of the amount attorneys collect from plaintiff's awards. Proponents of limiting these fees believe that through controlling the percentage or capping the amount that attorneys may charge, overall costs of litigation will decrease. Approximately 50% of the states limit fees in some way.[335]

Opponents of limits argue that by limiting fees, attorneys will only accept cases that have high probabilities of winning large awards and will forgo meritorious cases with small expected payouts. Those with the least access to representation now, the poor, may be penalized further by this system because they will not be able to pay the fees out-of-pocket.

Pretrial Screening

To reduce the number of claims that enter the litigation process, many states require cases to pass through some form of pretrial screening. Pretrial screening generally involves a hearing conducted by a panel of experts, including those in the health care and legal fields, which determines if the claim has merit. Although the decisions of these boards are not binding, the results are often admissible in subsequent proceedings; the procedure, therefore, discourages nonmeritorious claims.

Although screening procedures may be effective, they have been challenged successfully in the court system. Pretrial screening has been found unconstitutional in six states on the grounds that they infringe on the right to trial, and it has been repealed in five other states by the state legislatures.[336] Critics contend that screening only serves to add another layer of bureaucracy to the already cumbersome system.

Reforms to Legal Standards

Under the doctrine of *Res Ipsa Loquitur* (the thing speaks for itself), courts presume negligence if the injury would not normally have occurred in the absence of the medical intervention. For example, a patient would not be left with a sponge in their stomach had the surgeon not left it there. The presumption of negligence is intended to give the patient some help in a situation in which the plaintiff cannot have information equal to the defendant's (i.e., the patient may have been under anesthesia). Repealing or restricting application of this doctrine tightens the rules of evidence and discourages patients from filing of claims without decisive evidence. By 1989, thirteen states had outlawed or restricted the application of res ipsa loquitur in medical malpractice cases.[337]

Reforms That Limit or Alter Payments

Establishing limits regarding the amount of money that flows through the medical malpractice system offers the most direct solution to high expenditures.

Caps on Damages

Patients typically receive payment that compensates them for economic and other damages associated with their injuries, in addition to funds that cover the cost of medical care. Damages include payments for pain and suffering (i.e., reimbursement for fear, emotional loss, loss of ability to enjoy life), as well as economic loss, such as forgone income. Several states have implemented caps on these payments in various forms, from dollar cut-off of all damages to caps based on a scale of need and injury. Whereas some states have capped all damages, most restrict only the pain and suffering portion of the damage award. The Office of Technology Assessment identified caps on damages as "[t]he one reform consistently shown to reduce malpractice cost indicators," including claim frequency, payment per paid claim, and premiums.[338]

Critics maintain that this form of cost-containment is too blunt a tool to address the subtleties and the needs involved in individual cases. Furthermore, caps penalize the most severely injured patients, who should expect the highest awards. Finally, attorneys working on contingency may be reluctant to accept cases when the compensation is limited at the outset of trial, regardless of the length and complexity of the case.

Subrogation and Collateral Source Rules

Many plaintiffs, as a consequence of evidence rules that preclude entering information regarding patient insurance into the trial record, are able to collect reimbursement for injuries from several sources at once. Jury awards may be paid in addition to various public and private funds, such as sick-leave, health insurance, or disability insurance for loss-compensation. Some insurance policies and public funds, such as Medicaid and Medicare, regulate duplication of funds through a provision known as subrogation. Under subrogation rules, tort awards must be used to pay collateral insurers before the plaintiff receives the funds. The theory behind subrogation is that malpractice insurers, and not health or disability insurers, should bear the costs of malpractice.

Collateral source rules do just the opposite. If patients have health insurance, the coverage provided by those plans is subtracted from the malpractice award. This system, critics contend, rewards defendants by allowing them to benefit from a patient's wise decision to invest in health insurance. Accordingly, many states have adopted variations of the collateral source rule to allow juries and judges discretion in reducing awards.

Periodic Payments
Awards for malpractice claims are typically disbursed in a single payment that the patient can invest to provide funds throughout the life of the injury. There is no guarantee, however, that patients will invest wisely or spend slowly enough to cover medical costs. Spreading the payments to the victim over time minimizes the effect of award expenses on insurers and lowers the risk that patients will spend down funds that are needed for future medical services. Advocates of the periodic payment system argue that the structured system is more equitable because the payments can be halted should the patient recover. Furthermore, medical services payments can more accurately reflect the cost of the service provided at any given point in time. Currently, 14 states have provisions mandating periodic payments.[339]

Reforms to Streamline the Medical Malpractice System
Clinical Practice Guidelines
"Practice guidelines are 'systematically developed statements to assist practitioner and patient decisions about appropriate health care for specific clinical circumstances. [They are also] referred to . . . as 'practice parameters,' 'algorithms' or 'clinical indicators.' "[340] Guidelines are intended to serve several purposes. First, they can provide arbiters with clearly defined standards of care to facilitate the decision-making of judges and juries. Second, they may improve and systematize clinical care. Third, they can help cost-containment efforts. Finally, they can aid physicians in medical malpractice risk management. Many private and public organizations have developed protocols for a variety of procedures to help more carefully define acceptable standards of care.

Although many states are considering guideline legislation, programs in Maine and Minnesota have been the most far-reaching. Guideline legislation in these states allows physicians to introduce evidence that they followed guideline protocols as a defense against a medical malpractice charge. Plaintiffs must prove either that the physician violated the standards or that the standards were not applicable to prove negligence.[341]

Critics argue that comprehensive guidelines are of limited use. Because the U.S. adjudicatory process focuses on specific controversies, use of generally applied guidelines to determine relevant standards of care is limited by evidence rules. Yet, courts have become more liberal in allowing parties to rely on "statements contained in published treatises, periodicals, or pamphlets on a subject of history, medicine, or other science or art, established as a reliable authority . . . by judicial notice" as part of the full complement of evidence.[342] Critics also argue that the vast number of procedures and patient conditions create a daunting task of developing, updating, and standardizing guidelines. Furthermore, many new techniques are controversial, and finding the consensus to develop standards may prove impossible.

Radical Reform of the Malpractice System
No-Fault Liability

Recently, some policy experts have argued for replacing the tort system with a program removing the idea of fault from medical malpractice in a manner similar to the U.S. workers compensation system. Under a *no-fault liability* system, all patients who suffer iatrogenic injuries would receive some form of compensation to cover medical costs, lost wages, pain and suffering, or some combination of losses. Payments, made over time, would accurately reflect the value of needed services.

Under some plans, known as enterprise liability, sponsoring enterprises, hospitals, or health maintenance organizations, for example, would bear the liability for the injuries. In these plans, no-fault only applies at the physician level.

According to proponents, the no-fault system would lead to increased economic efficiency. Under the tort system, their argument proceeds, too many parties pay the costs of iatrogenic injuries. If a patient does not win a medical malpractice claim, the patient's family, community, or the state or federal taxpayer pays the cost of necessary care. No-fault better places the economic burden on the parties involved in the injury, including the physician, the hospital, and the patient because all harmed patients are compensated, and families and communities do not pay the burden of uncompensated harm. Furthermore, because patients will not have to undertake the expensive and complicated task of proving negligence or proximate cause, funds will flow to those who need them, not to complex and expensive litigation.

Critics argue that no-fault, enterprise liability removes the economic incentive to deter negligence. After all, under no-fault enterprise liability, hospitals and not doctors will directly pay the harmed patients. Others argue that the tort system has been instrumental in increasing the standards of medical care; each time a court defines a standard of care based on recent innovation it becomes precedent, and it holds the medical community to a new, and often higher, standard. Finally, most plaintiffs' attorneys argue that the no-fault system denies patients' rights to trial because no-fault systems involve administrative, rather than jury-based, determinations of damages. Equal protection may also be violated under this system if the compensation awarded under no-fault is not commensurate with that which the plaintiff could receive under tort.

Although many policy makers are investigating the no-fault system, only two states have adopted no-fault schemes. In reaction to the insurance crisis of the late 1970s and 1980s, legislators in Florida and Virginia instituted no-fault programs to cover obstetricians in the event of extreme, neurological infant impairment. Removing the high-risk exposure responsibility from the private insurance pool encouraged major insurers to re-enter the market. Currently, several other states are considering the experience of Florida and Virginia and designing farther-reaching programs.

Contract

Policy makers with a more traditional economic focus have advocated various forms of individual contracts between physicians and patients or patient representatives. According to supporters of contract liability, those parties directly involved in the services, patients and physicians, are best able to understand the value of the provided services and the loss due to injury. For instance, a physician and a patient can, together, explore the associated risks of a procedure and arrange a contract to reflect that risk and assign responsibility. A contract system offers flexibility to express important treatment preferences. As long as nonconsenting, third parties are not involved, mutually advantageous agreements can be constructed.

Opponents of contract liability criticize both the theoretical and the practical implications of the system. First, patients and doctors must have equal information and power to negotiate fairly. Neither condition holds in this case. Patients with equal treatment risks would not negotiate equal contracts. Instead, those most able to manage the negotiation would benefit. Cumbersome provisions would have to be made for children, emergency room patients, the senile, the mentally impaired, and others. The logical solution, allowing third parties to negotiate contracts en bloc, would compromise the accurate reflection of marginal benefits and costs to the direct participants.

Second, critics argue that third parties, and the public, hold legitimate interests in the malpractice process. Families, financial dependents, employers, and other individuals who depend on the patient have an interest in the compensatory aspects of the contract. Not only as individuals who know and depend on particular patients, but also as members of a society, we may have a legitimate interest in the doctor-patient relationship. We value a healthy population and work force enough that we provide care through a public system.

Not all contracts restrict liability. Contracts can be developed to specify procedure, such as different forms of dispute resolution in lieu of litigation, or enterprise liability rather than physician or insurer liability. Other contracts, such as those limiting damage recovery, could be effectively developed. Courts, however, have scrutinized such contracts carefully. No matter how tightly or carefully drawn, a patient's preferences after an injury are difficult, if not impossible, to assess before the injury occurs.

Alternative Dispute Resolution

Alternative dispute resolution, a catch-all title for several types of reforms, generally seeks to replace the tort system with a less expensive procedural system, to employ technically expert decision-makers, to limit the anxiety of participants, and to screen nonmeritorious claims. Although alternative dispute resolution proposals proliferate, no state has adopted a comprehensive plan. The proposals involve adjusting the process rather than the liability involved in malpractice.

There are several dispute resolution proposals in the medical malpractice realm. Neutral evaluation by an expert to assess a case offers potential litigants a clearer idea of the merits of their respective cases. If the parties do not reach an agreement, they may continue, with no prejudice, to more traditional litigation. Courts have also required nonbinding arbitration before parties argue in trial. In some cases, the court may admit the transcripts as evidence to facilitate a subsequent trial. Voluntary binding arbitration is meant to replace trials completely. Finally, some potential litigants hire professional mediators, some without legal training, to help parties reach agreements outside of the judicial system altogether. "The one extensive study, [conducted over a decade ago], comparing the experience of injured patients who had their claims arbitrated with the experience of those who litigated found that the claims of patients who suffered permanent disabilities tended to be upheld more frequently under arbitration th[a]n litigation; but the claims in which no physical injury, temporary injury, or fatal injury had occurred were upheld less frequently under arbitration."[343]

Alternative dispute resolution may not be effective at containing costs for several reasons. First, the very fact that extra-court proceedings limit transaction costs may raise overall spending. Parties settle because they perceive the costs of litigating to be higher than the expected gains. If the transaction costs are lower, as a result of screening panels or preliminary mediation, parties may be more willing to take their chance in court. Second, if litigants have the right to appeal to a court and demand a full trial, the preliminary attempts at resolution simply add to the overall costs. Finally, mandatory dispute resolution raises questions regarding the constitutional right of injured parties to find relief through court proceedings. "Of the 15 states with specific malpractice arbitration statutes, only Michigan has a formal program to encourage arbitration. . . . Participation has been disappointing. Only one-half of Michigan hospitals must participate and the remaining hospitals apparently see no benefit in entering the program and spending resources to train personnel to offer arbitration agreements. . . . Physicians say they are reluctant to offer patients pre-treatment arbitration agreements because they are uncomfortable discussing malpractice at that point and are concerned that such a discussion may undermine patients' confidence in their abilities."[344]

CONCLUSION ❖

Medical malpractice is an important part of the health care system and one many feel needs to be changed for the benefit of both patients and physicians. The Clinton Health Security Act of 1993 is a good example of what such changes may look like. Specifically, the plan called for:

✦ Mandatory alternative dispute resolution involving arbitration, mediation, and early offers of settlement before allowing access to the tort system.

✦ A requirement for certificates of merit to be issued before an enrollee of any health plan could pursue a lawsuit.

✦ Limitations on attorney's contingency fees.

✦ Reduction of awards for recovery from collateral sources.

✦ Periodic payments of awards.

✦ Two demonstration projects, one involving funding for enterprise liability and the other applying practice guidelines to medical malpractice liability actions.

Although the Clinton plan was not enacted, medical malpractice reform along these lines promises to remain a part of every health reform discussion.

❖ Suggested Reading ❖

Furrow BR, Johnson SH, Jost TS, Schwartz RL. Health law: cases, materials and problems, 2nd ed. St. Paul, MN: West Publishing Company, 1991.

Havighurst CC. Health care law and policy: readings, notes and questions. Westbury, NY: The Foundation Press, 1988.

Good general reviews of medical malpractice from a legal perspective.

Danzon P. Medical malpractice. Cambridge, MA: Harvard University Press, 1985.

An economic model of medical malpractice and tort.

Institute of Medicine. Medical professional liability and the delivery of care. Washington, DC: National Academy Press, 1989.

An interesting and informative collection of chapters on malpractice, such as medical, legal, public health, and economic issues, originally given as papers at a 1988 symposium on obstetrics and malpractice.

For other interest group perspectives, the following organizations have taken a variety of positions on malpractice tort reform: The American Medical Association, The Association of Trial Lawyers, and The American Association of Retired People. State and local bar associations may also be able to provide further information. The United States General Accounting Office has published several reports on many of the facets of the medical malpractice debate.

AIDS

Gretchen Schwarze and Deborah Cotton

By 1992, the acquired immunodeficiency syndrome (AIDS) had claimed the lives of more than 133,000 people in the United States (U.S.). In addition, more than 206,000 cases of AIDS had been reported, and an estimated one million people had been infected with the human immunodeficiency virus (HIV).[345] In this chapter, we look beyond the human tragedy represented by these numbers, and we examine the AIDS epidemic in the context of the U.S. health care system. More than any other disease in recent history, AIDS has highlighted both the capabilities and the shortcomings of American health care policy.

In this chapter, we first look at the changing nature of the AIDS epidemic, both in its incidence and its prevalence, as well as in the public perception of the disease. Then, we look at AIDS in the context of four different aspects of health care policy: public health strategies, health financing, health care delivery, and science and technology policy. In each of these areas, we look at how each area has been affected by AIDS, as well as how AIDS has changed the way we view these aspects of health policy.

EVOLUTION OF AN EPIDEMIC ❖

AIDS was first diagnosed in the early 1980s when a number of young, gay men across the country were found to have illnesses previously only seen in the elderly and debilitated. Since then, the disease has spread to include almost every part of the population, although it still affects predominantly those with certain risk factors. Although there is still no cure for the disease, there are an increasing number of treatments that can either slow its progression or help fight opportunistic infections. To understand the effects of AIDS on the health care system, we need to describe how these changes in demographics and treatment have changed our perception of AIDS as a disease.

Demographics

At the beginning of the epidemic, AIDS was a disease that primarily affected gay men and intravenous (IV) drug users. The occurrence of this disease in these socially marginalized groups explains the initially weak and inadequate policy response. More appropriate funding and policy initiatives became available as gay men increased their political visibility and as predictions that AIDS would spread to the general population as a whole increased.

Although the majority of persons with AIDS are still gay men, the greatest rate increase in cases has been among IV drug abusers or their partners, usually from minority and disadvantaged communities. Table 16.1 shows the change in the population afflicted with AIDS. This shift is illustrated in the increase of the number of AIDS cases in cities with large black and Latino populations. In 1988, Newark, New Jersey, had a 45% increase in the rate of reported cases. For that same year, San Juan, Puerto Rico, had a 78% increase in the rate of reported cases, whereas the increase of reported cases in San Francisco, with a predominantly white population, was only 12%.[346] This shift of risk of infection to disadvantaged members of minority groups has had profound implications for health care policy.

Treatments

Because of the lack of treatments available, for most of the 1980s, AIDS was viewed as a short-term fatal disease. In 1989, AZT and aerosolized pentamidine

Table 16.1 % Cases of AIDS by Risk Group

	Nov 1986	Oct 1993
Homo- and bisexual male	66	55
Intravenous drug user	17	24
Both of the above	8	6
Hemophiliac	1	1
Heterosexual	4	7
Transfusion related	2	2
Other	3	5
Total	27,390	334,344

Source: Weekly Surveillance Report, US AIDS Program, CDC.

were found to have significant prophylactic benefit for those who were HIV-positive but in whom full-blown AIDS had not developed. Because of these therapeutic advances, AIDS became more like a chronic disease "characterized by relatively brief acute episodes requiring hospitalization and longer periods when patients could be cared for in nursing facilities or at home."[347]

With these changes in the AIDS epidemic as a background, we look at the disease in the context of four areas of health care policy: public health, financing, delivery, and research policy.

AIDS AND PUBLIC HEALTH   ❖

The traditional public health approach to combating epidemics involves focusing efforts on those who have disease and those whom they may specifically communicate it to. Specific techniques include testing of populations at risk, reporting positive results to a central source, and tracing the contacts of those who test positive. Because of the social stigma and financial burdens placed on those with AIDS, as well as the political power of those initially afflicted with the disease, public health officials abandoned these traditional approaches for tackling infectious disease and prompted the adoption of an exceptionalist approach to tackle AIDS.[348]

This *exceptionalist approach,* which promoted mass education and voluntary testing, rather than targeted testing and contact tracing, was adopted in the belief that ". . . failure to adopt a course that would win the cooperation of those most at risk . . . would 'drive the epidemic underground.' "[349] Specifically, because AIDS affected marginalized populations who feared both state and federal governments, and because prevention of spread required modification of intimate behavior, many believed that traditional methods would not work. Thus, the primary force behind public health policy in the first decade of the AIDS epidemic was the protection of privacy.[350]

As the epidemic has evolved, however, this exceptionalist approach is being complemented by more traditional public health efforts, including testing, reporting, and contact tracing. In addition, many preventive efforts have been tried, although whether they work is somewhat controversial.

Testing

With the advent of effective early intervention in 1989, there was new hope for slowing progression and perhaps transmission of the disease, and previous alliances formed to protect privacy started to unravel, and new, more controversial, policies have been proposed. Gay men's activist groups, for example, such as Project Inform and the Gay Men's Health Crisis, joined the public health officials to launch more aggressive testing campaigns.[351]

Most recently, there has been a strong effort by obstetricians and pediatricians to initiate a program for mandatory screening of pregnant women and newborns. Such programs would follow models of programs that screen pregnant women for hepatitis B virus and syphilis, and those that screen newborns for phenylketonuria.[352] These initiatives not only reflect the shift in perception of AIDS as a plague to AIDS as a chronic disease with opportunities for intervention, but also reflect the shift in populations infected with this disease. Such proposals suggest that whereas the political clout of gay men was sufficient to preserve privacy, the political clout of more disadvantaged populations may not be enough to protect these groups from potential coercion and stigma.

Reporting

Although mandatory testing for certain groups is still a highly controversial issue, the benefits of early intervention have led states to favor policies that sanction reporting seropositivity while increasing safeguards to preserve privacy. With the recognition that early clinical intervention is incompatible with anonymity, the creation of laws that protect the rights of individuals with AIDS have become more important.[353]

Contact Tracing

From the start of the epidemic, the Centers for Disease Control (CDC) advocated contact tracing and reporting. Now with increased support for such measures from the American Medical Association (AMA), the American Bar Association, the President's Commission on AIDS, the National Academy of Sciences, and the National Institutes of Medicine, states have formulated varied responses. In general, individual partner notification has been more common in states with large numbers of AIDS cases, whereas provider notification is more often the policy in states with smaller numbers of AIDS cases.[354]

Criminal Prosecution

Finally, with the support of the President's Commission on AIDS in 1988, policy was created that linked the receipt of funding to the ability of each state to criminally prosecute those who knowingly expose or transmit HIV to unsuspecting individuals. Although only a small number of people have been prosecuted, those who have had guilty verdicts have received particularly harsh penalties.[355]

AIDS and the Physician

There are two major public health issues concerning AIDS and physicians. The first involves mandatory testing for physicians and other health care workers. In 1991, the case of Kimberly Bergalis, who had contracted AIDS from exposure to her dentist, inspired initiatives to establish mandatory testing for all health care workers. The CDC responded with guidelines for strict enforcement of universal precautions, which required health care providers to disclose seropositivity and to get informed consent from patients undergoing "risky" procedures. Groups such as the AMA were solicited to formulate a list of these "risky" procedures, but they refused to contribute to this policy, citing lack of proper evidence to establish an accurate list. In July 1992, the National Commission on AIDS recommended against health care provider testing and notification. They deemed such policy inappropriate because of the remote risk of transmission and the potentially devastating consequences for medical careers.[356]

Another issue for physicians concerns the duty to warn those who may be immediately at risk of contracting AIDS, specifically the partners of those infected with HIV. Physician-patient confidentiality, as well as many early laws regarding the confidentiality of people with AIDS, seemed to indicate a physician should not warn partners. In contrast, however, the Supreme Court in the *Tarasoff* case held a physician responsible for not warning the partner of a patient of his threats to kill her. These conflicting duties have been settled differently in different states, but in general there have been significant revisions of early confidentiality restrictions, and *most states have passed laws that give physicians the privilege, although not the duty, to warn unsuspecting partners about their risk of contracting HIV.*[357]

Prevention Strategies

Sex education and condom distribution continue to be hot political issues. The need to promote modification of sexual behavior has initiated academic interest in an area in which there had been little study previously. Still enshrouded in controversy, mass education about safe sexual practices continues to be a primary tenet for the public health campaign against AIDS.

The continued spread of HIV in the population of IV drug users, without signs of slowdown, points to a distinct failure to adequately address the problem of IV drug abuse. Proposals ranging from therapy on demand to needle exchange have been vigorously debated. Pilot programs suggest that these techniques may slow the spread of HIV infection without increasing drug use.

The AIDS epidemic, then, has posed considerable challenges to public health policy. Although the first response was based on an exceptionalist approach, technological and demographic realities refocused many initiatives toward a more traditional direction. Case reporting and partner identification have become accepted tools, whereas mandatory testing and screening efforts are still controversial. Even with this more traditional approach, the primary strategy for public health policy is mass education.

AIDS AND THE FINANCING OF HEALTH CARE ❖

AIDS has brought to light many issues concerning the financing of health care in the U.S., including the cost of health care and the distribution of who pays for that cost.

The Cost of AIDS

Initially, the projected cost to care for each patient with AIDS was close to $150,000.[358] Coupled with overestimates about the number of people who would be infected with HIV, this cost prompted concerns about how to pay for necessary treatment for all people with AIDS. Currently, more realistic estimates predict that each patient with AIDS will need $40,000 to $50,000 for health care over a lifetime (this is likely lower than current costs given the introduction of new therapies). Thus, projections for total expenditures for all patients with AIDS account for less than 2% of the national health care bill.[359] The question is more one of finance than of cost. *The issue is no longer how will we pay, but who will pay.*

Private Insurance

Paying for AIDS therapy has and continues to devastate people financially. Those who can afford private health insurance are nearly always denied access through policies of discrimination and pre-existing conditions. Nonetheless, patients with AIDS are often ineligible for government-sponsored insurance because their financial status keeps them from Medicaid, they are too young for Medicare, and they have not been sick long enough to qualify for disability insurance.[360]

Government Financing

People with AIDS not only meet difficulty securing private insurance, but also a large portion of those infected with AIDS are impoverished to begin with and rely on the Medicaid system for their care. Initially, states used existing Medicaid funding to finance AIDS treatment, but these funds quickly became inadequate. Emergency federal programs set up to pay for AZT and to provide additional support for Medicaid and other patchwork organizations were established, but they were not sufficient. Notably, financial strain created by the AIDS epidemic has the potential to cripple all social services and entitlement programs, because the urgency of this disease has pulled funding away from other important programs.[361]

At the state level, significant changes in Medicaid were created in response to this need, but improved federal support was lacking. In 1990, Senator Edward Kennedy, in cooperation with Senator Orrin Hatch, sponsored the Ryan White Emergency Comprehensive AIDS Resources Act, which granted ". . . federal assistance to localities most severely burdened by HIV."[362] The grant, similar to natural disaster relief, promised $2.9 billion for HIV over five years. The bill had overwhelming support (the votes were 95–4 in the Senate and 408–14 in the House), but funding was substantially reduced later in battles over the budget. Although the initiative still exists, it is unclear how much funding the federal government will ultimately provide.[363]

AIDS AND THE DELIVERY OF HEALTH CARE ❖

In addition to pointing out weaknesses in the financing of health care, AIDS has shown places where improvements need to be made in our health delivery system.

Outpatient Care

The AIDS epidemic occurred at a time when the efforts to control the cost of health care were increasing nationally. Patients with AIDS have a high demand for services, particularly high technology care. The participation of advocates for people with AIDS in the development of services for patients with AIDS combined with the high cost of in-patient care accelerated the movement for increasing outpatient services and opened the door to innovations in high technology home care. In addition, innovations in clinical therapy, such as the development of fluconazole (an oral antifungal for maintenance therapy of cryptococcal meningitis), advanced these efforts to manage AIDS in an out-patient setting.[364]

Hospice Care

Although most people with AIDS required long-term care, there were difficulties in bringing them into the existing system. For the most part, patients with AIDS were younger than the usual patients who required long-term care. There were also fears from other clients about the contagious nature of the disease, as well as problems of reimbursement. Finally, the varied intensity of care required by patients with AIDS was less suited to the format of typical nursing homes.[365]

Thus, *hospice* services became a more viable option. However, the needs of people with AIDS were not completely satisfied by the hospice format either. The care provided for terminal cancer patients was not appropriate for patients with AIDS, whose life expectancy was more difficult to predict. Thus, special hospice facilities for people with AIDS were developed to accommodate the special type of care required for this disease.

Community-based Services

The case management model, which pools a variety of community resources, has been pioneered by and refined for the care of persons with AIDS. This form of care has been highly supported by the federal government through the Health Resources and Services Administration and the Ryan White Emergency Comprehensive AIDS Resources Act of 1990.[366]

AIDS, SCIENCE, AND TECHNOLOGY POLICY ❖

AIDS has brought issues concerning medical research and procedures for drug testing to the public forum. Increased awareness of how the scientific process affects people with AIDS profoundly has forced scientists and policy makers to examine and to change policies that guide methods of research and study.

Policy regarding basic science research and clinical trials are more completely discussed in the next chapter, but it is important to note that the political efforts of advocates for people with AIDS have done much in the past decade to determine science and technology policy. The primary focus of these efforts has been in the area of drug testing and approval. Initiatives that challenge the traditional scientific methods and procedures, such as community-based trials and fast-track drug approvals, have been favored recently as political pressure and the urgency of this epidemic have opened these practices to public view.

CONCLUSION ❖

AIDS has required a strong response from health care policy makers. Examination of this epidemic points to the capabilities of the system as well as its failures. This epidemic has prompted considerable controversy, and it continues to present dilemmas concerning the best management of this disease. However, as tragic as the epidemic is, AIDS has accelerated and initiated policy innovations that will not only improve the care for people with AIDS, but also the care for all Americans.

❖ **Suggested Reading** ❖

Fox DM. Chronic disease and disadvantage: the new politics of HIV infection. J Health Politics, Policy and Law 1990; 15:341–355.

A brief overview of the evolution of AIDS from an epidemic primarily affecting gay men and IV drug abusers to a chronic disease affecting members of disenfranchised communities.

National Research Council. The social impact of AIDS in the United States. Washington, DC: National Academy Press, 1993.

A detailed collection of data and analysis of multiple aspects of the AIDS epidemic and its social consequences.

Biomedical Research Policy

David Morales and David Blumenthal

As we approach the year 2000, the face of clinical medicine and the role of biomedical research continues to change. The medical academic community must strive to meet the demands of a changing health care system and to ensure the continued growth and support of its academic ventures. It needs to ensure the training of physician-scientists who will continue to push forward the frontiers of clinical and scientific understanding through original contributions, and to provide new generations of teachers to rejuvenate aging faculty in medical schools across the country. The biomedical revolution of recent years has set a precedent of extraordinary discoveries at a pace unlikely imagined 15 years ago. Our understanding of the devastating disease, the acquired immunodeficiency syndrome (AIDS), increased at an astounding rate through the 1980s. Great strides have been made to elucidate the molecular pathogenesis of such genetic diseases as muscular dystrophy and cystic fibrosis. Important studies are under way to examine new treatments for many diseases, as well as improving therapy for many more.

Biomedical research has created unparalleled progress in basic science as well as in clinical pathophysiology. Generous support from the national government, the pharmaceutical industry, and philanthropic organizations has provided for new initiatives in scientific investigation, as well as training of exceptional young people over the years. How do they go about allocating their funds, and how do these three entities affect the biomedical research arena and the future of health care?

Not unlike the current health care system in the United States (U.S.), biomedical research has come under close scrutiny and re-evaluation of its goals, benefits, and costs. Scarce funding has become more restricted in its application, and

337

pressure exists to align research goals with what public perception values as a health care need. Some have suggested that the biomedical research climate is in a state of "crisis" regarding the funding of projects and the nurturing of fresh talent. Recruiting and training young investigators and faculty is an issue critical to the healthy future of medical education and biomedical research. The potential well-being of people in our nation, and around the world, can only be assured if we continue to champion medicine and biomedical science, while keeping mindful of social issues and ethical concerns.

In this chapter, we attempt to give a general overview of biomedical research in the U.S., touch on the major funding sources, and address some of the issues on the current agenda.

FUNDING   ❖

Where does the money for research and training come from, and who gets how much? The answer is as complex as the tangle of forms one must submit with a grant proposal to fund an original or a continuing project.

In general, there are three major sources of research and training funds: the federal government through the *National Institutes of Health (NIH)* and the *National Science Foundation (NSF),* the pharmaceutical research and development industry, and private foundations and philanthropic institutions. In fiscal year (FY) 1993, approximately $30.8 billion was spent nationally to support biomedical research.[367] It is estimated that private industry accounted for 50% of the funding for this research and development, whereas the NIH contributed approximately 32%. The remainder was supported by other federal and private agencies.

The National Institutes of Health

The NIH, located in Bethesda, MD, is the preeminent site of government-sponsored basic science and clinical investigation in the U.S. Composed of 24 separate science institutes and divisions, the sprawling campus just outside Washington, DC, is an incredible wealth of opportunity and resources. Some 4,000 faculty and junior investigators, and another 4,000 support staff, occupy approximately 287 laboratories and 10 million square feet of space. The Warren Grant Magnuson Clinical Research Center is the largest hospital in the world, it is devoted solely to clinical research, and it is located at the center of the campus. Another resource is the National Library of Medicine, noted as being the world's largest research library in a single scientific field or profession. The latest research institutes joining the NIH in 1993 were the National Institute on Alcohol Abuse and Alcoholism, the National Institute on Drug Abuse, and the National

Institute of Mental Health. The U.S. government supported health research and development in FY 1992 with a budget of more than $24.8 billion.[368] This figure included an NIH budget of more than $8.8 billion. Approximately 17% of NIH funds were used to fund intramural projects (i.e., projects done at the NIH campus). Part of this money also paid for management costs and upkeep of the buildings and the facilities. The bulk of the money, extramural awards, went to fund projects, training, and contracts outside the NIH campus, either associated or not associated with an NIH institute or center.

The NIH has multiple support mechanisms, which include research grants, research development, contracts, and training awards.[369]

The largest category of funding is *Research Grants.* This category supports the following four areas.

◇ *Research Projects.* The primary grant is termed an (R01) traditional research grant, and it is awarded to a domestic or a foreign institution to fund a principal investigator's specific research project in their area of competence. A second type is the (P01), which grants support to a group of coordinated investigators with a long-term, broadly based, and often multidisciplinary program objective. These two grant types are the bulk under this heading, although the following are also funded: (FIRST - R29) awards for new investigators to develop and demonstrate their research capabilities, (SBIR - R43 and R44) awards to small businesses that provide technological contributions, and (R35) outstanding investigator and (MERIT - R37) awards to extend research time to outstanding, experienced investigators.

◇ *Research Centers.* These grants fund multidisciplinary, long-term research programs at research centers that usually have a clinical orientation and are associated with an institute. This type of grant is awarded to the institute on behalf of a program director and a group of scientists working together.

◇ *Career Development.* Career awards, as well as academic research enhancement (AREA) awards, support scientists in training at science centers and at colleges that are not necessarily research intensive.

◇ *Other research and research-related programs* include grants for construction of new research facilities, repair and renovation of older facilities, as well as medical library grants to establish new resources and to improve existing ones.

Another large area of funding from the government is the *Research and Development Contracts* (R&D). These R&D awards are negotiated with domestic and foreign organizations, and they provide support for basic, applied, or developmental research, as well as funds to test and to evaluate a product for use by the research community.[370]

A third category, called *Training Awards,* funds training of scientists for careers in research, as well as helps professional schools establish and improve programs in continuing professional education. These awards include the National Research

Service Awards (NRSA) training grants and fellowships and the Minority Access to Research Careers (MARC) awards.[370]

Since FY 1983, extramural funding has more than doubled from $3.2 billion to its current amount of more than $8.8 billion. The majority of the extramural support since 1983 ($\approx$ 75%) has been used for research grants. The remainder was used for R&D contracts and training. California ($1,028M), New York ($788M), and Massachusetts ($772M) accounted for 35% of the total amount of extramural funds awarded to domestic institutions in FY 1992.[371] These top three recipients were followed, in rank order, by Maryland, Pennsylvania, and Texas. Figure 17.1 shows a geographical representation of the NIH extramural awards. Puerto Rico also received $17 million dollars in extramural awards in 1992. NIH institutes also receive extramural funds to support extramural projects. The National Cancer Institute, with a 1992 budget of $1.5 billion, had the largest extramural budget of NIH institutes or centers, followed by the National Heart, Lung, and Blood Institute ($1 billion).

Interestingly, 73% of NIH extramural awards in FY 1992 were presented to 458 institutions of higher learning.[372] The top 10 institutions for that year received between $115.7 and $209.0 million dollars each, accounting for 19% of all extramural awards.[373] Table 17.1 lists these top 10 institutions. Medical schools, specifically, received just more than half of all NIH extramural awards (Figure 17.2).[374] The top 20 medical schools received almost 49% of this amount (see Table 17.2). These totals are somewhat misleading because they do not include funds awarded

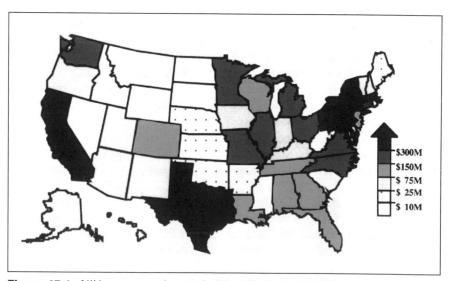

Figure 17.1 NIH extramural awards (in millions) in FY 1992, by geographical distribution. State variations in research funding do not take into account research intensity. Graph represents a mix of successful competition for funds and population size. (Adapted from NIH Extramural Trends FY 83-92.)

Table 17.1 NIH Support to Top 10 Institutions

Institution	Total Received (in Millions, FY 1992)
Johns Hopkins U.	$209.0
U. of Washington	166.4
U. of CA, San Francisco	165.8
Harvard U.	132.6
Yale U.	131.9
U. of Michigan	127.3
U. of CA, Los Angeles	124.3
Columbia U., New York	120.6
U. of Pennsylvania	119.9
Washington U.	115.7

NIH support to top 10 institutions of higher learning. (Adapted from NIH Extramural Trends FY 83-92.)

separately to teaching hospitals affiliated with each of these medical schools. For example, although Harvard Medical School is listed as seventeenth on this list, if one were to include extramural funds awarded to the Harvard teaching hospitals, the total amount for the Harvard medical system would swell to more than $339.2 million.[375]

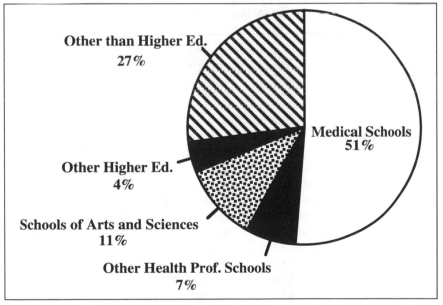

Figure 17.2 NIH extramural awards distribution FY 1992. (Adapted from NIH Extramural Trends FY 83-92.)

Table 17.2 NIH Support to Top 20 Medical Schools, 1992

Rank	Medical School	Total (millions)
1	Johns Hopkins U.	$157.5
2	U. of Calif., San Francisco	143.5
3	Yale U.	114.2
4	U. of Washington, Seattle	112.4
5	Washington U., St. Louis	107.8
6	Columbia U.	102.4
7	Stanford U.	94.3
8	Duke U.	93.0
9	U. of Michigan	91.3
10	U. of Pennsylvania	90.5
11	U. of Calif., San Diego	85.6
12	U. of North Carolina	77.0
13	U. of Calif., Los Angeles	76.5
14	Baylor College of Medicine	74.8
15	Albert Einstein College	70.0
16	U. of Alabama at Birmingham	69.6
17	Harvard Medical School	69.4
18	U. of Chicago Pritzker	66.9
19	Case Western Reserve	66.8
20	Vanderbilt U.	62.8
	Total—Top 20 Schools	$1826.3
	Total—All Medical Schools	3742.5
	Percent Top 20 Schools	48.8%

NIH extramural support to the top 20 medical schools in FY 1992. Totals exclude awards made separately to hospitals affiliated with each medical school. (Adapted from NIH Extramural Trends FY 83-92.)

Although budget increases of more than $5.6 billion over the last decade are impressive and have made the preceding magnitude of awards possible, when using the Biomedical R&D Price Index to account for inflation, a dollar in FY 1983 equals 64 cents in FY 1992, when purchasing services.[376] These biomedical purchasing costs increased faster (57%) in the last 10 years than costs for urban consumer goods and services (41%). This increase is significant when examining actual grant-dollar increases over the years. Inflation significantly erodes budget increases. For example, without accounting for inflation, from 1983 to 1992, the research grant dollars grew 130%, R&D awards increased 118%, and funds for training increased 87%.[377] After accounting for inflation in constant dollars, each only increased 47, 39, and 19%, respectively. This perspective has a tremendous impact when discussing funding trends, budgets, and costs. These issues are discussed later in this chapter.

The National Science Foundation

The NSF is an independent federal agency created by the National Science Foundation Act of 1950, a vision of the Truman administration. Its goal has been to encourage and advance scientific progress in the U.S. across all disciplines. Important scientific and technological contributions during World War II led to the creation of this foundation. The unique mission of the NSF makes it unlike other agencies created to support research in specifically focused areas.

The NSF funds research in all areas of science and engineering. It uses grants and contracts to award funding to more than 2,000 colleges and universities, as well as other research centers, nonprofit organizations, and small businesses. Approximately 25% of government support for basic research in academic institutions comes from the NSF, but, unlike the NIH, the NSF does not operate its own research laboratories.[378] However, it does support National Research Centers, oceanographic vessels, and research stations in the Antarctic. The NSF also provides aid for cooperative research ventures between universities and industry, as well as U.S. participation in international research efforts. In general, there are 10 areas funded by the NSF (Figure 17.3).

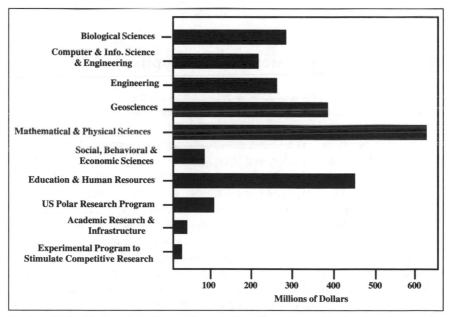

Figure 17.3 National Science Foundation financial table by funding areas in Fiscal Year 1992. Amounts in millions of dollars. (Source: NSF Annual Report, 1992.)

The President appoints an NSF Director and Board of 24 scientists and engineers to run the Foundation. It is structured into grant-awarding divisions for each discipline within science and engineering. An extended network of scientific advisors serves on formal committees, or as ad hoc reviewers of grant proposals, thus aiding core Foundation staff. This advisory system of more than 59,000 scientists and engineers lends direction to the NSF programs, and it supplies a reference faculty when reviewing grant applications. The NSF receives approximately 57,000 grant proposals each year for research, graduate and postdoctoral fellowships, and educational projects in other areas.[379] Ultimately, final award decisions are made by expert staff within each field.

Thus, although the fraction of the NSF budget dedicated for biological scientific research and technology is much smaller than the NIH budget, the NSF is still a vital source of research funding. Within the biological sciences, in FY 1992, the NSF appropriated $274.35 million for more than 3,200 awards. These funds were divided among projects in molecular and cellular bioscience, environmental biology, integrative biology and neuroscience, and biological instrumentation and resources.[380] The NSF is also an invaluable funding source for graduate fellowships and young scientists considering careers in research. The Foundation is committed to ensuring the nation's supply of scientists, engineers, and educators in science. For example, the NSF Presidential Young Investigator Awards funded 220 fellows in 1991 with $125,000 each, and they provided an additional $187,500 if investigators could match that with private funds.[381]

Pharmaceutical Research and Development

The ability of major pharmaceutical manufacturers to remain economically viable and competitive is dependent on their ability to develop innovative new drugs and market them. This is an expensive investment that is both time-consuming and involves significant risk. Yet, pharmaceutical corporations around the globe have met this challenge successfully, and they have developed a wide range of important new drugs, allowing them to remain a highly profitable industry. This industry is driven by research and development. In 1990, member companies of the Pharmaceutical Manufacturers Association reached worldwide R&D expenditures of $24 billion.[382] In 1992, that budget had increased by approximately $10.9 billion. In the U.S., major pharmaceutical manufacturers employ 40,000 people in R&D. Thus, in the U.S., as well as in many other developed countries, pharmaceutical R&D is regarded as having positive economic implications.

Yet the pharmaceutical industry is not without its own controversies. How much does it cost to develop a new drug from scratch? What is the cost of all the failed projects for every one of the few successful new drugs that go to market? Much discussion has focused on the R&D costs to manufacturers and how that translates into the market price for a particular product. In essence, how profitable is R&D in the long run? DiMasi and colleagues estimated that it takes

12 years, on average, and $231 million (in 1987 dollars) to synthesize a new drug and to obtain approval from the Food and Drug Administration (FDA).[383] Yet, stock in pharmaceuticals is considered to remain stable in the long run, with steady earnings, regardless of recessions or periods of growth in the economy. When one measures the percent return on the sale of a new drug, the drug industry is still one of the most profitable.[384] This profitability translates into an expense for many medicines that is attributed to the increasing costs of R&D, as well as to the high cost of losses sustained for failed projects that are spread onto the cost of successful products.

Although these are important discussions, they should not take away from the fact that highly significant research is being done by pharmaceutical companies. New drug approvals by the FDA are a testament to the innovation going on in pharmaceutical laboratories. From 1981 to 1990, the FDA approved 196 new chemical products, 92% of which were developed by the pharmaceutical industry (Figure 17.4).[385] Without doubt, this industry is the main source of most prescription drugs currently used. High levels of clinical research have produced drugs in a wide range of categories over the years (Figure 17.5).[386] Pharmaceutical R&D has had a major impact on current medical practice, and it has made significant contributions to the understanding of many clinical and basic science dilemmas.

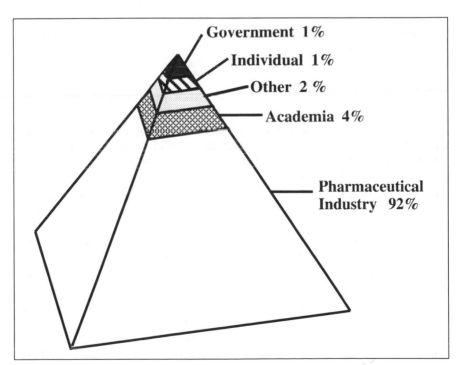

Figure 17.4 Relative sources of new chemical entities approved by the FDA from 1981 to 1990 (N = 196). (Adapted from Kaitin et al., J Clin Pharmacol, 1993.)

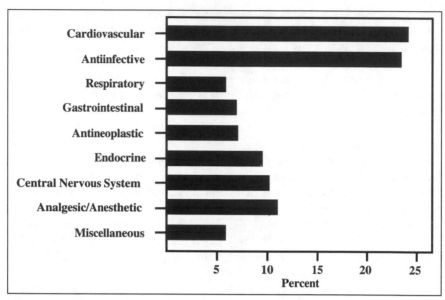

Figure 17.5 Percent of drugs, by therapeutic category, approved in the U.S. from 1976 to 1990. (Adapted from Kaitin et al., J Clin Pharmacol, 1993.)

One can surely expect that as the pharmaceutical industry increases support for R&D, so will its influence.

Private Foundations and Philanthropic Institutions

In the current competitive research arena, finding moneys to fund biomedical research demands skillful and strategic investigation of all available sources. An alternative source of funding that is becoming more heavily sought after are the private foundations and institutions established by wealthy philanthropists. These organizations are a relatively new, and largely American, phenomenon. There are currently more than 25,000 such foundations, each with its own application process and specific funding criteria. Although most are small, more than 90 of them have assets well over $200 million dollars.[387] Only in this century has the impact of these powerful foundations on medicine and general health been so apparent. Wealthy philanthropists, including names like Carnegie, Duke, Hughes, Rockefeller, Kellogg, Ford, Rosenwald, and Harkness, with large sums at their disposal, have influenced medical education and research in a major way. Table 17.3 outlines just a few of the major private contributors to current basic research.

The top two on this list are worth further mention. The Howard Hughes Medical Institute (HHMI) is now the largest organization of its kind in the world. Technically a medical research organization and not a foundation, as a result of careful investment of funds derived from Hughes Aircraft, it has generated assets in ex-

Table 17.3 Foundation Research Awards

Name	Founded	Awarded in 1990
Howard Hughes Medical** Institute	1953	$258M
Lucille P. Markey Charitable Trust	1983	$ 58.8M*
John D. and Catherine T. MacArthur Foundation	1970	$ 30.0M
W. M. Keck Foundation	1954	$ 14.0M
Whitaker	1975	$ 13.5M
James S. McDonnell Foundation	1950	$ 7.50M*
Pew Charitable Trusts	1948	$ 6.75M

Funds awarded for biomedical research by larger private foundations and **medical research organizations. *Awarded in year 1991. (Adapted from Baringa M., *Science*, 1991.)

cess of an astounding $7.3 billion.[388] Headquartered close to the NIH campus in a beautiful new facility opened in 1993, HHMI funds everything from basic research in cell biogenetics, immunology, and neuroscience, to medical student research endeavors through their Research Scholars Program. The second organization is a relatively newer organization, and it is certainly at a smaller scale than HHMI. The Lucille P. Markey Charitable Trust has funded new initiatives in broad range of biomedicine, and, until 1991, it also funded young scientists in training through its Markey Scholar Awards.[389]

That both these organizations fund young scientists in their early training years is exemplary of many of these organizations. For example, many foundations have not only focused on specific areas of research, but have also taken up the cause of young investigators. Thought to be at risk in the federal awards system, many young scientists are recipients of more than $35 million each year from such campaigns (Table 17.4).[390]

Foundations have given an incredible boost to research when they seek under-funded areas and projects. Yet, such investment does not come without added input and control by such organizations to determine how their money is spent. Unlike the NIH, which typically funds research in well-established areas, private foundations have more leeway, independence, and less bureaucracy than the government to distribute their funds. Many critics have suggested that this very freedom private institutions enjoy leads to an environment in which funding goals can change very quickly, depending on the popular and the political climate. Foundations have great latitude in selecting areas to fund. Yet many argue that all funding is vital. The degree to which many of these organizations and individuals have met areas of need in biomedical research is a testament to the extent private

Table 17.4 Private Support for Young Researchers

Name	Fellows	Awards per Researcher
Markey Charitable Trust	16	$543,000+
Packard Foundation	20	$500,000
Pew Charitable Trusts	20	$200,000
Searle Scholars Award	18	$180,000
Whitaker	60	$180,000

Examples of private support for young researchers. (Adapted from Baringa M., Science, 1991.)

citizens and foundations can provide valuable support to push forward scientific and medical knowledge.

CURRENT ISSUES ❖
The Research Funding Crisis

Many scientists involved with biomedical research have become increasingly concerned with what has been called the "crisis" in research funding. Well-known laboratories across the country have found it increasingly difficult to obtain support for new or continuing projects. Well-established scientists are losing funding, whereas young investigators are finding it more difficult to find a secure track within biomedical research. Much debate surrounds the research budget. Opinions differ on how much money should be spent and the best way to allocate it.

Several reasons have been suggested to explain the perception of crisis that has developed over the years. Likely, no single force alone has precipitated the crisis atmosphere in biomedical research. Budget deficit reduction, mandated by recent congressional action in an attempt to slow the sky-rocketing national deficit, has placed significant constraints on government spending, which in turn has limited funds available for biomedical research. Despite this pressure, the NIH budget has continued to grow steadily through the years. Unfortunately, inflation has offset much of these increases and diminished the purchasing power of the dollar. Inflation, therefore, is a force that limits the ability to fund more research projects, and the demand is certainly not decreasing.[391] In FY 1980, the NIH reviewed more than 14,000 applications for awards; in 1992, more than 20,000 applications were reviewed.[392] However, although the total number of grants awarded has increased since 1983, the percentage of grants awarded, from all applications reviewed, has actually decreased (Figure 17.6).[393] In FY 1983, 32% of applications were awarded funding, whereas in fiscal year 1992, only 29% received funds, despite a budget that more than doubled in the same period. The recent trend in the NIH budget in actual dollars, as well as in constant dollars accounting for inflation, is depicted in

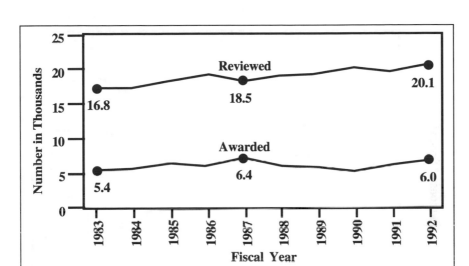

Figure 17.6 NIH competing research project grant applications reviewed and awarded for FY 1983–1992. (Adapted from NIH Extramural Trends FY 83-92.)

Figure 17.7. Inflation erodes the budget by making each funded project more expensive. The average R01 grant in 1983 cost $109,500 in current dollars; in 1992, average R01 costs increased 78% to $194,400.[394] When one looks at the relatively smaller research budget allocation in constant dollars, it becomes obvious that increases in the budget have served mainly to stay the effect of inflation.

Another factor suggested to contribute toward a sense of crisis is earmarking of the NIH budget by two different mechanisms that constrain spending. An increasing amount of each year's NIH budget is already committed to funding noncompeting continuing grants.[395] The first mechanism involves the length of award periods. Investigators in the early 1980s became concerned that research funds were awarded for too short a period to achieve long-term goals. No sooner had funds been awarded and work started than a new grant proposal had to be written to ensure ongoing funding for the project. Many complained that more time was being spent writing proposals instead of doing actual research. In the late 1970s, and through the early 1980s, the average length of individual grants, such as the R01, was approximately three years.[396] Responding to complaints, administrative policy was changed, and research grant awards were extended. Since 1987, funding awards have averaged more than 3.9 years (Figure 17.8), which in turn committed more of the anticipated growth in the federal health research budget to keep these longer running projects going. Due to these obligations on the anticipated NIH budget, the number of new and competing grants awarded has either decreased or stabilized in the last few years (See Figure 17.9A). These obligations preclude significant increases in the budget for competing continuation grants or new grants. Most of the increases in the new budget are earmarked for noncompeting continuation of awards already in progress (Figure 17.9B). This

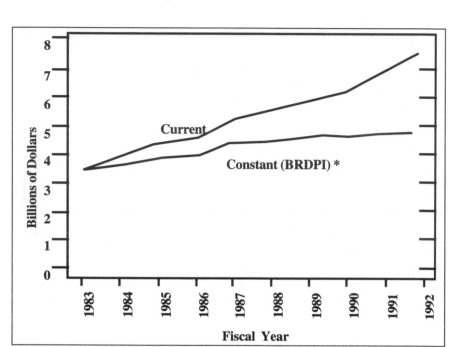

Figure 17.7 NIH funding in current and constant dollars, calculated by *BRDPI = The Biomedical Research and Development Price Index. (Data source: NIH Extramural Trends FY 83-92.)

effect was most noticeable in FY 1990, when 77% of the grants funded were non-competing continuations.[397]

Appropriations for specific health concerns is the second form of earmarking that limits funds and can contribute to the crisis. For example, AIDS has come to the forefront of research. To deal with this deadly disease, starting in 1982, Congress has designated a growing fraction of the NIH's budget to fund investigation in this area (Figure 17.10).[398] In FY 1992, the AIDS appropriation accounted for 9.4% of the NIH budget.[399] Similarly, appropriations for the much publicized Human Genome Project have set aside increasing amounts of each year's budget to fund research related to this area. The Human Genome Project, a multinational, cooperative effort to map the entire human genome, has sparked concern among biologists, who fear the impact of this project on traditional biological research and funding priorities. Congress is currently funding genome work both at the NIH and at the U.S. Department of Energy (DOE). The DOE, charged with monitoring inherited damage caused by low-level radiation exposure and other environmental hazards, perceives the Genome Project as the vehicle to accomplishing this task. Thus, considerable funds are being appropriated for the NIH to refine human genome mapping of clinical diseases and to study the genomes of selected model organisms.[400] The DOE has focused solely on the human physical map, on the

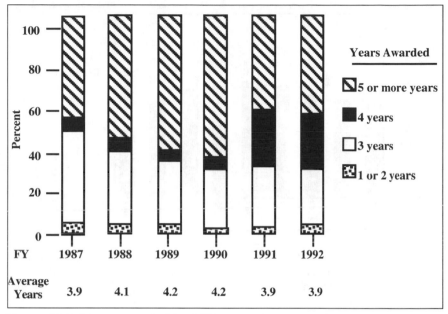

Figure 17.8 Years awarded for NIH competing research project grants and average length of project period from 1987 to 1992. (Adapted from NIH Extramural Trends FY 83-92.)

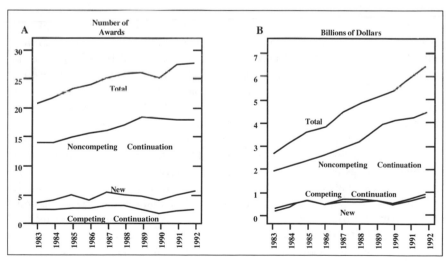

Figure 17.9 (A) Number of NIH research grant awards (in thousands) by type, for fiscal years 1983–1992. (B) Funding for NIH research grant awards (in billions) by type, for fiscal years 1983–1992. (Adapted from NIH Data Book 1993.)

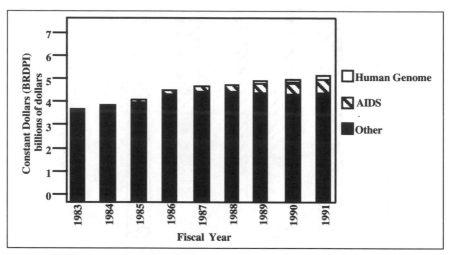

Figure 17.10 Annual relative NIH appropriations for the Human Genome Project, and AIDS research for FY 1983–1991, in constant dollars, as calculated by the Biomedical Research and Development Price Index, BRDPI. (Adapted from Petersdorf RG, Trans Am Clin Climat Assoc, 1992.)

development of new mapping and sequencing techniques, and on methods to handle the data being generated by the project. This analysis of specific budget appropriations is not to suggest that these are not worthy goals, but only that they limit the ability of institutions to fund projects outside particular fields. Figure 17.11 shows NIH budget appropriations in 1992 for a variety of other illnesses.[401]

Health care reform is another force that may be contributing to a sense of crisis in biomedical research. Streamlining our health care system, eliminating duplication of service, and increasing access to health care are needed goals, yet the various methods being discussed to reach these goals cannot be expected to take effect in a vacuum. Biomedical research, teaching, and clinical care are a complex interrelation. One cannot constrain one partner in the relationship without affecting the others. For example, in an effort to decrease hospital costs, more and more procedures are now being done on an out-patient basis. This approach decreases costs, but it also decreases the amount of revenue a hospital can generate, thus putting teaching hospitals at risk of not being able to internally subsidize their own research. Moneys that could have been used to start up a laboratory for a young researcher may no longer be available. Equally important is the loss of potential research study participants. Patients are often able to enroll in a clinical study and possibly benefit from participating in a clinical study, while helping researchers to better understand a disease process. The patients are no longer in the hospital and are therefore less readily available. This is but one simple example showing the complex interrelationship between research and the health care system. Any reform package of our health care system, if not carefully considered, could pose a significant threat to biomedical research.

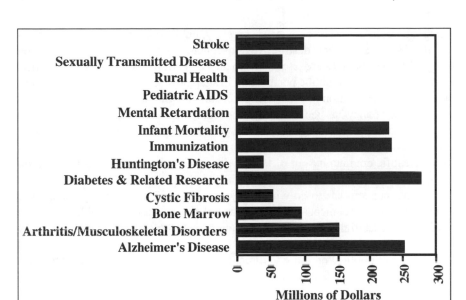

Figure 17.11 NIH FY 1992 obligations for selected diseases.

Thus, the crisis in biomedical research has likely been precipitated by a combination of all these forces: erosion of buying power by inflation, increasing cost per grant, increase in the number of applications, ear tagging NIH funds for specific illnesses, and budget obligations for continuing projects of longer duration, as well as some anxiety about the path of health care reform. To solve the problem, a greater understanding of the contributing forces must be sought. Some blame the grant-awarding procedure for the crisis, others blame administrators with inadequate prioritizing of goals, and still others see the problem stemming from expectations that exceed a reasonable capacity to fund projects. Most agree, however, that an integrated, long-term research funding strategy needs to be in place, which can only be achieved by a united biomedical research community.[402]

Public Concerns

Biomedical research, once thought of as indisputable good, has come under greater scrutiny in the last decade. Spending limited resources has become a more acute concern to more people. The general public, with increasing access to sources of information, has come to appreciate the incredible advances made in science; at the same time, they have come to expect and to demand more of the scientific community. In the 1980s, the public, demanding rapid action against an unknown, deadly disease, saw an unprecedented surge of scientific and epidemiological understanding about AIDS. Even earlier, in the 1970s, a "war on cancer" was declared, which, for better or worse, earmarked a substantial chunk of the NIH budget to research this disease. More recently, public concern about the use of illegal substances and their destructive consequences has been met with a "war on drugs." These examples are testaments to the power of public opinion and politics, and to the force of the public perspective in shaping science. This relationship has also led to some friction between the public and the biomedical research community. A discrepancy has been suggested between the community's expectations of science and the practical capacity of the government to fund enough projects.[403] The political climate is dominated by economic constraints and public perceptions of a scientific community out of touch with basic health care needs.[404] What do people expect for their money, and is it feasible?

Another concern has to do with the type of research that is being done: basic science research or clinical research. In general, the less-informed public perceives basic science as irrelevant mental ruminations with little direct benefit to society at large. Discussions focused on the NIH intramural programs have been fueled by significant political pressure to direct investigation toward a foreseeable clinical application. One clear example of this debate was alluded to previously, concerning the Human Genome Project. Arguments that the Genome Project, involving the immense task of sequencing a complex genome, will yield little direct benefit if we cannot correlate the map to any human disease and use it to treat illness. Others are convinced that the project's short-term cost is small relative to the long term and theoretically immeasurable benefits. The benefits, including everything from the complete human genome map and information it may yield, to improved technology, techniques, and expertise, are likely to be precipitated by-products of such a large, concerted scientific effort.

Arguments have been made to suggest that science has traditionally been isolated from the public.[405] The benefits of such a relationship were not lost to investigators. One could work on a particular topic without being encumbered with social and political value justifications. This association produced an astounding growth in our understanding of basic scientific mechanisms and their application to medicine. In contrast, this isolation led to the myth that science is solely a cognitive process, unaffected by social need and demand. The indisputable good produced by science is now being disputed. Given that value judgments are made concerning what is and what is not worthy of investigation even within science, it stands to reason that not all that is produced by science is necessarily of benefit. Yet, pressure to reshape all of science into a producer of marketable goods is equally flawed. Without advances in basic scientific knowledge, which may not have immediate clinical application, understanding would stagnate, and, in the long run, society would suffer greatly. The merit of original contributions in science should be recognized, and scientists must actively and effectively communicate and educate the public, as well as respond to social concerns. The biomedical research and academic medical communities must achieve a balance to resolve value issues raised by a public concerned with the high cost of medicine and science.

Another critical issue concerning the public is that of trust. Biomedical researchers have enjoyed a relatively privileged position dependent on the political process, congressional assurances, and public support. Multiple threats to public confidence have eroded the ability of researchers to effectively argue their position and to convey important scientific information. Cases of academic misconduct, misuse of federal grant monies, or disputes between investigators over intellectual property receive much press, and they cripple the public's faith in the merit of science and research.

Equally precarious as the issue of trust are the issues surrounding the relationships between the academic community and industry. Over the last decade, there has been an apparent growth in academic-industry relationships.[406] These relationships consist of an exchange between for-profit corporations and academic institutions. Generally, research, training, or intellectual property, such as patents or licenses to commercially useful techniques, are exchanged with private industry for financial compensation, such as research support, consulting fees, royalties, or equity.[407] The possible consequences of these alliances are unclear, and to what extent they should be encouraged, managed, or discouraged is uncertain.

Universities, private companies, and the government all have a role in this discussion. Biomedical research and technological advances precipitate products with wide application that hold significant implications for the public health, but also for our economy. Yet, the public seems wary of the idea that biomedical research in academic centers may be influenced by its association with commercial enterprise. Given that much research is sponsored either directly or indirectly through the government, it is unclear whether private corporations should be allowed to profit from public funding of research. Government is more closely scrutinizing the relationships between industry and academic institutions in an effort to refine federal policy. It is still too early to make a good assessment as to how these associations will affect biomedical research. The rewards of corporate sponsorship will likely be tempered by public concern to keep basic biomedical investigation independent of commercial interests, while preserving the economic and productive aspects of the academic-industrial relationship.

Training Physician-Scientists

In striving to meet the demands of a changing health care system, so too has the medical academic community been challenged to ensure growth and support of its academic enterprise and to train talented young investigators in research and in leadership roles. New generations of researchers, teachers, and administrators are needed to take full advantage of advances being made each day, as well as to add to the wealth of knowledge in the future. The training of an adequate number of physician-scientists is critical to the application of new strategies in treatment and prevention of many human diseases and in the future of scientific understanding.

Despite limited funds, this is an age of incredible opportunity in biomedical research. Advances in molecular genetics have created powerful technologies to study human disease. Burgeoning understanding of the immune system has precipitated multiple clinical trials investigating the efficacy of modulating the immune response in the treatment of many systemic diseases. Yet the message dominating attention is that of crisis and limited opportunity. Not surprisingly, the number of aspiring young physician-scientists is small. The potential for a shortage of new talent was suggested more than a decade age.[408]

The importance of training physician-scientists in research and leadership positions is unquestioned. It is expected that physicians, trained in the details surrounding human disease, are uniquely attuned to biological research, with potential implications for understanding and possibly treating or preventing illness. Obviously, the more engrossed one becomes with science, the more likely lasting fundamental contributions will be made. Thus, more and more medical students now incorporate a laboratory experience into their years of training. One or two years of full-time research has also become a required component of many residency training programs, as well as a desired prerequisite for many competitive subspecialties. Early exposure to research at the high school level has also become more pervasive. Hundreds of programs now offer competitive positions in laboratories to students interested in science, introducing them early to the independent research experience.

However, with all these programs designed to enhance the number of physicians in basic and clinical research, certain concerns of medical students, housestaff, and junior faculty still prevent many from exercising this option in their training. A questionnaire sent to these groups showed that more than half were interested in research and academic positions, but they were held back by three main concerns. First, limited resources in a more intensely competitive environment make funding more elusive and difficult to obtain.[409] Concern likely focuses on the ability of MDs, as principal investigators, to effectively compete against PhD applicants. Yet, analyses of RO1-type applications to the NIH have shown that MDs and PhDs are actually awarded at the same rate, making their funding success about equal.[410] PhDs do receive a greater cut of the pie, but only because more of them apply. The second concern had to do with the politics of academic medicine and research, as well as the perception that not enough faculty positions are available to merit their pursuit. The headaches and stress of academic responsibility are also thought to take away excessive time from clinical responsibilities. With this interruption from patients, as well salary caps placed on many academicians by the affiliated institutions, the burden of incurred educational debt becomes greater motivation to stay out of academia, finish quickly, and maximize their earning potential. Thus, debt responsibility is the third concern. Of those who do exercise the option to work in a laboratory during residency, or are required to do so, many spend a large fraction of their time away from the bench, moonlighting. This is a very real concern, and unfortunately, it detracts from the research experience and it makes significant contributions in science more difficult.

To address some of these issues in training physician-scientists, it has been postulated that residents would likely have to train longer, need to be paid higher salaries while in training, be less dependent on government funding, be more focused on population health issues, and be concentrated at research-intensive medical schools.[411] It is possible that with changing health care goals, government funding for resident training will be more limited, thus forcing teaching hospitals to maximize training in a minimal number of years. To meet this challenge, several subspecialties may need to accept medical students directly into their programs and to track them early, instead of doing a full residency before specialization. For example, a full medicine residency is not required to enter the field of dermatology or radiology. Residents entering orthopedic surgery or neurosurgery only do one or two years of a general surgery residency before focusing on their area of interest. Fields such as plastic surgery and cardiothoracic surgery, which have traditionally required general surgery Board certification prior to specialization, are starting to track this way as well. By tracking, the residency period becomes more focused on subspecialty relevance and possibly shortened, thus freeing up some time to pursue research interests without adding even more years to an already long training course. A focused, expeditious residency may also allay some fears of loan repayment, thus allowing more physicians to pursue academic roles.

Other programs designed to train doctors in science have been the MD/PhD programs started in the early 1960s. Summarized data regarding eight such programs found that of 760 graduates from MD/PhD programs from eight medical schools (Harvard, Duke University, Johns Hopkins University, Washington University in St. Louis, UCSF, University of Pennsylvania, University of Chicago, and Stanford), 62% had completed postgraduate training or a residency and, of these, more than 90% entered academic or institute research positions.[412] The success of these programs is attributed to careful nurturing and career counseling of very talented and motivated individuals.

These programs cannot produce enough scientists to meet the demand. Other programs make up some of the slack, like the NIH-sponsored *NIH Physician-Scientist Training Award* that trains MDs after residency. The *Howard Hughes Medical Student Research Scholars Program* and its *Post Doctoral Training Fellowships* also provide excellent research experiences. These are just two examples of the many programs that provide opportunities to meet the demand for people with a clinical background and strong scientific training.

CONCLUSION ❖

The opportunity to make original contributions in science, as well as to advance clinical practice, has never been greater. Many young people with exceptional qualifications are taking full advantage of research possibilities, as well as pursuing academic careers. Many investigators continue to thrive in science. Although restrained budgets for research have made the grant application process extremely competitive, research funds, both in the public and the private sectors, continue to grow. Scientists have become more creative and efficient in identifying funding sources. The scientific and medical-academic communities, together with industry, recognize the need for continued and expanded support for research activities to reverse negative perceptions. Likely, more and more funding will need to come from sources outside the government. Industry and private foundations will need to continue an aggressive role in tapping the resource of young talent. Greater government support in financing educational debt will certainly make academic training more palatable and feasible for many. A closer association between the public and the scientific community continues to improve and to lend stability to biomedical research endeavors that educate the public, as well as respond to social concerns. Many challenges have yet to be met, but like the health care system in the U.S., biomedical research policy likely stands to benefit from thoughtful analysis and critique of its methods to optimize results.

❖ Suggested Reading ❖

Strickland SP. Research and the health of Americans. Improving the policy process. Lexington, MA: Lexington Books, 1978.

Stickland SP. Politics, science, & dread disease. A short history of the United States medical research policy. Cambridge, MA: Harvard University Press, 1972.
A historical look at the development of the NIH and the policy and politics that underlie its funding.

National Institutes of Health, Division of Research Grants. NIH extramural trends, fiscal years 1983–1992. Pub. No. 93-3506, Nov 1993.

National Institutes of Health, The Office of Science Policy and Technology Transfer. NIH data book 1993. Pub. No. 93-1261, Sept 1993.

Science and engineering indicators, 1993, National Science Board. Washington, DC: U.S. Government Printing Office (NSB-93-1), 1993.
Easy-to-scan reports, tables, and graphs provide current broad based quantitative information about U.S. research activities and education funded by the NIH and the NSF.

Bellett AJD. Value issues in biomedical science: public concerns and professional complacency. Immunol Cell Biol 1992;70:363–368.

Cullinton BJ. Shaping science policy: what's happening to biomedical research in America. Acad Med 1991;66:188–191.

Porter RJ, Malone TE. Biomedical research collaboration and conflict of interest. Baltimore, MD: The Johns Hopkins University Press, 1992.
Discussions of current issues of public concern in biomedical research.

Mental Health Policy

Michael J. Murphy and Robert Dorwart

Mental disorders are among the most common human afflictions, and they are the cause of tremendous disability. The combined direct and indirect costs of mental illness amount to billions of dollars annually. Moreover, the ways in which the medical care and the social systems function and the policies by which they abide often reflect the ignorance about and misunderstanding of mental illness and the mentally ill. This chapter aims to provide a broad overview of mental health policy to describe the people, the institutions, and the policies that govern the current mental health care system.

We begin with a discussion of the epidemiology of mental disorders to define the population for whom these policies are created. Next, we discuss the structure and the function of the mental health care system, including how care is financed. We also examine the victims of substance abuse and homelessness, who are often mentally ill and treated by (or neglected by) the mental health system. Finally, trends in mental health policy are described, including a discussion of proposed reforms.

DEFINING MENTAL HEALTH POLICY ❖

For a number of historical and contemporary reasons, mental health policy is neither clearly in the realm of health care policy nor exclusively in the realm of welfare or social policy. Rather, it exists, in part, in both spheres. The "medicalization" of psychiatry (the period since the mid-1950s, in which there has been a movement toward increasingly biologically oriented treatment of people with mental illnesses) has prompted some policy makers to consider psychiatric services as part of general medical services and mental health policy as part of health care policy.[413] However, because the poor and the disenfranchised are disproportionately represented among the mentally ill, and, because of other historical reasons, the policies that dictate mental health care are closely tied to social/welfare policies. Put simply, mental health policy may be defined as the set of governmental systems and regulations that shape the way mental health services are financed and delivered in the United States (U.S.).

THE EPIDEMIOLOGY OF MENTAL ILLNESS   ❖

Mental illness, alcoholism, and drug abuse are pervasive in the U.S. According to the Epidemiologic Catchment Area (ECA) Study performed in the U.S. in the early 1980s, 32% of American adults have experienced one or more psychiatric disorders in their lifetimes. In any given year, 28.1% of adults meet the criteria for at least one DSM-III-R (*Diagnostic and Statistical Manual of Mental Disorders,* Third Edition, Revised) diagnosis.[414] The ECA study was a survey done on a large, randomly selected sample of the population in five U.S. cities, and it was designed to identify the incidence and the prevalence of psychiatric illness. The most prevalent disorder identified was phobia, with a 14.3% lifetime prevalence. Nearly as prevalent was alcohol abuse/dependence, with a 13.8% lifetime prevalence. Table 18.1 shows the lifetime and one-year prevalences for the major psychiatric disorders. This is a heterogeneous list of disorders, including both acute and lifetime disorders. The median age at onset for psychiatric illness is 16 (see Table 18.1). Whether the young person develops a chronic disorder or a more transient disorder with frequent recurrences, the costs of providing care for a mentally ill person are usually quite high because of the need for intermittent hospitalization and continuing care as an out-patient in the community for many years. Several groups of patients deserve special mention.

Chronically Mentally Ill

The so called chronically mentally ill are a heterogeneous group of patients, many of whom have schizophrenia and most of whom now live *outside* of mental hospitals. Schizophrenia, with a lifetime prevalence of 1%, is typically a chronic, debilitating mental illness that for some is characterized by a deteriorating course. Those with unremitting schizophrenia have a near-constant lifetime need for medical and social services, and they are frequently poor or uninsured because they are unable to work steadily. Bachrach estimated the total number of chronically mentally ill in the U.S. at 2 million.[415] Currently, they include older patients who may be former long-term residents of state mental hospitals and young adult chronic patients who have always lived in the community.[416] The chronically mentally ill constitute a large proportion of the urban homeless.[417]

Table 18.1 Prevalence and Median Age
of Onset of Selected Psychiatric Disorders

Disorder	Lifetime Prevalence (%)	One-Year Prevalence (%)	Median Age of Onset
Phobia	14.3	8.8	10
Alcohol Abuse/Dependence	13.8	6.3	21
Generalized Anxiety	8.5	3.8	
Major Depressive Episode	6.4	3.7	25
Drug Abuse/Dependence	6.2	2.5	18
Antisocial Personality Disorder	2.6	1.2	8
Obsessive Compulsive Disorder	2.6	1.7	20
Panic	1.6	0.9	23
Schizophrenia	1.5	1.0	19
Manic Episode	0.8	0.6	19
Somatization	0.1	0.1	15

Lifetime and one-year prevalence for the major psychiatric disorders. Includes acute and lifetime disorders. (Adapted from Robbins et al, An Overview of Psychiatric Disorders in America.)

The Elderly

The elderly constitute an increasing percentage of the U.S. population (12% in 1989). Among them, 0.1% suffer from dementia, which can be mild to severe, and it may involve varying degrees of difficulty with activities of daily living. They also experience psychosis, depression, and substance abuse, although less commonly than younger persons. The elderly are relatively low users of mental health services, but it is suspected that many who might benefit from such services are reluctant to seek them.[418] The majority obtain services from community facilities, and those with severe illness tend to be treated in nursing homes, where their care may be covered by Medicaid, rather than in hospitals.[419] Although many of the severely mentally ill elderly reside in nursing homes, few of the scarce resources in these homes are devoted to the treatment of mental illness, and many mental disorders in the elderly are not adequately detected or treated.[420]

Children

Mental disorders in children have been less amenable to classification than those of adults. Typically, problems will be identified by teachers. Some children exhibit childhood forms of adult psychopathology, some have developmental disorders such as autism, whereas others are simply labeled "maladjusted," having clear developmental or emotional problems that are not easily definable. The most significant risk factor for childhood mental illness is parental mental illness.[421] Children are treated in a variety of settings by psychiatric specialists, social workers, and correctional workers. However, psychiatric services are not equally available to all children. Cost of private services and lack of sufficient amounts of public services appear to be the factors that limit access for many children.[422] The need to combine medical with psychosocial services is apparent.

THE MENTAL HEALTH SYSTEM ❖
Who Provides Services?

Mental health services are provided in the U.S. by a wide variety of persons with varying degrees of specialized training in mental health. Psychiatrists and primary care physicians provide an extensive array of services to the mentally ill at a relatively high cost. There are more than 40,000 *psychiatrists* in the U.S. to whom patients are generally referred by other types of physicians. *Primary care physicians* see much of the most prevalent mental illnesses in their practices, yet they have relatively little training in psychiatry. *Clinical psychologists,* who have a doctorate degree in psychology but no medical training, often provide psychotherapy services or neuropsychological testing to patients, but they cannot prescribe medication or rule out organic pathology. They outnumber psychiatrists in the U.S. *Psychiatric social workers* have a master's degree in social work, often with focused training in mental health care. More numerous than both psychiatrists and psychologists, a majority of clinical social workers are employed by hospitals, public and private agencies, and mental health centers. *Psychiatric nurses* are either registered nurses or licensed practical nurses; some have a master's degree in psychiatric nursing, and they function as independent clinical specialists. *Mental health workers* may have a bachelor's degree, but they receive on-the-job training in mental health and are primarily employed in public and some private psychiatric hospitals. Finally, because suitable alternative care may cost more than a patient or their family can afford, or it may not be available at all, many of the mentally ill are cared for primarily by family members and friends.[423]

Where Are Services Provided?

There are a variety of settings in which mental health care is provided in the U.S. In-patient services are provided on psychiatric units of general hospitals (approximately 50,000 beds in the U.S.), in nonprofit or for-profit psychiatric specialty hospitals (40,000 beds), in state hospitals (100,000 beds), in Veterans Affairs Hospitals, and in some Community Mental Health Centers.[424] Out-patient care is provided by office-based physicians (primary care physicians and psychiatrists), office-based clinical psychologists, and by various mental health workers and professionals at walk-in mental health centers and in emergency rooms of hospitals. Alternatives to hospitalization in the form of *day hospitals* and *half-way houses* are increasingly being used to provide appropriate care for less money.[425]

MENTAL HEALTH CARE DELIVERY ❖
Initial Identification of Mental Illness

Mental illness may be detected by any one of many persons with whom the mentally ill person comes in contact; family, friends, colleagues, teachers, supervisors, police officers, social workers, family doctors, or clergy are the ones who may first encourage a person with psychiatric symptoms to seek professional help. Still, much pathology goes unnoticed or is ignored.[426]

Contacts with the Mental Health Care System

Primary care physicians are often consulted first after a problem is identified. Relatively few patients initially seek help from mental health professionals because of the stigma associated with mental illness; the lack of knowledge of, or prior contact with, mental health professionals; or the cost of seeking specialized assistance. Emergency rooms (both general and specialized psychiatric) are often the first site in which individuals with psychiatric disorders appear for initial treatment. Referral to a psychiatrist or a clinical psychologist may occur, but only a minority of the mentally ill see these professionals. Those who do not seek professional help do not do so because they can function without specialized mental health services, they lack adequate financial or sociocultural access to these services, or they choose not to go when referred to a psychiatrist.

Patients may also receive treatment from a mental health professional during an acute psychiatric hospitalization, during a psychiatric consultation for a medical/surgical hospitalization, during a criminal or civil court evaluation, in a variety of community-based clinics or programs, or in an institutional setting (e.g., prisons, nursing homes, hospices).

Delivery of Psychiatric Services Under Managed Care

Increasingly, mental health services are provided under some form of managed care. Managed care is any system of care in which something other than direct payment of physician and hospital fees occurs and in which the manager determines the necessity of care, the setting in which it is provided, by whom it is provided, and the fees charged (see Chapter 5 for more on managed care). The definition is necessarily broad because there are a multitude of different arrangements of financing and delivery of managed care.

Traditional indemnity plans that practice *utilization review* are practicing managed care, as are staff model health maintenance organizations (HMOs), albeit to different degrees. As under traditional indemnity plans, managed care plans typically have more restrictions on mental health coverage as compared with coverage for general health services. In addition to these restrictions, managed care plans institute varying degrees of *utilization review, case management,* and *gatekeeping* of mental health services.

The most comprehensive programs of managed care are found in HMOs. The HMO Act of 1973 required only minimal mental health and substance abuse benefits (specifically crisis intervention and outpatient services up to 20 visits). Coverage of in-patient care, chronic or recurring disorders, or substance abuse was not required. During the ensuing two decades, however, coverage by HMOs of mental health and substance abuse treatment expanded, primarily because of patient demand, but also because states required richer benefit packages as a condition of licensure.[427] HMOs also appear to have found that it is more cost-effective to allow subscribers direct access to mental health services rather than requiring initial evaluation by a primary care physician. A longitudinal study of a large number of HMOs found that only 22% of HMOs allowed self-referral for mental health care during the first two years of existence; 51% allowed self-referral after 2 to 5 years; and 80% allowed self-referral after 16 years.[428] Some research has been done on the quality of mental health services provided under the constraints of managed care.[429] Various delivery and financing mechanisms have been developed and tested, but very few have been rigorously studied, and little is known about their effect on quality of care.

MENTAL HEALTH CARE FINANCING   ❖

Approximately 12% of the $800 billion spent on health care in 1992 was devoted to the treatment of substance abuse and mental disorders.[430] These funds are from both private and public sources, and they are used in both public and private hospitals and clinics. The crisscross of financing in the system is illustrated in Figure 18.1.[431]

More specific data are available on how money is spent on organized mental health programs. These data exclude the costs of providing psychiatric care in private offices. Expenditures on organized mental health programs amounted to $18.5 billion in 1986. Approximately 34% of these expenditures were in state and county hospitals, 20% in Community Mental Health Centers, and 29% in both nonfederal general hospital psychiatric units and private psychiatric specialty hospitals.[432]

Nearly half of the $18.5 billion spent on mental health and substance abuse care came from non-Medicaid state funds (48%). Another 16.7% of revenue comes from patient fees (both insured and out-of-pocket). The remainder is derived from

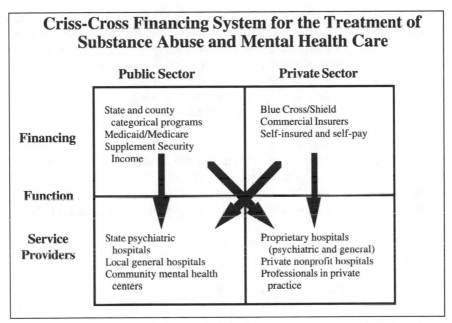

Figure 18.1 Criss-cross financing system for the treatment of substance abuse and mental health care. (Adapted from Textbook of Administration Psychiatry.)

non-Medicare, non-Medicaid federal funds (10.3%), Medicaid (9.0%), Medicare (3%), and local government funds (7.8%).[432]

Public Financing
Federal Funding

Prior to World War II, states were responsible for financing and provision of services to the mentally ill. Federal financing of mental health research, training of personnel, and assistance to states to develop new mental health programs began in 1946 with the passage of the National Mental Health Act.[433] Currently, the majority of funding for mental health care still comes from the states, but the federal government finances many services through Medicare (federally financed) and Medicaid (financed by federal and state governments), and it provides research funding through the *National Institute of Mental Health,* the *National Institute on Drug Abuse,* and the *National Institute of Alcohol Abuse and Alcoholism,* which are part of the NIH. *The Substance Abuse and Mental Health Services Administration,* a subset of the Public Health Service, funds research on the prevention of mental disorders and the delivery of mental health care.

Medicare
Medicare, which is described in Chapter 6, provides coverage under Part A for hospital care, extended care, and home health services. Coverage for psychiatric

disorders is similar to coverage for other medical disorders except for a limitation on lifetime reserve for those in a psychiatric institution. Part A covers 90 days of in-patient care per benefit period, with a 60-day interval between hospitalizations. Beneficiaries have access to a lifetime reserve of 60 days to be used as needed to extend any benefit period. If a patient is in a psychiatric free-standing hospital, however, coverage is limited to 190 days in a patient's lifetime.[434]

Part B is a voluntary enrollment portion of Medicare that covers physician services. Coverage for in-patient services by a physician are similar (80% with a 20% copayment), regardless of the diagnosis (medical/surgical/psychiatric). Coverage of out-patient psychiatric services was, until 1990, limited by dollar amount per year and included a 50% copayment, as compared with no yearly limit on out-patient medical visits and a 20% copayment. As of 1990, the yearly limit was lifted for psychiatric visits to adjust medication dosages, and the copayment was reduced to the 20% level.[435]

Increasingly, the federal government through the Health Care Financing Administration (HCFA) is allowing managed care plans to sign *Medicare risk-sharing* contracts. To enroll Medicare beneficiaries in private managed care plans, a contract with HCFA must be worked out that delineates the degree of financial risk that both parties (the plan and HCFA) will assume. Many initial attempts at Medicare risk-sharing failed, primarily because plan managers were not sophisticated enough about Medicare populations to manage their care properly. More recent contracts have been successful, and characteristics of successful contracts have become clearer.[436]

Medicaid

Medicaid, created in 1965 with Medicare, is financed with state funds and federal matching funds, but it is administered by the states. It covers the blind, the totally and permanently disabled, those receiving benefits from the Aid to Families with Dependent Children Program (AFDC), and the poor over age 65 not covered by Medicare. It pays for in-patient and out-patient care regardless of diagnosis, with the exception that it cannot be used for care of those aged 21 to 65 years in a psychiatric institution or a skilled nursing facility.[437] Medicaid is a major payer for mental health care providers for both out-patient and in-patient care. A total of 15% of Medicaid dollars were spent on mental health care in 1988.[438]

State Funding

The largest portion of financing for mental health care comes directly from states to fund state and county mental hospitals, Community Mental Health Centers, and their outreach programs. The degree of *privatization* of the public mental health system varies by state. For example, Massachusetts and several other states have begun to subcontract for the provision of mental health services in the private sector, in an effort to trim the cost of providing mental health services through market competition.[439]

Private Financing

In the past, mental health and substance abuse care for those who had various types of private health coverage was mostly financed by *retrospective payment* (i.e., after the service has been given) of a fee for each service. Hospitals and physicians set fees for their services, and they would send bills to third-party payers or patients. Traditional *indemnity* plans typically had *coverage limits* for mental health services that were more restrictive than coverage limits for medical/surgical care. Limits included restriction of the number of days/visits of in-patient/out-patient care per year, as well as *lifetime benefit limits.* Psychiatric care often was subject to more stringent *deductibles* and *copayments* than most medical care. These mechanisms were designed to rein in utilization and overall cost. Some authors have reasoned that limits on health coverage for mental illness were imposed by insurance companies because the demand for these services was perceived to be *price-sensitive,* and they are therefore more prone to overuse when price of services was shielded from the consumer by insurance coverage. Also, physicians had failed to agree on which services were most effective, so what exactly was to be covered was not as clear as in other areas of medicine.[440]

Increasingly, with the advent of more comprehensive forms of managed care, payment for mental health and substance abuse has become *prospective* and *capitated* (i.e., a fixed per capita amount charged per year regardless of the number of services provided). The traditional indemnity insurance plan is no longer as prevalent as in the past; instead, a myriad of prepaid health plans exist in which insurers/HMOs/self-insured employers contract with hospitals and doctors to provide care on either a capitated basis or a fee-for-service basis with strict *utilization review* imposed to monitor the necessity of care. A multitude of contractual arrangements exist for the provision of mental health care under managed care.

One popular arrangement in the U.S. has been the mental health *carve-out.* Carve-outs are arrangements in which particular types of services are subcontracted to be provided outside of an otherwise capitated payment system. The carve-out may call for those particular services to be paid for on a fee-for-service basis, under capitation, or through some other arrangement. For example, a large HMO that has a contract with a large *independent practice association* (i.e., a group of doctors willing to negotiate fees in return for guaranteed clientele), for the provision of primary care services for a capitated fee, might contract separately with a large private psychiatric hospital for the provision of out-patient and inpatient mental health care for a second capitated fee. The hospital and physicians under its employ would then be responsible for providing all the medically necessary mental health services for that population for the duration of the contract, regardless of the amount of actual services provided. This system has the effect of shifting the financial risk away from the HMO and the primary care physician onto the psychiatrists.

Out-of-pocket Financing

Private, office-based *psychotherapy* services are covered by some comprehensive health plans, but they are also under the scrutiny of utilization reviewers and subject to yearly and lifetime limits. Limits on psychotherapy may also be *provider-specific;* some HMOs/insurers may restrict access to the psychotherapy services of psychiatrists or clinical psychologists in favor of psychotherapy provided by less expensive mental health nurses or social workers, particularly for brief, goal-directed psychotherapy or interpersonal counseling. Psychotherapy, particularly long-term psychoanalysis (i.e., hour-long intensive sessions 3–4 times per week for several years with a physician who has received extensive postresidency psychoanalytic training), is, and always has been, paid for by individuals out-of-pocket.

PREVENTION OF MENTAL ILLNESS   ❖

The prevention of mental illness has been the focus of many public and private organizations throughout this century. In 1993, the Institute of Medicine was asked to review the literature on the prevention of mental disorders and to prepare a report with recommendations for future development of the field. In general, the prevention of illness and health maintenance is less well developed for mental disorders than it is for physical disorders. In its report, the Institute outlined three major recommendation areas:[441]

- ✦   Building the infrastructure to coordinate research and service programs to train and support new investigators.
- ✦   Expanding the knowledge base for preventive interventions.
- ✦   Conducting well-evaluated preventive interventions.

Greater attention is likely to be focused on the prevention of mental disorders in the future, as the U.S. tries to hold down the costs of health care and to decrease the federal budget deficit.

SPECIAL PROBLEMS   ❖
Substance Abuse

The abuse of and addiction to both licit and illicit drugs in the U.S. is a major public health problem. The combined lifetime prevalence of alcohol and drug abuse is approximately 20%. Substance abusers are found in all walks of life, but they are statistically most common among male, lower income persons with a family history of alcoholism. They also typically use more primary and tertiary health services than non-substance-abusing control subjects.[442] Treatment of substance abuse in the medical system is difficult and costly, with high rates of *recidivism.* There are numerous financial and sociocultural barriers to access to substance abuse treatment, particularly among those who need it most: addicted pregnant women, adolescents, and the poor.

The treatment system that currently exists is a complex array of public and private services that has evolved since World War II.[443] Some treatment began in prisons directed at those convicted of narcotics offenses, and it typically consisted of assisted withdrawal from drugs. In the community, treatment took the form of self-help groups, such as *Alcoholics Anonymous* and *Narcotics Anonymous.* The latter programs were designed to shape behavior through group support over a long period to prevent recurrence of abuse. Participants were thought to be continuously "recovering," and the self-help program provided ongoing social and psychological support to combat relapse.

Later, in the late 1960s and 1970s, *methadone maintenance* programs for narcotic addicts were implemented by the government in a move reflecting greater acceptance of the medical model of substance abuse as a disease rather than a social/criminal problem. During the Reagan era, federal support for the states' substance abuse programs was severely cut back, and the funding mechanism was changed from the traditional categorical funding to *block grants* for all mental health and substance abuse programs. The block grants, which are lump-sum funding packages without program specificity, gave the states more autonomy in devising programs, but they reduced the overall amount provided by the federal government. Much of the increased financial burden on the states was then shifted to the private sector. State mandates that required coverage of substance abuse treatment led to a large expansion of private treatment centers for substance abuse. By the late 1980s, most medium- and large-sized firms offered some kind of substance abuse treatment benefit.[444] Still, only one third of substance abuse treatment is funded through private sources nationwide.

The system that currently exists varies widely in capacity and quality by region. Some states tend to follow the criminal justice model for the treatment of illicit drug abuse, and they provide very little specialized medical treatment, whereas others devote most of their resources to medical treatment and rehabilitation programs.[445] There is an ongoing public policy debate about what balance of approaches works best for preventing and treating drug abuse in the U.S.[446]

Homelessness and Mental Health Policy

There is perhaps no more consistently vulnerable population in our country than those who are both homeless and mentally ill. Although there are no reliable estimates of the total number of homeless persons in the U.S. on a given day, estimates range from 250,000 to 350,000 to 3 million; the former is a 1984 estimate of the Department of Housing and Urban Development (HUD),[447] and the latter is extrapolated from several regional studies that estimate that the daily prevalence of homelessness is 1%.[448] The homeless have higher rates of mental illness than the general population as measured by rates of prior psychiatric hospitalization and positive screens for psychiatric symptoms. Studies indicate that 30 to 60% of the homeless currently have a serious mental illness.[449] Despite the high rates of mental illness among the homeless, it is important to note that the common misconception that homelessness was caused by deinstitutionalization is false. The multitude of factors that contribute to homelessness in the U.S. in general (e.g., lack of affordable housing, unemployment, inadequate social services, lack of family supports) are, however, compounded by mental illness. Mentally ill homeless persons are frequently disconnected from family and social supports, unable to support themselves, and they may not be coherent enough to seek appropriate financial and medical assistance. Mentally ill homeless persons may also be much less likely to receive assistance (financial or otherwise) from strangers because of the public's lack of understanding and fear of the mentally ill.

In an effort to provide long-term assistance to the chronically mentally ill, the federal government developed the ***Community Support Program*** (CSP) in 1977. This was a federal program that provided demonstration grants to states to encourage the development of innovative state and local programs to serve the rehabilitative and long-term care needs of the chronically mentally ill. Guidelines of the program specified essential functions that the programs must provide. Five of these functions were found to be especially important when dealing with the homeless mentally ill: outreach, case management, mental health treatment rehabilitation, continuum of residential assistance, and staff training. This model was unique among mental health programs in that it placed large importance on the *social welfare needs as well as the mental health needs* of the chronically mentally ill; therefore, it had the potential to be uniquely effective. Unfortunately, the cost of providing a continuum of social and medical services with housing that is appropriate for each stage of care (emergency, transitional, and residential) is enormously expensive. Therefore, the prospect of actually developing such a system for the homeless mentally ill nationwide seems unlikely, given the degree of fiscal constraint that currently exists in the health care system, as well as the reluctance of government to raise taxes.[450]

More recently, however, an experiment in New York City is under way to find more single room occupied (SRO) residences for the chronically mentally ill. Although SROs have met with some success in large cities, the heterogenous population of mentally ill will likely require a variety of interventions.[451]

TRENDS IN MENTAL HEALTH POLICY ❖
Historical Treatment of the Insane

Treatment of the mentally ill has varied in quality throughout history, and it has generally been based on the prevailing societal viewpoint toward those with mental disorders. In colonial America, mental illness was viewed as a punishment for moral turpitude or a result of demon possession. The mentally ill were considered the responsibility of the family and the community, and they were treated harshly for the "sins" they had brought on themselves. When there was no one available to care for the ill person, they would often be placed in an almshouse, where other societal dependents, such as orphans, the sick, the blind, and the unemployed, were kept. Some of the mentally ill were cared for in general hospitals, modeled after Europe. It was not until 1773 that the first institution devoted solely to the mentally ill was opened: the Eastern Lunatic Asylum at Williamsburg, Virginia. Treatment of the insane at that time was still largely punitive.

With the enlightenment of the late eighteenth century came a rethinking of the treatment of the insane. The French physician Philippe Pinel and the American physician Benjamin Rush independently called for unshackling of the mentally ill in almshouses and hospitals, calling for humane treatment, although treatment was still far from humane by current standards.[452] During the same period, a new type of institution for the mentally ill was being developed in Europe. William Tuke's Retreat at York, England, was founded by the Society of Friends in 1792. It operated on the concept that the mentally ill needed "moral treatment"; they needed to learn right from wrong through a reward-punishment system. The Retreat stimulated the establishment of several institutions for the treatment of the mentally ill modeled after the York Retreat: Asylum at Frankford, Pennsylvania (1813); Bloomingdale Asylum, New York City (1821); McLean Asylum, Boston (1818); and the Hartford Retreat, Connecticut (1824). These institutions were primarily run by the middle class for the middle class, and the poor were often excluded. During 1830 to 1860, there was a proliferation of public asylums that served the poor. Their superintendents boasted about the high rates of "cure" of public asylums by counting every discharge as a cure regardless of the actual state of the patient. This was a time of great optimism for cure or at least humane treatment of the mentally ill in a nonthreatening environment separate from society. Within just a few decades, however, confidence in the effectiveness of the asylum at rehabilitating the mentally ill waned. Overcrowding of asylums and an influx of immigrants, the poor, the criminally insane, and the mentally retarded contributed to the pessimism. The asylum had begun to assume a custodial function in society. By the turn of the century, however, with advancements in medicine occurring, there was a new-found optimism about the treatment of the mentally ill. This period, which lasted until World War II, has come to be known as the Mental Hygiene Period.[453]

Deinstitutionalization

Deinstitutionalization was the phenomenon associated with the community care movement that decried the kind of treatment common in overcrowded state hospitals. The phenomenon began in the late 1950s, with a sharp decrease in length of stay and only a small increase in rate of admission to state mental hospitals. This change led to a continuously declining census in the state hospitals throughout the 1950s and 1960s. The next phase of deinstitutionalization began in the 1960s, when the effectiveness of antipsychotic drugs became apparent; thereafter, closing of many of the hospitals to new patients began, and the rate of discharge continued to exceed the rate of admissions. The result was that the total census of state and county mental hospitals went from a peak level of 558,922 in 1955 to 193,436 in 1975.[454] Currently, there are approximately 100,000 patients in state and county mental hospitals nationwide. Many of the former state hospital patients experienced the phenomenon of transinstitutionalization by coming to reside in nursing homes and half-way houses,[455] whereas others joined their families, moved into community rooming houses, or became homeless.[456]

A fairly recent motive behind deinstitutionalization and the closure of large state hospitals has been the opportunity for states to shift part of the costs of caring for the chronically mentally ill to the federal government by releasing indigent, disabled persons from state care to the community where they would be eligible for assistance from Medicaid or Medicare, the public health care entities created in 1965.[457] Another motive has been pressure from civil rights advocates and the courts to have individuals treated in the "least restrictive environment." More recently, new advances in psychiatric medication (e.g., clozapine) have, once again, led to discharge of more institutionalized patients to community programs. Although the cost of such medications can be several thousand dollars annually, medication is more effective and less expensive than hospitalization. Third-party payers often will not pay for care in half-way houses or day-care programs, however, resulting in incomplete, unsatisfactory care for many of the mentally ill.

Community Mental Health Centers

An outgrowth of deinstitutionalization and the Community Mental Health Movement, the Community Mental Health Centers Act of 1963 and its subsequent amendments established federal matching funds for the creation and staffing of Community Mental Health Centers (CMHCs) across the U.S. The original intent of the Act was to provide community-based mental health care with an emphasis on prevention. CMHCs were required to provide in-patient, out-patient, emergency, partial hospitalization, and community educational services for the mentally ill in catchment areas of 75,000 to 200,000 people. Eventually, it was hoped, the states would take over the funding of CMHCs as each became an integral part of the community and state funds became available from decreased expenditures on the shrinking state mental hospital system. Unfortunately, substantial savings from the closure of state mental hospitals were never realized, and states seemed to have little incentive to take over the funding of CMHCs. By 1973, 493 CMHCs had been created with federal money, whereas state support of the centers, rather than increased, actually decreased. Despite these financial difficulties, CMHCs continued to grow (789 centers by October 1980), and several studies showed that they increased access to mental health services for the poor. Community Mental Health Centers still provide a large fraction of public mental health services, even though there are many hundreds of catchment areas throughout the country that lack a CMHC. Several uncontrolled outcome studies indicate that the services provided by CMHCs have a measurable positive impact on the functioning and quality of life of the mentally ill.

Privatization

Since the 1970s, there has been a significant shift from a time when the majority of in-patient psychiatric care was provided in public institutions to a time when fewer than 50% of psychiatric beds are government-owned. Privatization, the transfer of services from public to private organizations, has been spurred on by a number of factors. The advent of more restrictive prospective payments tied to fixed payments for illness categorized under diagnostic-related groups decreased occupancy of medical beds, and the relative profitability of psychiatric services in the health services market led to conversion of medical beds to psychiatric beds in many private community hospitals.[458] Deinstitutionalization of the mentally ill led to a concurrent increase in demand for psychiatry beds in general hospitals. State legislatures were also influenced by the common perception in the 1980s that public mental health care (along with other public services) was less cost-efficient than care provided in the private sector. States also loosened regulation of hospitals in the 1980s by eliminating the certificate of need for hospital expansion or creation.[459] Finally, destigmatization of treatment for mental disorders, which has come from increasing acceptance of mental health care as a part of general health care, has brought greater demand in the market for psychiatric services.

One result of privatization is that free care by physicians and hospitals has become less readily available than it was in the past for the millions of Americans who lack health coverage, because the "informal norms and practices upon which the poor and uninsured . . . have so long relied to pay for medical care are rapidly eroding in the face of competitive pressures within American medicine."[460] The solution, according to Dorwart and Epstein, is increased integration of public and private programs. Privatization has also changed the way many psychiatrists practice. Increasingly, psychiatrists are asked to assume, through managed care programs, some of the financial risk of their patients' care.

Mental Health Policy Reform

As the complex U.S. health care system is reformed, both by the private sector and potentially by the federal government, large-scale changes in the financing and delivery of mental health and substance abuse services are occurring. The private sector has clearly moved toward a managed mental health care model in many states in which managed care health plans have large market penetration. The Clinton Health Security Act proposes to eliminate the different coverage of mental and general health care by the year 2001. The accomplishment of this goal, many policy analysts claim, is dependent on the success of managed competition at controlling overall health care costs. Proponents of a single-payer model of health care reform argue that equitable coverage of mental and general health care would be provided under such a system without the intrusive micromanagement that is characteristic of many managed care plans. Global budgets, under a single-payer model, some argue, would promote payment for a system that maximizes health and minimizes cost. It is not clear, however, whether those seeking mental health care under a single-payer system would face longer queues to obtain care than those seeking general health care, despite theoretical "guaranteed" equal coverage.

CONCLUSION ❖

Mental disorders are prevalent, costly to society, and increasingly thought of as having a biological basis. The mental health care system is increasingly specialized and effective, yet it is inaccessible to many of the people who need it most. Universal, nondiscriminatory coverage of mental disorders under national health reform would likely be very costly, but the total direct and indirect costs to society of mental illness would, in the long run, decrease if mental disorders were appropriately covered.

❖   Suggested Reading   ❖

Rochefort DA. Handbook on mental health policy in the United States. Westport, CT: Greenwood Press, 1989.
The Bible of mental health policy. Twenty chapters covering many major topics in great detail, with plenty of historical references. Not a quick read, but an excellent resource.
Mechanic D. Mental health and social policy. Englewood, NJ: Prentice Hall, 1989.
A shorter, more readable book written by a well-respected sociologist who has written extensively about mental health. Provides a discussion of the basic aspects of the mental health and social systems and the policies that create and sustain them, as well as a much-needed balanced critique of the current mental health system.
Talbot JA, Hales RE, Keill SL. Textbook of administrative psychiatry. Washington, DC: American Psychiatric Press, 1992.
Excellent introduction to the rapidly growing field of administrative psychiatry. Covers basic management concepts, program development in the public sector, and administration in private sector, as well as legal and ethical issues, concluding with a discussion of evaluation of outcomes of care.
Institute of Medicine. Reducing the risks for mental disorders: frontiers for preventive intervention research. Mrazek PJ, Haggerty RJ, eds. Washington, DC: National Academy Press, 1994.

Landmark review of the literature on prevention of mental disorders by the Institute of Medicine, which was commissioned by Congress and published in 1994. The 484-page report draws on our understanding of the prevention of physical and mental illness (as well as on a group of four core sciences that contribute to our understanding of the prevention of mental disorders) to identify risk factors and to illustrate preventive measures for five major mental illnesses. The latter half of the book sets an agenda for prevention and health promotion efforts, particularly for research in these areas, for the coming decade.

19

Long-Term Care

Elizabeth Onyemelukwe and John Delfs

Over the last quarter century, the plight of the elderly and the disabled members of our communities have gained increasing public attention due to the lack of access to, the rising cost of, and the inability to ensure quality in long-term care.

This chapter begins with a discussion of why long-term care policy is important. The analysis then presents an overview defining long-term care, the population it serves, the forms of it, and who pays for it. And finally, the specific challenges facing long-term care and the policy recommendations to deal with them are reviewed.

WHY IS LONG-TERM CARE POLICY IMPORTANT? ❖

The American population is aging, and, as the "baby boomer" generation ages, they will need long-term care options that currently do not exist. In 1987, 29.8 million Americans (one in eight) were 65 or older. It is projected that by 2020, that population would reach 51.4 million (one in five Americans). Figure 19.1 estimates that the number of elderly needing assistance with activities of daily living will double to 13.8 million, and the number of elderly requiring nursing home care will more than triple to 5.3 million by the year 2030.

Due to the increasing number of clients needing long-term care, the percentage of health care dollars spent on long-term care will only increase. It was estimated that in 1988, the United States spent $52.8 billion on long-term care.[461] The Con-

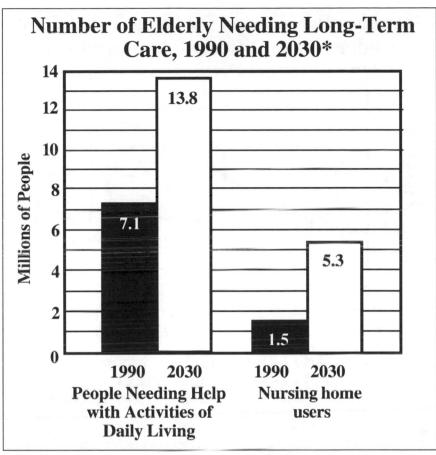

Number of Elderly Needing Long-Term Care, 1990 and 2030*

Millions of People

14
13.8
12
10
8
7.1
6
5.3
4
2
1.5
0

1990   2030   1990   2030
People Needing Help   Nursing home
with Activities of   users
Daily Living

Figure 19.1 Number of elderly persons needing long-term care, 1990 and 2030. (Adapted from Pepper Commission. A Call for Action; Final Report. Sept. 1990.)

gressional Budget Office projects that expenditures for long-term care could increase between 50% and 200% between 1985 and 2000.[462] The wide range in the estimated increases is due to the additive uncertainty of factors that affect costs, which include growth of the elderly population (demographics), escalating medical costs (prices), and trends of increased service needs per person (intensity). The projected spending based on these three factors is presented in Figure 19.2.

Currently, there exists a lack of access to long-term care for many Americans, and this problem is expected to worsen as the population of elderly increases in size. There is known to be wide variation between regions of the U.S. with regard to availability of nursing home beds and home care. Furthermore, long-term care insurance is too expensive for the majority of elderly and disabled.

Defining, measuring, and monitoring quality in long-term care facilities has long been a problem facing policy makers. Furthermore, measurement of quality

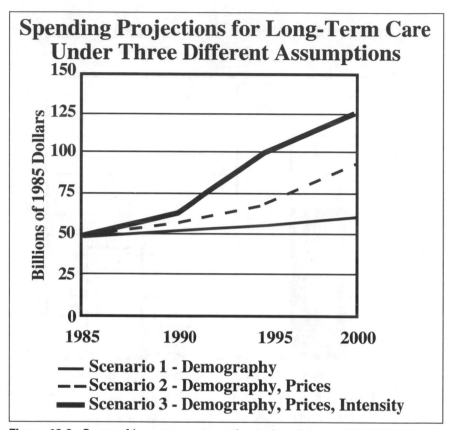

Spending Projections for Long-Term Care Under Three Different Assumptions

Figure 19.2 Costs of long-term care estimated to the year 2000. Wide range in estimates due to a variety of additive factors such as growth of the elderly population (demographics), escalating medical prices, and increasing service needs per person (intensity). (Adapted from GAO, Long term care for the elderly: Issues of need, access, and cost. GAO/HRD-89-4. Nov, 1998.)

placed too much emphasis on such things as structure, credentials, and written policies, and too little on quality-of-life issues. In addition, surveys have been unreliable and of questionable validity, a result of the forewarning of institutions and agencies, lack of use of opinions and experiences of recipients of care, and heavy weighting toward physical rather than emotional well-being.[463]

OVERVIEW OF LONG-TERM CARE ❖
Defining Long-term Care

The term ***long-term care*** was coined in the 1970s, a time in which the issue was rapidly gaining political and public attention. In their book, *Long-term care: prin-*

ciples, programs and policies, Kane and Kane define long-term care as "a set of health, personal care, and social services delivered over a sustained period of time to persons who have lost or never acquired some degree of functional capacity."[464] Central to this definition of long-term care is the concept of function. How much function does a particular person who is receiving long-term care have, and how can this be used to minimize the supports this person receives to maximize their physical and emotional well-being? The measurement of function has historically been limited to a physical scale. It is important to keep in mind, however, that function has important cognitive and emotional factors, which, although more difficult to measure, are crucial in the evaluation of the need for long-term care.

Due to the many variations in the definition of long-term care with regard to goals for functioning, focus of service, locus of service, mix of services and service providers, duration and intensity of care, and nature of public sector involvement, long-term care has remained a highly complex policy issue.

Measuring the Need for Long-term Care

The need for long-term care has traditionally been measured by evaluation of the performance of ***activities of daily living (ADLs)*** and ***instrumental activities of daily living (IADLs).*** The ADL index measurers the ability to perform basic functions of daily living, and it includes getting in or out of a bed or a chair, eating, using toilet facilities, continence, bathing, and dressing. The more ADL dependencies a person has, the more dependent they are considered; five to six dependencies is considered very dependent.

The IADL index measures ability to perform household and mobility activities, including meal preparation, taking medicine, managing money, making telephone calls, getting oneself around outside, and going places beyond walking distance. These factors are a measure of one's ability to manage independently in the community; therefore, they are not used with nursing home residents.

The ADL and IADL indices are not capable of providing information beyond basic yes/no answers about ability to perform the various activities measured. They also provide no information on the underlying reason for an inability to perform an activity, such as whether a person cannot independently bathe as a result of physical limitation or cognitive dysfunction. These are important issues of clarity that policy makers must consider, because they may profoundly affect the ability to make projections for the need for care, which should ideally take into account cognitive, physical, and psychological/emotional limitation.

Other more detailed indices have been developed in response to the problems of accuracy inherent to the ADL/IADL system. These systems include the OARS Multidimensional Functional Assessment Questionnaire and the Resource Utilization Groups (RUG) system. Both evaluation techniques use a much more detailed system than ADL and IADL indices to evaluate function. The RUG system, of which there are several variations, groups nursing home residents according to their service needs, and it serves as a basis for reimbursement of nursing home services.

Another problem in the needs assessment process is translation of measured functional disability into a set of services. Definitions of what comprises a specific service are lacking, and there is a problem in measuring whether a particular need is being addressed by a particular service. The implications of these problems for long-term care policy have been evident for many years, and they will continue to present serious challenges to policy makers.

What Is the Population Needing Long-Term Care?

According to a GAO Report in 1990, an estimated 9 to 11 million of the nation's population (one in 20 Americans) required help with ADLs or IADLS, or both. Approximately two thirds of this long-term care population were elderly (>65 years); the vast majority are members of the community, and approximately 20% live in nursing homes. The remaining third of persons requiring long-term care, those less than 65, resided predominantly in the community.[465] Figure 19.3 illustrates the age and residence breakdown of those needing long-term care. In addition, women were disproportionately represented, both in the population requiring home or community care and in the nursing home population.

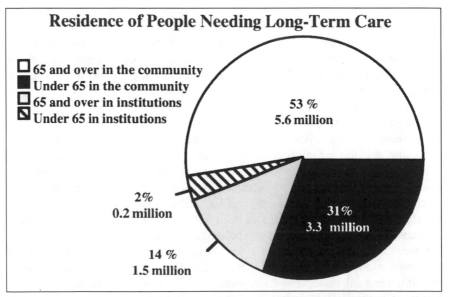

Figure 19.3 Residence of people needing long-term care. (Adapted from Pepper Commission. A Call for Action: Final Report. Sept. 1990.)

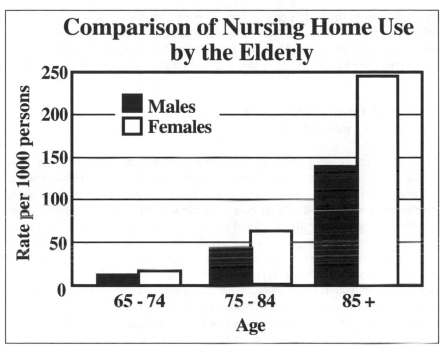

Figure 19.4 Use of nursing homes by the elderly in 1985. (Adapted from Kane and Kane, Springer, NY, 1987. Data source: Vital and Health Statistics, No. 135. DHHS Pub. No. (PHS) 87-1250. Hyattsville, MD: Public Health Service, 1987.)

The rate of utilization of long-term care services increases dramatically with age. The National Long-term Care (NLTC) survey of 1982 illustrated this well, showing three times as many people aged 85 and older reporting needs for help with ADLs as persons aged 65 to 74[466] (Figure 19.4).

A 1985 study by Cornoni-Huntley and associates showed age- and sex-specific rates of dependency with at least one ADL tended to double with successive 10-year age groups. The lifetime risk of entering a nursing home is approximately 20%.[467] Unfortunately, the bulk of work done on estimations of this risk for long-term care need has been cross-sectional rather than longitudinal. Projections of need have therefore been based on estimations of population growth combined with estimations of risk extrapolated from cross-sectional studies.

Much work on identification of the actual risk factors for entry into nursing homes has been done, although there are no definitive studies. Americans 65 and older represent the fastest growing segment of the U.S. population; of this segment, persons 85 and older are the most rapidly expanding group.[462] On the basis of these projections, it becomes clear that the need for long-term care will continue to increase into the twenty-first century, although, as mentioned, few longitudinal studies have been done.

Disabilities in the elderly population are most commonly the result of strokes or chronic illness, including heart disease, osteoporosis, and dementias, such as Alzheimer's. In the under-65 population, major causes include cerebral palsy, mental retardation, multiple sclerosis, and brain trauma resulting from accidents.

Forms of Long-Term Care
Formal vs Informal Care

Long-term care is categorized as either formal or informal care. *Informal care* refers to care given to dependents living at home, by family members or friends. An analysis of the NLTCS of 1982 revealed that up to 74% of persons receiving care at home received all of their care from friends and family.[468] Informal care, although not paid for by the individual receiving care, is nevertheless very costly, in terms of time and resources that go into the giving of such care. According to one survey done in 1987, an average of four hours per day were spent by care-givers of informal care doing such tasks as shopping, household work, and assistance with personal hygiene, among others. One half of these persons participated in administration of medicines.[469] Another analysis of the 1982 NLTCS showed that even with all this help from family and friends, a large number of elderly persons, especially those with higher levels of dependency, do not get sufficient care.[470]

Formal care includes care given both to the individual at home and to individuals in nursing homes. It refers to care given in the home by visiting nurses and home health aides, while including all nursing home care. The costs of formal care are tremendous, with bills of up to $25,000 per month for nursing home stays. Formal care services administered in the home are also substantial; average payments in 1982 for a severely disabled person were $439 per month.[462]

Home vs. Community Care

Home care is loosely defined as "the provision of equipment and services to the patient in the home for the purpose of restoring and maintaining his or her maximal level of comfort, function, and health."[471] The provider of home care is usually a family member or a friend, but it may also include physicians, nurse practitioners and specialists, registered nurses, physical and occupational therapists, social workers, rehabilitation workers, home health aides, and homemakers. Home care is most often provided on a short-term basis, and it is largely targeted to the acutely ill during the posthospitalization period.

During the 1970s and 1980s, there was a rapid proliferation of home health agencies (mostly skilled nursing facility–based home care and proprietary agencies) providing a wide range of services. The breakdown of services provided and the percentage of agencies providing those services are listed in Table 19.1. It is thought that much of the growth was in response to the Medicare Prospec-

Table 19.1 Types of In-Home Services
Provided by Home Health Agencies

Types of Service Offered	% Providing the Service
Skilled Nursing	100.0
Home Health Aide/Homemaker	94.5
Physical Therapy	83.0
Speech Therapy	65.4
Medical Social Services	52.8
Occupational	49.3
Nutritional Guidance	23.8
Appliances and Equipment	23.0
Pharmaceutical Service	6.4
Interns and Residents	0.8

Proportion of home health agencies providing various types of in-home services.
N = 4271. (Adapted from Kane & Kane, Springer, NY, 1987.)

tive Payment System, which provided an incentive for early discharge from hos
pitals, resulting in sicker patients being discharged to home, needing relatively
intensive care.

Community care refers to a wide range of services, from adult daycare and
respite care, to the Continuing Care Retirement Community (CCRC). Adult daycare is of two major types: social and medical. Social daycare centers care mostly
for elderly who are more functional, and they provide socialization, educational
programs, and various activities. Social centers are generally sponsored by church,
community, or government agencies, and they provide low-cost or free services.
Medical centers serve a more dependent population, and they are usually fee-for-
service agencies, often associated with nursing homes or lifecare communities
(CCRCs). Respite care refers to care provided to relieve informal caregivers, and
it may range from daycare to short-term nursing home stays.

The CCRC is a growing industry in the U.S. CCRCs combine insurance; primary, acute, and long-term care; and access to community physicians and geriatric
nurses. They typically provide three levels of care, including skilled nursing, personal care/assisted living, and preventive/ambulatory care. Residents of CCRCs
must, to receive the CCRC's guarantee of lifetime access to housing and needed
health care, pay a large entry fee (median fee in 1988, $47,000) and monthly fees
(median in 1988, $830). Fees have increased at approximately 6% a year since then.

National policies are needed that will reward CCRCs for implementing cost-
saving measures and preventive care rather than penalizing them. On Lok CCRC
in San Francisco is a successful program that has shown ability to care for residents with acute illness at lower cost than hospital care. CCRCs such as On Lok
are, however, prevented from undertaking early-stage prevention because they are
required to enroll people only after they are deemed qualified for nursing home
admission. In addition, programs are reimbursed less for treating people with acute
illness in their own facilities than if the residents were admitted to the hospital.[472]

Nursing Home Care

Nursing home care has changed dramatically over the last decade. The traditional nursing home, spanning all levels of care, from relatively acute medical care to custodial care, has steadily become less and less common. Rather, the impact of the Prospective Payment System is evident, and nursing homes have become much more specialized, dividing themselves into either skilled nursing facilities (SNFs) or intermediate care facilities (ICFs). Increasingly, nursing homes have developed units that specialize in the care of specific types of dependent persons, such as an Alzheimer's Unit. Persons requiring custodial care only are moving from nursing homes back into the community and receiving home care or moving to assisted-living facilities. Assisted-living facilities provide care to persons who are, for the most part, able to live independently, but need assistance with functions such as household chores, management of finances, shopping, and other such activities on the list of IADLs. Persons in assisted-living situations may also need some help with ADLs, more often due to physical rather than cognitive impairment.

By 1988, 76% of nursing homes were certified as SNFs or ICFs, or they were dually certified.[473] The care needs of residents at SNFs tend to be greater and of a more medical nature relative to those of residents at ICFs. As a result, certification requirements are much stricter for SNFs than ICFs. In 1985, approximately 75% of the nation's nursing homes (69% of the bed supply) were proprietary, and 41% of all facilities were affiliated with nursing home chains.[473] Figure 19.5 shows the characteristics of the different long-term care facilities, with regard to beds per 1,000 persons age 65 and over, occupancy rates, and average size.

Who Pays for Long-Term Care?

It is estimated that in 1988, $52.8 billion was spent on long-term care. In 1985, long-term care costs were shared between public and private sources (52 and 48%, respectively), and they were mainly for nursing home care.[462] Figure 19.6 shows that the vast majority of persons needing long-term care live at home, and yet the predominance of expenditures for long-term care occurs in the small percentage who lives in nursing homes. Given the extreme complexity of financing issues in long-term care, examination of the sharing of costs is perhaps most efficiently done by separating long-term care into the two broad categories of home/community care and nursing home care. Table 19.2 delineates national long-term care spending for 1988.

Home/Community Care

Home and community care are provided through unpaid informal care, by out-of-pocket purchasing of services, by insurers and private organizations, and through public programs, mainly Medicare or Medicaid. Figure 19.7 describes the sources of home care services for the severely disabled elderly in 1989. Estimates of total

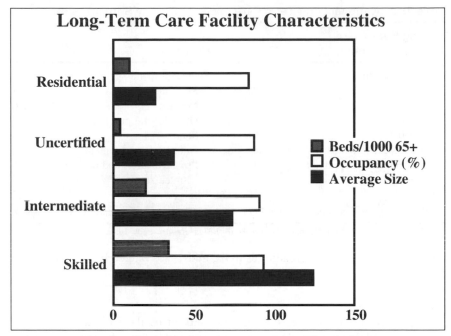

Figure 19.5 Characteristics of long-term care facilities, 1986. (Adapted from Kane and Kane, Springer, NY, 1987. Data source: Vital and Health Statistics, No. 135. DHHS Pub. No. (PHS) 87-1250. Hyattsville, MD: Public Service, 1987.)

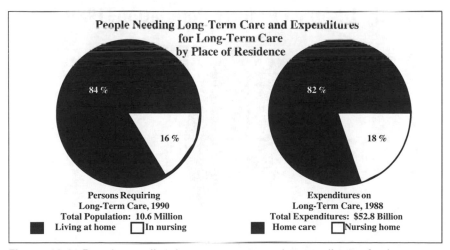

Figure 19.6 People needing long-term care and expenditures for long-term care by place of residence. (Adapted from Pepper Commission. A Call for Action: Final Report. Sept. 1990.)

Table 19.2 National Long-Term Care Expenditures, by Source, 1988

Nursing Home Care (Dollars in Billions)		Home Care	
Source of Spending		Source of Spending	
Medicaid	$19.2	Medicaid	$ 3.3
Medicare	0.8	Medicare	2.6
Other federal	1.0	Other federal programs	0.6
Other state	0.1	State	0.5
Out-of-pocket payments	20.8	Out-of-pocket payments	2.1
Private insurers and private organizations	1.3	Private insurers and private organizations	0.6
Total	$43.1*	Total	$ 9.7
*Numbers do not total due to rounding		Total long-term expenditures	$52.8

Adapted from Pepper Commission. *A Call for Action: Final Report.* Sept. 1990.

annual home health care expenditures in the mid-1980s ranged from $4 to $8 billion. Predictions of costs of up to $25 billion by 1995 have been made.[474]

Informal Care

As mentioned, informal care, although not paid for by the individual receiving care, does result in substantial costs to the nation and to the individuals providing care. Out-of-pocket expenditures for home health care (including nursing, speech, occupational, and physical therapy, home health aide services, and medical or

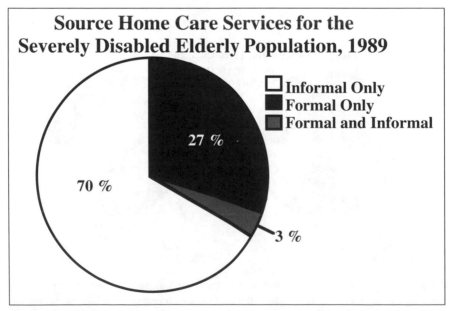

Figure 19.7 Source home care services for the severely disabled elderly population, 1989. (Adapted from Pepper Commission. A Call for Action: Final Report. Sept. 1990.)

social services; excluding adult daycare, meals, and transportation) were estimated at $3.7 billion in 1985, approximately half the total expenditures on home health care and approximately 80% of private home health care cost. Insurers or private organizations paid only 20%.

Medicare

There has historically been a great lack of support by public programs for long-term care services administered at home or in the community. Medicare, although it is the largest public payer for home services to the elderly, was designed primarily for and limited to acute or postacute care conditions. Coverage for daily home health care was extended to 38 consecutive days by the Medicare Catastrophic Coverage Act of 1988, but it was still limited to acute conditions. This act was repealed in 1989 due to intense opposition by the elderly led by the American Association of Retired Persons(AARP); the passing and repeal of this act is discussed in greater detail later in this chapter. Medicare is an entitlement program; it is therefore required to provide coverage for all persons who meet eligibility requirements.

By the mid-1980s, home care was described as the fastest growing Medicare service. Total payments were up to $2.0 billion by 1989. In 1987, Medicare national average home care costs were approximately $43 per day.

Medicaid

Medicaid is the state-based program for long-term care services. Medicaid pays for home care to low income persons. Individuals must qualify through a home health benefit (required by the federal government) and a personal care benefit (not required). States are given the authority to decide on the scope and the duration of services, payment rates, and eligibility for home health care. Medicaid personal care, offered by only half of the states, depends on individuals as opposed to agencies to provide care, subject to doctor authorization and nurse supervision. Medicaid long-term care dollars spent on home care total only approximately one tenth that spent on nursing home care.

Between 1982 and 1988, Medicaid expenditures for home care more than quadrupled. Much of this growth came as a result of personal care (defined as Medicaid-covered services delivered in the home by qualified professionals), a new category of service established in 1985.

Other Federal Funding

Three additional federal social service programs, the Veterans Administration (VA), the Social Services Block Grant Program, and Title III of the Older Americans Act, provide for a wide range of home and community-based long-term care services. Although eligibility requirements for these programs are not as strict as for Medicare and Medicaid, they are very limited in terms of dollars available for funding of care. The VA operates both an adult daycare and a hospital-based home care program. The block grant program allows states to provide adult daycare, adult foster care, and home health aide services. The Older Americans Act provides homemaker and home health services, in-home respite care, and adult daycare. Data on the Title III and the VA programs reveal that, compared with the number of dependent elderly in communities nationwide, a limited number of persons receive needed care.

Nursing Home Care

As mentioned, the vast majority of national expenditures on long-term care are spent on nursing home care. Figure 19.8 shows the 1990 breakdown of sources of payment for nursing home care.

Private Sources

Out-of-pocket expenditures in 1985 were approximately 96% of privately paid nursing home care ($16.2 billion). Other private sources covered the remaining 4% ($600 million).[462] Out-of-pocket payments for nursing home care increased at a rate of 420% between 1975 and 1985, as compared with a rate of 326% over the same period for Medicaid expenditures.[475] In the elderly population, expenditures on nursing homes are the major reason for catastrophic expenses. In 1990, for approximately 80% of elderly people, the monthly cost of nursing home care was

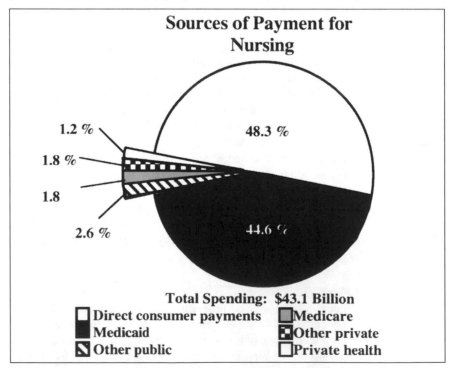

Figure 19.8 Sources of payment for nursing. (Adapted from Pepper Commission. A Call for Action: Final Report. Sept. 1990.)

greater than their monthly income from Social Security, pensions, and assets.[465]
The 1985 National Nursing Home Survey revealed that of elderly nursing home
residents, up to half depended primarily on personal income or family financial
support to cover the first month of nursing home care.

Medicare
Medicare only covers nursing home if the person needs daily physical therapy or
skilled nursing care. Again, these benefits are limited—100 days after at least a
three-day hospital stay, extended to 150 days per year by the Catastrophic Coverage Act. Cost-sharing, set at one eighth the cost of the Medicare hospital deductible, begins after the first 20 days of a nursing home stay. Up to 75% of people
receiving Medicare benefits stay on after the 20 days of full coverage. If a nursing
home resident does not require skilled care, they cannot receive Medicare benefits
at all. In 1990, this profile described up to one third of elderly persons entering
nursing homes. The Nursing Home Survey of 1985 estimated 4.9% of elderly
nursing home residents were relying on Medicare benefits to cover their costs.

Medicaid
In 1990, Medicaid covered 90% of public financing for nursing home care, more
than 40% of all nursing home revenues. Individuals qualify for Medicaid coverage if they are either disabled with low enough incomes to qualify for assistance
(under the SSI program) or if they "spend down" until they are eligible. As described by the Pepper Commission report, the spending down process occurs in
two stages. In the first stage, to get Medicaid benefits, a person's assets must be
lower than a certain amount. In the second stage, a person must, after exhausting
all their saving/assets, spend down their incomes to a certain level to receive benefits. All income, except for a very small amount (in 1990, typically $30/mo), must
go toward the cost of long-term care. The difference between personal contribution and the nursing reimbursement rate is covered by Medicaid.

Role of Private Insurance
Private long-term care insurance has historically not had a large role in the financing of long-term care. According to HCFA, only 1% of nursing home expenditures were financed by private insurance in 1991. The very nature of long-term
care, with the likelihood that claims will not be made for a long time after policies
have been purchased, leads to high levels (higher than in other insurance markets)
of uncertainty about costs of home or nursing home care, and it therefore creates
a major barrier to insurers considering entering the market. In addition, the economic problem of adverse selection, whereby people more likely to need long-
term care are more likely to buy insurance, represents a serious risk to insurers.
Furthermore, as described in the GAO report, there is widespread public belief that
Medicare and Medigap insurance cover long-term health costs, and that Medicaid
is a free long-term care program.

Between 1986 and 1989, the private long-term care insurance market expanded rapidly; the number of companies offering coverage increased from 15 to 118. Between 1987 and 1989, the number of policies sold increased from 423,000 to more than 1.5 million.[465] According to the GAO report, this figure represented coverage of only approximately 1.5% of the elderly population. By 1990, it was estimated that 3 to 5% of elderly owned policies.[465] A study by Rivlin and Wiener suggested that long-term care insurance will remain unaffordable to two thirds of the elderly by 2016 to 2020, partly because long-term insurance is generally sold to individuals rather than to groups, which results in higher premiums.[476]

Long-term care policies generally offer only partial coverage for nursing home or home care costs. In addition, those policies sold initially had several benefit restrictions, including exclusions for certain conditions (e.g., Alzheimer's disease), limited coverage for home care, requirements for a hospital stay, or skilled care before coverage of long-term personal care. Worse yet for policy holders, benefits were at a fixed dollar value at the time of purchase, meaning that claims made many years later might be entirely inadequate. Policies developed later offered broader coverage, including coverage of Alzheimer's. Many no longer required hospital stays or skilled nursing prior to nursing home coverage. During 1988 and 1989, there were further expansions in coverage; policies offered 50% of purchased daily nursing home benefit. State regulators made some effort to protect consumers: The National Association of Insurance Commissioners (NAIC) developed a regulatory framework for long-term care insurance.

Long-term care insurance has indeed continued to grow rapidly into the 1990s. In 1992, private insurance companies sold $1 billion in premiums. Despite this growth, HCFA estimates that in 1991 only 1% of the $60 billion in nursing home care costs were covered by private insurance.[477] Furthermore, in 1990, despite the efforts of the NAIC, many long-term care insurance policies still limited periods of coverage, and insurers were still permitted to raise premiums or to cancel policies if experience rating deemed it financially necessary.

LONG-TERM CARE POLICY CHALLENGES   ❖

We now turn to look at the specific policy issues involved in providing long-term care, then briefly examine the most recent attempt to reform long-term care, The Medicare Catastrophic Coverage Act of 1988. Finally we will look at proposals from several groups for improving the current provisions of long-term care.

Issues Specific to Home and Community Care

One of the major policy problems for home and community care is a lack of definition of what these methods of care comprise, as well as a lack of consensus on what their principal objectives and necessary elements are. One reason for this lack was the presence of two models of home and community care, the medical-postacute and the social-supportive.[478] This led to tremendous difficulties in determining whether the right people were being served.[479] Complicating these issues is the fact that these forms of long-term care are seen, and attention is focused on them only, as cost-saving options to nursing home care, rather than entities of value in and of themselves. Several studies looking into cost of home and community care have shown that they do not lead to savings; they are in fact often more expensive than nursing home care. In an analysis of demonstration programs, Weissert and colleagues concluded that broadened coverage of homemaker services is not associated with significant improvements in client function, and it significantly increased costs of care. Furthermore, a report by HCFA in 1981 showed that most home care would in fact not substitute for expensive nursing home care, but it would serve new populations.

Given concern about insufficient spending on home care, Section 2176 of the Omnibus Budget Reconciliation Act of 1981 authorized a waiver of Medicaid requirements, which, it was hoped, would encourage states to provide broader home services. The waiver allowed states to loosen eligibility requirements for coverage, but it permitted restriction of eligibility on a geographic and population basis. The states were required to keep the total number of people served and Medicaid long-term care expenditures at or below the levels that would have been reached without the waiver. All except eight states had programs as of February 1988. Unfortunately, the programs did not lead to the expected expansion of coverage of home services, mostly due to the difficulty faced by the states in meeting the federal limits on spending and number of persons served, as well as to constraints on state budgets. Furthermore, the assumption by the federal government that broader and less expensive home coverage would lead to savings did not take into account the fact that many persons living at home, who could more appropriately be taken care of in a nursing home, would qualify for home care, leading to increased total numbers of persons covered and increased total dollars spent on long-term care.

Introduction of the Medicare Prospective Payment System in 1982 forced more attention on home and community care. This system, which has been described as the definitive policy event for home care, significantly changed discharge incentives for hospitals. Sicker patients, needing intense and continuous home care, were now being sent home after shorter hospital stays. This practice not only impacted heavily on home care agencies, but also contributed further to the huge burden on informal givers of care. It was estimated that as a result of the prospective payment, dependent persons and their caregivers would have to absorb 21 million caregiver days annually.[480]

HCFA reports that thus far in the 1990s, 80 to 90% of home care is provided by informal networks of family and friends. Very little progress has been made in this area, and insurance companies have only recently begun to address the problem. Disability policies, developed by UNUM, a large insurer in Maine, allow beneficiaries to use benefits to pay providers of informal care.[480] Justification of home care as a cost-saving option to nursing home care was largely unsuccessful, as described earlier. There is, however, a need to demonstrate definitively the benefits of home care with regard to quality of life issues, as well as to improve efficiency of home care delivery, given that the vast majority of elderly and disabled prefer to be cared for at home or in the community.

A number of bills on home care were introduced during the late 1980s, all combining nursing home and home care coverage. The most important of these bills was the Medicare Long-term Home Care Catastrophic Protection Act of 1987, sponsored by Congressman Pepper. Included in the bill was a home care benefit financed by Medicare, based on dependency in two ADLs. This bill was defeated in 1988. Further attempts to provide increased home care coverage, none very significant, were made with the Medicare Catastrophic Coverage Act. The Pepper Commission did integrate the major features of the Pepper Bill, although in a more restrictive form, into its recommendations for long-term care. The other most prominent effort to expand home care was made by the Physicians for a National Health Program.

CCRCs presented serious problems of affordability, cost, and inadequate quality control. As Anne Somers points out in her article on CCRCs, another large problem was that of "(reconciling) essential regulatory and accreditation standards with the freedom needed to attract the necessary capital and entrepreneurial skills."[481] According to the book, *The CCRC: a viable option for long-term care?*, CCRCs would only be affordable to approximately 15% of elderly over 75 (the major target population of CCRCs) by the year 2000, and 25% of the same group in 2020.

Issues Specific to Nursing Home Care

The major policy problems of nursing home care have been issues of cost, access, and quality, all of which are closely related to payment systems. Fixed daily rates for care, especially of Medicaid recipients, has historically led to serious access problems for low income persons, because nursing homes tended to avoid the Medicaid-financed, especially those who were more dependent and required more intense care. Given that fixed per diem payment did not take into account differences in case mix among long-term care facilities, HCFA proposed changing the reimbursement system for SNF care into a prospective case-mix–based system, which would alter incentives to accept residents requiring lighter care.

A review by the Institute of Medicine in 1986 concluded that adequate reimbursement alone was insufficient to ensure adequate quality of care. Their report endorsed a stricter federal regulatory process, in addition to consolidation of SNF and ICF criteria into one set of standards. They also proposed a thorough revision of all standards, with greater emphasis on outcomes, civil rights, and quality of life.[482]

The reimbursement system of nursing home care with regard to differential reimbursement of SNF versus ICF care further contributed to the problems. Medicare covered care in an SNF, but not ICF care, which led to regional variations in the availability of different forms of nursing home care not based on need for care, but based only on reimbursement patterns. As mentioned, the nursing home industry was also profoundly affected by Medicare Prospective Payment.

The result of Medicaid requirements was frequently impoverishment of both nursing home residents and their spouses. An analysis of data in 1987 showed that seven of 10 elderly persons living alone would spend down their income below the federal poverty level within 13 weeks of admission to a nursing home, and those with incomes between $6,000 and $10,000 would be impoverished within six weeks. Even the changes introduced by the Catastrophic Coverage Act, although helpful in providing protection for spouses, were limited by the fact that the majority of nursing home residents were single and were still required to give up all their financial resources to pay for their care and to receive benefits. In addition, Medicaid was subject to wide variation from state to state in terms of amounts states would pay toward nursing home care, commonly resulting in discrimination against Medicaid patients.

In 1990, 20 states provided no Medicaid coverage for persons whose income exceeded a certain level, whether or not their income was sufficient to cover their nursing home care. The problem of spending down to Medicaid eligibility is still a major issue facing nursing home residents. In 1993, Medicaid paid for nearly half of all nursing home care. Regulations mentioned earlier did have some effect; spouses were permitted to protect up to $14,000. Some states allow couples to split assets evenly, providing even more protection. Two states have programs in which purchase of long-term care insurance allows people to protect their assets while receiving Medicaid benefits.[483]

Despite these changes, the problem of asset transfer, whereby people hide their wealth to qualify for Medicaid, is very present, although there is widespread disagreement on its extent. There is a report being written by the GAO on the issue, which will likely provide the first reliable data. Meanwhile, as groups such as the American Association of Homes for the Aged, representing nonprofit nursing homes, lobby to close the loopholes in divestiture policy, policy makers are busy searching for incentives that will stop the practice of asset transfer and encourage people who can afford it to pay for their long-term care expenses. Many argue that private insurance is the answer.

Medicare Catastrophic Coverage Act of 1988

This act was the largest expansion of Medicare since 1965. Catastrophic Health Insurance (CHI), as the act was abbreviated, had three main components: coverage of out-patient prescription drugs, expanded coverage of hospital care (Part A), and physician care (Part B). The act provided coverage of 50 additional days of nursing home care, as well 10 additional days of home care. The requirement of prior hospitalization for home care coverage was removed, and income protection for spouses of nursing home residents was instated. CHI established the U.S. Bipartisan Committee on Comprehensive Health Care, more commonly known as the Pepper Commission. The Commission was to make recommendations to Congress about the financing and delivery of long-term care services to the elderly and the disabled.

CHI was signed into law in July 1988, having won Congressional support by a large margin. One year later, in November 1989, it was repealed, again by a large majority. The intense opposition by the elderly, as described, was the major factor in the failure of the legislation. On close examination of the history of catastrophic coverage, however, it is clear that there were serious criticisms from both liberals and conservatives from very early on.

Despite its repeal, the Catastrophic Coverage Act did have some positive outcomes. With regard to long-term care, the spousal protection measure and the Pepper Commission were the only parts of the act to escape repeal. Perhaps its major impact was the added public attention on the issue of the serious shortcomings of long-term care for the elderly and the disabled. As John Rother, the legislative director of the AARP, stated, "If the catastrophic episode did anything it dramatized the need for a long-term care program for the American people. . .".

POLICY RECOMMENDATIONS ❖
The Pepper Commission

On the basis of their findings, the Pepper Commission concluded that federal action would be necessary to change what they called "the nation's fundamentally flawed approach to financing long-term care." They also concluded that government action should be an insurance-based strategy. The Committee unanimously adopted as their objective ". . . the development of public policies that give Americans of all ages access to coverage that provides them necessary long-term care and adequate financial protection." The Commission report states that "regardless of the strategy chosen, coverage should:

✦ Treat need for long-term care as an insurable event—that is, an event whose risk can be spread through private and/or public coverage.
✦ Be affordable to all Americans.
✦ Allow personal choice of care and setting.
✦ Assure quality care and provide for consumer protection."

In addition, the report states, "the Commission is equally committed to agreement on how to raise the financing required . . . through public and/or private means; to developing policies that control costs of current and future long-term care services, and to promoting research on preventing or reducing disabilities that create a need for long-term care."

The Commission's "Blueprint for Long-Term Care Coverage for All Americans" has nine parts, summarized as follows.

✧ Social insurance for home and community-based care and for the first three months of nursing home care, for all Americans, regardless of income.

✧ A floor of protection against impoverishment; protection of income for spouses, homes, and maintenance; and a sufficient allowance for personal needs.

✧ Measures to promote private long-term care insurance.

✧ Individuals must meet certain disability criteria.

✧ Reliance on case managers to develop and to oversee individual care plans.

✧ Social insurance portions of the public program to be fully financed by the federal government.

✧ Case managers allocate services and monitor service delivery within a budget set by the federal government.

✧ The plan is to be put into place a step at a time over a four-year period.

✧ The federal government should more aggressively contain costs and mitigate human suffering by funding a research and development program aimed at preventing, delaying, and dealing with long-term illness and disabilities.

The Commission was careful to provide an analysis of the costs of a federal limited social insurance program. The estimated new federal cost for the program was stated to be $42.8 billion—$24 billion for home care and $18.8 billion for nursing home care. The phase-in schedule and the estimated cost of the Pepper Commission Plan is shown in Table 19.3.

To raise the needed revenues, the Committee recommended three guiding criteria.

✦ Taxes should be progressive, requiring a higher contribution from those most able to bear increased tax burdens.

✦ Revenues should be able to grow fast enough to keep up with benefit growth.

✦ Contributions should come from people of all ages.

The Commission provided several suggestions for ways in which different types of taxes could be combined to come up with the necessary revenues. They emphasized, however, that there were only suggestions, and that the Committee did not endorse any particular option.

The Working Group on Long-term Care Program Design

One of the most prominent groups doing analyses of the long-term care issue and generating potential solutions is the Working Group on Long-term Care Program Design, of the Physicians for a National Health Program. In their article, "A national long-term care program for the United States," the group points out what they believe are the reasons that policy makers had for so long neglected the long-

Table 19.3 Phase-In Schedule and Cost of Commission
Long-Term Care Plan, 1990 Dollars

Year 1	
Provide limited home care benefit to all eligible persons**	
New federal cost	$10.8 billion
Year 2	
Provide initial three-month nursing home benefit	
Provide benefit for longer nursing home stays	
Begin to improve nursing home reimbursement, relative	
to Medicaid rates	
Additional federal cost from Year 1	$14.2 billion
Cumulative new federal cost, Years 1–2	25.0 billion
Year 3	
Expand home care benefit**	
Additional federal cost from Year 2	$ 7.8 billion
Cumulative new federal cost, Years 1–3	32.8 billion
Year 4	
Fully implement the home care program**	
Further improve nursing home reimbursement	
Additional federal cost from Year 3	$10.0 billion
Home care: $5.4 billion	
Nursing home care 4.6 billion	
Cumulative new federal cost, Years 1–4	$42.8 billion
Home care: $24.0 billion	
Nursing home care 18.8 billion	

*Cost estimates are presented as if each phase were fully implemented in 1990. Costs are not adjusted to reflect inflation or cost-containment savings.
**The full costs of the home care benefit reflect a budget based on a per capita payment that varies with participants' disability levels. Cost estimates assume that per capita payment for the most severely disabled would cover 1,300 hours of service per year, with lesser amounts for less severely disabled categories. Benefits would be phased in by limiting the volume of services provided to eligible individuals to lesser amounts—to 200 and 400 hours in Year 1 and Year 3, respectively. Adapted from Pepper Commission, *A Call for Action: A Final Report.* Sept. 1990.

term care issue: unwillingness to "accept long-term care as a federal responsibility in an era of cost-containment"; long-term care as a system would have to "emphasize social services, not just medical ones, with social service and nursing personnel rather than physicians often coordinating care—a model that some physicians and policy makers may find threatening"; long-term care needs are "largely invisible to policy makers because the majority of services for disabled people are provided by 'informal' caregivers, mainly female family members, neighbors, or friends."

The group proposed incorporation of long-term care into a publicly funded national health program. In coming up with their proposal, they looked at the Canadian provinces of Manitoba and British Columbia, where long-term care is a component of the health care entitlement of all citizens, without regard to age or income. In addition, they borrowed from several other proposals for long-term care in the U.S., including ones by the Pepper Commission and the AARP.

The proposal of this group is a component of the National Health Program proposed by Physicians for a National Health Program. Under this program, everyone would be covered for all medically and socially necessary services under a single public plan, which would consolidate all current federal and state long-term care programs. The benefits offered would include both home and community-based as well as nursing home care. Other services would include financial management, legal and protective services, and payment for providers of informal care. Preventive services would also be covered. The group emphasizes that services should promote independent living and support informal caregivers. They also point out the importance of culturally appropriate services.

With regard to the administrative structure of the proposal, there would be a federal mandate; each state would set up a long-term care system, with a state Long-term Care Planning and Payment Board and a network of local public long-term care agencies. This Board and the agencies would pay for covered long-term care services; the budget would be based on the number of elderly and disabled in the population, the case mix, and the cost of living. Each institutional provider (i.e., nursing home, home care agency) would negotiate a global operating budget with the local long-term care agency.

Eligibility would be based only on need, regardless of age or income. Entitlement to care would therefore replace means testing. The program would be financed by tax revenues alone, with no premiums, deductibles, copayments, or coinsurance. The group argues, as does the Pepper Commission, that removal of financial barriers to long-term care would increase demand for formal services. They refer to predictions of a possible 20% increase in nursing home use and a 50 to 100% increase in community and home health care utilization. To contain costs, they recommend utilization controls and overall budget ceilings, with incentives to local agencies to support cost-effective informal providers and community-based services. The group estimates that a total of $70 to 75 billion in new tax revenues would be needed to finance their program.

American Geriatrics Society

The American Geriatrics Society published a position paper summarizing their recommendations. Briefly, they outline five points they believe are central to the long-term care issue. They state that a comprehensive plan must be developed to establish minimum standards and a mechanism for the financing of care. They recommend a broad tax base to spread risk over the population, but they also emphasize encouragement of private funding to supplement public funds and to increase choice. The importance of linking funding to appropriateness and quality of care in home, community, and institutional settings is stressed. Finally, they strongly support inclusion of funds for education and research in long-term care.[484]

President Clinton's Health Security Act

The Health Security Act of 1993, President Clinton's proposed health care plan, has been recognized by many as the health policy proposal that has paid the most attention to long-term care issues in many years. The plan includes a home and a community care program for all ages to be included in the standard benefits package, with allowance for states to design their own community-based services system. Sliding-scale coinsurance is required in the proposed plan. In addition, HHS would set a national budget for home and community-based services, and it would allocate funds to the states, with annual increases the same as in the national budget. As with the rest of the proposal, there were few details on mechanisms of funding for long-term care.

The Clinton administration also stated that it intended to "tighten estate recovery rules, closing loopholes in order to ensure that those with substantial personal assets pay their fair share of long-term care." As a candidate, however, Clinton stated that "no Americans should have to impoverish themselves to qualify for long-term care." How these two arguably disparate goals would be reached has not been determined.

CONCLUSION   ❖

The Institute of Medicine appropriately summarized the issue of long-term care and its place in U.S. health policy: "Long-term care has been a chronic misfit in the U.S. health care and social service programs. There is no social consensus on either its definition or purposes."[485] As Somers points out, the "Catastrophic Coverage debacle left a legacy of frustration, bitterness, and Congressional distaste for any new health legislation for the elderly." Indeed, having examined the issue of long-term care and the many unsolved policy problems that remain, one realizes that over the past decade there have not been many changes in the financing and delivery of long-term care.

A major area of concern remains that of long-term care for persons under 65 years. Much of the progress made in long-term care, such as CCRCs, focuses on the elderly, who have a strong political voice in the AARP and other groups, such as United Seniors Health Cooperative in Washington, D.C. Younger persons needing long-term care have not traditionally been able to wield that political power; as a result, they have been frequently ignored in discussions of long-term care policy.

Clinton's health reform plan, which pays more attention to long-term care issues than any in many years, does offer some hope for the future of long-term care in the U.S. There is, however, much research that needs to be done to better direct long-term care policy makers. So many questions remain to be answered, from basic yet complex issues of definition of the different aspects of long-term care issues, to what cost-saving measures are most effective in each area of care.

❖ Suggested Reading ❖

Kane RA, Kane RL. Long-term care: principles, programs, and policies. New York: Springer, 1987.
> *An excellent review of the issues of long-term care. A good starting point for those interested in a more comprehensive look at the topic.*

GAO. Long term care for the elderly: issues of need, access and cost. GAO/HRD-89-4. Nov 1988.
> *Provides a look at many of the financial issues having to do with long-term care provision. A quick source of data on long-term care coverage/access issues and on the cost of that care.*

Pepper Commission. A call for action: final report. Sept. 1990.
> *An excellent primary source providing a historical review of Medicare, Medicaid, and long-term care insurance, as well as one of many viewpoints on possible solutions to the long-term care problem.*

Health and Public Policy Committee, American College of Physicians. Financing long-term care. Ann Intern Med 1988;108.
> *Provides useful data on the shortcomings of long term care financing so far, and describes another possible solution to the problem of long term care financing in the US.*

Further Reading

Chapter 1

Bergthold L. The fat kid on the seesaw: American business and health care cost containment, 1970–1990. Annu Rev Public Health 1991;12:157–175.

Coile RC Jr. The new medicine: reshaping medical practice and health care management. Rockville, MD: Aspen Publishers, 1990.

Enthoven A. Health plan. Reading, MA: Addison-Wesley, 1980.

Glassman JK. Is the government's health care cure really needed? Washington Post, 7 January 1994, G1.

Grey B. The profit motive and patient care. Cambridge, MA: Harvard University Press, 1991.

Herzlinger R. Creating new health care ventures. Gaithersburg, MD: Aspen Publishers, 1992.

Jones R. The supermeds. New York: Charles Scribner, 1988.

McKinlay JB, Stoeckle JD. Corporatization and the social transformation of doctoring. In: Salmon JW, ed. Corporate transformation.

Relman AS. The new medical industrial complex. N Engl J Med 1980;303:963–970.

Relman AS. The health care industry: where is it taking us? N Engl J Med 1991; 325:854–859.

Salmon JW, ed. The corporate transformation of health care. Amityville, NY: Baywood Publishing, 1990.

Wohl S. The medical-industrial complex. New York: Harmony, 1984.

Chapter 2

American Osteopathic Association. Yearbook and directory of osteopathic physicians, 1994 edition.

Association of American Medical Colleges. Medical school admission requirements, 1993–94. United States and Canada. Washington, DC: Association of American Medical Colleges, 1992.

Association of American Medical Colleges. Facts: applicants, matriculants and graduates, 1986–92. Washington, DC: Association of American Medical Colleges: Section for Student Services, 1992.

Personal communication. Association of American Medical Colleges, to be published in AAMC Databook on Statistical Information Related to Medical Education, Spring 1994.

Bergeisen L, ed. Minority students in medical education: facts and figures VII. Association of American Medical Colleges, Division of Minority Health, Education, and Prevention, August 1993.

Bickel J. Women in medical education: a status report. N Engl J Med 1988;319:1579–1584.

Bowman MA, Katzoff JM, et al. Estimates of physician requirements for 1990 for the specialties of neurology, anesthesiology, nuclear medicine, pathology, physical medicine and rehabilitation, and radiology. JAMA 1983;250;2624.

Bureau of Health Professions. Eighth report to the President and Congress on the status of health personnel in the United States. Washington, DC: Health Resources and Services Administration, Public Health Service, US Department of Health and Human Services, 1992.

Report of the Graduate Medical Education National Advisory Committee to the Secretary, Department of Health and Human Services, vol 1, September 30, 1980.

Bureau of Health Professions. Seventh report to the President and Congress on the status of health personnel in the United States. Washington, DC: Health Resources and Services Administration, Public Health Service, US Department of Health and Human Services, 1990.

Chassin MR. Explaining geographic variations: the enthusiasm hypothesis. Med Care 1993;31:YS37–YS44.

Council on Graduate Medical Education. Second report of the Council: the underrepresentation of minorities in medicine. Rockville, MD: Department of Health and Human Services, Bureau of Health Professions, August 1990.

Jacobsen S, Rimm A. The projected physician surplus reevaluated. Health Affairs 1987;6:48–56.

Mulhausen R, McGee J. Physician need: an alternative projection from a study of large, prepaid group practices. JAMA 1989;261:1930–34.

National Resident Matching Program (NRMP) Directory. Hospitals and programs participating in the matching program. Washington, DC: NRMP: Association of American Medical Colleges, 1993.

Physician characteristics and distribution, 1993 edition. Department of Physician Data Services, Division of Survey and Data Resources, American Medical Association, 1992.

Tarlov AR. HMO enrollment growth and physicians: the third compartment. Health Affairs 1986;5:23–35.

Wennberg J, Gittlesohn A. Variations in medical care among small areas. Sci Am 1982;246:120–134.

Wennberg JE. Variations in medical practice and hospital costs. Connecticut Med 49:444–453.

Wennberg JE. Future directions for small area variations. Med Care 1993;31:YS75–YS80.

Marder WD, et al. Physician supply and utilization by specialty: trends and projections American Medical Association Center for Health Policy Research, 1988.

Chapter 3

American Hospital Association (AHA). Guide to American hospitals and health care facilities. 1993.

American Hospital Association (AHA). Hospital statistics. 1993.

Curran WJ, Hall MA, Kaye DH. Health care law, forensic science and public policy, 4th ed. Boston: Little, Brown, 1990.

Eastaugh SR. Health care finance: economic incentives and productivity enhancement. New York: Auburn House, 1992.

Eastaugh SR. Medical economics and health finance. New York: Auburn House, 1981.

Feldstein P. Health care economics, 4th ed. New York: Delmar Publishers, 1993.

Frech HE III, ed. Health care in America: the political economy of hospitals and health insurance. San Francisco: Pacific Research Institute for Public Policy, 1988.

Harris JE. The internal organization of hospitals: some economic implications. The Bell Journal of Economics 1977; 467–482.

Lamb R, Rappaport S. Municipal bonds: the comprehensive review of tax-exempt securities and public finance. New York: McGraw-Hill, 1980.

Phelps CE. Health economics. New York: HarperCollins, 1992.

Starr P. The social transformation of American medicine. New York: Basic Books, 1982.

Weinsbrod B. The health care quadrilemma: an essay on technological change, insurance quality of care, and cost-containment. Journal of Economic Literature 1991; 29:523–532.

The sourcebook: the comparative performance of U.S. hospitals 1993. Deloitte & Touche and Health Care Investment Analysts (HCIA), October 1993.

Statistical abstract of the United States 1993. The National Data Book. U.S. Department of Commerce, Economics and Statistics Administration, and the Bureau of the Census, 1993.

Chapter 4

Economic report of The President 1994. Washington, DC: GPO, 1994.

Source book of health insurance data 1992. Washington, DC: Health Insurance Association of America, 1992.

Fein R. Medical care, medical costs, the search for a health insurance policy. Cambridge, MA: Harvard University Press, 1989.

Feldstein PJ. Health care economics. New York: Delmar, 1993.

Levit KR, Cowan CA. Health financing trends. Health Care Financing Review (1991); 13:83–94.

Newhouse JP. The economics of medical care. Reading, MA: Addison Wesley, 1978.

Starr P. The social transformation of American medicine. New York: Basic Books, 1982.

Sullivan CB, Rice T. DataWatch. Health Affairs 1991;104–115.

Chapter 5

Berkowitz ED, Wolff W. Group Health Association: a portrait of a health maintenance organization. Philadelphia: Temple University Press, 1988.

Fein R. Medical care, medical costs; the search for a health insurance policy. Cambridge, MA: Harvard University Press, 1989.

Ginzberg E, ed. The U.S. health care system, a look to the 1990s. Rowman & Allanheld, 1985:31.

Health Care Financing Administration. Notice of proposed rule making. The Federal Register 1993;58:38170–38184.

Hendricks R. A model for national health care: the history of Kaiser Permanente. Rutgers University Press, 1993.

Himmelstein D, Woolhandler S. Health policy in the Clinton era: the national health program chartbook, vol 2. The Center for National Health Program Studies, 1993:9.

Luft HS, et al. The competitive effects of health maintenance organizations. Journal of Health Politics, Policy and Law 1986;625–658.

Luft HS. How do health maintenance organizations achieve their cost savings? N Engl J Med 1978;298:1336–1343.

Manning WG, et al. A controlled trial of the effect of a prepaid group practice on use of services. N Engl J Med 1984;310:1505–1510.

Marion Merrell Dow Inc. Managed care digest: HMO edition. Marion Merrell Dow Managed Care Digests, 1993:5.

Marion Merrell Dow Inc. Managed care digest: PPO edition. Marion Merrell Dow Managed Care Digests, 1993:3.

Moore P. Evaluating health maintenance organizations. New York: Quorum Books, 1991.

The National Health Lawyers Association. The insider's guide to managed care. An NHLA Education in Print Publication, 1990.

The 93rd Congress. The Health Maintenance Organization Act of 1973. United States Code Congressional and Administrative News, 93rd Congress. First Session, vol 1, 1973. West Publishing, 1974.

Rubin HR, et al. Patient's ratings of outpatient visits in different practice settings. JAMA 1993;270:835–840.

Starr P. The social transformation of American medicine. New York: Basic Books, 1982.

Ware JE, et al. Comparison of health outcomes at a health maintenance organization with those of fee-for-service care. Lancet 1986;1017–1022.

Welch WP. The new structure of independent practice associations. Journal of Health Politics, Policy & Law 1987;12:723–739.

Greer W. Kaiser-Permanente Health Plan—why it works. The Henry J. Kaiser Foundation, 1971.

Chapter 6

Committee on Ways and Means. 1993 green book: overview of entitlement programs. Washington, DC: U.S. Government Printing Office, 1993.

Fee E. Disease and discovery: a history of the Johns Hopkins School of Hygiene and Public Health, 1916–1939. Baltimore, MD: Johns Hopkins University Press, 1987.

Fein R. Medical care, medical costs. Cambridge, MA: Harvard University Press, 1986.

Goudsblom J. Public health and the civilizing process. The Milbank Quarterly 1986; 64.

Health Care Financing Administration. 1993 data compendium.

Health Care Financing Administration. 1993 HCFA statistics.

Health Care Financing Administration. 1993 highlights.

Health Care Financing Administration. Medicare and Medicaid, brief summaries of Title XVIII and Title XIX of the Social Security Act. July 1992.

Health Care Financing Administration. The Medicare handbook.

Iglehart JK. The End Stage Renal Disease program. N Engl J Med 328; 366.

Iglehart JK. Medicaid. N Engl J Med 328: 896.

Iglehart JK. Medicare. N Engl J Med 327:1467.

Institute of Medicine, The Committee for the Study of the Future of Public Health. The future of public health. Washington, DC: National Academy Press, 1988.

Congressional Research Service. Medicaid source book: background data and analyses (a 1993 update). Washington, DC: U.S. Government Printing Office, 1993.

Merlis M. Medicaid: an overview. CRS Report for Congress. The Library of Congress, 1993.

The Robert Wood Johnson Foundation. Announcing the health care for the uninsured program. The Robert Wood Johnson Foundation, 1985.

Starr P. The social transformation of American medicine. New York: Basic Books, 1982.

Chapter 7

Altman DE, Morgan DH. The role of state and local government in health. Health Affairs 1983; 2:7–31.

Congressional quarterly guide to current American government, Fall 1992. Washington, DC: Congressional Quarterly Inc., 1992.

The economic and budget outlook: fiscal year 1995–1999. Congressional Budget Office, August 1994, p. 27–42.

Federal budget for fiscal year 1994. Washington, DC: U.S. Government Printing Office, 1993: (Appendix) 601–637.

How congress works, second edition. Washington, DC: Congressional Quarterly, Inc., 1992.

Kent C, Havighurst C. The FY95 budget for HHS: tough medicine while waiting for the cure. Medicine and Health 1994:1–4.

Kingdon JW. Agendas, alternatives, and public policies. Boston: Little, Brown, 1984.

Litman TJ, Robins LS. Health politics and policy. New York: Wiley Medical Publications, 1984.

For health care, time was the killer. New York Times, 8/29/94, p. A13–15.

Stanley HW, Niemi RG. Vital statistics on American politics, 3rd edition. Washington, DC: Congressional Quarterly Press, 1992.

Statistical Abstracts of the United States 1993, 113th ed. Austin, TX: The Reference Press Inc., 1994.

U.S. Government Manual 1993/94. Washington, DC: Office of the Federal Registrar, National Archives and Records Administration, 1993: 294.

Chapter 8

Aaron HJ. Serious and unstable condition: financing America's health care. Washington, DC: Brookings, 1991.

Aaron HJ, Schwartz WB. Rationing health care: the choice before us. Science 1990; 247:418–422.

Jonsson B. What can Americans learn from Europeans? Health Care Financing Review 1989; (suppl):79–93.

Letsch SW, Lazenby HC, Levit KR, Cowan CA. National health expenditures, 1991. Health Care Financing Review 1992;14:1–31.

Manning WG, et al. Health insurance and the demand for medical care: evidence from a randomized experiment. Am Economic Rev 1987;77:251–277.

Mendelson DN, Schwartz WB. The effects of aging and population growth on health care costs. Health Affairs 1993;12:119–125.

Newhouse JP. Medical care costs: how much welfare loss? J Economic Perspectives 1992;6:3–21.

Newhouse JP. An iconoclastic view of health cost containment. Health Affairs 1993;12 (suppl):152–171.

Reynolds R, et al. The cost of medical professional liability. JAMA 1987:2776–2781.

Reynolds R, et al. The cost of medical professional liability in the 1980s. Center for Health Policy Research, American Medical Association (internal document).

Rublee DA. Medical technology in Canada, Germany and the United States. Health Affairs 1989;8:178–181.

Schieber GJ, Poullier J, Greenwald LM. U.S. health expenditure performance: an international comparison and data update. Health Care Financing Review 1992;13:1–88.

Schwartz WB, Aaron HJ. The painful prescription—rationing hospital care. Washington, DC: Brookings, 1984.

Schwartz WB. The inevitable failure of current cost-containment strategies: why they can provide only temporary relief. JAMA 1987;257:220–224.

Schwartz WB, Mendelson DN. Hospital cost containment in the 1980s: hard lessons learned and prospects for the 1990s. N Engl J Med 1991;324:1037–1042.

Schwartz WB, Mendelson DN. Why managed care cannot contain hospital costs—without rationing. Health Affairs 1992;11:100–107.

Chapter 9

A call for action: final report. Washington, DC: U.S. Bipartisan Commission of Comprehensive Health Care, September 1990; 33–37; 101–114.

Aaron H. Serious and unstable condition: financing America's health care. Washington, DC: Brookings Institution, 1991.

Aday LA, Andersen R. Development of the indices of access to medical care. Ann Arbor, MI: University of Michigan Health Administration Press, 1975.

Aday LA, Fleming G, Andersen R. Access to medical care in the U.S.: who has it, who doesn't. Chicago: Pluribus Press, 1984.

Aday LA. At risk in America: the health and health care needs of vulnerable populations in the United States. San Francisco: Jossey-Bass, Inc., 1993.

American Cancer Society. Cancer facts and figures for minority Americans. New York: American Cancer Society, 1991.

American Cancer Society Subcommittee on Cancer in the Economically Disadvantaged. Cancer in the economically disadvantaged: a special report. New York: American Cancer Society, 1986.

American Medical Association. Medical care for indigent and culturally displaced obstetrical patients and their newborns. JAMA 1981;245:1159–1160.

Andersen R, McCutcheon A, Aday L, Chiu G, Bell R. Exploring dimensions of access to medical care. Health Services Research 1983;18:49–74.

Anonymous. Special report: access to health care in the United States: results of a 1986 survey. Princeton, NJ: Robert Wood Johnson Foundation, 1987.

Axinn J, Stern M. Age and dependency: children and the aged in American social policy. Milbank Memorial Fund Quarterly 1985;63:648–670.

Baquet C, Ringen K. Health policy: gaps in access, delivery, and utilization of the Pap smear in the United States. Milbank Quarterly 1987;65:322–347.

Bashshur R, Webb C, Homan R. Health insurance survey of Michigan on access to health care: final report. Lansing, MI: Governor's Task Force on Access to Health Care, 1989.

Battistella RM, Weil TP. National health insurance reconsidered: dilemmas and opportunities. Hospital Health Service Administration 1989;34:139–156.

Blendon R, et al. Access to care for the medically indigent: a resource document for state and local officials. Washington, DC: Academy for State and Local Government, 1985.

Blendon RJ, Moloney T. Perspectives on the medical crises. In: Blendon RJ, Moloney T, eds. New approaches to the medical crisis. New York: Frost and Sullivan Press, 1982.

Bodenheimer T. Sounding board: uninsurance in America. N Engl J Med 1992;327: 274–278.

Boone M. Social and cultural factors in the etiology of low birthweight among disadvantaged blacks. Social Sci Med 1985;20:1001–1011;1008.

Boufford J. Models for increasing access: strengthening community health centers and national health service corps. J Health Care for the Poor and Underserved 1990;1: 107–125.

Brown S. Barriers to the use of prenatal care. In: Brown S, ed. Prenatal care: reaching mothers, reaching infants. Washington, DC: National Academy Press, 1988.

Byrd WM. Race, biology, and health care: reassessing a relationship. J. Health Care for the Poor and Underserved 1990;1:278–296.

Centers for Disease Control. Measles—United States, first 26 weeks, 1985. MMWR 1986;35:1–4.

Children's Defense Fund. Unpublished data, 1986.

Chao S, Imaizumi S, Gorman S, Lowenstein R. Reasons for absences in prenatal care and its consequences. New York: Department of Obstetrics and Gynecology, Harlem Hospital, 1984.

David RJ, Collins JW. Bad outcomes in black babies: race or racism? Ethnicity and Disease 1991;1:236–244.

Davis K. Inequality and access to health care. Milbank Quarterly 1991;69:253–273.

Davis K, Gold M, Makuc D. Access to health care for the poor: does the gap remain? Annu Rev Public Health 1981;2:159–182.

Davis K, Reynolds R. The impact of Medicare and Medicaid on access to medical care. In: Rosett R, ed. The role of health insurance in the health sciences sector. New York: National Bureau of Economic Research, 1976:P391–435.

Enthoven A, Kronick RA. A consumer-choice health plan for the 1990s: universal health insurance in a system designed to promote quality and economy. N Engl J Med 1989;320:29–37;94–101.

Evans R, Lomas J, Barer M, et al. Controlling health expenditures—the Canadian reality. N Engl J Med 1989;320:571–577

Faller H. Perinatal needs among immigrant women. Public Health Report 1985;100: 340–343.

Foley J. Sources of health insurance and characteristics of the uninsured: analysis of the March 1992 Current Population Survey. Employee Benefit Research Institute Special Report (SR-16), Issue Brief Number 133, January 1993.

Freeman HE, Blendon RJ, Aiken LH, Sudman S, Mullinix CF, Corey C. Americans report on their access to health care. Health Affairs 1987;6–19.

Gordon N (Assistant Director for Human Resources, Congressional Budget Office). Testimony before the U.S. House of Representatives Subcommittee on Health and the Environment, April 15, 1988.

Grant JP. The state of the world's children 1986. Oxford: Oxford University Press (for UNICEF), 1985.

Greenberg E, Chute C, Stukel T, et al. Social and economic factors in the choice of lung cancer treatment. N Engl J Med 1988;318:612–617.

Grogan C. Deciding on access and levels of care: a comparison of Canada, Britain, Germany, and the United States. J Health Politics, Policy and Law 1992;17:213–232.

Hadley J, Steinberg E, Feder J. Comparison of uninsured and privately insured hospital patients. JAMA 1991;265:374–379.

Health Insurance Associates of America. 1986–1987 source book of health insurance data. Washington, DC: Health Insurance Association of America, 1987.

Hewitt Associates. Salaried employee benefits provided by major U.S. employers: a comparison study, 1979 through 1984. Lincolnshire, IL: Hewitt Associates, 1985.

Himmelstein D, et al. Patient transfers: medical practice as social triage. American Journal of Public Health 1984;74:494–497.

Himmelstein D, Woolhandler S. Cost without benefit: administrative waste in U.S. health care. N Engl J Med 1986;314:441–445.

Himmelstein DU, Woolhandler S. Writing Committee on the Working Group on Program Design. A National Health program for the United States: a Physician's Proposal. N Engl J Med 1985;320:102–108.

Hughes D, Johnson K, Rosenbaum S, Butler E, Simons J. The health of America's children: maternal and child health data book. Washington, DC: Children's Defense Fund, 1988.

Millman ML. Access to health care in America. Institute of Medicine (US). Committee on Monitoring Access to Personal Health Care Services. Washington, DC: National Academy Press, 1993.

Juarez Associates. How to reach black and Mexican-American women. Report submitted to the Public Health Service, Department of Health and Human Services. Contract No. 282-81-0082. Washington, DC, 1992.

Kalmuss D, Darabi KF, Lopez I, Caro FG, Marshall E, Carter A. Barriers to prenatal care: an examination of use of prenatal care among low-income women in New York City. New York: Community Service Society, 1987.

Katz R. Education as transformation: becoming a healer among the !Kung and the Fijians. Harvard Educational Review 1981;51:57–78.

Kinzer D. The real-world issues in access to care. The Henry Ford Hospital Med J 1990;38:154–157.

Knoll K. Barriers and motivators for prenatal care in Minneapolis. Minneapolis: Minnesota Department of Health, 1986.

Lurie M, Ward NB, Shapiro MF, Brook RH. Termination of Medi-Cal: does it affect health? N Engl J Med 1984;311:480–484.

McBride D. Black America: from community health care to crises medicine. J Health Politics, Policy and Law 1993;18:319–337.

Medical and Health Perspective Newsletter. Washington, DC: McGraw Hill, September 11, 1989.

Moloney TW, Rogers DE. Medical technology—a different view of the contentious debate over costs. N Engl J Med 1979;301:1413–1419.

Monheit A, Hagan M, Berk M, Farley P. The employed uninsured and the role of public policy. Inquiry 1985;22:348–364.

Newhouse JP. Medical care: how much welfare loss? J Economic Perspectives 1992; 6:3–21.

Nerenz D, Zajac B, Repasky D, Doyle P. Policy options to improve access to health care for the unemployed uninsured. Henry Ford Hospital Med J 1990;38:183–189.

Okada L, Wan T. Impact of community health centers and Medicaid on the use of health services. Public Health Reports, December 1980.

Peterson P. A time flow study: Hutzel Prenatal Clinic. Detroit: Wayne State University, 1987.

Reed W, Cawley K, Anderson R. The effect of a public hospital's transfer policy on patient care. N Engl J Med 1986;315:1428–1432.

Rosenbach ML. Insurance coverage and ambulatory medical care of low-income children in the United States, 1980. National Medical Care Utilization and Expenditure Survey, series C, analytical report no. 1, DHHS pub. no. 85-20401. Washington, DC: National Center for Health Statistics, 1985.

Rosenbaum S, Johnson K. Providing health care for low-income children: reconciling child health goals with child health financing realities. Milbank Quarterly 1986;64:442–478.

Rosenblatt RA. The perinatal paradox: doing more and accomplishing less. Health Affairs 1989;58–159.

Rowland D, Lyons B, Edwards J. Medicaid: health care for the poor in the Reagan era. Annu Rev Public Health 1988;9:427–450.

Schieber G, Poullier JP. International health spending: issues and trends. Health Affairs 10:

Schlesinger M, Bentkover D, Blumenthal R, Musacchio R, Willer J. The privatization of health care and physicians' perceptions of access to hospital services. Milbank Quarterly 1987;65:25–58.

Schroeder SA. Robert Wood Johnson Foundation, Annual Report 1991: access to health care. Princeton, NJ: The Robert Wood Johnson Foundation, 1991.

Schur C, Taylor A. Choice of health insurance and the two-worker household. Health Affairs 1991.

Scully D. Who controls women's health? 2nd ed. New York: Teacher's College, 1994.

Select Panel for the Promotion of Child Health. Better health for our children: a national strategy, vol 1. DHHS Pub. No. (PHS)79-55071. Washington, DC: Government Printing Office, 1981.

Skocpol T. Protecting soldiers and mothers: the political origins of social policy in the United States. Cambridge, MA: Harvard University Press, 1992:480–524.

Starr P. Medical care and the health of the poor. In: Rogers DE, Ginzberg E, eds. Boulder, CO: Westview Press, 1993:21–32.

Starr P. The social origins of professional sovereignty. In: The social transformation of American medicine: the rise of a sovereign profession and the making of a vast industry. New York: Basic Books, 1982:235–289.

Stone DA. Clinical authority in the construction of citizenship. In: Ingram II, Smith SR, eds. Public policy for democracy. Washington, DC: Brookings Institution, 1993:45–67.

Subcommittee on Human Resources of the Committee on Ways and Means. Subcommittee on the Increases in Poverty, Work Effort, and Income Distribution Data. Washington, DC: United States Government Printing Office, 1993.

Sulvetta M, Swartz K. The uninsured and uncompensated care. Washington, DC: National Health Care Forum, 1986.

U.S. Congressional Budget Office. Rising health care costs: causes, implications, and strategies. Washington, DC: U.S. Congressional Budget Office, 1991.

U.S. Department of Health and Human Services Report to the Secretary's Task Force on Black and Minority Health. Washington, DC: U.S. Government Printing Office, 1985.

U.S. General Accounting Office. Health insurance: cost increases lead to coverage limitations and cost shifting. GAO/HRD-90-68. Washington, DC: Government Printing Office, 1990:1–32.

U.S. General Accounting Office. Report to Congressional Requesters. Access to health care: states respond to growing crisis. GAO/HRD-92-70. Washington, DC: Government Printing Office, 1992:66–74.

Walker B. Resources for assuring access: health promotion and disease prevention. J Health Care for the Poor and Underserved 1990:1;126–129.

Wenneker MB, Epstein AM. Racial inequalities in the use of procedures for patients with ischemic heart disease in Massachusetts. JAMA 1989;261:253–257.

Wenneker MB, Weissman JS, Epstein AM. The association of payer with utilization of cardiac procedures in Massachusetts. JAMA 1990;264:1255–1260.

White House Domestic Policy Council. The President's Health Security Plan. Washington, DC: Government Printing Office, 1993.

Whittle J, et al. Racial differences in the use of cardiovascular procedures in the Department of Veterans Affairs medical system. N Engl J Med 1993;329:621–627.

Woolhandler S, Himmelstein D. Resolving the cost/access conflict: the case for a national health program. J Gen Intern Med 1989;4:54–60.

Woolhandler S, Himmelstein DU, Silber R, et al. Medical care and mortality: racial differences in preventable deaths. Int J Health Services 1985;15:1–22.

Zola IK. Medicine as an institution of social control. Sociological Review 1972;20:487–504.

Chapter 10

Berke RL. The health plan; rising expectations and fear of the bills create an opening. The New York Times 1993; 26 September: E-1, 6.

Berwick DM. Continuous improvement as an ideal in health care. N Engl J Med 1989; 320:53–6.

Berwick DM, Wald DL. Hospital leaders' opinions of the HCFA mortality data. JAMA 1990;263:247–249.

Blumberg MS. Comments on HCFA hospital death rate statistical outliers. Health Services Research 1987;21:715–739.

Brook RH, Appel FA. Quality-of-care assessment: choosing a method for peer review. N Engl J Med 1973;288:1323–1329.

Brook RH. Health care reform is on the way: do we want to compete on quality? Ann Intern Med 1994;120:84–86.

Brinkley J. U.S. releasing lists of hospitals with abnormal mortality rates. New York Times 1986; 12 March: p. 1.

Byer MJ. Faint hearts. New York Times 1992; 21 March, p. 23.

Caper P. Defining quality in medical care. Health Affairs 1988;7:49–61.

Chassin MR. The missing ingredient in health reform. Quality of care. JAMA 1993; 270:377–378.

Chassin MR, Brook RH, Park RE, et al. Variations in the use of medical and surgical services by the Medicare population. N Engl J Med 1986;314:285–90.

Chassin MR, Kosecoff J, Park RE, et al. Does inappropriate use explain geographic variations in the use of health care services? A study of three procedures. JAMA 1987;258:2533–7.

Cleary PD, Edgman-Levitan S, Roberts M, et al. Patients evaluate their hospital care: a national survey. Health Affairs 1991;10:254–67.

Codman EA. The Shoulder, Rupture of the Supraspinatus Tendon and Other Lesions in or About the Subacromial Bursa. Boston, MA: Thomas Todd Company 1934: pp. 5–11.

Daley J, Gertman P, Delbanco T. Looking for quality in primary care physicians. Health Affairs 1988;7:107–113.

Delbanco T. Enriching the doctor-patient relationship by inviting the patient's perspective. Ann Intern Med 1992;116:414–418.

Deming WE. Quality, productivity, and competitive position. Cambridge, MA: Massachusetts Institute of Technology, Center for Advanced Engineering Study, 1982.

Donabedian A. Explorations in quality assessment and monitoring, Volume I. The definition of quality and approaches to its assessment. Ann Arbor, MI: Health Administration Press, 1980.

Donabedian A. The quality of care. How can it be assessed? JAMA 1988; 260 (12):1743–48.

Donabedian A. Criteria and standards for quality assessment and monitoring. Quality Review Bulletin 1986;12:99–108.

Donabedian A. The end results of health care: Ernest Codman's contribution to quality assessment and beyond. The Milbank Quarterly 1989;67:1549–1556.

Dubois RW. Interview reported in Modern Maturity, August-September 1981, p. 35. Cited in Handbook of Health, Health Care, and the Health Professions, edited by David Mechanic. New York, NY: The Free Press, 1983, p. 400.

Dubois RW, Brook RH. Preventable deaths: who, how often, and why? Ann Intern Med 1988; 109 (7):582–589.

Dubois RW. Hospital mortality as an indicator of quality. In: Goldfield N, Nash DB, eds. Providing quality care: the challenge to clinicians. Philadelphia: American College of Physicians, 1989:107–131.

Dubois RW, Rogers WH, Moxley JH 3rd, Draper D, Brook RH. Hospital inpatient mortality. Is it a predictor of quality? N Engl J Med 1987; 317:1674–1680.

Epstein AM. The outcomes movement—will it get us where we want to go? N Engl J Med 1990;323:266–269.

Fink A, Yano EM, Brook RH. The condition of the literature on differences in hospital mortality. Medical Care 1989;27:315–336.

Freudenheim M. Business and health: software controls on health care. The New York Times 1992, 18 February, p. D-2.

Freudenheim M. Quality of care being measured. The New York Times 1990, 5 June, p. D-2.

Gardner E. Putting guidelines into practice. Modern Healthcare 1992, 7 September, p. 24.

Garnick DW, Fowles J, Lawthers AG, Weiner JP, Parente ST, Palmer RH. Focus on quality: profiling physicians' practice patterns. Journal of Ambulatory Care Management, April 1994.

Gerteis M, Edgman-Levitan S, Daley J, Delbanco T, eds. Through the patient's eyes. Understanding and promoting patient-centered care. San Francisco, CA: Jossey-Bass Publishers, 1993.

Gerteis M, et al. What patients really want. Health Management Quarterly 1993;15:2–6.

Goldman RL. The reliability of peer assessments of quality of care. JAMA 1992; 267:958–960.

Grumbach K., Keane D, Bindman A. Primary care and public emergency department overcrowding. American Journal of Public Health 1993; 83 (3): 372–378.

Hannan EL, et al. Adult open heart surgery in New York State: an analysis of risk factors and hospital mortality rates JAMA 1990;264:2768–2774.

Hartz AJ, Kuhn EM, Green R, Rimm AA. The use of risk-adjusted complication rates to compare hospitals performing coronary artery bypass surgery or angioplasty. International Journal of Technology Assessment in Health Care 1992;8:524–538.

Health Care Financing Administration, Health Standards and Quality Bureau, 1992. Request for Proposal: Cycle 4.0 (1 October).

Holahan J, Berenson RA, Kachavos PG. Area variations in selected Medicare procedures. Health Affairs 1990;3:166–175.

Iezzoni LI. Monitoring quality of care: what do we need to know? Inquiry 1993; 30:112–114.

Iezzoni LI, Greenberg LG. Risk adjustment and current health policy debate, in: Risk adjustment for measuring health care outcomes, Iezzoni LI (ed). Ann Arbor, MI: Health Administration Press, 1994.

Institute of Medicine, Access to health care in America. Millman, M. (ed). Washington, DC: National Academy Press, 1993.

Institute of Medicine, Division of Health Care Services. Medicare: A strategy for quality assurance, volume I. Washington, DC: National Academy Press, 1990.

Jencks SF, Wilensky GR. The health care quality improvement initiative. A new approach to quality assurance in medicare. JAMA 1992;268:900–903.

Joint Commission on Accreditation of Healthcare Organizations. The Measurement Mandate: On the Road to Performance Improvement in Health Care. Oakbrook Terrace, IL: JCAHO, 1993.

Joint Commission on Accreditation of Healthcare Organizations. Agenda for Change. JCAHO public information materials. Oakbrook Terrace, IL: JCAHO, 1993.

Jonsen AR. The new medicine and the old ethics. Cambridge, MA: Harvard University Press, 1990.

Juran JM. Quality planning and analysis: from product development through use. New York: McGraw-Hill, 1980.

Kahn KL, Rubenstein LV, Sherwood MJ, Brook RH. Structured implicit review for physician implicit measurement of quality of care: development of the form and guidelines for its use. Santa Monica, CA: The RAND Corporation, N-3016-HCFA. September 1989.

Kassirer JP. The use and abuse of practice profiles. N Engl J Med 1994;330:634–635.

Keeler EB, Rubenstein LV, Kahn KL, et al. Hospital characteristics and quality of care. JAMA 1992;268:1709–1714.

Knaus WA, Nash DB. Predicting and evaluating patient outcomes. Ann Intern Med 1988;109:521–522.

Koska M. Are severity data an effective consumer tool. JAMA 1989;63:24.

Kuhn EM, Hartz AJ, Gottlieb MS, Rimm AA. The relationship of hospital characteristics and the results of peer review in six large states. Medical Care 1991;29:1028–1038.

Lasker RD, Shapiro DW, Tucker AM. Realizing the potential of practice pattern profiling. Inquiry 1992;29:287–297.

Lawthers AG, Palmer RH, Edwards JE, Fowles J, Garnick DW, Weiner JP. Developing and evaluating performance measures for ambulatory care quality: A preliminary report of the DEMPAQ project. The Joint Commission Journal of Quality Improvement 1993;19:552–565.

Leape LL, Park RE, Solomon DH, Chassin MR, Kosecoff J, Brook RH. Does inappropriate use explain small-area variations in the use of health care services? JAMA 1990; 263:669–672.

Leary WE. More advice for doctors: U.S. guides on treatments. New York Times 15 April 1992, p. C-14.

Leary WE. U.S. issues guidelines on bladder problems. New York Times 24 March 1992: C-3.

Lohr KN. Outcome measurement: concepts and questions. Inquiry 1988;25(1):37–50.

Lohr KN, Donaldson MS, Harris-Wehling J. Medicare: A strategy for quality assurance, V: quality of care in a changing health care environment. Quality Review Bulletin 1992; 18:120–126.

NacNeil/Lehrer NewsHour. 3 December 1993. "Medical Breakthrough," reported by Greg Hirakawa of public television station KCTS-Seattle, Washington.

Margolis CZ. Uses of clinical algorithms. JAMA 1983;249:627–632.

McNeil BJ, Pedersen SH, Gatsonis C. Current issues in profiling quality of care. Inquiry 1992;29:298–307.

Mulley AG, Jr. E.A. Codman and the end results idea: a commentary. The Milbank Quarterly 1989;67:257–261.

Nash DB. Is the quality cart before the horse? JAMA 1992;268:917–918.

Neuhauser D. Ernest Amory Codman, M.D., and end results of medical care. International Journal of Technology Assessment in Health Care 1990;6:307–325.

New York State Department of Health, Cardiac Surgery in NY State. Albany, NY: NY Dept of Health, 1993:1–17.

Nuland SB. Doctors: the biography of medicine. New York, NY: Vintage Books, 1988, p. xv.

O'Leary DS. The measurement mandate: the report card is coming. The Journal of Quality Improvement 1993; 19:487–491.

Palmer HR. The challenges and prospects for quality assessment and assurance in ambulatory care. Inquiry 1988;25:119–131.

Park RE, Brook RH, Kosecoff J, et al. Explaining variations in hospital death rates, randomness, severity of illness, quality of care. JAMA 1990;264:484–490.

Podolsky D, Beddingfield KT. America's best hospitals. U.S. News and World Report 1993; 12 July, 115:66.

Physician Payment Review Commission (PPRC). Conference on Profiling. No. 92–2. Washington, DC: Physician Payment Review Commission 1992.

Reiser SJ. The era of the patient. Using the experience of illness in shaping the missions of health care. JAMA 1993;269:1012–1017.

Report on Medical Guidelines & Outcomes Research. Medicare launches effort to create HMO 'Report Cards'. 1993;4:1.

Restuccia JD, Kreger BE, Payne SMC, Gertman PM, Dayno SJ, Lenhart GM. Factors affecting appropriateness of hospital use in Massachusetts. Health Care Financing Review 1986;8:47–54.

Romano PS. Can administrative data be used to compare the quality of health care? Medical Care Review 1993;50:451–477.

Rubin HR, Rogers WH, Kahn KL, Rubenstein LV, Brook RH. Watching the doctor-watchers. How well do peer review organization methods detect hospital care quality problems? JAMA 1992;267:2349–2354.

Rubenstein LV, Kahn KL, Reinisch EJ, et al. Changes in quality of care for five diseases measured by implicit review, 1981 to 1986. JAMA 1990;264:1974–1979.

Schroeder SA, Kabcenell AI. Do bad outcomes mean substandard care? JAMA 1991; 265:1995.

Thomas L. The lives of a cell: notes of a biology watcher. New York, NY: Viking Press, 1974.

Thomas L. The fragile species. New York, NY: Collier Books, Macmillan Publishing Company, 1992.

Thomas JW, Holloway JJ, Guire KE. Validating risk-adjusted mortality as an indicator for quality of care. Inquiry 1993;30:6–22.

Topol EJ, Califf RM. Scorecard cardiovascular medicine. Its impact and future directions. Ann Intern Med 1994;120:65–70.

U.S. General Accounting Office. February 1991. Practice Guidelines: The Experience of Medical Specialty Societies Washington, DC: Government Printing Office, GAO/PEMD-91-11.

U.S. General Accounting Office. January 1993. Emergency Departments: Unevenly Affected by Growth and Change in Patient Use. Washington, DC: Government Printing Office, GAO/HRD-93-4.

Ware JE Jr., Berwick DM. Conclusions and Recommendations in: Patient judgments of hospital quality: report of a pilot study. Medical Care 1990;28:S39–S42.

Welch HG, Miller ME, Welch WP. Physician profiling: in-patient patterns in Florida and Oregon. N Engl J Med 1994;330:607–612.

Wennberg JE, McPherson K, Caper P. Will payment based on diagnosis-related groups control hospital costs? N Engl J Med 1984;311:295–300.

Wennberg JE. Which rate is right N Engl J Med 1986;314:310–311.

Wennberg JE. Sounding Board: Outcomes research, cost containment and the fear of health care rationing. N Engl J Med 1990;323:1202–1204.

Wennberg JE, Gittlesohn A. Variations in medical care among small areas. Scientific American 1982;254:120–134.

Wennberg JE, Freeman JL, Culp WJ. Are hospital services rationed in New Haven or over-utilised in Boston? Lancet 1987;1:1185–1189.

Wennberg JE, Freeman JL, Shelton RM, Bubolz TA. Hospital use and mortality among Medicare beneficiaries in Boston and New Haven. N Engl J Med 1989;321:1168–1173.

Wennberg JE, Gittelsohn A. Small area variation in health care delivery. Science 1973;182:1102–1108.

White House Domestic Policy Council. Health Security: The President's Report to the American People. The White House Domestic Policy Council, Washington, DC, 1993.

Williamson J. Evaluating quality of patient care. A strategy relating outcome and process assessment. JAMA 1971;218:564–569.

Winslow R. Network of doctors to market heart care for set fee. The New York Times 1993; 2 March: B-1, 4.

Woolhandler S, Himmelstein DU, Lewontin JP. Administrative costs in U.S. hospitals. N Engl J Med 1993;329:400–403.

Yasuda G. Computing health-care efficiency: use of 'practice patterns' divides medical community on cost issues. Orlando Sentinel Tribune, 1992; 6 January, B-12.

Zinman D. Heart surgeons rated. Newsday 1991; 18 December:32.

Chapter 11

Bergthold L. Purchasing power in health. New Brunswick, NJ: Rutgers, 1991.

Bergthold L. The fat kid on the seesaw: American business and health care cost containment, 1970–1990. Annu Rev Public Health 1991;12:157–175.

Califano J. America's health care revolution. New York: Random House, 1986.

Cantor JC, Barrand NL, Desonia RA. Business leaders views on American health care. Health Affairs 1991.

Coile RC Jr. The new medicine: reshaping medical practice and health care management. Rockville, MD: Aspen, 1990.

Glassman JK. Is the government's health care cure really needed? Washington Post, Jan 7, 1994, p. G1.

Hall W, Griner P. Cost-effective health care: the Rochester experience. Health Affairs 1993. The hospital. BusinessWeek January 17, 1994.

Iglehart JK. The American health care system. N Engl J Med 1992;326:962–967; 326:1715–1720, 327:10;327:742–747, 327:1467–1472; 1993;328:366–371; 328:896–900; 329:372–376; 329:1052–1056.

Jaeger J. Private sector coalitions: a fourth party in health. Durham, NC: Duke, 1982.

Jensen J. Employers look to hospitals to help control costs. Modern Healthcare, August 26, 1991.

Kenkel PJ. Business-led efforts to control costs. Modern Healthcare July 29, 1991, p. 48.

McArdle F. The changing health care market. Washington, DC: Employee Benefit Research Institute, 1987.

Politser P. US employers: the new pioneers of health care cost containment. Bull Am Coll Surg 1991;76:12–17.

Torichia M. How Twin Cities employers are reshaping health care. Business and Health, February, 1994, p. 30.

Warden G. Integrated regional health systems: models for health care delivery reform. Henry Ford Health System, Detroit, MI.

Chapter 12

Allen D. Health services in England. In: Comparative health systems. University Park: Pennsylvania State University Press, 1984: 197–244.

Blendon R, Humphrey T. Views on health care: public opinion in three nations. Health Affairs 1989:149–159.

Hsiao WC. Comparing health care systems: what nations can learn from one another. J Health, Politics, and Law. 1992; 17:613–645.

Iglehart JK. Canada's health system. N Engl J Med 1986:202–208, 778–784.

Moloney TW, Paul B. A new financial framework: lessons from Canada. Health Affairs 1989;148–158.

Peet J. A spreading sickness. The Economist 1991;6–18.

Phelps. International comparisons of health care systems. In: Health economics. New York: Harper Collins, 1992:483–509.

Reinhardt UE. What can Americans learn from Europeans? Health Care Financing Rev 1989;(suppl)97–103.

Reinhardt UE. West Germany's health-care and health-insurance system: combining universal access with cost control. Report Prepared for the U.S. Bipartisan Commission on Comprehensive Health Care, June 1990, p. 3–16.

Roemer MI. Canada. In: National Health Systems of the World. New York: Oxford University Press, 1991;161–170.

Woolhandler S, Himmelstein D. Resolving the cost/access conflict. J Gen Intern Med 1989; 4:54–60.

Chapter 13

Anderson G, Chaulk P, Fowler E. Maryland: a regulatory approach to health system reform. Health Affairs, Summer 1993.

Crittenden RA. Managed competition and premium caps in Washington state. Health Affairs, Summer 1993.

Fox DM, Leichter HM. The ups and downs of Oregon's rationing plan. Health Affairs, Summer 1993.

Government Accounting Office. Access to health care: states respond to growing crisis. GAO/HRD 92–70.

Knox RA. Hawaii touts health care that's working. Boston Globe, July 5, 1992, p. 1.

Leichter HM. Health care reform in Vermont: a work in progress. Health Affairs, Summer 1993.

Leichter HM. Minnesota: the trip from acrimony to accommodation. Health Affairs, Summer 1993.

Madden CW, Hoare G, et al. Washington state's basic health plan: choices and challenges. J Public Health Policy 1992; 81.

Moon M, Holahan J. Can states take the lead in health care reform? JAMA 1992; 268:1588.

Neubauer D. Hawaii: a pioneer in health system reform. Health Affairs, Summer 1993.

Rogal DL, Helms WD. State models: tracking states' efforts to reform their health systems. Health Affairs, Summer 1993.

Volpp KG, Siegel B. New Jersey: long term experience with all-payer rate setting. Health Affairs, Summer 1993.

Yawn BP, Jacott WE, Yawn RA. Minnesota care (health right): myths and miracles. JAMA 1993; 269:511.

Chapter 14

Alliance for Health Reform. Health care reform proposals: brief summaries of selected plans. November 1993.

Butler S, Haislmaier EF, eds. A national health system for America. The Heritage Foundation, 1989.

Sen. John Chafee, R-RI. Health Equity and Access Reform Today Act of 1993. Bill S. 1770.

President Bill Clinton. Health Security Act. Summarized in: Health security: the President's report to the American people. Simon and Schuster, 1993. Introduced as Bill H. R. 3600 by Rep. Richard Gephardt D-MO.

Rep. Jim Cooper, D-TN. Managed Competition Act of 1993. Bill H. R. 3222.

Ellwood, Enthoven AC, Etheredge L. The Jackson Hole initiatives for a twenty-first century American health care system. Health Economics 1992;1;149–168.

Enthoven AC. The history and principles of managed competition. Health Affairs 1993; (suppl). 24–48.

Enthoven AC. Why managed care has failed to contain health costs. Health Affairs 1993; 27–44.

Freudenheim M. Rochester serves as model in curbing health costs. The New York Times, August 25, 1992, p. A1.

Graig L. Health of nations: an international perspective on U.S. health care reform. The Wyatt Company, 1991.

Rep. Jim McDermott, D-WA, Sen. Paul Wellstone, D-MI. American Health Security Act of 1993. Bill H. R. 1200/S. 491.

Rep. Robert Michel, R-IL. Affordable Health Care Now Act. Bill H. R. 3080.

Schwartz WB, Mendelson DN. Eliminating waste and inefficiency can do little to contain costs. Health Affairs 1994;224–238.

Starr P. The logic of health-care reform. Whittle Direct Books, 1992.

Himmelstein D, Woolhandler S. The national health program book. Common Courage Press, 1994.

Chapter 15

Abraham KS, Rabin RL, Weiler PC. Enterprise responsibility for personal injury: further reflections. San Diego Law Review 1993; 30.

Bowsher CA. Testimony before the Sub-Committee on Health—Committee on Ways and Means—House of Representatives. Medical malpractice: a continuing problem with far-reaching implications. 26 April 1990. GAO/T-HRD-90-24.

Brennan TA. Improving the quality of medical care: a critical evaluation of the major proposals. Yale Law and Policy Review 1992; 10.

Danzon P. Medical malpractice: theory, evidence and public policy. Cambridge, MA: Harvard University Press, 1985.

Dayhoff DA, Cromwell J, Rosenbach ML. An update on physician cost shares. Health Care Financing Rev 1993; 14:3.

Defensive medicine: it costs but does it work? JAMA 1987;257.

Furrow BR, Johnson SH, Jost TS, Schwartz RL. Health law: cases, material and problems, 2nd ed. St. Paul, MN: West Publishing, 1991.

Gastel R, ed. Medical malpractice. Insurance Information Institute Reports, October 1993.

Glassman PA, Petersen LP, Bradley MA, Rolph JE. The effect of malpractice experience on physicians' clinical decision-making—Undated Report to the OTA.

Graetz MJ, Mashaw JL. Praise reform and start the litigation. N Engl J Med 1993;329.

Havighurst CC. Health care law and policy. Westbury, NY: The Foundation Press, 1988.

Hyams A, Brandenburg J, Lipsitz S, Brennan T. Harvard School of Public Health. Report to physician payment review commission: practice guidelines and malpractice litigation. January 25, 1994:7.

Institute of Medicine. Medical professional liability and the delivery of care. Washington, DC: National Academy Press, 1989.

Lawthers AG, Laird AR, Lipsitz S, et al. Physicians' perceptions of the risk of being sued. J Health Politics, Policy and Law 1992; 17.

Localio RA, et al. Relation between malpractice claims and adverse events due to negligence. N Engl J Med 1991;325.

Localio RA, Lawthers AG, Bengtson JM, et al. Relationship between malpractice claims and cesarean delivery. JAMA 1993.

Opinion Research Corporation. Professional liability and its effects: report of a 1992 survey of the American College of Obstetricians and Gynecologists. October 1992.

Sloan FA, et al. Suing for medical malpractice. Chicago: The University of Chicago Press, 1993.

Sloan FA, Mergenhage PM, Burfield WB, et al. Medical malpractice experience of physicians: predictable or haphazard? JAMA 1989;262.

Taragain MI, Willett LR, Wilczek AP, et al. The influence of standard of care and severity of injury on the resolution of medical malpractice claims. Ann Intern Med 1992;117.

Thompson LH. Testimony before the Sub-Committee on Health—Committee on Ways and Means—House of Representatives. Medical malpractice: experience with efforts to address problems. 20 May 1993. GAO/T-HRD-93-24.

Todd JS. Reform of the health care system and professional liability. N Engl J Med 1993; 329.

United States General Accounting Office. Medical malpractice: no agreement on the problems or solutions. February 1986. GAO/HRD-86-50.

United States General Accounting Office. Medical malpractice: six state case studies show claims and insurance costs still rise despite reforms. December 1986. GAO/HRD-87-21.

United States General Accounting Office. Medical malpractice: a framework for action. May 1987. GAO/HRD-87-73.

United States Congress, Office of Technology Assessment. Impact of legal reforms on medical malpractice costs. Washington, DC: October 1993. OTA-BP-H-119.

Weiler PC. The case of no-fault medical liability. Maryland Law Review 1993; 52.

Weiler PC. Medical malpractice on trial. Cambridge, MA: Harvard University Press, 1991.

Weiler PC, Hiatt HH, Newhouse JP, et al. A measure of malpractice: medical injury, malpractice litigation, and patient consent. Cambridge, MA: Harvard University Press, 1993.

Weiler PC, Newhouse JP, Hiatt HH. Proposal for medical liability reform. JAMA 1992.

Chapter 16

Bayer R. AIDS: the politics of prevention and neglect. Health Affairs 1991; 86–97.

Fox DM. Chronic disease and disadvantage: the new politics of HIV infection. J Health Politics, Policy and Law 1990; 15:341–355.

Institute of Medicine, National Academy of Sciences. Confronting AIDS. Directions for public health, health care, and research. Washington, DC: National Academy Press, 1986.

National Research Council. The social impact of AIDS in the United States. Washington, DC: National Academy Press, 1993.

National Research Council. AIDS, sexual behavior and intravenous drug abuse. Washington, DC: National Academy Press, 1989.

Chapter 17

Baringa M. The foundations of research. Science 1991;253:1200–1202.

Bellett AJD. Value issues in biomedical science: public concerns and professional complacency. Immunol Cell Biol 1992;70:363–368.

Blumenthal D. The price of success: promoting technology transfer through academic-industry relationships in the life sciences. Health Affairs, 1994.

Cadman EC. The new physician-scientist: a guide for the 1990s. Clin Res 1990;38:191–198.

Cantor CR. Orchestrating the human genome project. Science 1990;248:49–51.

Cullinton BJ. Shaping science policy: what's happening to biomedical research in America. Acad Med 1991;66:188–191.

DiMasi JA, Hansen RW, Grabowski HG, Lasagna L. Cost of innovation in the pharmaceutical industry. J Health Economics 1991;10:107–142.

Glaser RJ. The impact of philanthropy on medicine and health. Perspect Biol Med 1992;36:46–56.

Howard Hughes Medical Institute, Office of Communications. The annual report 1992; 1993.

Kaitin KI, Bryant NR, Lasagna L. The role of the research-based pharmaceutical industry in medical progress in the United States. J Clin Pharmacol 1993;33:412–417.

Kirschner M. The need for unity in the biomedical research community. Acad Med 1991;66:577–582.

Martin JB. Training physician-scientists for the 1990s. Acad Med 1991;66:123–129.

McKercher PL. Pharmaceutical research and development. Clin Ther 1992;14:760–764.

National Institutes of Health, Division of Research Grants. NIH extramural trends, fiscal years 1983–1992. Pub. No. 93-3506, November 1993.

National Institutes of Health, The Office of Science Policy and Technology Transfer. NIH data book 1993. Pub. No. 93-1261, September 1993.

National Science Foundation. National Science Foundation annual report 1992. Pub. No. NSF 93-1, 1993.

Pardes H. Assessing the past and planning the future to ensure support for biomedical research. Acad Med 1991;66:582–584.

Petersdorf RG. The crises in biomedical research funding. Trans Am Clin Climat Assoc 1992;103:182–190.

Vaitukaitis JL. The future of clinical research. Clin Res 1991;39:145–156.

Wyngaarden JB. The clinical investigator as an endangered species. N Engl J Med 1979;301:1254–1259.

Wyngaarden JB. The clinical investigator as an endangered species. Bull NY Acad Med 1981;57:415–426.

Chapter 18

Anonymous. Goodwin endorses severity-based mental health benefit reform. Mental Health Report 1994;18:33.

Bachrach LL. Asylum and chronically ill psychiatric patients. Am J Psychiatry 1984; 141:975–978.

Bennett MJ. The greening of the HMO: implications for prepaid psychiatry. Am J Psychiatry 1988;145:1544–1549.

Bigelow DA. Effectiveness of a case management program. Community Mental Health J 1991:27:115.

Bond GR, Witheridge TF, Wasmer D, et al. A comparison of two crisis housing alternatives to psychiatric hospitalization. Hospital and Community Psychiatry 1989;40:177–183.

Brotman A. Privatization of mental health services: the Massachusetts experiment. J Health Politics, Policy and Law 1992;17:541–551.

Brown P. The transfer of care: psychiatric deinstitutionalization and its aftermath. Boston: Routledge and Kegan Paul, 1985.

Ciarlo JA, Reihman J. The Denver Community Mental Health Questionnaire: development of a multi-dimensional program evaluation instrument. In: Coursey R, ed. Program evaluation for mental health, New York: Grune and Stratton, 1977.

Clinton JJ. Depression in primary care. JAMA 1993;270:172.

Cox GB, Brown TB, Peterson PD, Rowe MM. A report on a state-wide community mental health center outcome study. Community Mental Health J 1982;18:135–150.

Domenici PV. Mental health care policy in the 1990s: discrimination in health care coverage of the seriously mentally ill. Address to the American Psychiatric Association, 1991, Washington, DC.

Dorwart RA, Chartock L, Epstein S. Financing of services. In: Talbott JA, Hales RE, Keill SL, eds. Textbook of administrative psychiatry. Washington DC: American Psychiatric Press, 1992.

Dorwart RA, Epstein SS. Privatization and mental health care: a fragile balance. Westport, CT: Greenwood Publishing Group, 1993.

Eaton L. Eli Todd and the Hartford retreat. N Engl Q 1953;24:435–454.

Forsyth AB, Griffiths B, Reiff S. Comparison of utilization of medical services by alcoholics and non-alcoholics. Am J Public Health 1982;72:600–602.

Goldman H, Adams N, Taube C. Deinstitutionalization: the data demythologized. Hospital and Community Psychiatry 1983;34:129–134.

Harrington C. Factors that contribute to Medicare HMO risk contract success. Inquiry 1988;25:251.

Institute of Medicine. Mrazek PJ, Haggerty RJ, eds. Reducing the risks for mental disorders: frontiers for preventive intervention research. Washington, DC: National Academy Press, 1994.

Katon W. Depression: relationship to somatization and chronic medical illness. J Clin Psychiatry 1984;45:4–11.

Kiesler C, Sibulkin A. Mental hospitalization: myths and facts about a national crisis. Newbury Park, CA: Sage, 1987.

Kongstvedt PR. The managed health care handbook, 2nd ed. Gaithersburg, MD: Aspen Publishers, 1993.

Kosterlitz J. O.K., stick out your tongue and say 'taxes.' National Journal 1993;25:2668.

Koyanagi C. Operation help: a mental health advocate's guide to Medicaid. Alexandria, VA: National Mental Health Association, 1988.

Ladner S, Crystal S, Towber R, et al. Project future: focusing, understanding, targeting, and utilizing resources for the homeless, mentally ill, elderly, youth, substance abusers and unemployables. Rockville, MD: National Institute of Mental Health, 1986.

Lamb HR. The new asylums in the community. Arch Gen Psychiatry 1979;36:129–134.

Lamb HR, ed. The homeless, mentally ill; a task force report of the American Psychiatric Association. Washington, DC: American Psychiatric Association, 1984.

Leibowitz B. Mental health services. In: Maddox G, ed. Encyclopedia of aging. New York: Springer, 1987.

Levinson M. Once again, tiptoeing around the T word: why it's so hard to talk straight about new taxes. Newsweek, 1993;121:46.

Linhorst DM. The use of single room occupancy (SRO) housing as an alternative for persons with a chronic mental illness. Community Mental Health J 1991;27:135.

Mechanic D. Mental health and social policy. Englewood, NJ: Prentice Hall, 1989.

McGuire TG. Financing and reimbursement for mental health services. In: Taube C, Mechanic D, Hohmann AA, eds. The future of mental health services research. (DHHS Pub. No. ADM-89-1600). Washington, DC: National Institute of Mental Health, 1989.

Morrissey J. Deinstitutionalizing the mentally ill: process, outcomes, and new directions. In: Gove W, ed. Deviance and mental illness. Beverly Hills, CA: Sage, 1982.

Morse G, Shields NM, Hanneke CR, et al. Homeless people in St. Louis: a mental health program evaluation, field study and follow-up investigation. Rockville, MD: National Institute of Mental Health, 1985.

Office of National Drug Control Policy, Executive Office of the President. National drug control strategy: reclaiming our communities from drugs and violence. Washington DC: The White House, February 1994.

Owen WL. Analysis and aggregation of CMHC outcome data in a statewide evaluation system: a case report. Community Mental Health J 1984;20:27–43.

Pepper B, Ryglewicz H, eds. The young adult chronic patient. New directions for mental health services. San Francisco, CA: Jossey-Bass, 1982.

Regier DA, Narrow WE, Rae DS, et al. The de facto U.S. mental and addictive disorders service system: epidemiologic catchment area prospective 1-year prevalence rates of disorders and services. Arch Gen Psychiatry 1993;50:85–94.

Roberts MJ, Clyde A. Your money or your life: the health care crisis explained. New York: Doubleday, 1993.

Rochefort DA. Handbook on mental health policy in the United States. Westport, CT: Greenwood Press, 1989.

Roth D, Bean G. New perspectives on homelessness: findings from a state-wide epidemiologic study. Hospital and Community Psychiatry 1986;37:712–719.

Rutter M. Parental mental disorder as a psychiatric risk factor. In: Hales R, Frances A, eds. American Psychiatric Association annual review, vol 6. Washington, DC: American Psychiatric Press, 1987.

Sanderson WC. Syndrome comorbidity in patients with major depression or dysthymia: prevalence and temporal relationship. Am J Psychiatry 1990;147:1025.

Scheidemandel P. The coverage catalog, 2nd ed. Washington, DC: American Psychiatric Association, 1989.

Schlesinger M, Dorwart RA. Falling between the cracks: failing national strategies for the treatment of substance abuse. DAEDALUS Journal of the American Academy of Arts and Sciences 1992;195–237.

Sederer LI, Eisen SV, Dill D, et al. Case-based reimbursement for psychiatric hospital care. Hospital and Community Psychiatry 1992;43:1120–1125.

Shadle M, Christianson JB. The organization of mental health care delivery in HMOs. Admin Mental Health 1988;15:201–225.

Stuart P. Depression: hidden disorder in the workplace. Personnel Journal 1992;71:94.

Sunshine JH, Witkin MJ, Manderscheid RW, et al. Expenditures and sources of funds for mental health organizations: U.S. and each state, 1986. (Statistical note no. 193, DHHS Publ. No. ADM-90-1699. Washington, DC: U.S. Government Printing Office, 1990.

Talbot JA, Hales RE, Keill SL. Textbook of administrative psychiatry. Washington, DC: American Psychiatric Press, 1992.

Tuke S. Description of the retreat. London: Dawsond of Pall Mall, 1968.

Turner VE, Hoge MA. Overnight hospitalization of acutely ill day hospital patients. Intern J Partial Hospitalization 1991;7:23–36.

U.S. Congress, Office of Technology Assessment. Children's mental health: problems and services—a background paper. Washington, DC: U.S. Government Printing Office, 1986.

U.S. Department of Health and Human Services. The homeless: background, analysis and options. Washington, DC: U.S. Government Printing Office, 1984.

U.S. Department of Housing and Urban Development. A report to the secretary on the homeless and emergency shelters. Washington, DC: U.S. Government Printing Office, 1984.

Chapter 19

American Geriatrics Society Public Policy Committee. Financing of long-term care services. J Am Geriatr Soc 1990;38.

Institute of Medicine. America's aging: health in an older society. Washington DC: National Academy Press, 1985:23.

Benjamin AE. An historical perspective on home care policy. The Milbank Quarterly 1993;71.

Cotton P. Must older Americans save up to spend down? JAMA 1993;269:2342–2344.

Council on Scientific Affairs. Home care in the 1990s. JAMA 1990; 263:1241–1244.

Estes CL. Aging, health and social policy: crisis and crossroads. J Aging Social Policy 1989;1.

HCFA. Office of the Actuary.

Health and Public Policy Committee, American College of Physicians. Financing long-term care. Ann Intern Med 1988;108.

Home Health Care Market. American Demographics 1985;29–51.

Kane RL, Kane RA. Long-term care. Geriatric medicine text.

Kane RA, Kane RL. Long-term care: principles, programs and policies. New York: Springer, 1987.

Liu K, Manton K, Liu B. Home care expenses for the disabled elderly. Health Care Financing Review, 1985;7.

Pepper Commission. A call for action: final report. Sept. 1990.

Randall T. Insurance—private and public—a payment puzzle. JAMA 1993;269.

Rivlin A, Weiner J. Caring for the disabled elderly, who will pay? Washington DC: The Brookings Institution. 1988.

Somers A. "Lifecare": a viable option for long-term care for the elderly.

Stone R. Caregivers of the frail elderly: a national profile. The Gerontologist, 1987;127.

US GAO. Long term care for the elderly: issues of need, access and cost. GAO/HRD-89-4. Nov. 1988.

US GAO. Medicare: need to strengthen home health care payment controls and address unmet needs. GAO/HRD-87-9, Dec. 1986.

Waldo D, Levit K, Lazenby H. National health expenditures, 1985. Health Care Financing Review 1986;8.

Endnotes

[1]Relman AS. The new medical industrial complex. N Engl J Med 1980;303:963.

[2]Glassman JK. Is the government's health care cure really needed? Washington Post, 7 January 1994, G1.

[3]Relman AS. The new medical industrial complex, p. 964.

[4]Grey B. The profit motive and patient care, p. 16.

[5]Bergthold L. The fat kid on the seesaw, p. 160.

[6]Salmon JW, ed. The corporate transformation of health care, p. 133.

[7]The AMA Masterfile contains information on members and nonmembers, as well as all foreign medical graduates in the U.S. who meet the educational criteria as discussed in the text.

[8]Physician characteristics and distribution, 1993 edition. Department of Physician Data Services, Division of Survey and Data Resources, American Medical Association, 1992.

[9]Association of American Medical Colleges. Medical school admission requirements, 1993–94, United States and Canada. Washington, DC: Association of American Medical Colleges, 1992.

[10]L. Bergeisen, ed. Minority students in medical education: facts and figures VII. Association of American Medical Colleges, Division of Minority Health, Education, and Prevention, August 1993.

[11]Bickel J. Women in medical education: a status report. N Engl J Med 1988; 319:1579–1584.

[12]Council on Graduate Medical Education. Second report of the Council: the underrepresentation of minorities in medicine. Rockville, MD: Department of Health and Human Services, Bureau of Health Professions, August, 1990.

[13]Personal communication. Association of American Medical Colleges, to be published in AAMC Databook on Statistical Information Related to Medical Education, Spring 1994.

[14]American Osteopathic Association. Yearbook and directory of osteopathic physicians, 1994 edition.

[15]Bureau of Health Professions. Eighth report to the President and Congress on the status of health personnel in the United States. Washington, DC: Health Resources and Services Administration, Public Health Service, U.S. Department of Health and Human Services, 1992.

[16]Department of Health and Human Services. Report of the Graduate Medical Education National Advisory Committee to the Secretary, vol 1 (September 30, 1980).

[17]Bureau of Health Profession. Seventh report to the President and Congress on the status of health personnel in the United States. Washington, DC: Health Resources and Services Administration, Public Health Service, U.S. Department of Health and Human Services, 1990.

[18]National resident matching program (NRMP) directory: hospitals and programs participating in the matching program. Washington, DC, NRMP: Association of American Medical Colleges, 1993.

[19]Chassin MR. Explaining geographic variations: the enthusiasm hypothesis. Med Care 1993;31:YS37–YS44.

[20]Wennberg J, Gittlesohn A. Variations in medical care among small areas. Sci Am 1982;246:120–134.

[21]Wennberg JE. Variations in medical practice and hospital costs. Connecticut Med 49:444–453.

[22]Bowman MA, et al. Estimates of physician requirements for 1990 for the specialists of neurology, anesthesiology, nuclear medicine, pathology, physical medicine and rehabilitation, and radiology. JAMA 1983;250:2624.

[23]Marder WD, et al. Physician supply and utilization by specialty: trends and projections. American Medical Association Center for Health Policy Research 1988.

[24]Tarlov AR. HMO enrollment growth and physicians: the third compartment. Health Affairs 1986;5:23–35.

[25]Jacobsen S, Rimm A. The projected physician surplus reevaluated. Health Affairs 1987;6:48–56.

[26]Mulhausen R, McGee J. Physician need: an alternative projection from a study of large, pre-paid group practices. JAMA 1989;261:1930–1934.

[27]The AHA is the premier association representing hospitals in the United States. State and local hospital associations also serve the hospitals in their geographic area. Each year, the AHA publishes a Guide to American Hospitals and Health Care Facilities and Hospital Statistics, both informative data sources on the industry.

[28]Phelps CE. Health economics. New York: HarperCollins, 1992.

[29]Frech HE III, ed. Health care in America: the political economy of hospitals and health insurance. San Francisco: Pacific Research Institute for Public Policy, 1988:106.

[30]Feldstein P. Health care economics, 4th ed. New York: Delmar Publishers, 1993.

[31]Modern Healthcare, 7 February 1994.

[32]The AHA provides a summary of various hospital departments in *AHA Hospital Statistics*.

[33]Harris JE. The internal organization of hospitals: some economic implications. The Bell Journal of Economics 1977:467.

[34]Eastaugh SR. Medical economics and health finance. New York: Auburn House, 1981:329.

[35]In addition to providing needed services for the hospital, all these related health professions are a leading source of employment in the U.S. economy. Indeed, in 1993, one out of seven American workers were employed in health services. Health employment is also expanding at a rapid rate. For instance, between July 1990 and April 1991 although the U.S. economy lost 1.4 million jobs, jobs in health services grew by 4.9%, which meant 390,000 new jobs. Indeed, of the 30 occupations with the fastest projected rate of growth, more than half are in the health field. Thus, although expansion of the health sector in

general and of hospitals in particular may cause concern (see Chapter 8), this growth is not completely negative. (Damp D. Health care job explosion, Corapolis, PA: D-Amp Publications, 1993:12.

[36]Weinsbrod B. The health care quadrilemma: an essay on technological change, insurance, quality of care, and cost-containment. Journal of Economic Literature 1991;29:523–532.

[37]AHA Hospital Statistics.

[38]Health Care Review, D&T, October 1993.

[39]Chapter 9 of Lamb and Rappaport's *Municipal Bonds* gives a clear overview of tax-exempt bonds for hospitals. Eastaugh also provides an in-depth analysis of hospital bonds and financing, and this text is a good source for further reading.

[40]Fledstein, p. 95. Starting in 1948 and lasting for approximately 20 years, the Hill-Burton program, a federal act, subsidized the construction of thousands of hospital beds, costing billions of dollars. The Hill-Burton criterion for supporting hospital construction was that 4.5 hospital beds should be available per 1000 population in areas with more than 12 persons per square mile; that 5.0 beds per 1000 population should exist in areas with 6 to 12 persons per square mile; and that 5.5 beds per 1000 population should exist in areas with fewer than 6 persons per square mile. According to the Hill-Burton formula, population density was the sole determinant of beds per 1000 population.

[41]Modern Healthcare, 9 March 1992. The article refers to a study done by Rocie Luke, a professor at Virginia Commonwealth University.

[42]Curran WJ, Hall MA, Kay DH. Health care law, forensic science and public policy, 4th ed. Boston: Little Brown, 1990:650.

[43]Modern Healthcare, 3 January 1994.

[44]Fein R. Medical care, medical costs.

[45]Health Care Financing Review, 1991;13:83–94.

[46]Imagine that an act has several potential outcomes. For example, rolling a fair six-sided die has six equally likely outcomes. The law of large numbers states that as the act is repeated many times (e.g., the die is rolled over and over again), the frequency with which the outcomes actually occur approaches their estimated probability of occurrence. If the die is rolled 6,000 times, the law says that the observed number of rolls of each of the six numbers on the die will be very close to 1,000 (6,000/6).

[47]The Rand Health Experiment showed that people with catastrophic health insurance (i.e., they were responsible for all costs up to a certain limit—thus, a 100% copayment) spent 31% less on medical care than similar people with full insurance (i.e., free care with 0% copayment), with little or no ill effect on health status. Source: Manning WG, Newhouse JP, et al. Health insurance and the demand for medical care: evidence from a randomized experiment. American Economic Review 1987;7:251–277.

[48]See, for example, Chapter 4 of the 1994 Economic Report of the President for a description of the Clinton health care plan.

[49]Because moral hazard causes people to buy more health care than they otherwise would, moral hazard causes higher prices for health care. These higher prices raise the actuarially fair premium and therefore raise insurance costs. As we see in the discussion of adverse selection, higher insurance prices lead to less consumption of insurance. Thus, another effect of moral hazard is to reduce the level of insurance that people purchase.

[50]The Appendix to this chapter models consumers' willingness to pay for insurance. It briefly provides a more analytical treatment of the demand for insurance.

[51]Hendricks R. A model for national health care: the history of Kaiser Permanente. Rutgers University Press, 1993:5.

[52]Fein R. Medical care, medical costs: the search for a health insurance policy. Cambridge, MA: Harvard University Press, 1989:12–13.

[53]Greer W. Kaiser-Permanente Health Plan—why it works. The Henry J. Kaiser Foundation, 1971.

[54]Berkowitz ED, Wolff W. Group Health Association: a portrait of a health maintenance organization. Philadelphia: Temple University Press, 1988:54.

[55]Starr P. The social transformation of American medicine. New York: Basic Books, 1982:327.

[56]The 93rd Congress. The Health Maintenance Organization Act of 1973. United States Code Congressional and Administrative News, 93rd Congress. First Session, vol 1. West Publishing, 1993

[57]Ginzberg E, ed. The U.S. health care system, A look to the 1990s. Rowman & Allanheld, 1985:31.

[58]Marion Merrell Dow Inc. Managed care digest: HMO edition. Marion Merrell Dow Managed Care Digests, 1993.

[59]Welch WP. Journal of Health Politics, Policy and Law 1987:12.

[60]Rubin HR, et al. Patient's ratings of outpatient visits in different practice settings. JAMA 1993;270:835–840.

[61]Marion Merrell Dow, Inc. Managed care digest: PPO edition. Marion Merrell Dow Managed Care Digests, 1993:3.

[62]Luft HS. How do health maintenance organizations achieve their cost savings? N Engl J Med 1978;298:1336–1343.

[63]Manning WG, et al. A controlled trial of the effect of a prepaid group practice on use of services. N Engl J Med 1984;310:1505–1510.

[64]Moore P. Evaluating health maintenance organizations. New York: Quorum Books, 1991:36.

[65]Withdrawn.

[66]Luft HS, et al. The comparative effect of health maintenance organizations. Journal of Health Politics, Policy and Law 1986;625–658.

[67]Ware JE, et al. Comparison of health outcomes at a health maintenance organization with those of fee-for-service care. Lancet 1986;1017–1022.

[68]Bledsoe, Medical Care, #191.

[69]Fee E. Disease and discovery : a history of the Johns Hopkins School of Hygiene and Public Health, 1916–1939. Baltimore, MD: Johns Hopkins University Press, 1987.

[70]Fein R. Medical care, medical costs, Cambridge, MA: Harvard University Press, 1986.

[71]The statistics in this paragraph come from HCFA's 1993 HCFA Statistics.

[72]The Medicare Handbook, The 1993 Green Book, The Medicaid Source Book, and HCFA's Medicare and Medicaid, Brief Summaries of Title XVIII and Title XIX of the Social Security Act.

[73]HCFA has established pilot programs exploring the feasibility of Medicare Managed Care organizations as an additional choice for beneficiaries.

[74]HCFA's 1993 Data Compendium. Of these, 31.3 million are aged and 3.8 million are disabled.

[75]Iglehart JK. The End Stage Renal Disease program. N Engl J Med 328:366–368.

[76]The 1993 Green Book.

[77]Because these funds are used to pay current Medicare expenses, there is some concern that as America ages, the hospital insurance trust fund will be unable to meet the needs of the elderly.

[78]Iglehart JK. Medicare. N Engl J Med 327:1467.

[79]1993 HCFA Statistics.

[80]Medicaid Source Book, p. 328.

[81]Oregon was granted a waiver in 1993 that ranked the covered services according to a scale developed by the Commission, which enabled them to substantially reduce the scope of benefits to expand eligibility for Medicaid.

[82]Stevens R, Steven R. Welfare medicine in America. New York: Free Press, 1974:86, 92.

[83]Litman T, Robins LS. Health politics and policy. New York: Wiley Medical Publications, 1984:17.

[84]Statistical Abstracts of the United States 1993, 113th ed. Austin, TX: The Reference Press, 1994:107–108, 331.

[85]U.S. Government Manual 1993/1994. Office of the Federal Registrar, National Archives and Records Administration, Washington, DC, 1993:24.

[86]The Budget for Fiscal Year 1994. Washington, DC: U.S. Government Printing Office, 1993:(Appendix)610.

[87]Kent C, Havighurst C. The FY95 budget for HHS: tough medicine while waiting for the cure. Medicine and Health 1994:3.

[88]The economic and budget outlook: fiscal year 1995–1999. Congressional Budget Office, August 1994, p. 31.

[89]Calculated from the budget for fiscal year 1994. Washington, DC: U.S. Government Printing Office, 1993:(App.)601–615.

[90]U.S. Government Manual 1993/94, p. 301.

[91]The Budget for Fiscal Year 1994, p. (Appendix)614.

[92]Agency for Toxic Substances and Disease Registry, Public Relations Office, 8-8-94.

[93]U.S. Government Manual 1993/94, p. 303.

[94]U.S. Government Manual 1993/94, p. 302.

[95]The Budget for Fiscal Year 1994. p. (Appendix) 601.

[96]U.S. Government Manual 1993/94, p. 305.

[97]The Budget for Fiscal Year 1994, p. (Appendix) 602.

[98]U.S. Government Manual 1993/94, p. 307.

[99]U.S. Government Manual 1993/94, p. 310.

[100]The Budget for Fiscal Year 1994, p. (Appendix) 608.

[101]The Budget for Fiscal Year 1994, p. (Appendix) 611.

[102]The Budget for Fiscal Year 1994, p. (Appendix) 613.

[103]U.S. Government Manual 1993/94, p. 315.

[104]U.S. Government Manual 1993/94, p. 31.

[105]The Budget for Fiscal Year 1994. p. (Appendix)617–621.

[106]U.S. Government Manual 1993/94, p. 318.

[107]The Budget for Fiscal Year 1994, p. (Appendix) 622–623, 635–637.

[108]The Budget for Fiscal Year 1994, p. (Appendix) 623–628.

[109]U.S. Government Manual 1993/94, p. 297.

[110]The Budget for Fiscal Year 1994, p. (Appendix) 624.

[111]The Budget for Fiscal Year 1994, p. (Appendix) 629.

[112]U.S. Government Manual 1993/94, p. 296.

[113]Adapted from John W. Kingdon. Agendas, alternatives, and public policies. Boston: Little, Brown, 1984.

[114]Litman and Robins, p. 10, 11.

[115]Stanley HW, Niemi RG. Vital statistics on American Policics, 3rd edition. Washington, DC: Congressional Quarterly Press, 1992:175.

[116]New York Times, 8/29/94, p. A13.

[117]Altman DE, Morgan DH. The role of state and local government in health. Health Affairs 1983;2:10–25.

[118]Statistical Abstracts of the United States 1993, 113th ed. p. 293.

[119]American Medical Association. Physician Characteristics and Distribution in the U.S. 1992:36.

[120]Letsch LW, et al. National health expenditures 1991. Health Care Financing Review 1992;14:19.

[121]Schieber GJ, et al. U.S. health expenditure performance: an international comparison and data update. Health Care Financing Review 1992;13:5.

[122]Rublee DA. Medical technology in Canada, Germany and the United States. Health Affairs 1989;8:180.

[123]Manning WG, et al. Health insurance and the demand for medical care: evidence from a randomized experiment. Am Economic Rev 1987;77:251–277.

[124]Newhouse JP. An iconoclastic view of health cost containment. Health Affairs 1993;12: (suppl)156.

[125]Mendelson DN, Schwartz WB. The effects of aging and population growth on health care costs. Health Affairs 1993;12:119.

[126]Schwartz WB, Mendelson DN. Hospital cost containment in the 1980s: hard lessons learned and prospects for the 1990s. N Engl J Med 1991;324:1038.

[127]Schwartz WB. The inevitable failure of current cost-containment strategies: why they can provide only temporary relief. JAMA 1987;257:221.

[128]Ibid, p. 220. Much of this chapter—this section in particular—draws heavily on the work of William B. Schwartz.

[129]Schwartz WB, Mendelson DN. Why managed care cannot contain hospital costs—without rationing. Health Affairs 1992;11:104.

[130]Reynolds R, et al. The cost of medical professional liability. JAMA 1987;2776. Also, Reynolds R, et al. The cost of medical professional liability in the 1980s. Center for Health Policy Research, American Medical Association (internal document), p. 104.

[131]AMA Center for Health Policy Research. Socioeconomic Characteristics of Medical Practice (1992). pp. 134, 106, 124.

[132]Woolhandler 1989, p. 54.

[133]Aday 1984, p. 13; Millman 1993, p. 32.

[134]Aday 1993, p. 6; Davis 1991, p. 262; Freeman 1987, p. 9.

[135]Schroeder 1991, p. 15.

[136]Aday 1993, p. 15.

[137]Nerenz 1990, p. 185.

[138]Starr 1993, p. 27.

[139]Aaron 1991, p. 2; Monheit 1985, p. 348.

[140]Axinn 1985, p. 648; Woolhandler 1989, p. 54.

[141]Health Insurance Association of America 1987.

[142]White House Domestic Policy Council 1993, p. 4.

[143]Foley 1993, p. 1.

[144]Foley 1993, p. 1; Woolhandler 1989, p. 54.

[145]Schur 1991, p. 1; U.S. General Accounting Office 1990, p. 3.

[146]Sulvetta 1986, p. 1.

[147]Monheit 1988, p. 348.

[148]Bodenheimer 1992, p. 274.

[149]U.S. General Accounting Office 1990, p. 3; Woolhandler 1989, p. 54.

[150]Reed 1986, p. 1428; Woolhandler 1989, p. 55.

[151]Brown 1988, p. 75.

[152]Brown 1988, p. 77.

[153]Brown 1988, p. 76; Kalmuss 1987, p. 48.

[154]Brown 1988, p. 76; Faller 1985, p. 340.

[155]American Medical Association 1981, p. 1159; Brown 1988, p. 78.

[156]Brown 1988, p. 81.

[157]Boufford 1990, p. 111; Schroeder 1991, p. 16.

[158]Brown 1988, p. 70.

[159]Brown 1988, p. 71.

[160]Brown 1988, p. 73; Mayor's Advisory Board 1987, p. 1.

[161]Brown 1988, p. 74; Select Panel for the Promotion of Child Health 1981, p. 1.

[162]Mayor's Advisory Board 1987, p. 1.

[163]Mayor's Advisory Board 1987, p. 1.

[164]Boone 1985, p. 1008; Chao 1984, p. 1.

[165]American Medical Association 1981, p. 1159; U.S. Department of Health and Human Services 1985, p. 1.

[166]Lurie 1984, p. 480.

[167]A Call for Action 1990, p. 33; Greenberg 1988, p. 612; Wenneker 1989, p. 253; Wenneker 1990, p. 1255.

[168]American Cancer Society 1991.

[169]American Cancer Society study 1991.

[170]1993, p. 621.

[171]Rosenbaum 1986, p. 442.

[172]Blendon 1982, p. 1; Rowland 1988, p. 427; Woolhandler 1989, p. 54.

[173]Schroeder 1991, p. 19.

[174]Aday 1984, p. 25; Schroeder 1991, p. 15.

[175]Woolhandler 1989, p. 55.

[176]Nerenz 1990, p. 183.

[177]Boufford 1990, p. 109; Okada 1980, p. 1.

[178]Davis 1981, p. 159.

[179]Boufford 1990, p. 110.

[180]Boufford 1990, p. 108.

[181]Boufford 1990, p. 110.

[182]Medicine and Health Perspectives 1989, p. 1.

[183]Boufford 1990, p. 111.

[184]Schroeder 1991, p. 19.

[185]Boufford 1990, p. 124; Schroeder 1991, p. 19.

[186]Boufford 1990, p. 113.

[187]Byrd 1990, p. 278; Scully 1994, p. 1.

[188]Katz 1981, p. 57.

[189]Chassin MR. The missing ingredient in health reform. Quality of care. JAMA 1993; 270:377–378.

[190]Neuhauser D. Ernest Amory Codman, M.D., and End Results of Medical Care. International Journal of Technology Assessment in Health Care 1990;6:307–325. See also Berwick 1989, Donabedian 1989, and Mulley, 1989.

[191]Codman EA. The Shoulder. Rupture of the Supraspinatus Tendon and Other Lesions in or about the Subacromial Bursa, Boston, 1934: xxiii.

[192]Donabedian A. The quality of care. How can it be assessed? JAMA 1988;260: 1743–1748.

[193]Donabedian A. Explorations in Quality Assessment and Monitoring. Volume I. The Definition of Quality and Approaches to Its Assessment. Ann Arbor, MI 1980:100–101.

[194]Lohr KN. Outcome measurement: concepts and questions. Inquiry 1988;25:47.

[195]US GAO 1993 and Grumbach 1993.

[196]Berke RL. The health plan: rising expectations and fear of the bills create an opening. The New York Times, September 1988; E-6.

[197]Thomas L. The Lives of a Cell: Notes of a Biology Watcher. New York, NY 1974.

[198]Wennberg J, Gittelsohn A. Small area variation in health care delivery Science 1973;182:1102.

[199]See for instance Holahan 1990, Kaoharas 1990, Gittelsohn, Chassin 1986, and Wennberg 1984, 87, 89.

[200]Leape 1990, Chassin 1987.

[201]Wennberg JE, et al. Hospital use and mortality among Medicare beneficiaries in Boston and New Haven N Engl J Med 1989;321:1168–1173.

[202]Wennberg JE. Which rate is right? N Engl J Med 1986;314:311.

[203]Caper P. Defining quality in medical care. Health Affairs 1988;7:49–61.

[204]Freudenheim M. Quality of care being measured. The New York Times (5 June 1990): D-2.

[205]Winslow R. Network of doctors to market heart care for set fee. The New York Times 2 March 1993: B-1.

[206]Yasuda G. Computing health-care efficiency: use of 'practice patterns' divides medical community on cost issues. Orlando Sentinel Tribune, 6 January 1992: B-12.

[207]White House Domestic Policy Council Health Security: The President's Report to the American People, The White House Domestic Policy Council. Washington, DC: 1993:100.

[208]Koska M. Are severity data an effective consumer tool. J Am Hosp Assoc 1989;63:24.

[209]MacNeil/Lehrer NewsHour, "Medical Breakthrough," reported by Greg Hirakawa of public television station KCTS-Seattle (Washington 3 December 1993).

[210]Berwick DM, Wald DL. Hospital leaders' opinions of the HCFA mortality data. JAMA 1990;263:248.

[211]Jonsen AR. The new medicine and the old ethics. Cambridge, MA: Harvard University Press 1990.

[212]Nuland SB. Doctors: The Biography of Medicine. New York, NY 1988: xv.

[213]Daley, et al 1988.

[214]Delbanco 1992.

[215]Reiser SJ. The era of the patient. using the experience of illness in shaping the missions of health care. JAMA 1993;269:1014.

[216]Delbanco T. Enriching the doctor-patient relationship by inviting the patient's perspective. Ann Intern Med 1992;116:416.

[217]Byer MJ. Faint Hearts. New York Times, 21 March 1992:23.

[218]Iezzoni 1993.

[219]Palmer HR. The challenges and prospects for quality assessment and assurance in ambulatory care. Inquiry 1988;25:119–131.

Lawthers AG. et al. Developing and evaluating performance measures for ambulatory care quality: a preliminary report of the DEMPAQ project. The Joint Commission Journal of Quality Improvement 1993;19:552–565.

[220]Joint Commission on Accreditation of Healthcare Organizations. The Measurement Mandate: On the Road to Performance Improvement in Health Care. Oakbrook Terrace, IL 1993:245.

[221]Joint Commission on Accreditation of Healthcare Organizations. Agenda for Change. JCAHO public information materials, Oakbrook Terrace, IL 1993.

[222]Schroeder SA, Kabcenell I. Do bad outcomes mean substandard care? JAMA 1991;265:1995.

[223]Knaus WA, Nash DB. Predicting and evaluating patient outcomes. Ann Intern Med 1988;109:521.

[224]Goldman RL. The reliability of peer assessments of quality of care. JAMA 1992; 267:958.

[225]Brook RH, Appel FA. Quality-of-care assessment: choosing a method for peer review. N Engl J Med 1973;288:84.

[226]Donabedian A. Criteria and standards for quality assessment and monitoring Quality Review Bulletin 1986;12:99–108.

[227]Rubenstein LV, et al. Changes in quality of care for five diseases measured by implicit review, 1981 to 1986. JAMA 1990;264.

Kahn KL. et al. Structured Implicit Review for Physician Implicit Measurement of Quality of Care: Development of the Form and Guidelines for its Use," N-3016-HCFA. Santa Monica, CA, 1989.

[228]Rubin HR, et al. Watching the doctor-watchers. how well do peer review organization methods detect hospital care quality problems? JAMA 1992;267:2349.

[229]Institute of Medicine, Division of Health Care Services, Medicare: A Strategy for Quality Assurance. Volume I. Washington, DC, 1990.

Lohr KN, et al. Medicare: a strategy for quality assurance, V: quality of care in a changing health care environment. Quality Review Bulletin 1992:18.

[230]Berwick DM. Continuous improvement as an ideal in health care. N Engl J Med 1989;320:53,55.

[231]Gardner E. Putting guidelines into practice. Modern Healthcare September 1992:24.

[232]Health Care Financing Administration, Health Standards and Quality Bureau, "Request for proposal: Cycle 4.0" July 6 1992.

[233]U.S. General Accounting Office, Practice Guidelines: The Experience of Medical Specialty Societies GAO/PEMD-91-11 (Washington, D.C 1991) p. 13.

[234]Margolis CZ. Uses of clinical algorithms. JAMA 1983;249:631.

[235]Leary WE. More advice for doctors: U.S. guides on treatments, New York Times, 15 April 1992:C-14.

[236]Leary WE. U.S. issues guidelines on bladder problems. New York Times 24 March 1992:C-3.

[237]Restuccia JD, et al. Factors affecting appropriateness of hospital use in Massachusetts. Health Care Financing Review 1986.

[238]Freudenheim M. Business and health: software controls on health care. The New York Times 18 February 1992:D-2.

[239]Welch 1994, Lasker 1992, McNeil 1992.

[240]Physician Payment Review Commission. Conference on Profiling. No. 92-2 Washington, DC 1992.

[241]Garnick DW, et al., Focus on quality: profiling physicianss' practice patterns. J Ambulatory Care Manag, July 1994.

[242]Kassirer JP. The use and abuse of practice profiles. N Engl J Med 1994;330:635.

[243]Gerteis M, et al. What patients really want. Health Management Quarterly 1993;15:6.

[244]Cleary PD, et al. Patients evaluate their hospital care: a national survey. Health Affairs 1991;10:262.

[245]Gerteis M, et al. what patients really want. Health Management Quarterly 1993;15:3.

[246]Romano PS. Can administrative data be used to compare the quality of health care? Medical Care Review 1993:50.

[247]Epstein 1990, p. 267.

[248]Brinkley J. U.S. releasing lists of hospitals with abnormal mortality rates. New York Times, 12 March 1986:1.

[249]Blumberg MS. Comments on HCFA hospital death rate statistical outliers. Health Services Research 1987:21.

Dubois RW. Hospital mortality as an indicator of quality, in: Goldfield N., Nash DB. (eds)., Providing Quality Care: The Challenge to Clinicians. Philadelphia: American College of Physicians. 1989.

[250]Podolsky D, Beddingfield KT. America's best hospitals. U.S. News and World Report July 1993;115:66.

[251]Hannan EL, et al. Adult open heart surgery in New York state: an analysis of risk factors and hospital mortality rates. JAMA 1990;264.

[252]Zinman D. Heart surgeons rated. Newsday 18 December 1990:32.

[253]DOH Report. Cardiac Surgery in New York State. New York, 1993: p. 3.

[254]Chassin MR. The missing ingredient in health reform. quality of care. JAMA 1993;270:378.

[255]Woolhandler S, Himmelstein DU, Lewontin JP. Administrative costs in U.S. hospitals. N Engl J Med 1993;329:400–403.

[256]Iezzoni LI, Greenberg LG. Risk Adjustment and Current Health Policy Debate, in: Risk Adjustment for Measuring Health Care Outcomes. Iezzoni LI (ed). Ann Arbor, MI 1994:357.

[257]Nash DB. Is the quality cart before the horse? JAMA 1992;268:918.

[258]Keeler EB et al. Hospital characteristics and quality of care. JAMA 1992;268:1709–1714.

Kuhn EM, et al. The relationship of hospital characteristics and the results of peer review in six large states. Medical Care 1991;29:1028–1038.

Hartz AJ, et al. The use of risk-adjusted complication rates to compare hospitals performing coronary artery bypass surgery or angioplasty. International Journal of Technology Assessment in Health Care 1992:8.

[259]Park RE, et al. Explaining variations in hospital death rates, randomness, severity of illness, quality of care. JAMA 1990;264:484–490.

[260]Dubois RW, et al. Hospital inpatient mortality. Is it a predictor of quality? N Engl J Med 1987;317:1674–1680.

Dubois RW, Brook RH. Preventable deaths: who, how often, and why? Ann Intern Med 1988;109:582–589.

Fink A, Yano EM, Brook RH. The condition of the literature on differences in hospital mortality. Medical Care 1989;27:315–336.

Thomas JW, Holloway JJ, Guire KE. Validating risk-adjusted mortality as an indicator for quality care. Inquiry 1993;30:6–22.

[261]O'Leary DS. The measurement mandate: report card is coming. The Journal of Quality Improvement 1993;19:487.

[262]Brook RH. Health care reform is on the way: do we want to compete on quality? Ann Intern Med 1994;120:85.

[263]Topol EJ, Califf RM. Scorecard cardiovascular medicine. Its impact and future directions. Ann Intern Med 1994;120:65–70.

[264]Report on Medical Guidelines & Outcomes Research, "Medicare Launches Effort to Create HMO 'Report Cards," 4(19):p. 1. 7 October 1993.

[265]Ware JE Jr., Berwick DM. Conclusions and recommendations, in: Patient judgments of hospital quality: report of a pilot study. Medical Care 1990;28:5–39.

[266]Califano J. America's health care revolution. New York: Random House, 1986:10.

[267]Jaeger J. Private sector coalitions: a fourth party in health. Durham, NC: Duke, 1982:43.

[268]Iglehart JK. The American health care system. N Engl J Med 1992;326:963.

[269]McArdle F. The changing health care market. Washington, DC: Employee Benefit Research Institute, 1987:340.

[270]Cantor JC, et al. Business leaders views on American health care. Health Affairs 1991:98.

[271]McArdle, p. 368.

[272]Ibid, p.368.

[273]Ibid, p.340.

[274]Politser P. US employers: the new pioneers of health care cost containment. Bull Am Coll Surg 1991;76:14.

[275]Cantor et al, p. 98.

[276]Salick Health Systems Annual Report, 1993.

[277]McArdle, p. 8.

[278]Politser, p. 48.

[279]McArdle, p. 89.

[280]Kenkel PJ. Business-led efforts to control costs. Modern Healthcare 1991;48:17.

[281]McArdle, p. 376.

[282]Ibid, p. 356.

[283]Hall W, et al. Cost-effective health care: the Rochester experience. Health Affairs 1993;59.

[284]McArdle, p. 113.

[285]Ibid, p. 100.

[286]Kenkel, p. 48.

[287]The hospital. BusinessWeek, January 1994, p. 40.

[288]Coile RC Jr. The new medicine: reshaping medical practice and health care management. Rockville, MD: Aspen, 1990:20.

[289]Warden G. Integrated regional health systems: models for health care delivery reform. Henry Ford Health System Detroit, MI; p. 2.

[290]Glassman JK. Is the government's health care cure really needed? Washington Post, Jan 7, 1994, p. G1.

[291]Hsiao WC. Comparing health care systems: what nations can learn from one another. J Health, Politics, and Law. 1992; 17:620.

[292]Reinhardt UE. What can Americans learn from Europeans? Health Care Financing Rev 1989; (suppl) 99.

[293]Ibid, p. 97.

[294]Reinhardt UE. West Germany's health-care and health-insurance system: combining universal access with cost control. Report for the U.S. Bipartisan Commission on Comprehensive Health Care, June 1990, p. 4–9.

[295]Allen D. Health services in England. In: Comparative Health Systems. University Park: Pennsylvania State University Press, 1984; 208–223.

[296]Roemer MI. Canada. In: National health systems of the world. New York: Oxford University Press, 1991; 166.

[297]Iglehart JK. Canada's health system. N Engl J Med 1986;780.

[298]Phelps. International comparisons of health care systems. In: Health economics. New York: Harper Collins, 1992: 488.

[299]Government Accounting Office. Access to health care: states respond to growing crisis. GAO/HRD 92–70.

[300]Ibid., p. 50.

[301]Ibid., p. 64.

[302]Knox RA. Hawaii touts health care that's working. Boston Globe, July 5, 1992, p. 1.

[303]Ibid., p. 12.

[304]Volpp KG, Siegel B. New Jersey: long term experience with all-payer rate setting. Health Affairs, Summer 1993, p. 60.

[305]Ibid., p. 59.

[306]Leichter HM. Minnesota: the trip from acrimony to accommodation. Health Affairs, Summer 1993, p. 48.

[307]Yawn BP, et al. Minnesota care (health right): myths and miracles. JAMA 1993; 269:511.

[308]Freudenheim M. Rochester serves as model in curbing health costs. The New York Times, August 25, 1992, p. A1.

[309]The Program on Public Opinion and Health Care—Harvard School of Public Health and Marttila & Kiely, Inc. A survey of American attitudes toward health care reform. June, 1993:23.

[310]Office of Technology Assessment—Health Program. Impact of legal reforms on medical malpractice costs. September 1993:1.

[311]Weiler PC. Medical malpractice on trial. Cambridge, MA: Harvard University Press, 1991:102.

[312]OTA, p. 5.

[313]Weiler, p. 105.

[314]Dayhoff DA, et al. An update on physician cost shares. Health Care Financing Rev 1993; 14:122; 124.

315Opinion Research Corporation. Professional liability and its effects: report of a 1992 survey of the American College of Obstetricians and Gynecologists. October 1992:11.

316Ibid.

317Havighurst CC. Health care law and policy: readings, notes and questions. Westbury, NY: The Foundation Press, 1988:757.

318Furrow BR, et al. Health law: cases, materials and problems, 2nd ed. St. Paul, MN: West Publishing, 1991:127.

319Ibid., p. 199.

320Ibid., p. 199.

321Ibid., p. 167.

322Physician Insurers Association of American. Data sharing reports, cumulative reports, January 1, 1985–June 30, 1989. Lawrenceville, NJ: Physician Insurers Association of American Data Sharing Committee, 1989 (in OTA, 1993, p. 13. U.S. Congress, General Accounting Office. Medical malpractice: characteristics of claims closed in 1984. GAO/HRD-87-55. Washington, DC: April 1987.

323Weiler PC, et al. Proposal for medical liability reform. JAMA 1992; 267:2.

324Opinion Research, p. 17.

325Localio RA, et al. Relation between malpractice claims and adverse events due to negligence. N Engl J Med 1991; 325:245.

326Weiler, p. 2355.

327OTA, p. 16.

328Abraham KS, et al. Enterprise responsibility for personal injury: further reflections. San Diego Law Review 1993; 31:339.

329Gastel R, ed. Medical malpractice. Insurance Information Institute Reports, October 1993:8.

330Ibid., p. 8.

331Editors. Defensive medicine: it costs but does it work? JAMA 1987; 257:2801.

332Sloan FA, et al. Medical malpractice experience of physicians: predictable or haphazard? JAMA 1989; 262:3291.

333GAO, p. 7.

334OTA, p. 25.

335Ibid., p. 29.

336Ibid., p. 29.

337Ibid., p. 31, note 129.

338Ibid., p. 2.

339Ibid., p. 37.

340Hyams A, et al. Report to Physician Payment Review Commission: practice guidelines and malpractice litigation. Harvard School of Public Health, January 1994:2.

341OTA, p. 32.

342Hyams, p. 7.

343Weiler, p. 102.

344OTA, pp. 40–41.

345National Research Council. The social impact of AIDS in the United States. Washington, DC: National Academy Press, 1993): 1.

346Fox DM. Chronic disease and disadvantage: the new politics of HIV infection. J Health Politics, Policy and Law 1990; 15:345.

[347]Ibid.

[348]National Research Council, 1993, p. 10.

[349]Ibid., p. 26.

[350]Bayer R. AIDS: the politics of prevention and neglect. Health Affairs 1991; 87.

[351]Ibid., p. 88.

[352]Ibid., p. 88–89.

[353]Ibid., p. 90.

[354]Ibid., p. 91.

[355]National Research Council, 1993, pp. 36–37.

[356]Ibid., pp. 62–63.

[357]Ibid., pp. 33–34.

[358]Ibid., p. 68.

[359]Ibid., p. 69.

[360]Fox, p. 343.

[361]Bayer, pp. 94–95.

[362]Ibid., p. 94.

[363]Ibid., pp. 95–96.

[364]National Research Council, 1993, pp. 48–49.

[365]Ibid., p. 52.

[366]Ibid., p. 54.

[367]National Institutes of Health, The Office of Science Policy and Technology Transfer. NIH data book. Pub. No. 93-1261, 1993;3.

[368]Ibid., p. 7.

[369]National Institutes of Health, Division of Research Grants. NIH extramural trends, fiscal years 1983–1992. Pub. No. 93-3506, 1993;117–119.

[370]Ibid., p. 118.

[371]Ibid., p. 93.

[372]Ibid., p. 95.

[373]Ibid., p. 99.

[374]Ibid., p. 104.

[375]Ibid., pp. 127–135.

[376]Ibid., p. 13.

[377]Ibid., p. 17.

[378]National Science Foundation. National Science Foundation annual report 1992. Washington, DC: Pub. No. NSF 93-1, 1993;i–1.

[379]Ibid., p. i–1.

[380]Ibid., p. 38.

[381]Baringa M. The foundations of research. Science 1991;253:1202.

[382]McKercher PL. Pharmaceutical research and development. Clin Ther 1992;14:760.

[383]DiMasi JA, et al., Cost of innovation in the pharmaceutical industry. Health Economics 1991;10:107–142.

[384]McKercher, p. 760.

[385]Kaitin KI, et al. The role of the research-based pharmaceutical industry in medical progress in United States. J Clin Pharmacol 1993;33:412.

[386]Ibid., p. 416.

[387]Glaser RJ. The impact of philanthropy on medicine and health. Perspect Biol Med 1992;36:46.

[388]Howard Hughes Medical Institute, Office of Communications. The annual report, 1992; 1993;63.

[389]Glaser, p. 54.

[390]Baringa, p. 1200.

[391]Petersdorf RG. The crises in biomedical research funding. Trans Am Clin Climat Assoc 1992;103:182.

[392]National Institutes of Health, The Office of Science Policy and Technology Transfer, p. 70.

[393]National Institutes of Health, Division of Research Grants, p. 38.

[394]Ibid., pp. 28–29.

[395]National Institutes of Health, The Office of Science Policy and Technology Transfer, p. 63.

[396]Ibid., p. 71.

[397]Petersdorf, p. 186.

[398]Ibid., p. 182.

[399]National Institutes of Health, The Office of Science Policy and Technology Transfer, p. 26.

[400]Cantor CR. Orchestrating the human genome project. Science 1990;248:49.

[401]National Institutes of Health, The Office of Science Policy and Technology Transfer, p. 21.

[402]Kirschner M. The need for unity in the biomedical research community. Acad Med 1991;66:584.

[403]Cullinton BJ. Shaping science policy: what's happening to biomedical research in America. Acad Med 1991;66:188.

[404]Bellet AJD. Value issues in biomedical science: public concerns and professional complacency. Immunol Cell Biol 1992;70:363.

[405]Ibid., p. 363.

[406]Blumenthal D. The price of success: promoting technology transfer through academic-industry relationships in the life sciences. Health Affairs 1994,

[407]Ibid.

[408]Wyngaarden JB. The clinical investigator as an endangered species. Acad Med 1979;301:1254–1259.

[409]Martin JB. Training physician-scientists for the 1990s. Acad Med 1991;66:124.

[410]Vaitukaitis JL. The future of clinical research. Clin Res 1991;39:152.

[411]Cadman EC. The new physician-scientist: a guide for the 1990s. Clin Res 1990;38:191–198.

[412]Martin, p. 125.

[413]Domenici PV. Mental health care policy in the 1990s: discrimination in health care coverage of the seriously mentally ill, Address to the American Psychiatric Association, 1991, Washington, DC.

[414]Regier DA, et al. The de facto U.S. mental and addictive disorders service system: epidemiologic catchment area prospective 1-year prevalence rates of disorders and services. Arch Gen Psychiatry 1993;50:85–94.

[415]Bachrach LL. Asylum and chronically ill psychiatric patients. Am J Psychiatry 1984;141:975–978.

[416]Pepper B, Ryglewicz H, eds. The young adult chronic patient, New directions for mental health services. San Francisco, CA: Jossey-Bass, 1982.

[417]Roth D, Bean G. New perspectives on homelessness: findings from a state-wide epidemiologic study. Hospital and Community Psychiatry 1986;37:712–719.

[418]Leibowitz B. Mental health services. In: Maddox G, ed. Encyclopedia of aging. New York: Springer, 1987.

[419]Rochefort DA. Handbook on mental health policy in the United States. Westport, CT: Greenwood Press, 1989.

[420]Katon W. Depression: relationship to somatization and chronic medical illness. J Clin Psychiatry 1984;45:4–11.

[421]Rutter M. Parental mental disorder as a psychiatric risk factor. In: Hales R, Frances A, eds. American Psychiatric Association Annual Review 6. Washington, DC: American Psychiatric Press, 1987.

[422]U.S. Congress, Office of Technology Assessment. Children's mental health: problems and services—a background paper. Washington, DC: U.S. Government Printing Office, 1986.

[423]Kiesler C, Sibulkin A. Mental hospitalization: myths and facts about a national crisis. Newbury Park, Ca: Sage, 1987.

[424]Rochefort, p.

[425]Bond GR, et al. A comparison of two crisis housing alternatives to psychiatric hospitalization. Hospital and Community Psychiatry 1989;40:177–183; and Turner VE, Hoge MA. Overnight hospitalization of acutely ill day hospital patients. Int J Partial Hospitalization 1991;7:23–36.

[426]Stuart P. Depression: hidden disorder in the workplace. Personnel Journal 1992;71:94; Clinton JJ. Depression in primary care. JAMA 1993;270:172; Sanderson WC. Syndrome comorbidity in patients with major depression or dysthymia: prevalence and temporal relationship. Am J Psychiatry 1990;147:1025.

[427]Bennett MJ. The greening of the HMO: implications for prepaid psychiatry. Am J Psychiatry 1988;145:1544–1549.

[428]Shadle M, Christianson JB. The organization of mental health care delivery in HMOs. Admin Mental Health 1988;15:201–225.

[429]Bigelow DA. Effectiveness of a case management program. Community Mental Health J 1991;27:115; Sederer LI, et al. Case-based reimbursement for psychiatric hospital care. Hospital and Community Psychiatry 1992;43:1120–25.

[430]Talbot

[431]Talbot. Figure 12-1, p. 314.

[432]Sunshine JH, et al. Expenditures and sources of funds for mental health organizations: U.S. and each State, 1986. Statistical Note No. 193, DHHS Publ. No. ADM-90-1699. Washington, DC: U.S. Government Printing Office, 1990.

[433]Talbot

[434]Ibid.

[435]Ibid.

[436]Harrington C. Factors that contribute to Medicare HMO risk contract success. Inquiry 1987;25.

[437]Dorwart

[438]Koyanagi C. Operation help: a mental health advocate's guide to Medicaid. Alexandria VA: National Mental Health Association, 1988.

[439]Brotman A. Privatization of mental health services: the Massachusetts experiment. J Health Politics, Policy and Law 1992;17:541–551.

[440]Roberts MJ, Clyde A. Your money or your life: the health care crisis explained. New York, NY: Doubleday, 1993.

[441]Institute of Medicine

[442]Forsyth AB, Griffiths B, Reiff S. Comparison of utilization of medical services by alcoholics and non-alcoholics. Am J Public Health 1982;72:600–602.

[443]Schlesinger M, Dorwart RA. Falling between the cracks: failing national strategies for the treatment of substance abuse. DAEDALUS Journal of the American Academy of Arts and Sciences 1992;195–237.

[444]Scheidemandel P. The coverage catalog, 2nd ed. Washington, DC: American Psychiatric Association, 1989.

[445]Ibid.

[446]Office of National Drug Control Policy, p.

[447]U.S. Department of Housing and Urban Development. A report to the secretary on the homeless and emergency shelters. Washington, DC: U.S. Government Printing Office, 1984.

[448]U.S. Department of Health and Human Services. The homeless: background, analysis and options. Washington, DC: U.S. Government Printing Office, 1984.

[449]Ladner S, et al. Project future: focusing, understanding, targeting, and utilizing resources for the homeless mentally ill, elderly, youth, substance abusers and employables. Rockville, MD: National Institute of Mental Health, 1986; Morse G, et al. Homeless people in St. Louis: a mental health program evaluation, field study and follow-up investigation. Rockville, MD: National Institute of Mental Health, 1985.

[450]Levinson M. Once again, tiptoeing around the T word; why its so hard to talk straight about new taxes. Newsweek 1993;121:46; Kosterlitz J. O.K., stick out your tongue and say 'taxes.' National Journal 1993;25:2668.

[451]Linhorst DM. The use of single room occupancy (SRO) housing as an alternative for persons with a chronic mental illness. Community Mental Health Journal 1991;27:135.

[452]Rochefort DA. Handbook on mental health policy in the United States. Westport, CT: Greenwood Press, 1989.

[453]Ibid.

[454]Goldman H, Adams N, Taube C. Deinstitutionalization: the data demythologized. Hospital and Community Psychiatry 1983;34:129–134.

[455]Morrissey J. Deinstitutionalizing the mentally ill: process, outcomes, and new directions. In: Gove W, ed. Deviance and mental illness. Beverly Hills, CA: Sage, 1982.

[456]Lamb HR. The new asylums in the community. Arch Gen Psychiatry 1979;36:129–134; Lamb HR, ed. The homeless mentally ill: a task force report of the American Psychiatric Association Washington, DC: American Psychiatric Association, 1984.

[457]Roberts

[458]Dorwart RA, Epstein SS. Privatization and mental health care: a fragile balance. Westport, CT: Greenwood Publishing Group, 1993.

[459]Ibid.

[460]Ibid.

[461]HCFA. Office of the Actuary.

[462]US GAO. Long term care for the elderly: issues of need, access and cost. GAO/HRD-89-4.

[463]Kane RA, Kane RL. Long-term care: principles, programs and policies. New York: Springer, 1987.

[464]Ibid.

[465]Pepper Commission. A call for action: final report. Sept. 1990.

[466]Kane and Kane

[467]Health and Public Policy Committee, American College of Physicians. Financing long-term care. Ann Intern Med 1988;108.

[468]Liu K, Manton K, Liu, B. Home care expenses for the disabled elderly. Health Care Financing Review 1985;7.

[469]Stone R. Caregivers of the frail elderly: a national profile. The Gerontologist 1987;127.

[470]US GAO. Medicare: need to strengthen home health care payment controls and address unmet needs. GAO/HRD-87-9, Dec. 1986.

[471]Council on Scientific Affairs. Home care in the 1990s. JAMA 1990;263.

[472]Somers A. Lifecare: a viable option for long-term care for the elderly.

[473]Kane and Kane

[474]Edmonson B. The home health care market. American Demographics 1985;29–51.

[475]Waldo D, Levit K, Lazenby H. National health expenditures, 1985. Health Care Financing Review 1986;8.

[476]Rivlin A, Weiner J. Caring for the disabled elderly, who will pay? Washington, DC: The Brookings Institution, 1988.

[477]Randall T. Insurance—private and public—a payment puzzle. JAMA 1993;269.

[478]Benjamin AE. An historical perspective on home care policy. The Milbank Q 1993;71.

[479]Kane and Kane

[480]Estes CL. Aging, health and social policy: crisis and crossroads. J Aging and Social Policy 1989.

[481]Somers.

[482]Kane and Kane

[483]Cotton P. Must older Americans save up to spend down? JAMA 1993;269.

[484]American Geriatrics Society Public Policy Committee. Financing of long-term care services. J Am Geriatr Soc 1990;38.

[485]Institute of Medicine. America's aging: health in an older society. Washington, DC: National Academy Press, 1985:23.

Index